BUILDING THE CLIENT'S RELATIONAL BASE
A multidisciplinary handbook

Mark Furlong

First published in Great Britain in 2013 by

The Policy Press
University of Bristol
Fourth Floor
Beacon House
Queen's Road
Bristol BS8 1QU
UK
t: +44 (0)117 331 4054
f: +44 (0)117 331 4093
tpp-info@bristol.ac.uk
www.policypress.co.uk

North American office:
The Policy Press
c/o The Universi-ty of Chicago Press
1427 East 60th Street
Chicago, IL 60637, USA
t: +1 773 702 7700
f: +1 773-702-9756
sales@press.uchicago.edu
www.press.uchicago.edu

British Library Cataloguing in Publication Data
A catalogue record for this book is available from the British Library.

Library of Congress Cataloging-in-Publication Data
A catalog record for this book has been requested.

ISBN 978 1 84742 861 5 paperback
ISBN 978 1 84742 862 2 hardcover

The right of Mark Furlong to be identified as author of this work has been asserted by him in accordance with the Copyright, Designs and Patents Act 1988.

The statements and opinions contained within this publication are solely those of the author and not of the University of Bristol or The Policy Press. The University of Bristol and The Policy Press disclaim responsibility for any injury to persons or property resulting from any material published in this publication.

The Policy Press works to counter discrimination on grounds of gender, race, disability, age and sexuality.

Cover design: Qube Design Associates, Bristol
Front cover: image kindly supplied by istock.com
Printed and bound in Great Britain by Hobbs, Southampton
The Policy Press uses environmentally responsible print partners.

FSC
www.fsc.org
MIX
Paper from
responsible sources
FSC® C020438

There is nothing more powerful
than an idea whose time has come.
Victor Hugo

Contents

List of vignettes, tables, figures, and reflective exercises

Vignettes

Tables

Figures

Reflective exercises

Acknowledgments

Tom Paterson was crucial in the development of this contribution. Similarly, my friends and former colleagues – especially Dianna McLachlan, Amaryll Perlesz, Pam Rycroft, Jenny Smith and Jeff Young – were, and still are, a wellspring. More recently, it is not possible to adequately acknowledge the support and thoughtfulness I've received from Pam Trevithick.

Students, particularly those I worked with in an elective that focused on social connectedness, were tremendously generous in allowing me to workshop many of the raw exercises that eventually found themselves refined and included in this text.

Of course I owe much to many many clients over a great number of years. These people, I'm sure, often looked after me as much or more as I supported them. Other practitioners I have worked with – sometimes only once, often over some years – have also shared a great deal. Most often, this has happened without me letting them know how much I've appreciated our cooperative learning.

Lastly, my local mob – friends and family – you make it all worthwhile. To Liam and Casey, Robyn and her close crew Sarah and Anna, and to those who have been close but whose presence now has a different register, this book is dedicated.

About the author

Mark Furlong is a senior lecturer in the School of Health and Social Development at Deakin University in Melbourne. Previously, he practiced for nearly 20 years in therapeutic and protective settings. Mark has consulted broadly, taught in multidisciplinary education and has published in mental health, family therapy, family studies, psychotherapy, social work and primary health.

1
Introduction

Aims of the text | Policy and practice | Origins of the work | Structure of the book

This is a book for non-specialists and senior students. It is designed for the majority of practitioners, irrespective of their discipline of origin, whose daily work involves meeting with single clients. Hopefully, specialists who work with groups, couples or families will find much of the material original and stimulating, but the primary purpose is to equip practitioners to be more able to practice in ways that acknowledge the importance of the *relational base* of their clients. Amongst the larger set of professional tribes, for case managers or general practitioners, advocates or community nurses, social workers or occupational therapists, psychologists or counselors, this invitation could open a new horizon. If you are prepared to go beyond the silos of knowledge that act as the established knowledge base of your discipline there will be something for you.

Before beginning, a question must be asked: why should practitioners intensify their efforts to strengthen the relational base of their clients? Practitioners are already busy, dealing with many demands. They are told to be evidence-driven, to be guided by clear models, to pro-actively manage risk, to efficiently negotiate their workloads, and to coordinate professional relationships and information transfers within and beyond the immediate practice context. Whatever the discipline or role, they are urged to deeply engage with their clients, to clarify, and to strive to achieve, clear goals, and to be outcome-driven. With so many demands is it really possible to give a higher priority to stimulating clients' connections with their past, current and prospective significant others?

Mindful of this demanding background, this text makes a case for focusing on social connection given the striking findings of contemporary research. Recent reports have concluded that Western citizens are becoming more lonely (Cacioppo and Patrick, 2008), less involved with others (Putnam, 2000), less empathic (Szalavitz and Perry, 2010), and more self-absorbed (Howard, 2007). This trajectory is particularly worrying as it is now statistically established, and has been accepted by social planners in all the so-called developed nations, that individuals are healthier and happier if they are well connected (Berkman and Glass, 2000; Ryff and Singer, 2001; Hawkley et al, 2010; Wilkinson and Pickett, 2010).

It is now beyond dispute that good quality social connection acts to ward off problems such as heart disease and cancer and, in the event that someone becomes ill, good quality relationships act to maximize the chance of recovery and to minimize the sequelae of disease (Berkman and Glass, 2000; Ryff and

Singer, 2001). Similarly, mental health problems, such as depression, are mediated in their prevalence and outcome by the quality of a person's relational supports (Cacioppo et al, 2010). Intimate local community does not guarantee immunity, but it certainly helps.

Unfortunately, the lives of an increasing proportion of the population are at odds with the findings of social epidemiology. Emerging over the last 15 years, this research has proven that human beings benefit from being 'linked in': 'Together we do better' (VicHealth, 2010), as a recent health promotion campaign put it. Yet, what is actually happening in terms of relationships is that the trend is going in the opposite direction – many individuals are having less regard for, and are having less secure attachments with, others. This is especially, but not exclusively, the case for those who are already marginalized and disadvantaged.

Irrespective of discipline or role, it therefore makes good sense that practitioners seek to catalyze their clients' capacity to build and maintain high quality connections with their current and prospective significant others – whether the client is young, adult, or elderly it makes sense to stimulate relational embeddedness. Whether practicing directly with clients, for example, as care coordinators, protective workers or as occupational therapists, or acting indirectly in an expert, tertiary level role, in each instance practitioners have reason to be committed to doing whatever it takes so that their clients are able to realize a good enough measure of relational connection. The importance of this goal applies equally, whatever the role or disciplinary backgrounds. Practitioners have all long wanted their clients to be included and respected, and there is now evidence to warrant this sentiment becoming a legitimate professional goal.

This goal has yet to become a high priority, however. Why this is so, and why this book has relevance, is that relationships have less of a voice than individuals. Everyone can see you and me, the her and the him. Individuals stand out. They are obvious and exist at the foreground of our awareness. In contrast the relational – the reality which affiliates and locates, holds and contextualizes – is hard to discern. One cannot directly 'get to grips' with the relational . This reality does not have obvious dimensions, such as weight or voice, which can be measured and appreciated, re-imagined and reorganized. Moving the relational from the background of awareness to the foreground is a key concern in this book. The aim is to give personal relationships – the relational can take many forms – a greater profile in awareness. A second aim is to incite the ambition to believe that relational capacity can be improved.

Currently, what tends to have status and immediacy is that which is concerned with improving the autonomy and self-determination of clients. If it is about maximizing personal choice and control, there is a buzz for practitioners and citizens alike. If the focus is on relationships, this objective seems murky, awkward and indecisive. Specific nodes, rather than the networks that sustain them, are where the action is seen to be.

Few practitioners or practitioner groups are therefore prepared to put their hands up to say 'We are *not* in the business of giving consumers control of their lives.' However impossible the dream of autonomous freedom may be, its lingering thrall provides much of the context of what follows. It may hurt to recognize this premise, but in the real world each real partnership requires a degree of compromise, even surrender. This is not an appealing picture. Indeed, the truth of 'sustainable relating' is more sobering because secure attachments have an essential condition: peer-to-peer relationships are robust only as long as each participant understands that the other, as well as the 'me', will not insist on winning, on getting what is wanted, in each interaction. Even the best partnerships, it must be expected, will be experienced as imperfect, at times even as infuriating. This is in stark contrast to the air-brushed image of romance and friendship with which citizens have become so familiar.

Aims of the text

This text presents a contrasting account of the professional project to the traditional focus on improving individual functioning. Rather than according priority to improving client autonomy (or its synonyms: empowerment, self-determination, locus of control, agency, choice, and so forth), the starting point is the assumption that the wellbeing of clients depends on each person having a good-enough quality of connectedness to balance their capacity for independence. Simply put, the assumption of this work is that professionals can be optimistic that clients can develop the values, attitudes, and skills for thoughtful and fair relationships – for what might be framed as the capacity for 'accountable relating'.

The assumption in what follows is that it only takes one improved, or one new, relationship to make a positive difference to the quality of a client's life. Reviving a link with an old friend, or learning the skill to renegotiate just one difficult aspect in a current relationship, can enrich a person's relational base to a crucial degree. Even a minor shift in a client's disposition towards relationships can prompt a 'virtuous cycle' (Wender, 1968) of improved relating. According to the psychoanalyst, Carl Jung (1946), we all have 'kinship libido', a hunger for an abiding and energizing interpersonal affection in our lives. This appetite can be frustrated, a mal-adaptation which leaves people impoverished and vulnerable. It is investigating, and venturing into, this territory that is the concern here.

To put it another way, the aim here is to promote forms of professional practice that seek to acknowledge and develop the client's 'relational self' (Mathews, 1995). If it is seen at all, this aspect of 'the self' is usually relegated a secondary status and is regarded as an inferior, shadow side to identity. In contrast to this denigration, this work argues that the client's intimate social self needs to have sufficient vitality to balance the power of its converse, the client's 'autonomous self' (Mathews, 1995; Paterson, 1996). The proposition that these two aspects of the self need to be balanced, and that there is a creative tension between them, is at the core of this book.

Relational poverty has a disproportionate presence in the lives of those people who are currently excluded and disadvantaged. A holistic appraisal would have this impoverishment prominently on the radar for providers and planners, along with the client's access to citizenship rights, material wellbeing and personal agency. No amount of assertion training, not even secure accommodation and regular employment, substitutes for clients receiving, and in turn offering, affection and respect within circles of attachment and belonging. Internalized stigma, patterns of response that inadvertently ward off others, self-absorption – these are some of the phenomena that sustain loneliness and isolation. Interpersonal in their operations, these are the subjects of a relational focus.

What does 'relational' mean?

In this text it is assumed that practitioners are visitors in the lives of their clients and that the client's network, or absence of network, predates and outlasts the practitioner's involvement. Given this transient place it is unlikely that any single practitioner will provide a 'corrective emotional experience' (Alexander and French, 1946) that will permanently reorganize the client's life into one of health and wellbeing. Within this understanding the professional's involvement – variously termed the 'working alliance', 'the relationship' or the like – is a factor that should be recognized as important (Rogers, 1969; Trevithick, 2003), but it is only, at best, a means towards the client securing a degree of change.

This is an especially relevant consideration if the goal is to develop the client's relational base. Unlike the assumption found in some 'therapo-centric' formulations (Furlong, 1995), there is no reason to prioritize the practitioner–client relationship as if this linkage was a condition that is somehow sacred. Rather, in most circumstances it is preferable that professionals set out to carefully limit, to constructively minimize, the intensity and impact of the practitioner–client relationship (Paterson, 1996), although it should *always* be acknowledged as crucial.

It is not presumed here that an in-depth professional relationship is necessarily the axis around which effective practice turns. In this specific sense the ideas presented here are discontinuous with what has been termed the 'relational approach' in the psychoanalytic sense (Greenberg and Mitchell, 1983; Mitchell, 1988) or more discipline-specific sense (see, for example, Ornstein and Ganzer, 2005, or Ruch et al's 2010 accounts of 'relationship-based practice' in social work).

These authors privilege the practitioner's relationship with their clients. This preference has a clearly warranted claim within particular traditions and presenting situations, yet care needs to be exercised in order that short-hand versions of the term – the 'relationship' or 'relationship-focused practice' – do not inadvertently excise the interpersonal from the everyday social world and project it into a purer and more specialized identification with the therapeutic project. It would be a confused situation if the term 'relationship' was de-natured and became identified with what expert professionals do in individual sessions with single clients.

The 'relational' is a basic dimension of the everyday material-symbolic world. For this reason the term should remain primarily associated with what clients, and citizens more generally, do amongst themselves on a daily basis. As a point of difference the term 'relational' is used here in this latter sense; in contrast with the vision of therapeutically oriented practitioners engaged in undertaking one-to-one 'relational' work with individual clients, here 'the relational' has been reclaimed from the clinical realm to that of everyday social experience. In this latter sense each person is engaging in the 'relational' in all his or her interpersonal exchanges.

This usage represents, at the conceptual level, not so much a cleavage of perspectives as a pragmatic concern with respect to the site where client change is thought to occur. In therapeutically oriented practice the crucial site is understood to be the practitioner–client relationship, whereas here the crucial site is understood to be the non-clinical world of everyday life. What is central here is the day-to-day social world of the client, the place where there are better or worse interactions and social relations. Contact with a practitioner can accentuate the social functioning of the client, but this person's prospects will ultimately be determined by their interactions within their social sphere rather than centered on their interactions with a professional.

Policy and practice

A concern for relationships and interdependency, for the ebbs and flows of the locally social, aligns this text with emerging policy priorities that have gained acceptance across a range of Western nations. In distinct national contexts increasing policy attention is being given to questions of social inclusion and the impact of inequality and stigma on the citizen's capacity to participate in employment, recreation and, more generally, in the full spectrum of civic life. This attention is especially evident in the innovations that are taking place in the fields of public health and health promotion. Evidence has accumulated that health and wellbeing is heavily contingent on a set of social factors, not least of which concerns the quality of a person's social network. In this text a central argument is that practitioners working face to face with clients should be informed by the same macro-level evidence.

In taking up this challenge two points are clear. First, a concern for relational health has a politics that transcends the left–right divide, at least in so far as the latter is driven by traditional, rather than neoliberal, convictions. (An example of this crossover appeal is the Relationships Foundation in the UK; see www.relationshipsfoundation.org/Web/.) Second, it is also clear that no one profession has a monopoly on pursuing the relationship-building agenda. For this reason the material in this book is not directed at one single profession. The intention is to offer practical ideas that are relevant to a broad range of actors: to professionals who define themselves in terms of their profession of origin (as psychologists, nurses, social workers, and so forth) as well as to those whose professional titles are conferred by their agency (as case managers or outreach workers, as protective workers, or as discharge planners). Necessarily, as the concrete role the professional occupies specifies their point of contact with the client, the core business that different professionals seek to advance varies.

Distinct presenting problems and diverse agency roles demand differing approaches and often call on different knowledge and skill sets. The core task might focus on emergency care or it might concern the facilitation of the process of longer-term recovery; the degree of contact with the client might be that of a one-off exchange, consist of a medium-term involvement, or it might necessitate an intense ongoing relationship. The role might not even involve any direct client contact as it might involve non-clinical case management or service planning, secondary consultation, or program management. Whatever the role, there will nearly always be some capacity to assume that all clients have a need to be well connected with one or more significant others and to practice in relation to this principle. All who have clinical and direct practice roles, as well as those who are active in service design, management, and evaluation roles, are well positioned to creatively 'practice for relationships.' To do this is to align with the research findings that index health and wellbeing to the quality of a person's interpersonal relationships and the difficulties that are the consequence of social exclusion (Morris and Barnes, 2008; Ward, 2009). The opposite also applies: not being interested in promoting connectedness is, in effect, to act in denial of these findings.

Of course, being an insider in a group is not always a blessing or, more likely, might be a mixed blessing. An ongoing theme here is that there are risks, as well as benefits, in being part of – think of the word 'belonging to' – a strong network. For example, groups of young women with a diagnosis of anorexia came to refer to themselves as the 'Annas' and took to swapping tips on the internet about how to efficiently lose weight and avoid the attention of health authorities. Another example might also cement this point: as is well recognized, those with substance abuse difficulties have reported that 'hanging out' with others who have a similar background can sometimes result in conversations that recall (as one insider told me) "good scores and high times," a circumstance that can evoke and intensify old cravings. Group membership can be a tremendous resource, but there is always a suspicion that the 'mob' brings out the worst in humans. (This ambiguity is given a particular focus in Chapter 9.)

For now, what is important to acknowledge is that there is no one who is not sensitive to peer pressure. Often this influence is obvious, as in the group dynamics so obviously in play in the schoolyard. At other times this influence is not visible but consists of internalized voices so that even supposedly 'I don't care what anyone thinks about me' individualists, such as lone wolf entrepreneurs, are continuously subject to the approval, or disapproval, of their peers and heroes. This gallery is one these individualists pray to, and are prey to, inside their own heads. For example, apparently macho men, really 'rugged' types, are vulnerable to the living death of humiliation and being seen to be the fool. The influence of group membership is universal, mindful it can bring out the best and the worst in us. As inevitably social creatures, presumably the less conscious an individual is of the power of group dynamics, the less they are likely to identify choice points and to have the capacity to make active decisions.

Us and them

Another purpose taken up in this book is to challenge practitioners to have similar expectations for their clients as they do for themselves with respect to the importance of relationships. That is, in so far as each practitioner values their own personal relationships, so this should also be the case in their thinking about their clients.

To a profound degree each professional indexes their own self-worth to the quality of their bonds with their important others. We know our happiness depends on having, and deserving to have, the affection and respect of our partners, parents, children, friends, neighbors, and colleagues. Our self-respect is, as we subjectively know, related to feeling we are contributing, not just taking, within these linked sub-ecologies. We all know we feel better about ourselves if we feel we are accountable and deserve respect.

Despite this knowledge of what is personally important to us, it seems there is sometimes a disconnect when practitioners are thinking about clients: that they often feel it is their role to rescue clients from those who do not understand them well or who might abuse their interests. Rather than build on what is present relationally, it can often seem more vital to focus on enhancing clients' sense of control and agency, to help them get more of what they want. In so doing the practitioner takes the client's side and advocates their interests to their family and friends. Furthermore, they press the client's case to any person or organization that is not supporting and understanding the client as well as they do. To think this way seems almost an instinct, a kind of professional second nature. This individualizing seems more sensible, even natural, than it is to see clients as people who want to be loved and to respect themselves for being reciprocally involved with others.

This can be a problem. To ignore or discount the relational is to 'other' the client, to see them as essentially different (Levinas, 1987). What makes this tendency more prominent is that thinking and acting with respect to the relational dimensions of the client's life is generally not recognized as a core responsibility in many roles or in the conception of many tasks (Furlong, 2010b). A concern for the relational may be seen as a marginal task or, more commonly, might not be understood as any kind of legitimate concern at all. At least, this is how 'the work' has traditionally been understood.

That the design of many tasks is amnesic of the client's relational needs does not mean a concern for relational health cannot be a positive, albeit non-conventional priority in the way professionals choose to go about their practice. On the contrary, an abiding concern for the client's relational needs can complement the realization of the professional's official task. This creative attention to the matter of relational wellbeing entrains important processes that add long-term value to that core task – whatever it is that is accepted as the regular, day-to-day focus on which the professional has to concentrate.

There is a good reason to be so ambitious as to seek to go beyond what is usually attempted, and it is a modest one. Despite the tendency to assume it is the relationship between practitioners and the client that is at the center of the client's interests, in nearly every case professionals are temporary, even fly-by-night companions in their clients' lives. As noted earlier, in contrast to the practitioner's short-term visa, the client's social circumstances, and most particularly the 'circumstance' that is their interpersonal relationships, outlast any involvement practitioners might have as professionals.

In this situation if, for example, the professional has a short-term role such as assessing client needs in an aged care milieu or, if they are a cognitive behavioral therapy (CBT) practitioner, working with private clients who are referred for a specific problem of living, it is quite possible to complement the proximal focus, the immediate presenting problem, with the goal of enriching the clients palette of (non-professional) relationships. Such a goal might involve seeking to:

- prompt a new relationship between the client and a potentially supportive other;
- deepening an ongoing acquaintance or friendship;
- encourage a new appreciation of an existing relationship that is currently taken for granted or even disparaged; or
- raise the question of interpersonal accountability.

In so far as this action has a positive result, this outcome is likely to produce positive effects that will outlast the involvement the professional might have irrespective of their success, or otherwise, in addressing the presenting problem. Some practitioners, particularly those who have a more obvious purchase on engaging with the client's relational prospects, for example, actors who work as longer-term support workers or therapists, can find an abiding concern for promoting the client's relational health offers a tonic, perhaps even a wellspring of inspiration, in how everyday practice is envisaged and conducted.

Origins of the work

Central to the development of this text was the process of, and the results generated in, a recent doctoral program. The empirical component of this research investigated how practitioners viewed the importance of their client's significant others. This investigation concluded that the multidisciplinary sample of practitioners who were surveyed in the study paid surprisingly little attention to the client's connections with their significant others. Furthermore, the attention that was paid tended to be critical and pessimistic in its tone. This study provided a base for this current project and key findings from, and an elaboration of, this enquiry is woven into what follows. Similarly, the critical reading program undertaken for this project was highly relevant.

Another important reference was the development and delivery of a unit on 'social connectedness' over a five-year period. The focus of this subject was to present options that 'just graduated' professionals, those at the lowest level of the hierarchy, might employ to develop the client's local social network. This material was designed for practitioners who had received no advanced training in family or group work and were located in 'ordinary' base grade positions undertaking case management and discharge planning roles, outreach, or protective work. In this unit many ideas and exercises were extensively workshopped and much of this material is recycled here. This stock includes a range of teaching aids, such as 'vignettes', 'thought experiments', 'sequenced case studies', and 'reflective exercises'. Of particular note was the input of Grant Burkhart and Lisa Wright, professionals who are employed in a specialized forensic psychiatric service. The approach that Grant and Lisa presented, ideas for practice that have a strong relationally developmental bias, are cited here (see Chapter 9).

At an earlier point another input to the current project was the 'family sensitive practices' research I was committed to throughout the 1990s (Furlong et al, 1991; Perlerz et al, 1992). Initially this project focused on mental health and acquired brain injury before broadening outwards into a larger set of practice fields, such as alcohol and drug services. Across this period a key theme remained consistent: the organization and practice norms of many established services tend to suspect, neglect, or even disturb, the families of those who were the service's primary client. In a number of important ways the approach set out in this book grew out of this focus on families. This being stated, the ideas presented here re-contextualize the earlier work in that the current material does not privilege, nor does it discount, the importance of families.

More politically, this project arose from a commitment to contest an ideological and professional context that is increasingly individualistic. This agenda is brutally apparent in the deformation of positive psychology that holds each individual as wholly responsible for his or her health and wellbeing. Ehrenreich (2009) has urgently critiqued how the cult of positive thinking has reached the point where those with cancer, for example, feel persecuted by professionals programed with this ultra-exaggerated message from positive psychology: 'Your outcome is determined by your attitude.' This example is all too obviously nasty but it is only a more extreme expression of the ideology of self-reliance that has become so much part of the larger cultural climate.

In this climate each citizen is subject to the discipline that is self-determination, and those who are seen to fail this test, to not come up to the expectation of self-reliance, are increasingly castigated and may even be materially punished. Emerging public policies, concerning, for example, welfare dependence and the need for income management of social security recipients, officially express this trend. Needy citizens can now be abandoned with the rationalization that 'Some people are just not interested in helping themselves.' As in the era of the Poor Laws, of the deserving and the indigent, there remains both a moralism and disavowed violence in many supposedly technical debates concerned with public policy.

A different kind of driver in the origins of the material has been my experience teaching and consulting over many years. In this contact with multidisciplinary practitioners already in the field, as with undergraduates, it is clear there is always a keenness to learn how to work well, or better, with clients – yet there is something else that seems increasingly to be present. Teased out in many discussions, this less easily expressed aspect concerns a discomfort with the expectation that practitioners are expected to have the 'tools' to fix any and all presenting problems if they are to be judged as, and to judge themselves as, properly competent. Given that many practitioners believe there are often complex, less local problems that are the context of the client's personal issues, it follows that a standalone undertaking between one professional and one client feels like it is an unsteady project. Private solutions are not always possible.

On the one hand, practitioners already in the field, as well as those in training, feel it is essential to have a vigorous, even muscular, sense of professional agency. *If I am any good, I can 'do it' to, and for, my clients.* This is positive expression of professional pride and the 'can-do' attitude. Yet this feeling also reflects a projected pressure, a referred expectation from the many different audiences who are involved. These stakeholders include clients themselves, funding bodies, and those who are supervising managers and educators. Also watching are peers and the general public. Individual practitioners, and the professional associations who represent each competing discipline, passionately want to impress these different audiences with their professional utility. In this context it is necessary to be successful in projecting the message that the individual practitioner, and the group of which this person represents, is able to deliver the technically effective fix.

Different intervention models and host settings frame their methods and preferred remedies using a varied nomenclature. It is claimed that this, or that, intervention is best because it minimizes risk, can generalize across fields, has been standardized, can be readily learned, and so forth. This, or that, method, it is claimed, results in clients managing their anger responsibly, being able to gain greater control over their lives, has the outcome that clients remain out of hospital longer, are less subject to disabling symptoms, because of its supposed technical superiority. Evidence from standardized trials demonstrates, it is claimed, that X results in less disturbing delusions, a more positive self-image, less negative self-talk, that clients are more job-ready, stable in their accommodation, more able to effectively budget. And so on. This pressure to present as utile is so urgent that it often feels like we should be believers in, that it is necessary to sign up to, whatever supposedly sure-fire method will deliver the goods. Expressing, and ever more deeply constituting, this pressure different brands of intervention vigorously advertise themselves, and this proselytizing has a clear appeal to those who want to belong.

On the other side of the ledger, despite the evangelism that is so prominent, there is often a high level of background anxiety, even a wistfulness, for those who have made their professional commitment. Although it is often difficult to express their misgivings directly – to do so can seem close to traitorous – there seem to be many trainees and practitioners who have come to doubt the integrity of the advertising they have been subject to. At times this skepticism is grounded in a concern that contextual, rather than purely therapeutic or clinical factors, should be considered. More recently, a different kind of criticism is also being voiced.

In contact with counselors and therapists this concern has been stated in terms of a worry that many of their private clients are already so self-absorbed, so often 'on about themselves' and their wants, that to encourage them to identify the irrational beliefs that are constraining them, to be more in touch with their feelings, to claim more entitlement, to recognize the 'wounded child' within, to take back their projections – to name but a few of root metaphors – amounts to agitating a dog to chase its tail.

Less clinically oriented practitioners, for example, those who are in training for, or who are currently employed in, care coordination and case management roles frame their skepticism with the orthodox approaches they have naturalized in a similar way: for sure all the referrals that are offered, all the support that is given, the advocacy that is pursued, these services we provide to the client, are essential but they are not enough if someone is lonely and unhappy. What vulnerable, put-down people also need is someone or something they know they are contributing to, as well as one or more friends amongst whom there is companionship, intimacy and care. This kind of feedback has been a primary influence in mobilizing practitioners' motivation to execute this current project.

The author's professional background

My professional experience has powerfully framed this text. This experience includes 20 years practicing across a diverse range of fields, including experience with in-patient and community mental health settings, protective work, family therapy, acquired brain injury, and those burdened by chronic illness and other longer-term conditions. For many years I acted as clinical coordinator at a multidisciplinary family therapy agency that offered diploma, graduate, and postgraduate university-accredited training as well as consultative and specialist services (this center is now called the Bouverie Centre; see www.bouverie. org.au/). More recently, I have taught in social work educational programs and continues to undertake research with a focus on social connectedness and relationally based practice.

My background includes considerable experience with different theoretical approaches including the application of systemic, narrative, psychoanalytic, and experiential theories, as well as organizational theory and a familiarity with the legal and policy realities of contemporary professional practice. I have published broadly, including in specialist psychiatric, family therapy, psychotherapeutic, social work, and primary health journals as well as in more magazine formats (such as *Arena, Dissent* and *Overland*).

Structure of the book

The book has three sections. The first walks the ridge lines of two distinct theory traditions and comprises the first two substantive chapters of the book (Chapters

2 and 3), surveying the key conceptual formations that inform the material that follows in the second and third sections.

Chapter 2 draws on two central sources and one less developed, but still influential input. First, the research on the 'social determinants of health' that has emerged from social epidemiology is summarized. This statistical evidence has confirmed what many have long suspected: supportive relationships are implicated in health and wellbeing just as conflict relationships are deleterious. (For example, loneliness is almost as much a risk factor to health as smoking.) The other source has a very different background and nature.

This second tradition is taken from social theory and consists of an explanation of, and a summary of the effects of, what has been termed 'the process of individualization.' Developing its momentum over the last decades, this process concerns citizens being acculturated to believe that they should hold themselves responsible for the state and conduct of their own lives. Referenced to the idealization of choice, this process has 'downloaded' to each individual a relentless responsibility for every detail of life: from the choice of career and lifestyle to more intimate questions concerning values, sexual expression, and personal relationships. A third input, one that is less substantive in its volume, has been taken from feminist and critical scholarship. This influence has been orienting in impact and is unfortunately only able to be briefly sketched in Chapter 2.

The first section sets out the basic floor plan for what is to be developed. Building on this structure is a segment of the mid-level theorizing. This in-between material comprises four relatively brief chapters designed to act as the bridge between the basic theory that informs the book and the practice-specific material that follows. Each of these chapters is schematic; each has its own clear domain.

Chapter 3 engages with the experience and dynamics of loneliness. Social exclusion and inequality are examined and the relationship between attachment and the client's sense of wellbeing is reviewed. Central to this discussion is the idea that many clients develop a defensive attitude to relationships. Frightened that they may be hurt or rejected, it is contended that many of these people learn patterns of behavior that lead to problematic exchanges with others and worse: the increasingly prevalent conviction that isolation is the less dangerous option.

Chapter 4 locates the discussion of loneliness and exclusion within the larger idea that the nature of human relationships may itself be on the move. This change to the nature of affinity can be linked to the process of individualization examined in Chapter 2. That is, given that this process is said to have produced greater self-centeredness and self-promotion, and a diminished quantum of empathy, the prospects for secure attachment have been reduced. In this context the key question is: can the faux solutions and self-defeating behavioral cycles produced by social exclusion and individualization be interrupted? The chapter concludes with the optimistic argument that more hopeful relational attitudes and skills can be learned.

Moving from a broader concern with social analysis to the everyday world of therapeutic and human service practice, Chapter 5 introduces a different, more

---

local focus. This chapter investigates the possibility that there may be factors, such as an implicit theoretical heritage or accepted taken-for-granted habits, that might incline professionals towards inadvertently neglecting, discouraging, or even disrupting the client's embeddedness in their networks. This provocative material reviews shibboleths – self-actualization; confidentiality, etc – and identifies difficulties that practitioners face in being able to work creatively with clients who are isolated and/or relationally challenged. The chapter invites readers to 'paint themselves into the picture' by engaging in exercises that assist individuals in reflecting on their own personal biographies and attitudes about personal relationships.

Complementing this focus on professional issues is a review of the organizational and systemic factors that constrain relationally sensitive practice. That is, Chapter 6, which examines how funding arrangements and case recording formats, amongst a very large suite of accepted customs, 'set the stage' in such a way as to have practitioners act as if the client is an island of exclusive and abiding concern. Differences between the cultures of clients and organizations are considered before the argument is presented that there are advantages to professionals, and also to the bodies they represent, if practitioners are not limited to the information they receive from, nor only see themselves as agents of, the single clients with whom they meet.

The first six chapters, these first two sections, set the foundation for a third, more extensive engagement with practice that begins in Chapter 7. This practice-directed material begins with a basic orientation to relationally based practice, offering a number of guidelines concerned with considering practitioners' type of role and the length of contact with clients this role entails. Attention is given to the importance of, and several possibilities for, undertaking assessments of the client's relational status and how this process can be linked to goal setting.

Chapter 8 intensifies the focus on practice and includes case studies that offer practical demonstrations of the way a 'relationally oriented approach' might be enacted. Scenarios are presented where the practitioner assists the client in developing relationships beyond what is currently in place, particularly with significant others with whom the client does not currently experience a good-enough quality of relationship. Here, distinctions are made between 'reviving', 'rehabilitating' or 'remodeling' current relationships and attempts to create new relationships. Exercises that assist clients in imagining and actualizing preferred relationships are outlined.

To a degree, these ideas are challenging for the reader as it is argued that it is necessary to have profitable contacts with those who are, or might be, the significant others of their primary clients as well as with clients in their own right. This challenge includes the importance of the practitioner being able to engage in basic conjoint work where it is necessary to develop 'multipartial alliances' with more than one person. Observations on the role manager, planners, and supervisors can play in facilitating relationally oriented practice are also outlined.

Chapter 9 brings the earlier material into a higher point of focus. Several innovative exercises are introduced that can be used in diverse settings, including residential contexts, and two detailed case studies are presented. The first of these concerns the use of information and communication technology (ICT) in relationally oriented practice – a mode of social relations that is reshaping how interpersonal connection is understood, experienced, and conducted. Mindful of the dangers associated with mediated communication, this case study and its examination offers general pointers to the use of ICT in relationship-building practice.

The second and more extended example engages with the practical question of whether the approach is relevant in highly constrained practice contexts, environments where it would be assumed there would be disinterest, even hostility, to the aim of deepening the client's relational base. The example chosen to investigate the viability of the approach is that of an in-patient, forensic psychiatric setting. Here, the authorities have an abiding concern with risk and the patients (or is that prisoners?) are regarded by the public as both 'mad' and 'bad'. It is argued that if the approach can work in this setting, it can work anywhere.

Chapter 10 completes the text. In a new register this chapter reprises the themes and the argument that has been presented, and begins with a form of guided fantasy.

The aims of the exercise are ambitious. Analysis and theory is not cited as if knowledge of this material will itself modify either the practitioner or the client. Rather these abstract formations are mined for the practical purpose of detailing a framework within which a description of a set of practice applications can find coherence and meaning. As the text develops, it should become clear that there is an active dialogue between the theory that was initially presented and the ideas and schemas for professional practices that are subsequently set out. The ambition is to have an arc, an obvious trajectory, in the logic of the text.

In developing this logic the issue of confidentiality has been used at different points in the text as a test site, as a kind of laboratory, to illustrate the linkages between theory and practice. Confidentiality concerns the question of what will be held as 'mine' and what will be understood as 'ours'. This is a highly symbolic matter, as it is also an intensely pragmatic subject for practitioners, clients, and their significant others, because confidentiality exists as a phenomenon that operates at the interface of autonomy and relatedness – a location that will always remain sensitive, even talismanic in Western ideology. Given this context, researching and rehearsing how confidentiality might be performed differently becomes a key arena (see especially Chapters 4 and 6).

Hopefully, readers will be simulated and, at times, challenged. The material is offered with respect: practitioners are all doing the best they can with the knowledge they have in the circumstances they find themselves in. Marx observed many years ago that humans "are free to make their own decision, but do so in conditions that are not of their own choosing" (as quoted by Bauman, 1992, p 7). So it was, as it will always be.

2
Anchor points

You can't 'just do it': practical theory | Social determinants of health | Process of individualization | Principles from feminist and critical scholarship | Generalizing about 'normal' and at-risk populations

You can't 'just do it': practical theory

No Nike-like instinct ever warrants professional action: practitioners cannot 'just do it.' Just as a practitioner is informed by his theory, this chapter sets out a formulation – a multidimensional analysis – that underpins and informs the practice ideas to be presented in the latter half of the book. To put it slightly differently, the practice ideas presented later require a location and a purpose, and this chapter sets out this theory foundation.

Three anchor points secure this formulation and give the central argument its 'floor plan'. These footings comprise:

- findings from social epidemiology and the social determinants of health research that emphasize the importance of personal relationships;
- a focused stream of literature that has examined 'the process of individualization' – a trend which has, as one of its principle effects, that personal relationships are becoming increasingly fragile;
- themes concerning interdependence and personal accountability derived from the principles of feminist and critical scholarship.

As each of these sources consists of an extensive, developing, and relatively independent body of scholarship it is only possible to present a working outline of this material. This is especially the case with respect to the third category, feminist scholarship and the critical tradition in sociology, where no effort has been made to develop a general summary. Rather, a particular theme from feminism and the critical tradition has been taken up as a guiding point, an abiding value, to orient the larger exercise.

At this early point this material is presented in a relatively abstract form. To some degree the ideas may be challenging, yet there are two particular reasons why the reader's tolerance is sought. Most obviously, it is necessary to track the summarized literature as the bodies of thought surveyed inform later chapters.

And the second, less concrete purpose to working through this theorizing, is that, irrespective of the practitioner's specific role, theoretical persuasion or degree of commitment to the current text, this chapter retails an analysis that will be timely to many.

What is presented is an update, an attempt at a meta-view, for those dedicated professionals who feel their working lives are close to, if not right on, the edge. As the urgency of day-to-day, case-by-case demand rises up and threatens to overthrow practitioners' sense of adequacy, the analysis that follows is designed to help hold against, and to keep in place, the agitation that accompanies their immersion in the practice torrent. How might this analysis, any analysis, be useful to practitioners who are struggling? To misquote an old psychodynamic saying, there is nothing more practical than a new perspective.

Being in a dangerous swamp the most urgent demand, perhaps the only imperative, is to prevent yourself from capsizing and going under. When it feels like you are in it up to your neck, when the feeling is of murky water and the looming threat of alligators, where there are constantly contradictory demands and hard-to-contain anxiety, this is where it is near impossible to maintain enough distance to see the 'pattern that connects' (Bateson, 1973). Although the ideas put forward in what follows may initially seem abstract, this material is designed to offer enough elevation to see that there is a tidal pattern that is regulating the surges and hazards that are so intensely immersive.

Social determinants of health

Despite the established status of clinical medicine, a social model of health is rapidly establishing a profile. With its interest in relative inequality and social exclusion, disadvantage and stigma, the premises of this approach have long been attractive to those with alternative, left-leaning views. This is no longer true as the social model of health has become an approach with mass appeal. Currently, respectable, even prestigious, researchers from bodies such as the Harvard Center for Public Health (for example, Kawachi and Berkman, 2003) are presenting statistical findings that are so persuasive that the ear of governments and pragmatic social planners has been attracted whatever their political stripe. But what is being reported that is so compelling?

It is now clear that the cost of the traditional, clinically based model of specialist care is becoming, perhaps already is, unsustainable. Western governments now recognize this fact as multiple factors (for example, the growing burden of chronic disease; the spiraling cost of high-tech medicine; the emergence of a new generation of expensive medicines; an aging population) stipulate that health costs will become prohibitive in the near future. Like the arms race that occurred in the cold war, keeping up with an exponential rise in costs could bankrupt any regime. Without resorting to quackery or neglect, given this prospect, is there some kind of complementary approach that could under-gird wellbeing and health based on a non-specialist, low-tech approach?

Derived from a statistical base in social epidemiology, the axis around which this new approach turns is the idea that there are social determinants, non-clinical factors, that are fundamental to health outcomes. Qualitatively different to the traditional interest in variables, such as the number of hospital beds per 100,000 population units, such factors are said to mediate population-based figures. Most notably identified in Richard Wilkinson and Kate Pickett's flag-flying *The spirit level: Why more equal societies almost always do better* (2009), there is now a body of research that offers a contesting paradigm to the established, expert-centered template for healthcare. Using the analysis of comparative international data as its core, Wilkinson and Pickett's findings undermine the expectation that greater health expenditure leads to better overall health outcomes. An analogy might make this clearer: these authors have found that developing ever more specialist, clinically expert responses to healthcare is like looking for your keys where the light is brightest rather than where the keys are lost. For example, health outcomes in Cuba and the US (life expectancy, infant mortality, etc) are similar, yet the US spends in the order of 10 times what is spent in Cuba. Even more interesting, Wilkinson and Pickett do not confine their focus to the traditional indicators of health – those concerned with morbidity and mortality. Rather, they investigate an astonishingly broad suite of what they refer to as 'health and social problems' – homicides, imprisonment rates, literacy levels, mental health problems, obesity, teenage pregnancy, and so forth – and argue that the prevalence of these problems correlates closely to the presence of inequality – a steeper 'social gradient' – in a given society.

In their analysis, the steeper the gradient of inequality – with the most unequal countries being the USA, Portugal, the United Kingdom and Australia (in that order) – the higher the rate of social and health problems. And the converse also applies: the lesser the gradient (in countries such as Japan and Denmark), the less these problems present. Within the bracket of the 20 most affluent countries, not only does the rate of health and social problems not correlate with a nation's health expenditure, Wilkinson and Pickett argue that it also has little or nothing to do with differences in the average income between these nations.

Other researchers, such as those whose orientation is taken from economic history, have noted something similar. For example, Offer (2006) argues that improvements in the economic status of citizens in the poorest countries definitely enhances the quality of life of these populations – although it does not follow that those in the more affluent nations, those who are currently well off, will experience an improved quality of life if they are further enriched. If societies have high levels of aggregate choice, Offer contends, patterns of consumption are associated with an absence of self-control, as is seen in rising rates of obesity and gambling, for instance, more than in the enhancement of health and subjective wellbeing.

This analysis is provocative at several important levels. In significant ways these ideas align with deepening concerns about health expenditure that governments across the Western sphere are experiencing. This alignment can be seen in the policy attention many Western governments are giving to, and to an extent the funding that is now being directed into, programs concerned with health promotion, social inclusion, and the programs that are being designed to manage chronic disease in community settings (Wilkinson and Marmot, 2003; Marmot, 2005). Before examining this research further, the question of definition requires some attention.

What is meant by 'health' and 'social factors'?

The field is characterized by ambiguous terms and unstable meanings. At the center of this difficulty is the word 'health' itself. Being well, or not well, for example, involves using a reference that has multiple meanings. In everyday speech someone might ask 'How are you, are you well?' You might reply 'I'm a bit tired, you know, I am not feeling fine – but I am not ill.' In everyday language health is as an attribute – even if it is often talked about as if it is a state – just as illness exists as a more or less transitory condition or misfortune. For example, a person might tell you 'I've gone down with a nasty bug' or 'My mum has been diagnosed with X [a specific illness].'

This semantic minestrone has recently been complicated by the increasing use of the term 'wellbeing' in professional, semi-professional, and everyday speech. It connotes a quality of being that is both more technical, and yet somehow more global in its ambit, than the simple term 'health' (at least in its absence-of-disease usage). Rudely put, 'wellbeing' is rather like a less familiar, albeit shadowy, big brother to health. Fortunately, in lived experience and daily conversation exact meanings are not necessary: implicit conventions are observed which order perceived meanings even if the words themselves are inexact.

Separate to everyday talk there is the material complication that there are diverse types of health agencies. These services and programs all use the reference 'health' but do so in such inconsistent ways as to embed a troublesome ambiguity. Most obviously, there are general medical practitioners, familiar providers of what is termed 'a primary health service'. Yet even with this everyday example, there is ambiguity as 'primary health' can also be used to denote basic, as opposed to professional, health service provision. Within the larger health sector there is also the high profile suite of what are termed 'tertiary' or 'specialist' health services. The above service types are all concerned with the direct delivery of care, but there is another category of health service altogether: health promotion.

The health promotion project is an indirect, preventive enterprise which seeks to modify health-related behaviors, for example, by way of public education concerning the dangers of obesity and benefits of exercise. More recently, a new area has developed within the health sector: a concern for, and programs to ameliorate, 'chronic illness and its management'. Lastly, there is 'aged care', a rapidly growing service network ambiguously located within, and yet also definitely extending beyond, the health sector. Along with the ever-expanding realm of high-tech health service, planners and policy makers anticipate it is these latter subfields where the financial liability will increasingly be found. That is, as the 21st century unfolds, Western governments fear that increases in health expenditures will skyrocket far and away beyond any expected productivity and tax increases. Such a trajectory is said to be financially unsustainable and invites attention being given to the promotion of wellbeing: let us ensure good health by cradling health prospects within an allegiance to good living.

This is the context that explains why the emerging data on the 'social determinants of health' has attracted a ready audience amongst politicians and senior administrators. Clearly, from an instrumental point of view, this research has a number of provocative facets, not least of which is the finding that social factors, such as a person being a member of an at-risk group, is a health issue. For example, those in social groups that are subject to racism, or other forms of stigma, as well as those who have poor or conflictual interpersonal connections, do far more poorly and are a disproportionate impost to the system. Social factors powerfully mediate the incidence and severity of a range of health and mental health problems.

The term 'social factor', it should be noted, is itself a rubric that is unstable and contested. Depending on the operational definition, this term is inclusive of an extensive number of dimensions, which range from structural categories, such as class, gender, and employment, to more traditional public health concerns, such as patterns related to nutrition and exercise.

What is particularly innovative in recent formulations, and what is of crucial importance here, is the active regard that is now being given to 'the locally social', such as the presence and quality of personal relationships. Reputable research centers are now reporting that a person with significant relational support will have a diminished likelihood of illness, not by a few percentage points but a factor or two or more times those who do not have such a level of affectionate support. Conversely, a hostile local social setting amplifies risk. No longer able to be summarily dismissed as a leftie-hippie bias, the importance of 'the locally social', of having, and giving, affection, of being respected for making a contribution to one's significant others, and so forth, has now received epidemiological, and to some extent, empirical validation. Such findings have created a new set of headlines.

The big news

Social epidemiologists have recently reported results that many have found quite shocking. The claim is that prevalence rates for a broad profile of serious illnesses, such as diabetes, stroke, heart attack, and even cancer, are, to a very significant degree, socially determined. Further, if a person happens to become ill, a positive interpersonal network will ameliorate the severity and sequelae of this condition. In addition to Wilkinson and Pickett's work, allied high-profile reports include Ryff and Singer's *Emotion, social relationships, and health* (2001), Uchino's *Social support and physical health: Understanding the health consequences of relationships* (2004), and Cacioppo and Patrick's *Loneliness: Human nature and the need for social connection*

(2008). The latter authors go so far as to report that "loneliness [is] on the list of risk factors for ill-health and early death right alongside smoking, obesity and lack of exercise" (Cacioppo and Patrick, 2008, p 108).

These findings are boldly surprising, especially to those who have naturalized the idea that the individual is a biologically enclosed island. This recent research on physical health complements the material that has been available since the mid-1980s with respect to mental health, where high-profile reports have long supported the case that prevalence and recovery statistics are highly correlated with social factors: see, for example, Warner's *Recovery from schizophrenia: Psychiatry and political economy* (1985) and Brown and Harris' *Social origins of depression* (1984) Recent research, for example, around anxiety and depression, has only deepened this interest (Pilgrim et al, 2009).

Social exclusion and stigma are important social factors. The research reports that groups who are targeted for their difference, such as traditionally dressed Muslim women and gays in conservative neighborhoods, are at risk. How could this be? How can the impact of disregard have a negative effect on a person's health prospects? Putting physical danger to one side, Wilkinson and Pickett (2009) argue that being regularly bullied, abused, or simply ignored, for example – being 'dissed' – by those you don't know, has its effects. Acts of dehumanizing disregard cued by the perception that a person is viewed as unsightly, a loser, or in some other way the wrong kind of person tend to lead to lowered self-appraisal and higher levels of stress – a stimulation that incites the produces cortisol ('hydrocortisone'), a steroid hormone. If this over-stimulation persists over time, immune function is impaired and a spiralling sequence of health consequences is entrained. Central to this negative spiral is the suppression of the immune system, which is both a symptom and a cause of a slide towards vulnerability and ill health. Micro-transactions and, even more so, their importance, can be difficult to track but to be stared at, or pointedly ignored, can be a powerful experience, and most of us have had occasion to recognize how aversive this can be.

However persuasive the case has become that social factors are influential, there continues to be high-profile advocacy for a strictly illness-based conception of health. Established professional and industry bodies have a strong grip on public attention and tend to agitate for a radically clinical approach. For example, a vigorous recent public campaign in the UK has advocated the mass introduction of cognitive behavioral therapy for depression. For example, Layard (2005), a high-profile 'happiness' author, has argued that one in six adults suffer from this disorder and that it is generally amenable to "short, forward-looking treatments that enable people to challenge their negative thinking and build on the positive side of their personalities and situations" (LSE, 2006, p 3). Similarly, in Australia, Beyond Blue, a not-for-profit advocacy and treatment body, has led an enormous campaign to normalize depression as a mental illness. In both these examples depression is understood as a private mental illness, a disorder whose etiology and context is a non-issue because the only priority is to ensure that efficient clinical treatment is available (Pilgrim, 2011, offers a thorough review of this matter).

In contrast to an illness-based framing, for those who believe there are important social determinants to health it is clear that illness and recovery, vulnerability and resilience, cannot be well understood, and attempts to respond appropriately conceptualized, without acknowledging the importance of the immediate, as well as larger, social context. This attitude de-centers the traditional, clinical approach to healthcare. It also disturbs the received image of the active expert acting on the supine patient. Some argue these are progressive developments, but there remain stubborn problems, not least of which is the above-mentioned issue of nomenclature.

There is no stable conceptual vocabulary for articulating the relevant social context at the macro, or micro level, or for theorizing the connection between these levels. For example, there is no common language practice across the disciplines for denoting 'the socially relational'. Terms are used willy-nilly. Often the preferred term is 'supportive relationships' but there is, of course, reference to 'networks', 'families', 'neighborhoods', and 'communities'.

More abstract terms, such as 'social connection', 'social attachment', and 'social capital' (both 'bridging' and 'bonding' subtypes) are also in use, albeit in ways that remain definitionally uncertain. Most likely, this is an inevitable issue. Formally defining, trying to tie down and classify, the mandala that is the relational is like trying to subordinate the irrepressible. In what follows non-specific, deliberately inclusive terms are used to reference linkages in 'the locally social'. The generic 'significant other relationship' is often preferred for discussing more intimate relationships, but affinities and connections, contacts and conflicts, that act to deepen or attenuate the client's relational base, can also involve incidental, one-off interactions.

A cautionary note

Conceptual uncertainties will continue to persist, yet from a policy perspective, if there is empirical evidence that the 'social determinants of health' are influential, then these determinants are a potential site for intervention. That is, if the set of factors that is implicated can be identified, this set might be positively manipulated in order to reduce the incidence, and perhaps the severity, of ill health presentations, a circumstance that will, in turn, have a positive budgetary significance. This interest is animated by the well-established concern for the costs involved in 'carrying' those with chronic conditions, allied with the cost concerns that derive from the prospect of an aging population.

There may be no consensus about how 'the social' should be theorized; nonetheless it has become conventional to understand that a person's 'family and friends' are a resource, an asset that is there to buttress the prospects for the individual. Supportive relationships, it is reported, tend to ward off the physical and psychosocial threats to health and wellbeing, and, if you do happen to contract a virus, a disease, or suffer from a mental health problem, supportive relationships will help you recover quickly or, at least, not succumb as deeply. Interpersonal connections, it is thought, can be opportunistically taken advantage of when the 'user' needs them. In the discourse favored by health promotion bodies, personal relationships are a kind of prophylactic medicine.

This thinking is evident in many public health campaigns. Advertisements pasted in men's lavatories in Australia exhort the reader to check whether a friend might be depressed and, if so, to set about supporting this friend. Posters in rural settings tell the reader 'Times are tough. If you haven't heard from your mates for a while, give them a call. Keep talking.' Sponsored by the Together We Do Better public health campaign, advertisements in newspapers show a picture of jolly young men sitting around talking and drinking with the caption 'Master therapists at work.'

The message is clear but, at the same time, it is naive. Supportive relationships may be a foundation for health but they cannot simply be 'delivered'. Unlike commodities or legal rights, supportive relationships have a particular character and can only be learned and earned rather than conferred or guaranteed. Although thought of as assets, as resources, no one can "access" supportive relationships, to exactly recycle the language used by one leading health promotion authority (VicHealth, 2005). A person can access a parking space, be delivered a meal, or have a right to a ticket to the football but this logic does not, and should not, be misapplied to relationships. To propose that supportive relationships can be delivered is as useful as distributing menu cards in a famine, to repurpose one of Freud's delightful lines. And to see positive relationships as an asset, as a 'personal resource', instrumentalizes the interpersonal (Furlong, 2009b).

The locally social is the interpersonal

What is the particular contribution of the 'locally social'? What role do family, friends, encounters with strangers, workmates, neighbors, and the like play within the larger field included in the social determinants of health? To examine this question it is necessary to approach this matter using a multi-theoretical set of sources. This rubric seeks to name the intricacies of relationship on which higher orders of action articulate, including the social determinants of health.

As acknowledged earlier, 'the social' is a wondrous and indivisible matrix. For this reason it is quixotic to attempt to construct an inclusive and coherent summary. For the current purpose, a limited engagement with 'the locally social' can be initiated from a modest premise: *humans are inherently social beings and interpersonal contact is an irreducible expression of this sociality.* Although it is not restricted to this location, 'the locally social' can be seen to consist of local ensembles within which interpersonal relationships cluster and are expressed. Within these ensembles are conducted:

• interactions, including acts of affection and reciprocity, exploitation and violence, with those with whom an individual is very familiar, or might even have intimate relations;

- everyday experiences of material life that take place between the intimate and the incidental, such as exchanges with those a person has some degree of closeness or familiarity with, but where there is no symbolic or emotional charge;
- informal, incidental interactions that hail/address the person as a particular kind of identity, such as encounters in queues or on public transport;
- highly charged symbolic ceremonies, such as interviews for employment or appearances in court, that occur infrequently but which have a definite significance.

Many traditions, including symbolic interactionalism (Blumer, 1986), narrative (White, 1994, 2007), and social theory (Frazer and Honneth, 2003), agree that it is within these dynamic local sites where crucial relational transactions takes place. Summarizing a large claim, these interactions are a context for identity appraisal. Here, accounts of the self are vetted and, if the individual is judged positively, a sense of positive identity is confirmed: yes, you are a loyal daughter; yes, you have dignity and worth, and so forth. Yet, in these encounters negative appraisals can be made, or worse, can be confirmed: no, your violence stamps you a failure as a father; no, you look so bad, you are definitely still not one of us.

Melodramatically put, encounters are foundries where identity can be reproduced or recast. You can be recognized – acknowledged and affirmed – or misrecognized – rendered invisible or spoiled (Frazer and Honneth, 2003). Interactional exchanges between a person and another, between a person and a group, or between groups are therefore performative of identity. Weingarten (1991, p 289) wrote:

> ... the experience of the self exists in the ongoing interchange with others ... [in that] the self continually creates itself through narratives that include other people who are reciprocally woven into these narratives.

It is within these local exchanges that a crucial dialogue takes place: the exchange between 'What I say I am' and what those who I encounter 'Tell me I am.' Such meetings have a key role in confirming or contradicting a person's self-description. This is the arena where formalities and informalities jostle and interpenetrate, and where primary calculations of a person's worth are conducted. Judgments around respect, status, level of contribution, reputation, and the degree of inclusion, amongst a larger set of actions, act to support or contest a person's private self-evaluation. The result can be positive self-esteem or its opposite – dishonor, shame, and ostracism. It is often a mix of each of these values that is performed. Over time, a person's prospects for wellbeing are correlated with these calculations that constitute social identity. As White noted (1994, p 78), identity is negotiated, and renegotiated, in exchanges with others. This can occur whether these others are intimates or strangers, authority figures, or peers.

Within all relationships 'emergent' characteristics, to use the language of systems theory, are generated (Miller, 1978). That is, specific patterns – what can broadly be termed local norms or even cultures – develop and which then persist over extended periods. These characteristics can be glimpsed in the protocols that an outsider can observe (but which tend to be unclear to those who have become acculturated within these circles). There is an active politics in play in which individuals are listened to, which specific person speaks first, who speaks less, and who talks last. In a particular ensemble there will be patterns about whose sensitivities act as the axis of the relationship and whose interests are marginalized. In other words, repetitive patterns develop around the weight that is given to which specific participants and, more generally, how respective roles and responsibilities are allocated. Over time, local customs cement questions of etiquette. Such empirical detail tends to determine how the interactional is experienced, understood, imagined, and conducted in a given relationship.

Here the interest is in the spectrum of social exchanges that take place between people in dyads and small groups, whether these interactions may be familiar or incidental. Historically, these patterns tend to have an embodied character, a 'presence' that is immediate. More recently this character has tended to become mediated (Sharp, 2009) as texting and email, gaming, and all manner of net-based exchange have become progressively more naturalized.

What might be said of the day-to-day encounters we have with strangers, intimates, or associates, that whole suite of contacts and relationships that take place across the wide spectrum of our affinities inclusive of whether the contact is mediated or face to face?

Although exchanges embedded in a common history and recurrent pattern of interaction are the more obviously significant, in a material sense each meeting, even if it is fleeting, impersonal, and barely noticed, can be considered a variation on the category 'relationship'. As in established connections, in these momentary relationships important transactions can occur, implicit performances concerned with identity and reality construction. With (at least) a million years training in being sensitive to the nuances of group dynamics, a human can be affected by a moment in a crowd or another's gesture whilst standing in a queue (Douglas, 1995). Amongst a jostling mix of momentary exchanges, a person can unexpectedly catch the eye of, or be meaningfully ignored by, the driver in the lane next to them when both cars are gridlocked together at an 'intimate' distance.

This theatre may be reciprocal in its enactment of status and concern – it may be 'civil' – or it may be asymmetrical, iniquitously distributing socio-personal costs and rewards. A particular performance may maintain the participant's identity and self-esteem, or it might endanger, even disturb, these categories. In their cumulative effects, or their potential to have a particular psychodramatic power, under certain conditions chance encounters have a traction, a heft, that can have important effects. The effects of these impersonal, yet personal, transactions may be potent, but they tend to be harder to notate than those that occur, for example, in more formal encounters: between a priest and a parishioner or a grandmother and a grandchild. It is only recently that there is evidence that if people are regularly looked down in their encounters with strangers, this can compromise wellbeing and health (Wilkinson and Pickett, 2009).

There is a spectrum of interactions within which humanness is realized and health and wellbeing is either honored or poisoned. Whilst it is likely that larger socio-structural formations, for example, ideology, gender, religion, and law will shape the actions and meanings that occur within personal interactions, the 'locally social' can never be totally determined by these larger influences. Moreover, the division between the local and the socio-structural is, at best, a kind of 'regulatory fiction' (Khan, 1975, p xvii).

The 'social determinants of health' research is progressive in that it identifies, and gives weight to, the importance of positive relationships in the maintenance of health and wellbeing. What is odd is that this view only became respectable when it was seen to have a firm statistical warrant. Strangely, a millennium of human experience and reflection had not been seen to have previously vouchsafed this knowledge. This is odd as even the most feckless person – the so-called blind man on a galloping horse – has long known that a key ingredient for securing health, wellbeing and a positive quality of life is to know you are making a contribution, to feel respected, accepted and cared for. To people who are 'un-educated' it is common knowledge that good quality relationships offer a degree of protection against, as Shakespeare put it, 'the slings and arrows of outrageous fortune' – what is now referred to as physical, psycho-social and psychological stress. And, of course, it makes sense to the 'uneducated' that supportive relationships act as protective factors. That is, many people assume that having good friends and a close family offers a person a degree of insulation from the negative impacts of illness and bad luck – what professionals term physical, psychosocial and psychological stress. Intuitive knowledge and folk wisdom would also expect that if a person did become unwell, positive relationships would be likely to minimize the duration and extent of this difficulty. Similarly, what is the news value in the idea that a poor relational context, or a relational context that is stressful or conflicted, will act as a 'risk factor' to health and wellbeing? This should be our common knowledge, but it has only recently become scientifically respectable.

Everyday and at-risk populations

If interpersonal factors are important for 'normal' citizens, it follows that these factors will be even more decisive in relation to the clients with whom health and human service professionals work. Clients tend to be vulnerable and excluded and are more likely to have experienced trauma and stigma, illness or disability, exploitation, and isolation. It is therefore logical to consider that a consideration of the client's current, and also their future potential for, personal relationships, will have significance. It is in the particular interest of the more vulnerable to be well connected as the longer-term health and welfare of those who are at greatest risk is presumably strongly correlated with the adequacy of their contexts to provide practical support and symbolic meaning. On this basis it is a sensible, even compelling, goal to work towards these clients experiencing a quality of inclusion, mindful that there is no recipe for what mix of connections will best serve the interests of any one individual.

That humans are interdependent and not autonomous is well understood in everyday personal experience. This interdependence has also long been a key theme in literature, the arts, and more recently in the popular media. For example, in Bernard Wolf's science fiction classic *Limbo* (as quoted in Clark, 2003, p 13), the narrator says:

> The human skin is an artificial boundary: the world wanders into it, and the self wanders out of it. Traffic is two way and constant.

Sadly, Western ideology and the more recalcitrant disciplines have propagated the contrary view: that humans are, and should act as, autonomous beings. The emerging paradigm introduced by Wilkinson and Pickett (2009), amongst a larger band of epidemiologists and neuro-scientists (Cacioppo and Patrick, 2008), goes a long way towards acknowledging the social being-ness of humans.

A process of individualization

The second anchor point securing this current exercise is a theoretical formation that has been termed the *process of individualization*. This notation can initially feel alienating: "the *process of individualization!* That sounds grandiose – too posh and clear as mud." To some readers, particularly those who have studied child development, *individuation* is so close to *individualizations* as to be outright confusing.

The *process of individualization* is an interpretative construct, not a thing that can be seen or weighed. Despite its abstract nature it can be summarized relatively easily and, once introduced, comes to take on a 'Yes, that seems sensible, even familiar' quality. There are debates concerning its definition and use value, complexities that will be noted shortly, yet in its essence it is a construct that is both important and intuitively valid to those who are the citizens of a globalized world. Unlike *individuation*, which is a psychological concept related to the infant's development of differentiation and uniqueness, *individualization* is a sociological force which is tending to typecast personal subjectivity so that each citizen increasingly feels responsible for determining his or her own fate. Church, family, science, convention, tradition, whatever authority, or set of authorities, used to govern the lives of people, these larger bodies no longer write the rules and own the game. Now, our globalized culture holds as self-evident the principle that each person has to take charge of deciding his or her own behavior and biography.

What is referenced in the phrase the *process of individualization* is a historical and ideological development, a powerful tide producing a series of profoundly standardizing effects. Of central concern in this process is the idea that citizens hold themselves accountable for managing their private and public life on the basis that what I am and what I do is the product of an endless succession of personal decisions. Where our grandparents, and in many cases even our parents, knew what they could expect their lives to be, modern citizens are now expected to take responsibility for establishing their own values and priorities. Place of birth, gender, class, religion, these and other structural variables once authored and anchored the lives of the majority. In contrast, it is now being said that each of us must put ourselves in the driver's seat of our own life.

This is a position that involves both privilege and anxiety. There is privilege as it was once only the select few who were free in life; anxiety as it is lonely and burdensome to have no relief from the day-to-day, year-by-year demand to be self-managing. It is exciting not to be subject to higher authority, but it can also be scary. Skiing ahead of an avalanche is thrilling, but it is tiring if this pursuit is never ending, if there is never the prospect of rest.

With more of a base in critical theory than empirical research, *the process of individualization* refers to a very different kind of knowledge than is associated with the social determinants of health. The reason it is so central here is that it represents a pervasive development, an amalgam of ideological force, actual sociological change, *and* subjectively altered experience, that is directly antagonistic to the prospects for social embeddedness and secure relationships. If this assertion is taken for the moment as true, that the modern citizen is increasingly disembedded and isolated (Giddens, 2002), this presents as a very large irony: at the very moment empirical research has confirmed for the first time that interpersonal connections are crucially important to health and wellbeing, a dynamic contemporary process is reported to be producing a rising degree of human separation. As the 'social determinants of health' framework demands good quality human connection as the condition for wellbeing, it is being argued by some formidable thinkers that an intensifying global force is endangering, and practically eroding, this very possibility. Before developing this argument further it is necessary to detail the construct of individualization more precisely.

Background to the process of individualization

What is the process of individualization? At its core individualization is an ideological program that stipulates the terms within which each person *should* act and think. This program obliges each citizen to behave as if they were a self-managing company, a kind of mobile and self-interested corporation. Just as the pre-eminent management guru Peter Drucker (Rosenstein, 2011) argues that each corporation's chief executive should manage by objectives, exercise self-control, be rigorously disciplined in their use of time, and so forth, so each individual should conduct their own private life, attitudes, and choices.

Individualization has this content, but it also involves a specific and cogent individual experience. Those who have internalized this content subjectively experience its force in how their private consciousness is framed and focused:

consciousness is narrated in terms of persistent lines of thought, such as 'What are my choices?', 'Am I living up to my potential?', 'Can I do better?', 'What are the costs and benefits of this relationship?' This line of thinking is premised on the value of self-reliance. The inner world, its preoccupations and processes, strive to, and are evaluated in terms of, the citizen's success in creating a total life that is organized in terms of a person's more or less preferred choices.

As can be expected, amongst scholars there remain contests around definition (Howard, 2007), as there is also dispute regarding the overriding benefits and costs of this program. Yeatman (2007), for example, argues that the process of individualization offers significant advantages to some sub-populations, especially those who have traditionally been disenfranchised. As such individualization is a phenomenon that presents a number of consensual, as well as disjunctive, evaluations and consequences. However these larger questions may be addressed, central to the operations of individualization is the premise that personal choice is the most cherished of all values (Offer, 2006).

Consistent with this belief, and stated very starkly, individualization can be understood to download to the lowest level entity – you and me – total freedom of our own fate. No longer can we rely on higher authority, such as government or tradition, church or family, to make decisions as to what should be done. This being clear, the writ of individualization goes much deeper. Disputes can still be found in degree, but the story of individualization broadly states that the old categories – gender, class, ethnicity, dis/ability, location – all these and more no longer have the power to write a person's biography. It is the individual who is the author of what they are and what they might choose to become. Circumstances cannot be blamed nor excuses found. Individualization entails the belief, a 'knowledge' that becomes internalized by each individual citizen to the effect that outcomes and accountability must rest with the private self.

Personal responsibility and the calculation of costs and benefits are central themes in the operations of individualization (Bauman, 2003; Beck and Beck-Gernsheim, 2002; Giddens, 2002). Amongst an almost endless list of items requiring attention, each person is responsible for, and must be held to be responsible for, making the decisions that will determine their lifestyle, their career, where they will live, how their sexuality will be expressed, where they should live, their superannuation arranged, how their health will be managed, and what, if any, relationships will be chosen and maintained. For example, rather than fall back on notions of loyalty and commitment, each person in a romantic relationship has to calculate on a daily basis whether they experience, for example, sufficient sexual satisfaction and personal affirmation.

In the event that this calculation is 'in the red', it is the individual's responsibility to decide whether it is preferable to be live an unsatisfied life with respect to, say, their degree of sexual satisfaction or to bargain for more, to leave the partnership, or to remain coupled but to source one, or more, parallel sexual and/or affectionate inputs. As this process of reflexive decision making can never be finalized, no relationship represents more than a provisional arrangement, an association of convenience that each party understands comes without guarantee (Kipnis, 2003). *I love you, I feel committed to you, but only as long as the lights stay green.* Before exploring the question of relationships and the process of individualization more deeply, the leading themes in the history and character of individualization need to be introduced or there will not be a clear context within which it is possible to focus in on the relational.

The history of individualization

According to Elliot and Lemert, (2006, p 7), the grammar of individualization:

> ... remains the master idea of modernity for a whole host of reasons, not least because ideologies pertaining to the free and autonomous individual have been essential to the patterning of relations between self and society throughout the capitalist west.

What are the roots of this 'master idea'? Where and how did this practical philosophy, this ideology for the living of one's life as an opportunist, arise? It is possible to go back a very long way in tracing this story. Strands of this theme can be found in the ideas of the 19th-century English economist, Adam Smith, who stipulated in *The wealth of nations* that each citizen must be a merchant; to Ralph Waldo Emerson in the US, who was so influential in valorizing the ideal of 'self-reliance'. Of course one could go back far earlier, to Thomas Moore and the Protestant revolt, to Shakespeare's depiction of his protagonists, but such an investigation is beyond this current exercise.

Elliot and Lemert (2006) propose that the process of individualization has been gaining momentum over hundreds of years, albeit intensifying steeply more recently. Preceding the hyper-individualism of our current neoliberal period was the ordinary 'liberal' individualism of the preceding era, the period of modernization that continued from Victorian times, say the late 19th century to the beginning of the 1990s. Although a time of accelerating urbanization and industrialization, this was a period of continuous and, in some ways, linear modernization in the West. The process of modernization established the circumstances within which the flows and transformations now taking place in relation to how personhood is experienced and conducted can be understood. Especially after the Second World War, living standards quickly rose and a new expectation developed: there should be ready access to consumer goods (Offer, 2006). New needs were established, such as when–you–want–it mobility, as the rights of the consumer-citizen gained a far higher profile. In one sense these changes culminated in the 'alternative' selfhood that became available within the counter-culture of the late 1960s and early 1970s – what Tom Wolfe (1975) memorably termed the 'me-decade'.

Individualizing modernization has become an insistent soundtrack since the Second World War. Although its thematic wellsprings can be identified in earlier sources, over this period the 'Don't fence me in' theme became a repeated motif in popular culture, such as in music and cinema. The iconography of the misunderstood teenager, the outsider rebel, and the Clint Eastwood-type lone action hero have been popularized and romanticized over these decades and became normalized as they have been consistently recycled. More recently, this 'naive' individualization has been replaced by a sterner, less romanticized version.

Central to the logic of contemporary, aggressive individualization is the imperative that each subject undertakes personal appraisals of what it is that they most want. This reflexive process of review and reappraisal needs to be constantly executed and to be undertaken without sentiment. Goals must be constantly set, reviewed, and adjusted, or replaced; pragmatic plans set out that deliver the desired outcomes, and so forth. This is the life of the reflexive, strategizing contemporary self – the skilled agent – that Giddens has described so powerfully (1991, 1992).

Illustrating the non-sentimentality of this process is the idea that the knowing (and privileged) subject has to choose in which city and in which country it is in their best interest to live. In the past, famine and war, for example, created the conditions for mass immigration from time to time. Putting such pressures to one side, the great majority of people remained, and expected to remain, embedded geographically and interpersonally. Location and networks were continuous. Today, according to Richard Florida, a high-profile futurist and demographic commentator, the choice of where to live is the most important decision an intelligent and truly modern person has to make. Each of us has to take responsibility for deciding which city and which country presents the greatest suite of advantages for achieving our interests and talents (Florida, 2008). Consistent with the bard-nosed ethic of individualization, Florida contends that this is not a task that feelings, such as attachment to friends and family, location and state, should be allowed to colonize. Rather, due process requires place-finding to be rationally calculated by a subject who owes it to him or herself to be a ruthless and persistent opportunist. Relationships – to intimates, to location – should never be overvalued, and can always be dissolved and reconstituted as desired.

Nikolas Rose (1989, 1999) argues that this configuration includes a moral as well as a pragmatic dimension. Citizens who believe the neoliberal mantra, that it is possible to be 'in charge of your life', 'to make the most of your talents and opportunities', and so forth, endow these self-help metaphors with the status of a creed. More than mere guidelines, they are both obligations and injunctions: 'If I can *be* master of my own fate, I *ought to be.*' In a context that is shaped by the process of individualization, how individual people experience, put into words – 'language'– and imagine themselves is woven, at least to a large degree, with these terms and themes as their key elements.

Why focus in on the process of individualization and its effects if the overall subject is that of personal relationships and the importance of social connection? This material has been introduced as the changing practices of the self associated with the process of individualization are having material effects on how relationships are understood and conducted by contemporary citizens. In brief, the process of individualization teaches each person to say to him or herself, 'What's in it for me?' and 'Can I do better?' In such a process individuals put themselves at the center of their consciousness. Such a pattern of thought is injurious to the prospects for relational stability as it sidelines a commitment to others and disrupts the chance that individuals will achieve and maintain interpersonal competencies, such as securing an ongoing appreciation of the other as an ends rather than as a temporary, ad hoc means.

Individualization is a rhizome with many shoots. Concomitant with the valorization of independence is the creation of its mirror – the hatred of dependence. This reflex hatred plays a crucial role in public politics and is expressed in areas such as so-called 'welfare reform'. Captured in such an ideological regime you hold yourself to be and, in turn, are held by the state to be totally responsible for, your own fate. This is an unrealistic fantasy, a mythopathic 'dream of the autonomous subject' (Furlong, 2008a), as interdependence remains a core condition for a satisfying and accountable human life. Of particular note, the process of individualization has spawned a male-stream imagining of the self (O'Brien, 1981) that can be seen in the qualities popularly put forward as the elements that make up the psychologically healthy self. The well adjusted self:

- is independent
- is autonomous
- is self-determining
- has an internal locus of control
- rationally sets and reviews his or her own goals
- has firm personal boundaries
- audits his or her own personal performance
- possesses an adequate degree of personal distance
- is sufficiently self-confident and resilient to stay on a chosen course despite life's inevitable setbacks.

Such qualities are persistently idealized, but only within a psychology that privileges separation rather than connection. Foucault (Rose, 1989, 1999) termed such attributes 'specifications of the self', and if these qualities, these dots, are joined together, they trace a stable outline of the template for positive identity. This tracing describes a certain kind of being, one that is definitely more concerned with personal agency than interpersonal connection. That the process of individualization has taken deep root in our thinking and our institutions can be sensed in the degree to which these specifications have become naturalized. As cross-cultural commentators Trompenhaars and Hampden-Turner (2002) note, it is a measure of how taken-for-granted a cultural assumption has become that people experience irritation, or even confusion, if this taken-for-granted fact is queried: '*Of course, each of us is meant to be independent: what are you talking about?!*'

The current context for relationships

As discussed above, in earlier periods the great majority of citizens understood they could expect a stable role in life and, misfortune to one side, what their future would hold. This is no longer the case. There is now far less occupational, geographical, and relational certainty. Uncertainty is the condition of life and a globalized, increasingly post-industrial landscape has established a less linear personal prospect than ever before. Western citizens now tend to experience their lives as unwritten, and this scenario is being narrated using a language of choice and self-determination: you can become an astronaut, or decide to be a hermit. It is up to you, at least that is what the well-adjusted are expected to believe. Don't limit yourself, dream large.

The heady prescription that each of us is now totally in charge of what we are and do has been termed 'the project of identity' (Giddens, 1991). You have not been cast, your life is fluid, and you are the master, the driver, of what it is to be. That individuals can live according to their own wishes is the positive argument that accompanies the process of individualization (Howard, 2007). Clearly, there are advantages that arise from this program. Proudly using the 'politics of identity' as a wellspring, a number of groups who have experienced stigma and marginalization, such as those with 'diverse' sexualities or physical difference, have claimed the right to define themselves and to write their own scripts. For those who have benefited from this emancipatory process the result has been a greater sense of possibility and public respect. This is not a benefit that should be underestimated as the results of this startling freedom are, in many senses, progressive and exciting. Class, gender, sexuality, these categories, and more, which for so long have restricted the options of many, have become less restraining than ever before.

Given this escalation in freedom, some enthusiasts believe Western societies have reached a new plateau of development. According to neoliberal proponents, such as Davidson and Rees-Mogg (1997), it is now possible for ordinary citizens to be the 'sovereign' of their own lives for the first time in history. Where once this kind of freedom was the province of the few, particularly the very privileged or the truly outcast, advocates assert all citizens can now make of their lives exactly as they will in this 'era of the self' (Vejleskov, quoted in Sommer, 1998, p 316). Such statements may be over-ripe and ideologically loaded, but they make an important point.

These advantages acknowledged, in its extent and its power the process of individualization has also produced unwelcome consequences. For those who have been acculturated to hold themselves accountable for their own lives, a pressure and an anxiety accompanies this boundless freedom. If I feel anxious and isolated, a well-established trope would see this 'private trouble' as reflecting a common 'public issue' (Mills, 1959). Using this logic, Ulrich Beck (1999, p 40) argues in the context of non-stop fluidity, of unrelenting change, the experience of personal anxiety has become a 'mass sentence'.

But is this to over-state the current situation, to paint with too broad a brush a negative scenario? Presumably most citizens in the (so-called) first world continue to enjoy reasonably stable relationships and the excitement of greater personal possibility. And what of national, let alone regional, differences? Beck, a German scholar, comments on the experience of his compatriots, but also seeks to make a case that purports to be relevant to all developed nations. Similarly, Zygmunt Bauman (2001, 2003) and Anthony Giddens (1991, 1992, 2002) comment on the situation in the UK, yet both make a similar, broad stroke argument to Beck.

If a broad argument is to be framed it is in the US, where, more than anywhere else, competitive individualism has a stronger, more valorized place in a nation's culture and ideology. It is here that the value of self-reliance has been termed 'that American religion' (Bloom, 2003) and the notions of 'self actualization' and 'self-fulfillment' originated and found their sacred altar. (These psychological ideals are investigated at some depth in Chapter 4.) This is not to say that, for example, neighborhood and solidarity, class consciousness, and community spirit, has no place. Rather, for a set of complex reasons it is in this nation that the case for individualization presents its boldest face.

But what of other national environments? In this respect Australia presents as an interesting 'test case' when it comes to considering whether the process of individualization warrants its claim to universality across the Western sphere. With its national slogan 'The fair go', its strong history of trade unionism, and its social democratic tradition, it might be expected that the process of individualization would struggle to find root.

In a substantive, in-depth qualitative survey of 'life, politics and the future of their country', Brett and Moran (2006) interviewed hundreds of 'ordinary' Australians. To their surprise these encounters did not reveal a norm of solidarity, of locality, or of other-orientedness. On the contrary, the authors state:

> [I]f there is one big conclusion we draw, it is that the politics of ordinary people are grounded in pragmatic, common sense individualism. They see people as responsible for their own lives, as they feel themselves to be. Time and again people answered questions about collectivities and groupings with answers about individuals. (Brett and Moran, 2006, p 7)

According to these authors, self-reliance now 'trumps' interdependence and solidarity as the predominant, if not preferred, template for living internalized by Australian citizens.

No doubt, variations are present between different Western countries as there also exist competing trends and country examples within nations, regions, sub-regions, and groups. This said, a strong case could be put that the process of individualization has and will continue to influence how individuals experience themselves and their world. Reflecting on this theme, Michael White (2002), a narrative therapist, wrote evocatively of the many clients he worked with who regarded themselves as 'personal failures'. No matter how much they had achieved or endured, no matter the impact of events outside their control, many clients felt they were just not measuring up. (The implications of this trend for social policy and the understating of the marginalized and disadvantaged are examined shortly.)

Fluid modernity, to use Bauman's term, no longer allows the recourse to social obligation or abiding tradition. Accordingly, there is no end to each individual's need to make decisions and there can be no release from the expectation of total self-reliance. In summarizing this situation, Nikolas Rose (1989, p 213) says the modern subject is 'obliged to be free'. In this framing Rose deliberately recycles a principle developed by the existential writer Jean-Paul Sartre who argued each human is essentially condemned to be free. To the terror that Sartre said accompanied a life of unremitting self-determination, Rose adds moral scrutiny to this sentence: not only is there existential freedom, the ideology of individualization insists each citizen has a moral duty to vigorously take up this responsibility to him or herself.

Hatred of dependence: individualization and its discontents

Bauman (2000, p 5) noted that '"Dependence" has become a dirty word: it refers to something decent people should be ashamed of.' In the 'can-do' modern era, the mirror image of the successful, self-directed entrepreneur is the 'loser'. These individuals are perceived as so deficient, so lacking in self-reliance, that they are unable to look after themselves. In a period of steepening individualization those who do not conform to the expectation of self-sufficiency are a blank screen onto which are projected the darkest images. They are even turned into caricatures of what it is to be properly human. Losers are unsightly; they deserve to be mocked. Having suffered whatever misfortunes have befallen them, and then used these as excuses, it is said they need to have a good hard look at themselves: if Oprah Winfrey can pull herself out of where she came from, if she can rise above her traumas and achieve success, those who refuse their obligation to work up an effective degree of self-reliance deserve no sympathy. Such is the vitriol, 'losers' are now close to criminalized.

Why is there such little compassion? Individualization maps identity and subjectivity to highlight independence, even aggressive autonomy. Those who fall outside this spotlight are in trouble as it is assumed that they have put themselves into the position they are in. *Each of us is responsible for our own fate and, if people will not pick themselves up if they fall over, they only have themselves to blame.* The period of individualization has its particular vocabulary and its own harsh grammar.

As discussed above, in the current era individualization has taken up a moralistic tone. *It is a fact: each of us has the obligation to make the best of our talents.* You may not be regarded as a high-flyer, but as long as you can afford it, pretty much anything goes. Unfortunately, not everyone can afford to be idle, and not everyone who does not have work, or enough work, chooses this. These people are dependent, are 'on the welfare', and they are despised.

The last decades have witnessed a series of changes in 'the presentation of self in everyday life' (Goffman, 1971). Much of what was regarded as inappropriate only a generation ago, even diagnosed as an indication of personality disorder, is now accepted or has even become celebrated. For example, consistent self-congratulation, a behavior regarded by our grandparents as boastful and egotistical, even labeled as exhibitionism or narcissism, is now understood as a sign of vitality and confidence (Westacott, 2011). Being driven to achieve a goal, in other words, having an exclusive focus on 'What I want', was once the preserve of elite athletes and artists, scientists, and visionaries, but is now celebrated as an everyday attribute – even this results in people acting in ways that are inconsiderate to, even exploitative of, important others.

If the presentation of the self is changing, what is occurring with social relations? One new setting for relating is social networking where, for example, Facebook has more than 800 million users. Billions of contacts occur on Facebook everyday, which means that the frequency of person-to-person exchanges has grown powerfully. Yet, it is argued that there is a less positive side to this phenomenon, where Facebook operates to commodify relationships in each user's 'network' (Hodgekinson, 2008). Mark Zuckerberg and the platform's other designers take the view that a user's network is an asset, an instrumental resource, that seamlessly blends friendship with business. Interestingly, in his history of friendship, Silver (1990) concluded that it was the codification of commerce in the 18th century that allowed business associations to be distinguished from friendships. Now, with mixed effects, this idealized distinction has become notably more uncertain.

Another change has seen 'geeks', those who are intelligent but interpersonally unaware, become acceptable, even special, as long as they are economically successful. Modeled on Bill Gates, one of the world's most successful men, the profile of the 'autistic savant' becomes ever brighter (Furlong, 2009d). Amongst these are the so-called best and the brightest, the 'quants', who invented the new financial service products which have so destabilized the markets. These heroes gave the world derivatives, CDOs (collateralized debit obligations), amongst other exotic instruments, and have become the new elite, the financial engineers, the designers and the computer programmers, at the hub of the new economy. As traditionally defined these people may have few social skills but they are 'hot'. Similarly, the corporate flyer, the careerist in a hurry, has long been with us, but the 'snake in a suit' psychopath (Babiak and Hare, 2006) is more frequent, and more accepted, than was ever previously the case. A new book asks the reader to consider – and it is not an ironic request – *The wisdom of psychopaths* (Dutton, 2012).

There is a mix of progressive and problematic aspects in these new inclusions to acceptable selfhood. What is crucial to the current argument is that one factor unites the disparate aspirants to social inclusion: any new entry has to pass the test of economic viability. At the very least, financial self-reliance is required, but far better, the particular presentation of self up for review should be associated with success and celebrity. A representative of an aspiring group can now get away with being rude, nerdy, ugly – a whole lot of unhappy things – if this person is a financial winner or if it is thought they have a good chance of achieving success in the future. Of course, being able to talk a good game helps, but this is not entirely essential.

The association of economic success with social acceptability has allowed a number of previously excluded personal profiles entry to the club of social inclusion, but what does this mean for those groups who cannot advance such a claim? Particular groups are still barred, but there are variations in the extent and flavor of this ostracism. Some of those who have long been excluded have made minor headway: people with a mental illness, such as schizophrenia or manic depression, may be slightly less stigmatized, but most of these people can't help being economic dependents. Similarly, those who are cognitively impaired due to developmental or traumatic injury can never jump the bar into the fold, even though they can't be held accountable for their condition. The achievements of those who are physically impaired, such as the champions who compete in the Paralympics, have lifted the status of this group. In our more civilized, supposedly pluralistic communities, the only groups who deserve to be castigated are those who are thought to have brought their misfortune upon themselves. And who is included in this outlier group who does not deserve compassion?

Of those who are deemed worthy of castigation, of being 'other-ed' (Dominelli, 2002), it is the poor who are the most obvious target group. They are unsightly and, it is assumed, their plight would be resolved if only they got off their backsides. For the same reason smokers and those who are unhealthy and overweight are others who have only themselves to blame. Refugees, although not in exactly the same category, do also not deserve to be respected: they are queue jumpers. And there are more. Those who make no apology for refusing to assimilate are asking for trouble: think of those who wear the hijab or who hang around with their own kind, like aboriginal Australians. Unkempt homeless people have shelters to go to so why do they threateningly loiter in the parks and the streets making law-abiding citizens feel unsafe? Beggars, gypsies, drug addicts – these people, indeed everyone, are equally 'authors of their own individual destiny and their own success', according to a leading Australian politician (Abbott, 1999). Therefore, if a person is seen as a failure, they will not be respected, which, as Wilkinson and Pickett (2009) have demonstrated, leads to being 'dissed'. If a person is so named this is not only bad for self-image, it is bad for the immune system and, over time, for health prospects. If you exist outside the authorized territory, if you and your kind are on the other side of the perimeter, there are many dangers.

Am I to blame if I am excluded?

There is a terrible further dimension to semi-official, culturally sanctioned social exclusion: those at the bottom end tend to buy into this story. Not only do disadvantaged people have less opportunities and material resources, they tend to blame themselves for their situation, as Bageant (2009) has colorfully documented. Even as a person is looked down on, even chastised, by those who assume themselves their moral betters, those who find themselves the subject of a 'bad press' do not have a private language to narrate and contest their position. Whilst solidarity and class consciousness are still, to a significant degree, part of the subjectivity of many, the vocabulary and grammar of individualization has pervaded consciousness far more thoroughly than ever before. For much of human history there was said to be dignity, even a degree of nobility, in honest poverty, but this sentiment has dimmed if not been entirely replaced.

As a vigorous rhizome the roots of the ideology of individualization are colonizing every space, every conduit of thought, and this is no less the case with its victims. Individualization has each of us scrutinize ourselves relentlessly. It follows that those at the bottom end of the hierarchy (it is assumed) are there because they have not engaged in behavior that is sufficiently positive, have not been strategic enough in their thinking, have not been persistent enough in their efforts, have not set the right goals, have been too diffuse in their focus, have not sought out what is inspiring. W. Mitchell, like Oprah Winfrey, another North American who has overcome calamity and disfigurement to become a multi-millionaire and motivational speaker, tells us: 'Before I was paralyzed there were 10,000 things I could do; now there are 9,000. I can either dwell on the 1,000 I've lost or focus on the 9,000 I have left' (Mitchell, 2011). Mitchell's position is captured in the title of his pop-psychology motivational classic, *It's not what happens to you, it's what you do about it.*

Chanting to one side, holding each individual accountable for the situation they find themselves in is like blaming the cabin boys for the sinking of the Titanic. Not only is it not possible for anyone to be 'self-reliant', it is human to be interdependent, and circumstances will statistically determine the probability of human outcomes. However illogical, the celebration of independence and its obverse, the hatred of dependence, presents as a material social fact – as a 'discursive formation' (Foucault, 1972) that has material consequences. This disturbed narrative frames the psychosocial context to the debates that are heard around 'welfare dependence' (Frazer and Gordon, 1994; Hoggett, 2001).

Like the law and order debates that occur before elections, debates about welfare dependence have a strident, race-to-the-bottom character where there is often an unpleasant, even nasty, undertone. Where once poverty and disadvantage were not seen as sins, the ideology of individualization sets up the public and its politicians to think it right to look down on, and then to punish, those who are said to refuse its logic. Rather than the solidarity that was said to be characteristic of the 1930s depression, there seems more polarization and division, less compassion and empathy for those who are struggling than might be expected. But could this be true, could people and social relations ever really change?

Do people and their personal relations really change?

An old Arabic saying, one that has been traced to medieval times, has it that 'Men resemble their times more than their fathers.' Whilst it is tempting to assume 'human-ness' is timeless and unchanging, and that we may discover but can never create who we authentically are, it seems much more likely that cultural and historical variables do mediate identity and human behavior, including how we experience and understand our social relations. This is not to argue that humanness is endlessly malleable. Rather, it is to say that we adapt to, and are adapted by, our current social circumstances.

In considering how forms of personhood are representative of different cultures and points in history, the literary critic Harold Bloom (1998) famously argued that the works of Shakespeare created the modern self. No doubt aware his claim is exaggerated, Bloom was nonetheless making a telling argument about a mechanism that is intrinsic to the evolution of selfhood. Bloom proposed that Shakespeare's characters and plot lines, such as Cordelia and Lear and the drama played out in *King Lear*, presented emergent and tellingly prescient images of woman and men, characters mired in the deepest travails of life, that the modern character – the 'we' of yesteryear – eventually grew into.

Narrative paintings in the medieval period were used to tell religious stories that conveyed deep messages to pre-literate subjects. Similarly, Bloom argues that Shakespeare's major characters, in all their tragic flaws and with all their magnificent qualities, came to be naturalized in the centuries after he composed them to be timeless representations, essence-like depictions, in relation to which audiences came to recognize key aspects of their own selves and lot in life. For example, Shakespeare has Hamlet famously say 'Unto your self be true.' This stipulation, over time, came to represent a new model for proper humanness, a specification that idealized the notion of personal authenticity that has come to eclipse the older, previously conventional ideal of honor and obligation.

Focusing on more recent times it seems almost certain that identity and subjectivity are, to an observable degree, distinct from, say, two generations. In so far as this is so, it follows that the process of individualization has also affected the conduct of, and the prospects for, personal relationships. As with 'the human', it can be argued that relationships – intimacy and friendships, everyday cordiality, and good manners – are timeless and unchanging, but to take this view is to propose an a-historic, even quixotic position. If the opposite position is taken – that identity and subjectivity will change from period to period and from place to place – it follows that relational patterns will also shift. Given that the process of individualization is an example of a radical transformation, how might this process have affected, and be affecting, contemporary relationships?

There are advantages and disadvantages in how the process of individualization may have affected personal relationships. Advantageously, there is far less pressure to remain in exploitative or abusive relationships, and there is less likely to be constrictions around the 'But what will the neighbors think' ethic of Victorian times. At least on the espoused level, there is encouragement to speak up, to be assertive, with family, workmates, and friends. There should be less sexism, homophobia, and racism in a world where the process of individualization has taken root. More ambiguous in its mix of benefits and difficulties is the way certain traits, for example, 'shyness' and 'modesty', have been repositioned. In the era of individualization, to be rude, to be 'out there', is to be in good health, and this is fine in so far as this disrupts old mores around the importance of 'minding your place'. The relational consequence of this evolution is that there should be less hierarchy and more democracy in what is voiced and who talks.

Less advantageously, self-restraint and quietness can be pathologized. 'Shyness' – social phobia – is being considered as a possible diagnostic category in the next *Diagnostic and Statistical Manual* (American Psychiatric Association, 2002). The idea of 'manners' also becomes moot, which can have both advantages and disadvantages. Yet, there are also clear dangers. Crudely put, it is logical to expect that the well-adjusted product of the process of individualization will have learned to practice a self-referential pattern of thought. For example, it is sensible for the well-adjusted, autonomous person to continually ask themselves the following kinds of questions: *What is in it for me? What do I want? Is this relationship working for me?* There is much good sense in this, but it can get out of hand.

In an extreme case, if an individual's horizon of awareness extends no further than 'me', in so far as the 'I' has become the key referent in thinking, feeling, and behaving, then relationships will be transacted differently to those where the key referents were obligation and duty, other-orientedness and honor, as was traditionally the practice. If a reflex develops where more individuals ask themselves 'What are my options here?' or 'I feel awkward, I'm out of here', this is discontinuous with earlier frames that privileged loyalty and reputation. An *I-referenced* pattern of thought makes it less likely, even impossible, to be able to 'put yourself in others' shoes.'

As caricatures, the made-up woman and the self-made man of individualization are types of psychopath as they purely exist on a 'what's in it for me?' diet. More likely, the pure product of the process of individualization will be thoughtless about others and will simply act in ways that are interpersonally non-accountable. Again, this is to over-state an argument and to cede far more ground than the process of individualization has actually taken. As Giddens (1991, pp 2, 8) notes, there are 'exceptions and counter-trends' but, nonetheless, it seems hard to dispute that there are new patterns in human relating that are consistent with the values and practices of individualization.

This is a large problem for the prospects for secure affiliation. Unlike more collectivist civilizations, the culture of the West has never privileged a nuanced appreciation of relationships, even in earlier times. Perhaps this lack of relational sophistication was best summarized by Louis Dumont, a French anthropologist who devoted the majority of his career to the study of Indian culture. Dumont (1986, p 9) concluded that, 'western ideology grants real existence only to individuals and not to relations, to elements and not to sets of elements.' That is, we of the West are practiced at focusing on 'her' or 'him', 'me' or 'it'. We have naturalized the practice of thinking about individual people as if it is axiomatic that a person is a standalone site properly described with static attributes: what she is doing, what he is like, what it is I am thinking and feeling. We have the vocabulary, as we have the inclination, to frame our thinking in terms of individuals, as this seems entirely natural.

In this way Eastern citizens tend to be practiced at separating people from their contexts and their relationships. This is a kind of 'second nature' within the cultural logic that is hegemonic to this period (Jameson, 1991). The generalization holds at each of the different levels of Western practice: psychiatry classifies individuals; gossip magazines focus on 'Rachel's fat shame'; social science academics examine subjectivity and identity; motivational spruikers inspire ordinary citizens to achieve success; I try to make the best of my talents and minimize my exposure to 'downside risk'. Ours is a culture that, more and more, privileges separation above connection. Against this background, it follows that the process of individualization it is not a positive influence when it comes to promoting 'social intelligence' (Goleman, 2006), and the prospects for secure and accountable attachments. Whilst the above analysis is broad, later in the development of this text this theorization provides a context that informs and locates the practice-based ideas that are the focus for the larger exercise.

Principles from feminist and critical scholarship

The construct of individualization and the social determinants of health framework present as the most obvious theoretical footings for the current project, but these reference points do not stand alone. Amongst a larger set of inputs, critical theory and feminist scholarship has also been crucially influential.

Of particular note are specific readings around gender and culture which have generated the attitude to 'the locally social', to 'interpersonal politics' that is so fundamental to the exercise. Whilst it is impossible to properly consider these influences within the current limits, it is possible to acknowledge and schematically present several of the primary references that have been taken from this scholarship given the role they have played in constructing the argument on which the 'practicing for relationships' approach depends.

Feminist influences

Initially associated with the work of the Harvard Project and the Stone Center in the US, a range of authors within the feminist tradition have introduced the idea that women's selfhood is relationally natured, for example, in the centrality of mother–daughter connectedness and the idea of the 'self-in-relation' (Gilligan, 1982; Jordan et al, 1991).

According to Carol Gilligan (1982), women have, in general, an innate preference for closeness, a quality that is (in part) due to women's capacity for empathy, emotionality, and other-orientedness. It is argued that this is palpable in how women's groups function, how women interact in same, and mixed-sex, groups, and is especially seen in relations between mothers and daughters. According to Gilligan, mothers and daughters tend to have a closeness, an enduring affinity, so profound that this quality distinguishes this dyad, and its respective participants, from all others.

Much, if not all, of the above material assumes there is a quality of powerful connectedness between mothers and their children, and between women in general, notwithstanding that there is a particular quality to relationships between daughters and their mothers. In Gilligan's (1982) hugely influential *In a different voice*, the point is made that women's mode of being has a characteristic locus in the relational domain. This is not understood as simply a facility with the relational, that is, it should not be understood as a skill or reduced to the status of a behavioral competence. Rather, as a sex women's mode of being is, in part, characterized as inherently 'relational'.

This argument advances an essentialist position that rests on the claim that women exclusively possess a claim on the relational mode. This question of essentialism – that women and men are, or are not, qualitatively different entities in terms of their respective modes of being – recalls the explosive debate between Lawrence Kohlberg and Carol Gilligan in the early 1980s concerning moral development. The starting point of the debate was Kohlberg's supposedly scientific finding that men's moral development was superior to that of women. Gilligan powerfully dismantled this claim by arguing that men were not in anyway superior to women; rather, she contended, women and men operated with different sensibilities with respect to moral reasoning.

In this debate both Kohberg and Gilligan advanced claims that were essentialist, albeit where Kohberg contended superiority for one cohort whereas Gilligan argued that there were differences, rather than superiorities, based on sex (Longres, 2000). Whilst acknowledging Gilligan's critique of the language of science and, more generally, her argument that established social biases tend to denigrate women and to idealize men, it is not a logical necessity to assert that women 'own' the relational mode, a position that is embedded in her attack on Kohberg. An alternative view is that men either have a potential for a distinct, yet equally valid, relational self, or that all humans, including men, are embedded social entities irrespective of whether this is immediately assessable to consciousness or not (Weingarten, 1991). That is, it is possible to remain committed to furthering the feminist critique and the feminist cause without this allegiance stipulating that one gender – women – be granted superiority within the relational domain.

Different feminist authors give this theme differing accents, even distinct formulations. Hall (1990, p 13) states that

> … as social beings our humanity is a product of interaction, not isolation. The one and the whole are inextricably interrelated [and] Interdependency is a central characteristic of human nature.

This view contends that (what might be called) the 'social self' or the 'self-in-relation' is a universal phenomenon, albeit one that may be more or less performed with respect to gender. Whether one believes that there is a typical, or even an essential, 'female' and 'male' mode – with respect to the development of moral reasoning, with respect to 'the relational', and so forth – for the current purpose it is sufficient to simply acknowledge that feminist scholarship, in conjunction with feminist advocacy, has made a far more positive place, even an honored place, for a relational mode of being. This is clearly in contrast to the typical accounts from bourgeois psychology and mental health that cast down 'the relational' as 'undifferentiated' and/or as an indication of 'personality disorder, dependent type'.

Feminism's re-appropriation of interpersonal-connection-as-health offers a compelling alternative to received Western thinking on the nature of selfhood and normalcy. Whilst the feminist tradition is not alone in asserting this position – for example, anthropologists have also long argued this point: see, for example, Heelas and Locke (1981); Gergen (1994); Triandis (1995) – feminist contributions have led the way in terms of promoting this position academically. This said, it seems logical to reject the premise that either gender has dominion over 'the relational' (or any other realm) and to welcome an attitude that normalizes thoughtful connectedness and denigrates separateness. Given this legacy, it is no longer possible to assume it is healthy and self-respecting – manly? – to be self-reliant and to expect that each well-adjusted person should be capable of standing alone on their own two feet. (Of course, this is what the social determinants of health research summarized earlier also concluded.)

At a more obviously political level, the feminist tradition has made another crucial contribution to the present exercise. This contribution is more straightforward and less foreboding than the question of how the self and normalcy should be understood: feminist authors have long drawn attention to the matter of fairness. This commitment to justice has been vigorously pursued with respect to larger structural matters, such as educational and economic opportunity, but it has also been associated with a persistent interest in the investigation of the locally social, that arena that might be termed 'interpersonal politics'. In this effort feminist researchers and activists have scrutinized the domestic and intimate realm extensively and critically.

This action has, at the more public level, directed attention to domestic injustices such as violence and abuse, but it has also resulted in mounting the more general argument that personal relationships should be fair and accountable. For example, leading researchers, such as Hochschild (1990, 2003), have concluded by way of innovative, multimodal investigations that practical tasks and 'emotional labor' tend to be unfairly distributed in households. Although it should be noted that it is not exclusively feminists who privilege the principle of fairness in relationships – see, for example, moral philosophers such as Colgate (2004) – it is the feminist tradition that has put this issue on the map in terms of public attention.

The feminist slogan 'The personal is the political' was well chosen given 'the structures of society become the structure of our own consciousness … [and] society penetrates us as much as it envelopes us' (Thompson, 2001, p 17). Similarly, it can be said that 'The interpersonal is the ideological', and it is in the analysis of personal relationships that the political becomes more visible and open to ethical reflection. In the moorings of its attitudes and priorities, the approach advocated here is put in place by the feminist allegiance to fairness.

Critical theory

Feminist analysis identified how interdependence has been denigrated. By way of unpacking the process of 'othering' (Dominelli, 2002), critically minded theorists have also investigated how different modes of selfhood and relationship have been ideologically and culturally inferiorized. For example, 'Orientals', the peoples of the East, have long been denigrated by Western explorers and 'experts' as evasive, inscrutable, irrational, feminine, and so forth (Said, 1978).

Said, and other post-colonial thinkers, argue that this denigration is based on the practice of universalizing Western norms, one of which has involved privileging the norm of attributing primacy to 'the individual', and simultaneously denigrating contrasting norms that privilege the broader group/collective. More collectivist cultures tend to privilege shame (the need to 'keep face'), showing restraint and the primacy of reputation much more than individual agency and private conscience. Group solidarity, rather than individual action, is preferred. Critical reflection enables one to see how often 'we of the West' have read, heard, or said to ourselves, 'Why won't they stand up and look you in the eye like any self-respecting wo/man should!'

Critical thinking also helps recognize how the ideologically and culturally preferred shape of personhood creates a shadow world, a place that is the mirror image of what is esteemed. If independence is the norm, if this specification is accepted as the key criteria, being dependent becomes a status that is unacceptable, inappropriate, even transgressive. What is idealized and what is derided are simply two sides of the same coin.

This is the either/or of an overly normative discourse (McBeath and Webb, 2005) where a 'regime of the normal' reigns (Duberman, 2002). Like what occurs with gender and culture, what is 'other' is inferiorized: dependence is denigrated and autonomy idealized. Marx said, more or less, that each person could be considered an ensemble of social relations (as quoted in Leonard, 1984, p 23). This manner of framing personhood – that each human entity is essentially social rather than private – tends to make an immediate, intuitive sense to Indigenous Australians and the First Nations people of North America. Yet, to those who are properly acculturated Western citizens, to those who apprehend themselves and the world as different realms where the former is the active agent, and the latter is the inanimate site for action, the idea that 'the person' is a collective noun probably sounds odd, even bizarre.

In so far as a person is well adjusted to the realities of a globalization and individualization, a unitary setting will be perceived. This location will be understood in terms of its resources and its difficulties, its uses and its challenges. If subjectivity is desired that contests this pattern, a starting point is to inspect our language and to ask: how sufficient is the Western vocabulary for envisaging people as interdependent rather than as independent beings? Rather than dogs chasing their tails, it is altogether more sensible to paint ourselves into the picture and to understand ourselves as inherently relational entities. Informed by the kind of critical refection found in texts that contest the taken-for-granted stratus of Western ideology, this current exercise finds its fourth pillar.

Generalizing about 'normal' and at-risk populations

Not so much a theoretical as an ideological matter, a further point requires attention: in terms of personal relationships is the situation of clients, those with indexed difficulties who are deemed impaired or misadjusted, qualitatively distinct from those who are said to be normal? This brings into focus the question of generalizing.

What specific individuals experience and believe, ask and reply, is mediated by structural factors (culture, location, gender, and the like) as well as by the person's specific life situation (personal biography, generational status, specific life circumstances, disposition, intelligence). For this reason even 'good' generalizations can only offer an initial orientation, a formative schema, and act as possible starting points. This acknowledged, the lines of thought built up in this chapter have been based on the premise that nobody narrates or conducts their life using a private language. How we think about ourselves, and how we communicate with others, uses the common conceptual vocabulary we have been given:

> We do not personally construct every situation in which we participate. Instead, we most often identify the appropriate conventional frame for a situation and how others are participating in it, and then we work within the demands, constraints, and opportunities that these provide to construct our own roles. (Coyne, 1985, p 342)

For this reason how people understand themselves, how they talk their way through life to themselves and to others, can never be a private invention. This is so whether it is you or me, her or him, whether we are 'normal' or 'diagnosed'.

Gergen (1994, p 210) has argued that the "narratives of the self are not personal impulses made social, but social processes realized on the site of the personal." For generations this dialogue between self and society has been examined more richly by anthropology and sociology, fiction and biography, poetry and refection, theatre and movies, than by empirical research. This is not to denigrate, for example, the importance of double-blind trials or properly matched research samples. Rather, it is noted in order to acknowledge that different methodologies, different truth strategies, are required in different types of enquiry. In the relational world interactions are so dynamic, so reciprocally causative, that it is a folly to insist that it is only properly conducted laboratory-style investigations, methods of study that require all but one or two variables to be 'controlled' for the research to be respectable. To be a methodological purist is to risk being captured by the game.

Excising complexity and ambiguity in order to be able to claim objectivity results in findings that trade simplification for what has the greater power – accounts that offer range, intuitive satisfaction and a density of suggestion.

Complexity is particularly an issue given the subject is the investigation of personal relationships. The premise of the current exercise is that some connections nourish and insulate whilst others are correlated with impoverishment, even poisoning. In this case it is not sensible to divide off clients from non-clients or to shear off interpretations between 'the haves' and 'the have-nots'. Similarly, it is not sensible to assume all those who are disadvantaged and marginalized will have common characteristics, sensibilities, and experience. A refugee from Somalia has a different biography and consciousness to a homeless Western citizen with substance abuse and mental health problems. And those within the rubric 'disadvantaged and marginalized' have no monopoly on poor relationships as there is every indication that the relatively affluent, even the clearly privileged, can also experience alienation and exploitation in their interpersonal relationships.

This complication is not an idle point as the major current commitment is to those who are most excluded and at risk, to those who have been labeled and stigmatized. Nonetheless, the analytic logic of this book also applies, if not in degree at least with respect to pattern, to those who are thought of as society's insiders. Particularly relevant here is the assumption that the language of individualization patterns the consciousness of those who are homeless as much as it does those who are winners, even as the lifestyle and material prospects of each group diverge. This can be illustrated in the following 'gallery'.

Castells (2004) famously proposed that the life world of an unemployed, homeless person with mental ill health in Manhattan has more in common with a homeless, unemployed person with mental ill health in Mumbai than it does with those of Manhattan's elite. His view is that there are now sub-populations within the 'first world' who are captured within a 'third world' mode of existence to such an extent that the privileged New Yorker is starkly set apart from the life world and life prospects of a street person in their own city. If you are at the bottom of the pecking order, irrespective of where you live, you experience a fundamental quantum of inequity and exclusion no matter what language you happen to speak or which laneway you sleep in.

This is a provocative idea, a proposition that speaks to the transformations that are reshaping the 21st century. Acknowledging Castells' central point, perhaps the New York aristocrat and the street person do have more in common than simply their geographic location. The street person's lived experience may be of boredom and deprivation, of a flattening routine that is occasionally interrupted by acts of intimacy and violence, whilst those who are wealthy remain highly cocooned. This is a tremendous difference, yet both are likely to have internalized the language of individualization. That is, in so far as the street person has been incited to blame themselves for their situation – 'I am responsible for my own life' – the wealthy ill also tend to blame themselves if they feel dissatisfied – 'Isn't everybody, including me, the product of their own decisions. Isn't it common knowledge that each person is in charge of their own life? If I am not happy, I am the problem.'

Given there are commonalities, as well as clear differences, between those who are formally defined as clients and those who are supposedly normal, the reader is asked to consider something unusual. In what follows the attempt is made to track 'the pattern that connects' (Bateson, 1973), as well as to discern points of departure, between these different populations when it comes to loneliness and relationship. Although this might seem odd, to do otherwise would manufacture a "dividing practice" (Dreyfus and Rabinow, 1982, p 208) and execute a process of 'othering' (Dominelli, 2002) which cuts off the supposedly normal from the so-called abnormal.

However much it is usual in practice-oriented texts to disaggregate insiders from outsiders, to construct a cleavage between ordinary and needy people – and to also assume that professionals are different to the populations they serve – the opposite is attempted in what follows. We often feel safer when we talk about 'cases', those 'over there' who have a file and a diagnostic code. This preference objectifies the other and distances us from the 'bad' or 'mad', the traumatized, and the damaged. As least to a large degree, identity is defined in opposition to the other, and in some small way it seems sound to de-centre, even subvert, this practice.

However awkward it may feel, because the outlier and the insider are distinct and yet are, in the systemic sense, *also* indivisible, the reader is asked to 'work the loop' (Wender, 1968) in order to recognize that the normal and the non-normal dynamically interrelate. Relationships are always dynamically embedded in a larger social context, a context that is itself transforming, even careering, along its developmental trajectory. Keeping an eye on the ways the normal and the pathological, the weird and the everyday, interpenetrate allows for a depth of field in the perception of relationships and the politics that is their essential context.

3
Isolation and its accomplices

Are interpersonal attachments necessary? | 'Kinship libido' |
Loneliness and autonomy | Social inclusion and social exclusion |
Dynamics of isolation

Are interpersonal attachments necessary?

Before proceeding, a question has to be asked: are close personal relationships really necessary? Laura Kipnis, for example, argues against sentimentality (Kipnis, 2003). Who now needs, she says, an obligation to others? For her, all domestic relationships are a prison, and each interpersonal connection should never be understood as permanent.

Kipnis, a kind of post-feminist provocateur, proposes that it is outdated, even superstitious, to value relational constancy in our brave new world. In her view individuals have the same relationship with those with whom they talk, have sex with, work with, travel with – all those with whom we communicate in any way – as we have with a buffet (Kipnis, 2003). Relating is, in her view, simply another form of consumption, an activity that is no more than a moment of choice in a take-it-or-leave-it loop. In this attitude her views align with those of Mark Zuckerberg, the founder of Facebook, who regards personal relationships as assets, as commodities, that exist to be employed rather than sentimentalized (Hodgkinson, 2008).

These views might seem disturbing when presented starkly, just as ideas like 'strategic friendship' (Pierce, 1996) seem overly cold. Nonetheless, there is an undoubted allure in the ideal of radical autonomy, a desire that has perhaps never been so powerfully felt as it is now. Stimulated by the dream that each individual is a 'sovereign' being (Davidson and Rees-Mogg, 1997), it can be argued that we now have no need for secure attachments.

From a different base, but with a similar disregard for the conventions of affiliation, the mission of Nick Bostrum (2005) and his followers is to accelerate the development of the 'post-human'. These unsentimental advocates consider human biology as an imperfect prototype, as a vehicle that should simply be understood as a work-in-progress. Towards advancing the utility of the body they believe that technological intervention – gene splicing, hybridizing implants, and the like – will advance human capacity. For this group humans are not social beings, not collective and emotionally connected entities, in the accepted sense. Rather, the adventure is to advance the biology and let the rest, such as our received notions of romance and loyalty, of the common good and fairness, look after themselves.

Outliers to one side, the great majority of researchers now accept that high quality interpersonal connections are necessary for healthy human life. This finding would not surprise any anthropologist or sociologist. Anticipating its empirical verification, Emile Durkheim (1997, p 196) said more than 100 years ago, that 'conjugal society is, in itself, harmful to women' but that it advantages married men. In his sociological imagination Durkheim recognized as a brute reality that there was a relational context in traditional households where husbands iniquitously benefited from the support and devotion they received from their wives. That sociology recognizes that a person's relational context is an axis for wellbeing echoes what philosophers have long considered a truism. For thousands of years, and across all cultures, to those who have been the accepted spokespeople, the primacy of affection and respect, love and reputation, affinity and obligation, has long been recognized.

Epicurus, the Greek philosopher who identified with the celebration of the sensuous life, is quoted to have said 2,500 years ago:

> Of all the things that wisdom provides to help one live one's life in happiness, the greatest by far is the possession of friendship. Eating or drinking without a friend is the life of a wolf.

Around the same time Aristotle said 'Without friends no one would choose to live, though he had all other goods.' From a very different time and place, a Zulu proverb states 'You are a person only because of other people.' More recently, and again colloquially, the ex-Australian cricket captain, Steve Waugh, denied he was infatuated with the achievement of material or statistical goals: "At the start, you want to get all these test centuries and [to] have a great average. Then you see more of the world, see people struggling and you think *it's only a bloody number.* In 20 years time, it is not going to comfort you if you haven't got any mates" (as quoted in Baum, 2003).

A person's general assessment of the value of relationships, and of the value attributed to different types of relationships in particular, is likely to vary across the life course. This noted, perhaps this appraisal is never sharper than when a person is near life's end:

> When the body sinks into death, the essence of man is revealed. Man is a knot, a web, a mesh into which relationships are tied. Only those relationships matter. The body is an old crock that nobody will miss. I have never known a man to think of himself when dying. Never. (Antoine de Saint-Exupery, 1900-44)

The author of *The Little Prince* never worked in a palliative care unit, yet his life as an adventurer pilot convinced him how highly personal relationships rate in life's most poignant calculations. Kipnis, Bostrum, and other extremists to one side, a person would have to be extraordinarily unreflective, committed to the post-human, or inordinately in love with themselves to disagree with de Saint-Exupery.

John Donne said more than 300 years ago that 'No man is an island [sic]' (Meditation XVII). Whether it is acknowledged or not, each and every human lives within a relational matrix, however flawed or facilitative. These relationships are with friends, work contacts, neighbors, the people we come to know in various 'service industries', with particular people in the clubs, pubs, and gyms where we feel comfortable, and so on. This array of possible contacts is extensive even before we consider the relationships we have with our family of origin and with those we relate to as romantic, day-in-and-day-out 'significant others'.

A roll-call of your, or your client's, significant others includes the friends and family who are not seen regularly or, in fact, are not seen at all: think how there is a living quality to the relationship a person might have with a sister who now lives 13,000 kilometers way in Montreal (or Perth or London), or a relative who was once abusive and who the victim knows they will never talk to again. A realistic account of a person's *being in relationships* cannot be based on where their important others happen to live or how frequently there is contact between these people. The importance of a relationship is not measured by the physical proximity or the frequency of contact. The quality of a relationship is an intersubjective attribution that is generally invisible to an outside observer. Those who have migrated can, and usually do, have rich connections with those who remain. A diaspora does not lead to disconnection.

This relational matrix of a person's 'now and then' contacts also includes those internalized connections a person has with key people who are no longer alive. These past relationships may be considered fondly, they may feel aversive, or they may be mixed in their emotional charge. There can be the aunt who was so positive about you or an especially favorite teacher; there might be the employer who sacked you unfairly or the stranger who accosted and robbed you. 'Here and now' contacts are important, and so can occasional, or even 'in the past', relationships be significant. That Westerners organize their experience of the world and of themselves in terms of 'the individual' – the me and the you – is a constant, if illogical, premise, yet it is a non-negotiable reality that all humans are interdependent and are 'beings in relationships'. We may not generally think about it this way, but it is literally impossible to be 'not in relationships'. However vibrant or unhealthy, ordinary or attenuated, a person's social connectedness has an existence that is both material and symbolic.

Kinship libido

Carl Jung, a renegade psychoanalytic thinker, proposed that humans had an ineradicable 'kinship libido'. This appetite for connection prompts us to bond closely with others and is a desire that is neither sexual nor exploitative. Rather, it is what animates and conjoins siblings, friends, and comrades (Jung, 1946, para

431). A need to belong is not simply about fearing what will happen if we are rejected from the nomad herd; it is in our nature to have a hunger for the giving, and the receiving, of affection and respect.

This tendency to affiliate has been characteristic of human behavior across all human history. Far from it being self-destructive, the satisfaction of this need does us good. Recent research may have confirmed this, but airy-fairy statistics to one side, how many people really need to be told there is truth in these newly minted findings? Intuitively, this knowledge is held as self-evident right down deep in the bones.

If humans have a need to relate, and it is good for us, how is it that many people – probably more than ever before – are now lonely and isolated? This chapter examines this question. In brief, a set of suspects are interrogated. These suspects make up a diverse crew. They come from different locations, have different aliases, and present in different guises. Included in this group are some apparently good sorts – we all know how popular *autonomy* and *being in charge* are – but there are also some seedy types. Social exclusion and defensiveness are very fine coaches of loneliness, but are hard to locate, let alone pin down. All will be vigorously quizzed.

The examination of loneliness and isolation is presented as the next step in the developing arc of the book. Where the larger, anchoring concepts were discussed in the last chapter – in particular, the social determinants of health and the tide of individualization – and the next chapter begins to zero in on the practical by taking a hard look at the context of practitioner–client contact, this chapter focuses on a half-way zone: the interpersonal experiences of clients and non-clients. In this space there seems to be a changing dance, an evolving pattern of interpersonal action. What is put forward is the idea that, as people change in their attitudes and behavior, so do their relationships, at least to a degree.

Like a mobile in a nursery, selfhood and social relations are conjointly on the move. For example, a number of studies have indicated that many of us are less practiced at being empathic and are more likely to be self-referential in how we understand the social space. These studies are discussed later but for now, imagine how the prospects for cooperation and connection would be affected if each participant equally felt the need to be in control. A vignette from a popular television sit-com draws out this point.

Who's in charge of the relationship?

In a *Seinfeld* episode Elaine became interested in, even deeply smitten by, an avant-garde jazz musician who she saw as deeply attractive. Unfortunately, Jerry let this suitor know she was very keen. When Elaine heard Jerry had done this she was distraught. Incensed that Jerry's indiscretion had blown her playing-it-cool cover, and more pragmatically because she assumed this slip would result in her being seen by her suitor as less desirable, she fronted Jerry. This exchange began with Elaine positively screeching at Jerry.

At this point viewers would not have been surprised Elaine was angry and wanted to berate Jerry, but the intensity of her feelings and the clarity of her argument was wonderfully informing. Her outburst centered on a specific claim, a claim she loudly yelled directly into Jerry's face: "Do you have any idea how terrifying it is not to be in control of the relationship?"

On hearing this Jerry saw her point, or at least she thought he did. Wracked at the humiliation her emotional nakedness signified, Elaine went close to bailing out of the nascent romance but, fortunately, she held her nerve and viewers got to hear the good news that it did work out, at least for this single episode.

Reflecting on Elaine's outburst it is not hard to see her point. Elaine thought she had had her prospects blighted, that she was so exposed as to be transparent and defenseless. Holding this idea, but reflecting further, a second and less empathic line of thought arises: who does she think she is? Does she think the relationship is only about her? Of course, this is only a television show, a brilliant, if worryingly prescient, social satire. Elaine is no more than a certain type of character, a knowingly constructed representative image. In this representation what have the savvy writers depicted as the truly modern subject? Someone who is always thinking *I must be in control*.

That participants might 'play it cool' is not unusual in the pursuer–pursued dance that is conducted in the early stages of a romance. This is fine as long as it is recognized that one party in a romance, a friendship, indeed *any* relationship, should ever have, or aspire to have, unilateral control. Acting as if a single participant ever has the right to be in total control is to model intimate relationships on the master–slave or consumer–provider dynamic. Neither of these metaphors is appropriate in any kind of reciprocal personal relationship. This being clear, if one, or both, parties are over-sensitive to 'not being in control', this will disturb, even disrupt, the prospects for genuine partnership.

Loneliness and autonomy

Having presented the conceptual base in the previous chapter, the focus of this chapter is to examine isolation and loneliness, exclusion and ostracism. To do this is to venture broad-brush statements, outlines of trends and shifting patterns. The intention is to find some higher ground and to walk along a ridge line observing the general lay of the land. According to the anthropologist Clifford Geertz (1995, p 78), from this vantage point complexities seem 'clear at a distance' yet, when you get into the detail, when you are immersed in the immediate, these apparently clear patterns become disturbed, and it is 'jumbled up close'. What Geertz meant is that distance is a precondition for clarity, but this apparent lucidity is illusory and naive. Similarly, the line of argument developed in this chapter is always in danger of simplification and over-reach. When the subject at hand is complex and ambiguous – in this case statements about the changing nature of isolation and connectedness, exclusion and intimacy – conclusions become overly generalized.

Exceptions and counter-examples, outliers and anomalies, defy the correctness of any set of descriptions. It can never be right to declare what any person – 'this woman' or 'that man' – subjectively thinks or feels, or how any particular person, or people, will behave interpersonally. Given the level of generalization being considered it is especially important the reader remains skeptical about the broad argument that is put forward. Review and contest what is presented in the light of your own knowledge and experience.

One fact that is clear is that the fastest growing housing category across the Western world is 'single person occupancy' (OECD, 2003). In part, this reflects the availability of a creative new option as many people desire this choice and no longer feel it is stigmatizing to live on their own. Rather than being seen, for example, as an unmarried and unhappy woman, or a difficult and lonely man, having a place of your own represents autonomy and day-in, day-out control. For these people making a decision to avoid the compromise and irritation of domestic life is experienced as performing the kind of personal independence that realizes an exactly modern specification. Others who live alone, such as older people or those with a disability, may do this without it being a preferred choice: being on your own is not always a freely taken decision whose aim is to have dominion over your living conditions.

In so far as an increasing number of individuals actively choose domestic independence, it is possible to understand this movement as representing the confluence of complex social processes as much or more as it purely expresses a freely chosen private desire. Perhaps there is diminishing access to the values, attitudes, and skills required to live well with others, a trend that speaks to the effects of major social transformations such as the rise of techno–consumerism, and that a private desire for control experienced by a sub-population might reflect, amongst other possibilities, the creation of a demand for a certain market-driven lifestyle.

However it is interpreted, that many who are affluent now find it less tolerable to negotiate and haggle, reasonably let go, or thoughtfully take up their differences with cohabitants represents a shift, even a rupture, in relation to earlier generations. Domesticity is, and always has been, irritating, at least from time to time. Compromising is rarely easy. And managing differences is not just about feelings. Successful coexistence also requires a suite of attitudes and skills that, when they are harmonized, generates a practical magic where the circle is squared so that two, or more, actually live better than the sum of the parts. A set of elements can form an ensemble that generates a shared sense of purpose, identity, and pride.

But what of those who are not well off? Is it different for those who are disadvantaged and stigmatized? Such citizens have fewer material options with respect to housing than those who are more affluent. For example, if you leave the supported accommodation you have been lucky enough to be granted, if you have a persistent mental illness or you are a refugee who does not speak the local language, you almost certainly won't have enough money to compete in the commercial property market. This material circumstance is a fact, but there is also a second level of context to take account of: what are the chances you will have the kind of values, attitudes, and skills that are conducive to making and keeping friendships and family contacts, irrespective of your financial resources?

There is no straightforward answer to this question. Certainly, if practitioners review their current caseloads, and/or look back over the many clients with whom they have had contact, it is possible to identify a good number of clients who have 'the gift of the gab' or who have had enough personality, even charisma, to stay well connected. Some people have a lucky streak or, somehow, have an appeal or energy that has them seen as attractive company. Other clients have friends and family who are so steadfast that there is always a safety net and a font of affection. For the rest, and it is likely to be at least a sizable minority, isolation and loneliness is a common and persistent feature of their lives.

In everyday terms, those who are the recipients of services, who are at the lower levels of the social hierarchy, often do not present the skills, attitudes, and values that are associated with making and sustaining relationships. Amongst a larger set of behaviors, these people often trust far too little, or way too much, and/or are so frightened and suspicious that this static keeps others at bay (Cacioppo and Patrick, 2008). Many who are anxious and defensive will 'get in first' and exit – a group, a new associate, a budding friendship, a romance – in order to avoid the possibility of rejection and hurt. Such relationship patterns are a learned form of defense, are 'attempted solutions', which have a counter-productive effect as they are 'problem maintaining' (Watzlawick et al, 1974). This is a poignant and troubling concern.

Billie

Billie is a 48-year-old woman currently living alone in a public housing unit. She has a long history of homelessness and alcohol abuse and has been subject to repeated assaults from those she tells you were her "mates", her drinking buddies from the days she was in hostels and on the streets sleeping rough. She says she hated how violence "just happened", but that she mostly "gave back as much as I got" when it did. She tells you she now misses this company for the "good times when we had a few quid, when we partied hard, never spooking ourselves worrying about tomorrow." Although relatively mild, Billie has an acquired brain injury from her drinking and the violence she has suffered. She has undoubted warmth about her, but this glow is dimmed and kept close. "I've got the drawbridge right up. What else can you do?"

The last of these assaults found her (once again) in the local Accident and Emergency (A&E) department. With a great deal of assistance, from there she eventually took the path to the semi-supported accommodation where she now resides. Backed up by a dedicated homelessness service, Billie's very limited finances are managed for her. She has, on her own account, "no mates, no friends now" and states she does not want any: "Like a dumb dog I trusted people, gave what I had to whoever asked for it. No more. I just want to be safe. That last time in the hospital really freaked me out when I saw what had happened to my face. Fuck it, I hate being on my own, but what can you do? Better be on your own because everybody turns on you don't they? I just don't know how to be with others without it all going wrong."

Social inclusion and social exclusion

It is hard to identify the factors that lead individuals to find personal relationships difficult, if not self-defeating. Reflecting on a particular person's struggles as these have an impact on their prospects for relationships is important in itself, yet these reasons are unlikely to be unique. At a higher level of analysis each person-to-person exchange can be theorized with respect to the larger cultural, sociological, and economic processes within which particular difficulties occur.

In the past few years a key construct that has been used to link broader social conditions with the personal experience of individuals is that of social inclusion and social exclusion (Todman, 2004; Morgan et al, 2007). Much of this linkage work has emphasized access to economic participation, particularly as this is related to the prospects for securing civil rights, stable accommodation, and adequately paid employment. In this emphasis attention is given to educational attainment, geographical location, ethnicity, disability, gender, the absence of citizenship documentation, and so forth. Taket et al (2009) offer a formidable review of this complex interplay.

The construct of social in/exclusion now plays a central role in understanding how groups of people – such as those who are homeless or who have serious mental health problems, those who are carers or single parents – find themselves without adequate access to material and symbolic capital. This has led to social interventions being devised and implemented that are informed by the developing inclusion/exclusion literature. Mindful there remain definitional and ideological uncertainties with the construct (there are 'horizontal' and 'vertical' versions, 'strong' and 'weak' formulations, etc), many OECD (Organisation for Economic Co-operation and Development) governments and many research bodies now focus considerable attention on the interplay of mechanisms that are said to influence, if not determine, how certain categories hold, and are maintained in, a socially excluded status. French authorities and social planners, for example, have long been concerned about the large number of citizens who live in the high-rise, racialized, and distinctly criminalizing public housing enclaves that ring Paris. In contrast to elsewhere in France, employment prospects and educational levels in *les banlieues* – the deprived outer suburbs – are poorer, levels of poverty, violence, and disaffection are high, and it assumed that these exclusory conditions will be self-sustaining unless satisfactory campaigns can be created to address these problems.

That 'social exclusion' has become such a significant interpretative framework is itself an interesting phenomenon. Some critics consider this popularity a cause of suspicion, and argue that the in/exclusion flag can reflect a politically conservative instinct as they see it conflates paid employment, however marginal or even exploitive, with social inclusion as if the two were synonymous (Jones, 2001). In some quarters it has also been argued that there is an instrumental interest in using programs tagged with the high-sounding motto 'Promoting social inclusion' to disguise a narrow concern with public order rather than with the concern for justice per se. Actions based on this narrow and conservative frame could aim for nothing more progressive than simply inhibiting outbreaks of disaffection, such as those that occurred in Paris in 2005 or in London in 2011.

It seems fair to conclude that there is a mix of conservative and progressive thought which has led to the establishment of commissioners for social inclusion in the European Union (EU), Social Inclusion Units in many OECD countries and the diverse programs that have been established to reduce the marginalization of excluded groups such as those with mental ill health or the homeless, the Roma, or refugees. As argued in the previous chapter, there is an economic driver behind these developments as it is understood that the more a group is excluded, the greater the scale of their health and social problems which, in turn, are expected to create a greater demand on limited health and human service budgets over the long term. Irrespective of whether the driver is a concern for public order and/or a concern with costs, the question of justice also arises. If groups are marginalized because of their ethnic character or are disenfranchised due to unemployment, housing, illness, access to education, or political rights, this is unfair.

The discourse of social in/exclusion is centrally relevant here in an important yet nuanced manner. Briefly put, structural issues alone are insufficient to explain, and inform interventions with respect to addressing the problems of, loneliness and isolation. For example, according to one peak body (VicServ, 2008, p 56) there are five dimensions to social exclusion:

i) relational exclusion: refers to poor social ties or connectedness with respect to friends, family, neighborhood, etc;
ii) economic exclusion: refers to an impeded access to employment and its pathways;
iii) institutional exclusion: inequitable access to rights and to the range of services that underwrite wellbeing;
iv) geographic exclusion: the impact of location on opportunities and risks;
v) symbolic exclusion: refers to a poor sense of belonging, purpose, agency, and identity.

None of these interrelated factors should be under-acknowledged. With this understood, the current exercise is particularly concerned with (i) and (v), where the former is relevant to the importance of the immediately interpersonal and the latter as it concerns the higher order interest humans have in belonging, purpose, agency, and identity.

Exclusion is, as Taket et al (2009) argue, the antithesis of connection, and it is in this sense that the essence of inclusion is played out in what is conducted between people. This is the case not just where it might be expected, in those exchanges that occur between the kith and kin who interact closely, if not always frequently or face to face, but also in the quality of exchanges that take place in informal, everyday contacts such as those that occur between strangers who cross paths on the street. In such exchanges, if there is a pattern where a person is looked down on because they are poorly groomed, speak roughly, or if they appear obviously different in 'race' or dress, a pattern of social exclusion is present. In moving about their environment, if people are 'dissed' by those they have never met, this is the antithesis of an inclusive society. *All* relationships matter whether they are informal, official, or intimate (Wilkinson and Pickett, 2009).

Are personal relationships central to inclusion and recovery?

Examining how social exclusion is understood introduces a contested point. Taket et al (2009, p 12) argue that 'an individual may be excluded, [but] they may also experience strong social networks and connections.' This statement seems to imply that authentic exclusion has to have its source in the economic and rights dimensions of life. Summarizing Szreter and Woolcock (2004), Taket et al (2009, p 12) argue there is a decisive role social capital plays in the presence, or otherwise, of social exclusion, as this 'facilitates individuals to gain (or lose) access to resources.' Rather than privilege economic participation and access to opportunities, an alternative is to conceptualize exclusion as a multidimensional phenomenon where an absence of one dimension, in this case 'high quality interpersonal attachments', is as central to the definition of exclusion as are economic, rights, or other structural variable (VicServ, 2008).

In how social exclusion is understood structural variables must be acknowledged *and* a place also found for the intimate and informal aspects of social connection. A person's relationships are empirically and subjectively significant, and it follows that recognition of this status should be present at both a theoretical and operational level. Regrettably, it seems that structural variables – those that concern employment, housing, access to opportunities, social stigma, and the like – have so far been accorded an almost exclusive status as *the* focus for those interested in social exclusion. A clear indication of this bias can be seen in how current measures of social inclusion have been constructed (Barnes, 2005; Atkinson and Marlier, 2010). Although there are exceptions (Crisp, 2010), most reports that are based on this thinking place structural variables in the foreground and render affectionate social connection a not-to-be-recognized status.

A similar disregard is present in how measures of recovery are constructed in the mental health field. For example, in a meta-review, Burgess et al (2010) identified a total of 22 recovery measures and narrowed this field to a sub-group of eight that represented the 'best practice' instruments. A total of 48 'domains'/'areas' were nominated as key concerns in these leading instruments, and each of these was set out in an extended table. Only three from this group of 48 had a focus on any aspect of social connectedness.

It is worrying that personal relationships have a marginal status in the thinking that informs health and welfare practice, but it is not unexpected given the rhizome that is the process of individualization (see Chapter 2). What is striking is this: in an impartial study designed to review recovery measures, the authors do not even raise as a possibility the idea that affectionate relationships might have a subjugated status in the construction of these instruments. This possibility is hidden in plain sight even when the authors of this study Burgess et al explicitly quote Patricia Deegan, a foundational thinker in the recovery movement: 'the aspiration to live, work and love in a community in which one makes a significant contribution' is inherent to the possibility of recovery (Deegan, 1988 as quoted in Burgess et al, 2010, p 6). These reviewers make a point of featuring this quote early in their study, yet do not appear to take her words seriously. In this elision it would appear that representatives of the research industry have reproduced the individualizing culture they inadvertently represent. It is a stubborn fact that the quality of a client's relational base is a variable that is often marginalized, or completely falls off the radar, for researchers, despite an occasional espousal of its importance and the value that is placed on intimate social connection by consumers.

If the focus is shifted from the field of mental health to that of sexual abuse, the same pattern emerges. The first report that mainstreamed the term 'recovery' with respect to the trauma of sexual abuse was published 20 years ago. This landmark publication stated that a pre-condition for recovery was the 'the creation of new connections': 'capacities for trust … and intimacy' that were needed to compliment the 'autonomy, initiative, competence [and] identity' that also had to be re-established (Herman, 1992, p 133).

The same argument is being made in other fields, such as intellectual disability (Clegg and Landsdall-Welfare, 2010; Hall, 2010), and refugee/asylum-seekers. According to van der Veer (2000, p 10), 'traumatized people are those who don't have a social network and … the primary objective (of recovery work) should be to build up social connections.' It should be clear that affectionate social connection is intrinsic to the prospects for a person being able to recover or be included. Irrespective of whether you are a refugee or a homeless drug user, elderly and ill or able bodied but unemployed, Deegan's lived experience tends to resonate with many.

Being singled out

Clients are frequently lonely and feel left out. Many tend to have little sense of solidarity and secure companionship which, to any vulnerable person, is a particularly telling experience. If you know in your heart you have been ostracized, it is far harder to cope with this if you are not part of a sub-group with whom you positively identify. Stigma, like honor, is a public rather than a private emotion. Worse still is if you do not have a single mate to connect with. Humans have a vulnerability to being singled out: we have all known this from the crib to the school playground, from your first day at university to your last day on the planet. So how can this knowledge not be front and centre in how practice and social policy is understood and delivered?

There are, of course, a number of reasons this is the case. Not least of these is that there remains a vital cultural energy that celebrates independence and its expression in the idealization of 'independent living'. If it is not constrained, this force acts as a gas that expands to displace the attention that can be given to the indeterminate construct that is social connection. There is a buzz around autonomy, whereas belonging and connectedness seems fuzzy and impractical. Key figures in the practice field, like those who design instruments to measure inclusion and recovery, often find themselves in thrall to autonomy's allure just as the broader current culture celebrates independence as sexy and the 'quest for autonomy' as noble (Seedhouse, 2002).

Yet, there are 'switch-points' (Rose, 2000, p 326) where autonomy's opposite – that which concerns loyalty, compassion, and community – is dramatically summoned. For example, when an elderly person is found dead and alone in their home, television commentators will rail against those who are said to have failed their frail neighbor; where it is asserted 'our' troops in Afghanistan have been let down by the proper authorities newspaper headlines shout out the accusation that a civilized society should never allow its loyal soldiers to be betrayed; when innocent young people take their own lives well-meaning spokespeople bemoan the lack of community. In such difficult moments the importance of obligation and caring is often righteously evoked and thrust onto center stage.

Reflecting on this phenomenon points to an unstable dynamic between the allure of independence and the demand for community. At one moment autonomy and independence take pride of place; then an unexpected reverse occurs and the primacy of connection and belonging becomes the imperative. Cronen et al (1982, p 101) say such figure-and-ground inversions signal the presence of what they term a 'strange loop'. This vexed dynamic is problematic for politicians, planners, practitioners, and citizens alike.

A case in point concerns the use of the phrase 'independent living' in health and human service practice. At first glance this phrase hums with positive appeal. For example, it is often said that 'this client should learn independent living skills', and few in the sector would not see this as a sensible service goal. This agreement is consistent with the fact that the term 'independence' evokes positive associations. Quite literally, the valorization of autonomy is often embedded in the brochures and mission statements of service agencies: one Melbourne agency in Australia, targeted to work with disadvantaged, homeless young people, has its masthead, its mission statement: 'Our goal is for each young person to become independent.' It follows that a successful case outcome would involve each client 'living independently' in that they had secured paid work and stable accommodation. Yet, such an aim is simplistic, even possibly misguided.

The allure and the horror of independence

In public housing estates in Sydney and Melbourne so many people have died alone and unnoticed that state-funded programs have recently been introduced. These deaths are troubling because it is often weeks (or more) before the dead person is missed and their death reported. In many cases this news is only signaled by a decomposing body becoming so malodorous that the immediate neighbors, or passers-by, take offense and call the local authorities. Apparently, there is literally no neighborly contact, no friend, or relative, who has become aware that 'this woman' or 'that man' has died. A similar phenomenon has also been reported in Japan and the Netherlands. Reports in the popular media of these horrors recoil and seek to cast blame: 'Where are the neighbors, where are the families?!' The instinct to trust in community is never far away.

It is disturbing that lonely deaths are on the increase, yet the larger meaning of this phenomenon can be uncomfortably linked to the official goals of this book. Older people, people with chronic illness, those with a mental illness as well as homeless young people are commonly assessed as having a successful outcome if they are judged as 'living independently'. To be able to live alone is represented as a positive outcome given the goal 'independent living' sounds functional, even positive, mindful this ideal can so easily slip into a life that is lived in dangerous isolation.

Successful living for the young and old alike should be understood as contingent on the client attaining a 'good-enough' quality of interdependence. Young people, indeed all people, require a pattern of relating that is commensurate with their particular life stage. As Carter and McGoldrick (1999, p 9) note, 'healthy development requires finding the optimal balance between connectedness and separateness, between belonging and individuation, accommodation and autonomy.' If this view is accepted, independence is an impossibility and its pursuit is counter-productive. DiNicola (1997, p 199) proposes that 'independence is a myth', as the playwright George Bernard Shaw was quoted as saying more than a hundred years ago. However illogical, it is a feature of Western ideology to conflate independence with adulthood and to equate autonomy with health and wellbeing.

When an assumption becomes so embedded as to become invisible, this often disguises a problem (Trompenaars and Hampden-Turner, 2002). An example from cross-cultural practice makes this point clearly. Barnett (as quoted in Furlong, 2008a, p 202) recounts:

A team of rehabilitation staff was working with aboriginal Australians who had received treatment in the Central Australian Blindness Project in the late 1970's. We explained that even a little mobility and orientation training would enable an elderly visually impaired person to become independent. This person could then, for example, make their own way to the local shop on their own. The reaction of the elderly people, and their extended families, to this good news could only be described as complete horror. They declared that what we were suggesting was unbelievably cruel and that it invoked the history of the stolen generations. How could we be so heartless as to want an old person to have to go around on their own? What they wanted were ways of increasing their interdependence – not the isolation of independence.

At the level of culture, as at the level of the services that represent and seek to further this culture, it is independence rather than interdependence that tends to be celebrated. Expressed in a privileging of economic autonomy and access to material wellbeing, this bias can be found in the literature that is committed to social inclusion. Rather than accentuate the primacy of social connection this bias tends to dull the prospects of positive and reciprocal relationships. More dramatically put, and however inadvertent, the championing of independence is a 'vector' for the spread of the disease of isolation.

Dynamics of isolation

Jasper and his dad

It is not going well for son or father. Jasper, a 16-year-old, feels neither listened to nor cared about. In reaction to this perception, the younger person withdraws more, yells more loudly, and rebels with increased vitally. At his end Brett, Jasper's dad, is adamant that his soon-to-be adult, but-not-yet teenager, is treating him disrespectfully: he sees his offspring's behavior as objectionable, as out of order. In reaction to this interpretation the father pushes back harder, talks more loudly, disperses punishments, or simply withdraws his attention, feeling hurt and unloved. In response to this the young person feels even more aggrieved, and then righteously retaliates – and the cycle intensifies.

Father and son in this example are each having a parallel experience. They do not know this, and each acts in exactly the best way to make it worse. Inadvertently, participants in a 'symmetrical process' (Bateson, 1973) exchange the same behaviors and do to each other what they think the other is doing to them. In seeking to explain systemic thinking, Hoffman (1985, p 283) asks: 'is there a first horse on the merry-go-round?'

In this same way those who are lonely tend to invite, sometimes even insist, in their behavior a replication of the steps of a dance where participants reciprocally tread on each other's corns. Put more theoretically, and using a lens that observes dynamics from a distance, what is experienced subjectively can be theorized systemically (although, of course, such an interpretation discounts the phenomenological experience of being excluded and stigmatized). For example, if a person assumes they will be rejected – given this is over-learned perception of the prevailing pattern – it is more than understandable that the person will get in first and reject the other. And why try at all? Alternatively, this individual might not have learned the skills to relate well, has forgotten them, or has lost sight of their value.

As it has arced though the lives of the disadvantaged and and those who are relatively well off but who worry about their neuroses – the so-called 'worried well' – the process of individualization tends to produce subjects who are unable to understand the mysteries of relationships. Bounded by a mode of thought that is 'I-referenced', but still subject to the realm of intense emotions social relationships cue, many of us are increasingly in trouble. Front and centre in our thinking is the neoliberal principle that 'I want to get on with my life: I need to be in charge!' Yet, over and over, many of us find the intense feelings stimulated by personal relationships, or the lack of them, overthrows this contrived logic. Citizens have been told that we should always be rational, but relationships beat to the rhythm of a different drum.

A good example is where individuals find themselves repeating, or repeatedly avoiding, what is awkward and mistaken around relationships endings. This can be so extreme as to form a pattern that repeatedly cartwheels through people's lives. You will probably have experienced or witnessed people 'get in first', being overly eager to say 'This relationship is not working for me – I'm out of here' to avoid being hurt. Most of us do not do this, or at least not very often, but it is also true that each of us can relate to the attractiveness of this position – of the logic of withdrawing in ways that are defensively self-protective. 'Filtered through the lens of lonely social cognition, other people may appear more critical, denigrating, or otherwise unwelcoming' (Cacioppo and Patrick, 2008, p 15).

We have all slipped away unobtrusively, left a workplace, a party, or a last meeting without saying our goodbyes. Such examples are common, even if the underlying pattern of avoidance is more likely to be present in clients' lives. If the attention is shifted from the 'normal' to the 'disadvantaged', although the matter of social status and resources may vary between the two, it is quite possible that both will work to the same rational calculation: I have been bitten before, have felt hurt, etc, therefore I will (i) refuse to connect, or (ii) get out first to minimize the emotional risk. Either option, of course, diminishes the prospects for relationship as each option is interpersonally illiterate. 'What makes loneliness especially insidious is that it contains this Catch 22: Real relief from loneliness requires the cooperation of at least one other person, and yet the more chronic our loneliness becomes, the less equipped we may be to entice such cooperation' (Cacioppo and Patrick, 2008, p 33).

As noted earlier, the process of self-scrutiny is particularly intense for those who have been judged to be at risk or as 'eligible for a service'. In this context it makes sense that the process of casework contests the effects of disconfirmation and seeks to re-pair the person with a sense of connectedness as well as of self-respect. Mindful of this dynamic, practitioners have some capacity to be the co-creators of new maps and to invite clients into dances that connect rather than distance.

4
How are we getting along?

Insiders and outsiders | Experience of individualization | In and out of control | Vitamin me | Can the cycles of loneliness and isolation be interrupted?

Insiders and outsiders

Mostly 'the interpersonally local' (Furlong, 2010a) simply hums along routinely, but it has a power to hurt or please that can jump up unexpectedly. Taken by surprise, everyone has had the experience of finding themselves on the edge of, or perhaps having fallen right into, an intense argument. Form time to time each of us has acutely felt a sense of loneliness suddenly welling up, even as we are in the company of another. Yet, this same interpenetration between self and others can also be the source of positive feelings. Without warning, I can experience a heady joy, a feeling of being opened up, when another person's thoughtfulness, or simply the fact that this person is there, renews me with a springtime feeling of optimism.

As members of nomad groups, agrarian collectives, feudal systems, in modern cities and nations, in every historical period and location, a million years of evolution has hard-wired humans to the importance of our relationships with others. That we generally roll along taking our relationships for granted, that we are mostly unaware of the symbolic and practical power in these attachments, may be true, but this is no way disavows their empirical status.

The findings of the social determinants of health research have identified the key role supportive relationships play in human health and wellbeing. This research identifies two particular points about personal relationships:

- that conflictual relationships are deleterious to health and wellbeing; and
- the absence of affectionate relationships is injurious to those who are lonely and isolated.

This brings into focus a practical, albeit grand, question: what's going on with how we are getting along?

If the set of personal relationships that Wilkinson and Pickett (2009) argue are important are considered as an aggregate – that stock of intimate, affectionate, and everyday social relationships that are transacted between people – it is possible to make a broad judgment of the quality and robustness of this stock. Given it is accepted that each person does better if they are loved and respected, if they are embedded in secure attachments within which they contribute and feel honorably accountable, in so far as a person is respected rather than looked down on or ignored ('dissed'), what is the current report card? There is no possibility of an exact measurement as it is impossible to 'drill down into' this question or to quantify an answer.

On the one hand, Anthony Giddens (1991) has argued that the modern person is now freer than ever before to have 'pure relationships' and to make creative choices in how they wish to design and conduct their personal connections. In so far as this is so, it should be the case that the outlook is increasingly bright and the stock of quality relationships should be on the rise. Unfortunately, the empirical evidence gathered by researchers such as Putnam (2000) points to a less than shiny picture. Summing up this evidence Ulrich Beck, a prominent researcher who has written extensively about relationships and the process of individualization, takes a much darker view. He argues:

> What emerges from [our] fading social forms is naked, frightened, aggressive ego in search of love and help. In search for itself and an affectionate sociality, it easily gets lost in the jungle of the self.... Someone who is poking round in the fog of his or her own self is no longer capable of noticing that this isolation, this 'solitary confinement of the ego' is a mass sentence. (Beck, 1999, p 40)

In considering if those who chose to live alone are disadvantaged, or more broadly, in reflecting on the generalization that 'modern citizens are more isolated and less well embedded than previously', what is to be made of the influence of ICT? Shouldn't it be argued that mobiles, email, texting, and social media such as Facebook, Bebo, and Twitter – that developing suite of innovative ICT-based applications – have resulted in an aggregate enhancement of social connection? It was reported by Nie (2001, p 433), amongst others, that the introduction of mobile phones, and ICT more generally, has resulted in a 'substantial and meaningful enhancement in interpersonal connectivity.' In a 24/7, ICT-connected world, proximity and geography no longer have the same power that they once had when distance so dominated the prospects for communication. Yet, it has also been reported that ICT-based relationships can be fractious and insecure, lacking both presence and robustness (Sharp, 2009; Eldred, 2010).

For more than a century it has been reported that modernization has had a detrimental effect on social relationships. For example, Marx theorized that late capitalist conditions led to complex forms of alienation with respect to oneself, one's labor as well as in relation to others. The aggregate deterioration in social connectedness became a key reference point in the distinction Ferdinand Tönnies proposed in the mid-19th century between *Gemeinschaft* and *Gesellschaft* social relations. This idealized binary distinguished between pre-modern social life, a mode of life that was based on close interpersonal bonds. He termed these *Gemeinschaft* relations. In contrast, 'modern' relations – what has evolved, broadly, since the enclosure movement and the industrial revolution – he characterized as *Gesellschaft* relations. These relations, he argued, are grounded on formal, often legally warranted impersonal associations (Tönnies, 2001). Also in the late 19th century, Emile Durkheim famously posited that *anomie* – the separation of self from one's peers and society as a whole – was, more or less, the individual's lot in modernized, now post-industrial societies (Rapaport and Overing, 2000).

In the later part of the 20th century this theme began to assume a mainstream status. Finding its emblematic statement in David Riesman's *The lonely crowd* (1956), sociologists reported that modern citizens in the (so-called) developed nations were increasingly likely to feel, and often to be, isolated rather than well connected. Obviously this is a grand generalization – there must be, as there always will be, considerable variations, even counter-trends in certain social fields – but this broad conclusion has found confirmation in several key recent studies. Amongst those who have argued this worrying conclusion, Robert Putnam's (2000) work has achieved the highest profile. In the immensely popular crossover text *Bowling alone*, Putnam puts an empirical case that North Americans are more isolated and less civically connected than ever before.

Putnam's work has prompted considerable debate. Critics have queried the definitional integrity of the constructs 'bridging' and 'bonding' social capital (Healy and Hampshire, 2002). Others have found his approach nostalgic, even repressive (Mowbray, 2004). And at least one critic has argued that Putnam's focus depoliticizes development by concentrating far too much on the economic dimensions of social life (Harriss, 2002): Putnam did his PhD fieldwork in Italy and contrasted what he said was the industrial, more trusting and enterprising North to the less developed, more suspicious South. Whatever opinions may be on this proposition, the note that he hit that reverberated so persistently across the policy and academic worlds was simple and evocative: US citizens are more isolated than ever before.

Giddens (2002), meanwhile, has argued that human relationships have become 'de-distanced' and are therefore far less subject to physical constraints. This argument makes clear sense but there remains a fierce debate as to whether, on balance, ICT-based communication is conducive to, or attenuating of, secure attachments. One point of view is that digitally based contacts with others are mediated, anonymous, and precarious in ways that face-to-face encounters are not. There are tensions, ironies, even paradoxes that are introduced with ICT where, ambiguously, we may have more contacts but where the nature of these contacts amount to 'touching from a distance, further and further all the time,' to re-purpose a poignant lyric (Curtis et al, 1979).

Later, in Chapter 9, where we look at how new technology can be used to develop the client's relational base, productive uses of ICT are considered. For now, it should be noted that ICT-based communication does not necessarily lead to constructive relationships and may, at least in some circumstances, hollow out and negatively reshape the quality of human interaction (Eldred, 2010).

In seeking to overview the larger question, 'How are we getting on?', there are a number of clear problems presented here, not least of which is the issue of nomenclature. Marx talked of *alienation* and Durkheim of *anomie*. More recently, Maris (1998) examined the idea of *social attachment* and Putnam (2000) of *social capital*. Over the past 20 years, the frames of *social inclusion* and *social exclusion* have dominated (see Chapter 3). If terminological and theoretical uncertainties are put to one side, it is possible to stand above the fray and observe the larger trends: despite the optimism expressed by Giddens and some others, and without going too far beyond the data, it is reasonable to observe that the relational world is not in good shape for many, say for at least a sizable minority. Although it is impossible to find a stable empirical base line, it seems likely, even very likely, that there has been an increase in loneliness and of relational precariousness (Cacioppo and Patrick, 2008; Wilkinson and Pickett, 2009). In so far as this is true, this is not good news for the health of those who are poorly embedded.

Broadly in agreement with Putnam's conclusion there is a diminishing stock of social capital in the US, even conservative commentators note that it is not just the 'losers' who are alone and isolated. In *America: Land of Loners*, the conservative columnist Daniel Akst bemoans the general decline in friendship, especially for men, in lives ruled by the 'cult of conspicuous busyness' (Ehrenreich, 2010; as quoted in Akst, 2010; p 24). He also refers to the finding that that the average citizen in the USA has only two friends with whom they could 'discuss important matters of spend free time' (Christakis & Fowler, 2009; as quoted in Akst, 2010; p 24). Compared to 20 years ago, "Americans have a third fewer non-family confidants ... and a quarter of us no confidents at all" (Akst, 2010, p 2). Perhaps citizens of the US are more isolated than those of other nations, but isolation and loneliness is a universal experience if not a universal pattern of experience.

How could this 'dysfunctional' condition have become so widespread? Structural issues temporarily put to one side, at an interpersonal level, to a significant degree isolation and loneliness are the consequences of, are the mirror image of, inappropriate values and of poor attitudes and skills with respect to relationships. On this premise, if professionals and their agencies can act in ways that result in their clients having a greater relational capacity, this will produce clients with a stronger relational base and therefore a higher quotient of interpersonal connection. Such an outcome promotes more 'function' in whatever area is the focus of specialist attention. In a nutshell, this is the rationale for this book.

That many clients are insufficiently embedded in a sustaining interpersonal matrix, that these people experience persistent social precariousness, converges with the account that critical sociologists are presenting with respect to the position of the greater, supposedly normal population. Giddens (2002) tells us that no matter how well off a citizen may be, no matter how normal, an abiding feature of contemporary life is that this person no longer senses their world as secure and stably moored. Being dis-embedded, he argues, is a general characteristic of contemporary life. A person's resources, a catch-all that includes private, social, and cultural capital (Bourdieu, 1986), will mediate how vulnerable they are, yet, according to Giddens (2002), no one can escape the anxiety and material danger that goes with being on the 'runaway train' of globalization and individualization.

It may seem a strange proposition but those who are understood to be 'normal', as with those officially deemed to be more-or-less in need or at risk, are co-participants in a set of conditions that encourage anomie and social attenuation (see Chapter 2). What unites the group of citizens who live 'independently' as an act of choice, those who wish to be in charge of, and therefore provisionally connected to others, and those who have little or no choice in their living situations, is that everyone is on the same train careering along the same railway line. There will be differentials in the extent of relational precariousness, but there is also an increasingly likely commonality.

The following reflection seeks to outline some of the sources of this commonality. This statement seeks to articulate how the processes taking place at the level of culture and ideology can be linked with everyday subjective experience and interpersonal conduct. This is important to do if the life world of 'clients' is not to be split-off from the life world of the 'normal' citizen – a domain that includes the sub-group 'practitioners.'

The experience of individualization

According to Bauman (2001, 2003), Beck and Beck-Gernsheim (2002), and Howard (2007), amongst a larger group, the case can be made that post-modern citizens experience two contradictory emotions. On the one hand, the contemporary subject experiences:

- *being weightless:* if I am the 'boss of me now' this is both an exciting and a precarious condition. There is no access to security or legitimation, to a priori values or received codes of ethics and behavior. If it is only *my* conscience that guides me, how can I be sure?
- *being burdened:* from managing your superannuation to 'owning' your sexuality, it is up to you as every choice, every risk, has been downloaded onto the lowest entity-level unit – the individual – where once forms of traditional and collective responsibility tended to take responsibility for decision taking. There can be no holiday from self-responsibility for those whose life is their enduring project.

Novelists such as Milan Kundera and Michel Houellebecq have examined this phenomenon and their literary accounts speak directly to the subjective experience of many citizens. Bridging the literary with the clinical, an Oxford literary scholar and former clinical director of London's Bethlem Royal and Maudsley Hospital put it even more graphically. He said we "occupy an increasingly fragmented, de-contextualized world marked by unwarranted optimism mixed with paranoia and a feeling of emptiness" (McGilchrist, 2011, p 6). Individualization is a transformative social process that has direct consequences for inner life.

The norm of autonomy has not led to a sense of security, the feeling that *I-am-a-well-bordered-state*. Rather, the converse seems to be present. Subjects who are "obliged to be free" (Rose, 1989, p 213) cannot escape the contingency that is the legacy of this norm's regime of choice. Always precarious:

> ... the norm of autonomy produces an intense and continuous self-scrutiny, self-dissatisfaction and self-evaluation. [In our] ... striving to live our autonomous lives, to discover who we really are, to realize our potentials and shape our lifestyles [we have] become tied to the project of our own identity. (Rose, 1999, p 93)

Never good for our blood pressure (Hawkley et al, 2010), this project is relentless. Framed in this way it is also a task that has to be performed in each minute of every day just as Sisyphus, a miscreant in Greek mythology, was condemned to the endless task of pushing a rock up a hill when, once he had reached the top, he had to turn and follow it to where it came to rest so he could recommence his labours once more.

If theorizing the process of individualization speaks to the experience of many 'ordinary' citizens, what might be said about the prospects for the interpersonal, the intimately social, in this regime? In *Liquid modernity* and especially *Liquid love*, Bauman concludes that as 'normal' people are tending to feel burdened, vulnerable, and non-trusting, this has led to relationships that are, and are expected to be, insecure, even fractious. Bauman sets it out like this: if I am always considering 'is this relationship working for me?' it follows that the other will be asking themselves the same question. If each of us know the relationship is always and forever open to question, it is not possible to have the experience of a secure attachment.

Being relationally provisional does not apply to everyone equally. In elective communities, in more or less traditional families, in groups, in book clubs, in many and varied expressions of affinity, people continue to connect. New technology can facilitate linkages, but it also offers the perfect template for the contingency that is increasingly built into modern relating. If I become bored or uncomfortable with an exchange I am having on the net, I can simply drop off: out of sight, out of mind. The single 'user' is in control and has unilateral choice about whether to persist with any connection. In this new context some have found it tempting to look to idea of 'the family', even in its traditional patriarchal forms, with nostalgia.

Decades ago Christopher Lasch (1977) suggested that the family had become a 'haven in a heartless world.' Taking a different tack, Bauman (2003, p 6) appears to positively quote Ulrich Beck in his view that "family' (along with class and neighborhood) are now no more than 'zombie categories', 'zombie institutions', that are 'dead and still alive.' A more nuanced position was put forward by Barrett and McIntosh (1982, p 213) many years ago. These authors suggest that 'it is not so much that the family is dying or evil, but that we have perhaps asked too much of the family.' Finding the right one, setting up a home, and having children positively generates meaning, which is a fine accomplishment, but this dream can be privatized and over-invested with expectations. In such ways we expect more from 'the family' than this buffeted institution can be reasonably expected to deliver.

What, then, of those who are disadvantaged, excluded, and stigmatized? Many in this larger group have had negative experiences early in life characterized by insufficient or disturbed attachments and multiple traumas. Given such developmental histories one view tells us that developmental injury inevitably results in a kind of physic determinism, a domino effect where the 'wounded child' (Miller, 1983) is doomed to perennially repeat their early disasters in all their subsequent relationships. Simply put, psychoanalytic determinism means 'as it was, so it will always be.' It seems impossible to dispute that this is the case with those clients who have suffered the most severe damage. This acknowledged, there is a danger in over-generalizing, in assuming that there is an outright psychological negation to new possibilities for relationship for a majority of clients unless intense, long-term psychotherapy is received.

Resilience, indeed constructive resistance, can be found and possible strengths identified in many people including those who have been subject to extreme difficulties (Ungar, 2005). Unlike deficit-centered perspectives, approaches that are informed by a sociological and strengths-based imagination leads to a less negatively deterministic prospectus. Helpful here too is the Jungian notion of 'kinship libido' (Jung, 1946), discussed on p 49. The notion of kinship libido can be glimpsed in many everyday ways where a person strikes a bond with a neighbor or a casually met stranger. Nearly all humans have a talent for relating given the right circumstances, regardless of the fact that no one has ever had an ideal upbringing.

In and out of control

Personal relationships may be as important to clients as they are to practitioners, yet it is likely that those on the lower rungs of the social hierarchy frequently have a less robust purchase on the values, skills, and attitudes that are associated with making and sustaining relationships. At the observable level it is clear many clients:

- trust far too little, or much too much;
- are so frightened of closeness and relationship that this static wards off others;
- cement their social anxiety into a form that resembles suspicion – a state that leads them to act as if under siege;
- do not offer the interpersonal initiatives that start up conversations ('anticipatory postures') or, if they do, these will seem odd and inappropriate;
- do not respond reciprocally when another presents the start-up gestures that have the role of signaling an openness to exchange;

- do not often offer the 'free information' that assists conversations, and therefore allows relationships to build;
- play it safe by not readily, if ever, lowering the drawbridge to declare their attachments;
- seem to be resolutely concrete to the extent that they appear to lack empathy – which is unattractive to others;
- are so self-referential as to be unable to sense the other's feelings and interests;
- will 'get in first' and exit – a class or meeting, a new associate, a budding friendship, a romance – so as to avoid the possibility that they will again be hurt.

Much more than reflecting a neuro–cognitive deficit (see Chapter 6), in my view such behaviors are better understood as defensive, over-learned patterns. Sadly, these patterns can be understood as attempted solutions that are problem maintaining when it comes to loneliness and isolation. People who are vulnerable tend to be skittish about getting involved in relationships for good reasons, even if these reasons are no longer valid or in their best interests. To a degree, it also seems that well-adjusted 'normal' citizens are increasingly availing themselves of the same suite of behaviors and vulnerabilities.

How might this reticence to being linked to others be understood? Clearly there is no single answer to this as there must be multiple factors in play. In the era of individualization not least of these factors is that 'being in a relationship' requires a degree of vulnerability, even surrender, which is a particularly worrying prospect for those whose sense of independence is fragile but whose aspiration for autonomy is high.

In general, autonomy, and its negation, has a totemic meaning in Western culture, where there are major social norms, deeply ingrained conventions related to one's age and stage of life, that have resulted in citizens having the experience that autonomy and self-determination are sacred. Think of the devastation felt by older people when they lose their license to drive: as well as a pragmatic concern, an event that has deep material consequences, it also signifies loss of independence. As Tony Abbott, an Australian conservative political leader, wrote in his book *Battlelines*, owning, and being licensed to drive a private vehicle to wherever I choose to go by the authorities, confers a 'sense of mastery' to people. This is similar to Margaret Thatcher's old quip that she looked down on anyone over the age of 25 she saw waiting for a bus. To be awarded a license is to have undergone a rite of passage and to lose it is to regress through a ritual of degradation.

More generally, a full legal status guaranteeing independence, what is called 'being autonomous', is granted when someone reaches the age of 18. When a person reaches this age they are granted the right to vote, to drive a car, to drink, to sign contracts, to formally make their own decisions. And, if to be an adult is to have autonomy, to have this status voided is to become a non-adult, to be deemed an identity that is in breach of age and stage expectations of rightful citizenship. Against this general background, there is a steepened sensitively to autonomy, and its loss, for the majority of mental health consumers precisely because nearly all these individuals have had the actual experience of their 'autonomy' being publicly breached, or at least meaningfully threatened. That is, they have been declared by the competent authorities to lack self-management capacity, to be unfit guardians, to be mentally incompetent and in need of certification, to be subject of a guardianship order, and so on.

Such formal processes communicate that the citizen-who-is-about-to-become-a-client is, in effect, not 'in working order' to such an extent that they are unable to look after themselves. Many may even have had the experience of being told where to live, what to do, and what is said to be appropriate for them and what is not. Some have even been told that they cannot take care of themselves, even perhaps that their self-hygiene is inadequate: think about the meaning of being told you are "pongy". Given these kinds of experiences many become sensitive, often over-sensitive, to the issue of 'losing control'.

In a heady mix this over-sensitivity acts to resonate with their inner experience of having their boundaries breached and their autonomy compromised. This is especially serious to some groups – to those who have been in prison, to those who are elderly and who have been judged to be cognitively impaired, to those who have a mental illness where they have experienced delusions of reference, of thought insertion, broadcasting, of being rushed by, even completely overwhelmed by, the onset of psychosis.

The issue of autonomy is central because relationships are sites where a person's sense of 'being in control' is threatened. In any meaningful partnership, for example, when one agency really collaborates with another, in a personal relationship each party is required to 'give over' a degree of control to the process that a partnership entrains. This is scary as a person is now 'not really in charge': of the other, of where it all will go and, perhaps most worrying, of themselves as they are now not able to be in control of their own feelings. For this reason the prospect of 'losing control' in relationships is a problem for many clients – but an aversion to 'losing control' is also becoming a broader phenomenon. Think back to the example from Seinfeld on p 50.

The client as 'loser'

When autonomy has a quasi-sacred status it becomes dishonoring to be officially declared deficient and in need of help because you lack the capacity to self-manage. However much this is an unintended consequence of service provision, this is what happens if your intelligence is measured and you and your relatives are told you function below the accepted threshold; or if your mental status is assessed and you are found to be abnormal; or, if your 'job-readiness' is appraised and you are told that your competence or your attitude is below par. Once judged by the competent authorities as eligible for a service, the person's autonomy has been reduced and a lesser status is the effect of this process. This is because a ritual of symbolic disconfirmation has been conducted – achieving public 'clienthood'

(Alcabes, 1985) involves being subject to a formal procedure that re-grades a person's status that reframes them as an entity who is problematic.

This outcome tends to intensify the sense of self-scrutiny discussed in the previous chapter with respect to how 'normal' citizens experience the process of individualization (Rose, 1999; Bauman, 2001, p 2003). White (2002), a narrative therapist, theorized that this self-scrutiny was directly expressed in the number of clients who presented with a sense of personal failure, whether they were well resourced or not. These people told him they felt they were not making the most of their lives, not living up to their potential, were not sufficiently making good their lives, and so forth. This theme links White's work to that of Zygmunt Bauman, Ulrich Beck, Anthony Giddens and Nicholas Rose, writers who have been so prominent in developing the analysis of the process of *individualization* examined in Chapter 2.

What distinguishes White's work from this scholarship is that he was a practitioner who was informed by, but was not bounded by, an academic role. White wrote of clients who felt the sense of rupture and fragility that the theory predicted was characteristic of the post-structural subject, even as his commitment was to develop practices that involve 'taking back' an accountable form of personal agency (White, 2002). What the historian of ideas Michel Foucault offered White, and other narrative practitioners, was the idea that a careful use of language could have a key action in combating the operations of individualization and governmentality, that de-centralized, privately internalized mechanism by which the modern Western citizen comes to act as their own subjugator.

But it is worse if a person is not an 'ordinary citizen' but someone the competent authorities have subjected to a naming procedure, the effect of which has been to downgrade that individual's personal status. These rituals are commonplace, albeit always symbolically significant: children's courts that have marked a parent as 'neglectful' or 'unfit'; mental health experts who have conferred upon a person a psychiatric diagnosis; rehabilitation specialists who place upon a person the label 'head injured'; or, more generally, all those who are eligible for a service as they have been deemed 'excluded' or 'currently at-risk'.

Following such a definitional ceremony (White, 1992, 2000), it makes sense to expect that the person is likely to suffer a more intense process of self-interrogation than is usual for the general citizen. Moreover, this self-scrutiny occurs within a context where a relentless media stirs the pot further. Often boosted by concerned expert professionals, the popular media underlines the problem of 'broken homes', 'failed marriages' and 'dysfunctional families'; singles out those who are 'dole bludgers', 'benefit scroungers' or 'bad mothers', those who accused of reproducing 'the poor parenting' they themselves received, and so forth. Spurred by this attention, the net of self-suspicion wraps itself ever more punishingly around, and into, those who have been castigated. Over time, these helpfully conferred labels tend to become the labels and badges of a person's lived identity.

According to critical theorists, these labels become the inscriptions of a demoralizing self-report, a branding that comes to haunt the subjectivity of so many. Being haunted, even stalked, by that which disqualifies – by dividing practices that operate on simplistic yes/no criteria, judgments that are constitutive of an absolute moral nomenclature – makes for a difficult inner experience of the self and, in all likelihood, a compromised behavioral life. Bringing this process of disqualification into sharp relief is the interaction that occurs when this person–culture interpenetration interacts with the 'technical' systems of classification found in human services. As Saleebey (2009, p 7) notes: 'Many traits and capacities that are signs of strength are hidden by the rubble of years of self doubt, the blame of others and, in some cases, the wearing of a diagnostic label.'

If the newly minted client comes to take what the agency understands is a receptive and cooperative attitude, what is often referred to as being insightful, this person will internalize a self-description that is, at least with respect to normal expectations, a disabling self-description. Having insight might sound positive but it also involves being burdened by a telling weight. For example, if the specialist sits you down and informs you that 'the diagnosis is autism [or depression, unfit parent, alcohol dependency]', this can negatively totalize the person's identity. On the other hand, if the person balks at the label conferred by the expert, the expert and their agency reserves the right not only to maintain they were correct in assigning pathology but to add an additional disqualification: the person is deemed resistant, un-cooperative, in denial, and ignorant. Asking the client to agree with the expert is therefore dangerous because "… the diagnosis, the assessment, [can] … become the cornerstone of an emergent identity" (Saleebey, 2009, p 238).

Such vexing processes test, and often exhaust, the client's sense of autonomy. In this context the client tends to be sensitized to, and fearful of, signals that convey to them that their capacity to self-manage might again be in danger. Being over-sensitized to the experience of being 'taken-over', 'intruded upon' or 'not acknowledged' does not align with the reality that personal relationships are about give and take. Relationships are a form of partnership, a mobile equation where both parties have to be prepared to change, to alter their behavior and position, in order to achieve the dynamic balance that keeps the ensemble steady. If one, or both, parties insist on being in control – like Elaine did in the Seinfeld episode discussed on page 50 – there is a disconnect. It is an intrinsic feature of the relational world that a degree of compromise, even surrender, is part of the deal. Enigmatically, if a relationship is to be containing, the participants have to understand it is a reliable context, yet for a relationship to be reliable its participants have to be prepared to let go – and to be able to cope with the emotional vulnerability that this entails.

If this going-along-to-get-along condition is not present, a number of problematic scenarios arise. For example, if one party feels their autonomy is not being respected, or even if they are primed to be on the lookout that this might occur, they will tend to read the evolving interaction with a strict focus on this concern. If this bias is present, it is not merely an abstract matter concerned with the person being self-referential in their thinking. Rather, this mindset will lead the person to acting in a way that appears to be unappreciative, even paranoid and resentful. In this event being other-oriented – for the moment, but only as a segment in a longer-term reciprocal cycle – is not an option as it feels like giving in, like not having a voice or rights. Here, being considerate comes to feel like you are throwing in the towel. Better to stand up for yourself – which is likely to come across to the other as self-centered and alienating.

A second possibility is that a person can be so relationally needy as to be overly other-oriented. That is, if I feel I am not self-sufficient, if I know that I get lonely and anxious and this experience is aversive, I will tend to back down at all costs. This is a recipe for exploitation and relational volatility and is prejudicial to the chances of healthy and secure attachments. (An informal schema for assessing clients' relational styles based on this idea is presented in Chapter 7.) This is the flipside of the *I-will-not-back-down* maneuver. Each of the above dispositions tends to sabotage the chances of relational utility.

Vitamin me

A recent study compared the self-appraisals of US college students 25 years apart (Twenge and Campbell, 2009). Baseline data was drawn from a large sample of young adults from San Diego State University in 1982; the second sample from a similar sized cohort who attended the same university in 2007. What made the study methodologically interesting was that the sample size was not only respectable (approximately 1,600 young adults in each group) but the T1-T2 interval of comparison approximated a generation in its period. Comparing the initial to the recent data, Twenge and Campbell concluded that a third more respondents now report that:

- 'I think I am a special person', or
- 'I like to be the centre of attention.'

These findings were published under the provocative title *Egos inflating over time*. This is a catchy title, one that seeks to play into the much discussed Generation Y question, yet a spirit of skepticism prompts one to question the sloganeering. Perhaps the results might represent 'a set effect': that respondents reported what they thought was the appropriate attitude: *isn't it expected that I believe I have what it takes, that it is right and proper to be confident and alive to my talents?* Further, Twenge and Campbell's findings might be native to the US, an emblem of that nation's 'indigenous psychology' (Heelas and Lock, 1981), and have pertinence to this one place and its cultural satellites.

Differences in culture and class, gender and faith, across different sites would have the effect of mediating how much their results could be generalized, although there seem likely to be convergent characteristics within a rapidly globalizing world. Just as patterns in global markets have local economic effects, how personhood is conducted, experienced, and understood is likely to realize an international dimension. Assuming the findings were not flawed in their interpretation and they do, in fact, represent validly drawn and internationally relevant conclusions, who is to say an increase in the perceived self-appreciation of young adults is any kind of problem at all? Rather than deride those who participated, isn't it better to regard a positive self-image as much more a virtue than it a fault? A little 'vitamin me' is surely a good thing, but 'more' can easily become too much.

The last decades have seen a transformation where self-confidence has become progressively more valued as a personal trait. This is the case at two levels: confidence is now valorized as a subjective attribute, and as a behavior in the presentation of the public self. Presumably, this has occurred to varying degrees in different national and cultural particular locations, but this trend seems likely to be a relatively common tendency. The mirror image of this trend is also observable – that shyness, modesty, self-deprecation, reticence, and so forth have become less preferred, even pathologized. Gender and generation, as well as cultural and class variables, mediate these developments but they do not negate them.

A minor illustration of this evolution took place in Australia in the mid-1970s. Written and recorded by a bright and ambitious local band, "Ego is not a dirty word" was a hit pop record that became a self-styled anthem. Initially perceived as startling, even to a degree transgressive, this catchy ditty referenced a game-changing adjustment in what was considered 'cool' in the presentation of self. *Don't be backward: be bold and think big of yourself.* Now little more than a dated relic, occasionally recycled on heritage rock radio, before its sentiment became embedded as a naturalized muzak, the cultural norm had held that 'blowing your own trumpet' was not the thing to do.

As well as appearing more confident, more 'out there' as it is said, many in the modern West have developed more self-awareness and a greater sense of entitlement compared with, say, their forebears in Victorian England. Self-affirmation, believing in oneself, has become a virtue. Unless suffering stigma and disadvantage, one would expect the modern citizen to be more assertive and confident, less uptight and less conforming, than their relatives who lived three generations earlier. Mostly, it is good to be self-aware, but at what point does self-awareness metastasize into self-absorption? Adolescents can be exquisitely self-conscious but this is not the kind of awareness that is either healthy in itself or facilitative of secure, reciprocal connections with others.

To be self-affirming seems sensible. It is productive and sound to feel good about yourself. Intuitively, to be self-loving feels right, at least to a degree. All this is credible, yet the problem of self-absorption is an occupational hazard of those who are self-referential and immoderately self-centered. If I interpret everything that happens around me as about me, this is bound to cause a range of big problems, not least with respect to personal relationships. And if I deem too much, or too little, of what is happening around me as directly relevant to me, this will lead to difficulties of a greater or lesser order. At one end, a person can become paranoid; at the other end, oblivious. As is often the case, it is all about getting the balance right. You don't want to be out of touch with your own feelings, needs, and interests: self-awareness and a sense of your own worth is essential. Yet, too much emphasis on 'me' – on what I want and need, on how bad I feel and what my worries are – does not encourage personal accountability. Not only is a me-first attitude ethically problematic, it is also likely to be alienating for those with whom I would like to have relationships.

Putting too much emphasis on *me* can also make you both vulnerable to, and exploitative of, others. Particularly when the internal monologue runs on themes such as *I am special* or *I like to be the center of attention* there is the prospect of slipping from self-affirmation to narcissism. Narcissism is a much voiced, but diffuse, pejorative construct. Its original use was in theorizing one kind of defect in human development. This defect produced in its stronger iteration a disorder of the self (to use the lingua franca of Freudian psychiatry) or, in its lesser expression, characteristics that are less than healthy or even moderately dysfunctional in terms of mental ('psychic') structures.

Refracted in many different ways, the construct is now often used in informal, less clinical instances. The key example of this broader sociological use is probably Christopher Lasch's landmark text *The culture of narcissism* originally published in 1979. In this work Lasch famously argued that over the preceding decades Western citizens have been subject to a general process that has led many towards a state of progressively greater self-absorption, a condition that approximates pathological narcissism. This thesis has much in common with the more recent literature on the process of individualization (see Chapter 2) that has already been cited. There is a general argument that narcissism, which was originally a psychological concept concerned with deficiencies in the development process that are said to lead to difficulties in the organization of personality, have much in common with, but where there are also differences to, a sociological perspective that seeks to explain broad scale transformations in personal identity and the individual's experience of subjectivity.

This is tiger country where observation, commentary, and speculation jostle and contend. Alternative judgments and interpretations, not least contesting understandings of ideology, abound. Is it self-centeredness or personal freedom that is being considered? Is it narcissism or individual control that is at issue? Is there a positive new paradigm for relationships emerging, one that privileges individual choice over obligation and restraint? Or is this reading little more than a rationale for, and a pseudo-warranting of, atomization and isolation and the demise of personal accountability and loyalty?

A sensible analysis displaces this kind of 'either/or' thinking. As Giddens noted, there are always exceptions and counter-trends and it is not helpful to totalize contemporary life as if there is a 'a single world [which has] a unitary framework of experience' (Giddens, 1991, p 5). There are emerging developments, but the 'vanguard tendencies' of high modernity should not be allowed to completely characterize how identity and subjectivity, interaction and relationships, are depicted. And if the subject is relationships, if the focus is on the person's capacity to relate well, if that someone has a strong sense of personal confidence, perhaps is to a degree even cocky, it does not follow that this person will necessarily be less concerned about, or less able to care for, others. Confidence and self-affirmation are not antithetical to good relating – but self-absorption and an asymmetric sense of entitlement are.

Empathy

A point of engagement with the above is to consider the question of empathy. Simply defined, empathy is the capacity to emotionally and cognitively understand, and then to compassionately respond to, the other. Such a capacity is, according to Donald Winnicott, a 'sign of health in the mind is the ability of one individual to enter imaginatively and accurately into the thoughts and hope and fears of another person; also to allow the other person to do the same to us' (as quoted in Phillips and Taylor, 2009, p 97). Goleman (2006) argues that empathy is a key attribute of what he calls 'social intelligence', the wherewithal to get on well with others.

Empathy is a slippery construct and has been defined and measured in many ways over many decades (Gerdes et al, 2010). Currently, there seems a reasonable consensus that empathy has both an emotional and a cognitive dimension, what social neuroscientists Decety and Moriguchi (2007, p 4) have concluded involves a capacity for 'affective sharing', 'self awareness', 'perspective taking' and 'emotional regulation'. This understanding recalls, and then elaborates, the much earlier psychoanalytic idea that empathy operates as a form of 'vicarious introspection' (Kohut, 1959, p 82).

So, how are we doing with empathy: is it on the rise or the wane? Bruce Perry, a child psychiatrist and neuroscientist with a particular commitment to the child protection field, makes a strong case that empathy is essential but it is endangered. Amongst a suite of empirical and more anecdotal reports, he quotes researchers from the University of Pennsylvania who have examined empathy levels in a series of longitudinal studies. Unhappily, the comparative scores for empathy reported in these serial studies is not good news: empathy scores amongst college students have almost halved in the past 10 years (Szalavitz and Perry, 2010).

In theorizing this apparent decline, one obvious suspect is the increased use of ICT, as noted earlier. Whilst mobile phones, email, texting, and the like have a clear potential to increase communication, and therefore to potentially enhance the quality and quality of relationships (a subject that is specifically developed in Chapter 7), there is some evidence that the intense use of ICT, especially when this involves multitasking, diminishes empathy in and of itself. Watson (2010), for example, argues in *Future minds* that 'screenagers' develop a splintered concentration span and that the anonymity of the web erodes the capacity for empathy.

Compared to face-to-face, synchronous interaction, the argument runs, the use of ICT attenuates the presence of the other because there are insufficient cues to prompt an adequate level of empathic response. There is a consensus that the majority of inter-human communication is non-verbal as it relies on tone of voice, physical setting, the nuances of body language, including eye contact, proximity, and so forth. (The calculation varies with some saying more than 90 per cent of communication is non-verbal: see, for example, Mehrabian, 2007, p 193.) It follows that text-based, asynchronous, and mediated communication provides a thin data stream that endangers the prospects for empathy.

Moreover, there is a developing body of research from neuroscience that posits that the exact social-neurological wiring that humans have evolved over hundreds of thousands of years that allows us to be empathic – to merge – is being coopted to hook us into a different kind of bonding: with our ICT devices. According to Jason Mitchell (2009) from Harvard University's Social Cognition and Affective Neuroscience Laboratory, humans have a set of processes for inferring what those around us are thinking and feeling.

This capacity for mind reading has been crucial in humans being able to 'coordinate large groups of people to achieve goals that individuals could not.' (Mitchell, as quoted in Carr, 2010, p 213). Unfortunately, this capacity for intuiting with other minds involves a 'chronic over-activity of the brain regions implicated in social thought' and can result in humans endowing sentience where none exists, including into inanimate objects such as computers (Mitchell, as quoted in Carr, 2010, p 213). Just as mirroring is essential to ordinary empathy, we can project onto technology, and take from technology, human characteristics. Our facility with computers, for example, extends our capabilities, but in this interplay we are also altered neurologically, as Greenfield (2008) has discussed. Based on her own neuroscientific research, Greenfield has controversially concluded that an immersion in gaming and other ICT applications re-wires the neural patterning in our brains.

Important theorizing and research is taking place concerning the impact of technology on selfhood and sociality. A good deal of this work is critical, but to single out ICT as the reason for diminishing empathy scores makes little sense. There are other transformations in play, not least of which is the intensification of individualization, consumerism, and disparity. These tides affect the circumstances within which the human talent for, and the actual conduct of, human sociality is realized. Human nervous systems may still be as hard-wired to 'merge' as ever, but the conditions that shape how this potential is expressed are decisively important. In reflecting about this issue it seems that 'vitamin me' is a likely confidante of isolation even as it might initially seem harmless, or even fun. On deeper review it is likely there is something darker to this character than first meets the eye.

Can the cycles of loneliness and isolation be interrupted?

'[W]ith a little encouragement, most anyone can emerge from the prison' of isolation, report Cacioppo and Patrick (2008, p 19). This is a terrifically optimistic position, especially if the trend lines on some key indicators, such as the average level of empathy, are in decline. Yet, rather than be discouraged, this bad news should be heard as a prompt for action. As Szalavitz and Perry (2010), Goleman (2006), and others argue, empathy, amongst a larger set of relationship-building attributes, can be encouraged and learned. This is especially potent for those clients who have had good reason to make their self a fortress: if you have been excluded, if you have been stigmatized, you tend to have your drawbridge up and your defenses on high alert. (This point is elaborated in Chapter 7 with respect to exercises that seek to improve the person's capacity to 'perspective take'.)

Doc, one of John Steinbeck's protagonists in *Cannery row*, remarked:

> 'It has always seemed strange to me,' said Doc. 'The things we admire in men, kindness and generosity, openness, honesty, understanding, and feeling are the concomitants of failure in our system. And those traits we detest, sharpness, greed, acquisitiveness, meanness, egotism, and self-interest are the traits of success. And while men admire the first, they love the produce of the second.' (Steinbeck, 1965, p 438)

Just as Steinbeck wrote these thoughts in the 1930s, so it is today. To a degree we have become more hardened and self-absorbed, but to accede to pessimism – to take the view that the young, indeed all of us, are now more superficial and narcissistic, that men have become dishonorable and callous, that women are now more materialistic and less caring – is to negatively generalize.

Co-existing with the rising tide of me-first opportunism there are contesting, even antagonistic, currents. These oppositional flows to the neoliberal tide are present in a diverse range of locations: in virtual communities, in what have been termed horizontal families, in same-sex parenting. Norms around gender, culture, values, and ideology are being disputed in these creative examples. If professional practice can be understood as a type of research, as an action research project that commits itself to aligning with the exceptions and counter-trends that contest the larger tide, we 'study acts of resistance rather than acts of power' (Wodak, 1997, p 49). According to 'Foucault ... and others' this is to engage in 'liberating research' (Wodak, 1997, p 49).

Even those who seem most excluded are never completely outside of relationships. As social beings it is inevitable that there will be an interpersonal dimension to life, no matter however limited or unsatisfactory this might be an optimistic, albeit perhaps naïve, view contends that the nature of positive social relations, such as friendships, may change in their expression over time but will nonetheless maintain their robustness and supportive character. Unless one is an advocate of the post-human, following the thinkers discussed earlier (Kipnes; 2003; Bostrum, 2005), such old fashioned hopefulness has a certain appeal. Yes, it's possible that affiliation will look after itself and be both stubborn and also fungible. Unless you are an advocate of the post-human, following the thinkers discussed earlier (Kipnis, 2003; Bostrum, 2005), it is hard to take issue with this hope. Social connectedness may prove to be far more stubborn than many fear.

It has been said that "[t]he propensity to make strong emotional bonds to particular individuals [is] a basic component of human nature" (Bowlby, 1988, p 3). Being so bonded can be likened to being in a small craft on a stormy sea where, to repurpose Paris' old mottos, the boat will often be rocked but will not capsize. The question then arises: are professionals doing all they can to strengthen the relational base of clients? However heretical, perhaps, they might be doing the opposite: being accomplices to the process of atomization. The next chapter investigates this question.

5
Questioning professional norms

Painting ourselves into the picture | Agents of connection or
separation? | Problematic professional norms | Practice wisdom
and the culture of practitioners

Painting ourselves into the picture

Clients and ordinary citizens alike are able to improve the quality of their
relationships. Individualization and the effects of social exclusion may corrode
the prospects for relationships, yet as a species we have continued to form bonds
with one another. It continues to be in our interest to be so: there is a health and
wellbeing dividend that makes it smart to contest defensiveness and the incoming
'I-me-my' tide. This stance requires a degree of optimism and commitment, but
it is indisputable that good-enough attachments help the swimmer stay afloat
during the difficult transitions encountered across the life course. If the fantasy of
radical autonomy is acknowledged as captivating, and then archived, it opens space
for professionals to prioritize the creation of local instances of social connection.

Consistent with this thinking, the next step in this book is to take what has
been presented so far and to bring this material into a pragmatic engagement with
the domain of practice. At first, this appears a straightforward task. Everybody is
willing: clients want to be included and acknowledged, to be loved and lovable,
and professionals want the same things for their clients. Or, maybe it is not so
simple. It is not possible to drive straight and fast down a twisty lane, so, before
starting off, assuming that relationship-building practice is no more than an
unproblematic add-on, an extra that can be glued onto current approaches, a
process of critical review is required. What is needed is an assurance that the
accepted assumptions and patterns of action, the taken-for-granted norms that
underwrite the professional project really do square with the principles of a
relationship-building agenda. However comforting or confronting this review
turns out to be, it has to be done.

Good will can be assumed. Practitioners really do want their clients to be
linked in. This desire is a pragmatic aim and represents much more than a feel
good kind of attitude or the workings of sentiment. Practitioners want the people
they work for to be loved, respected, and included, and that their clients make
personal contributions, contributions that are recognized, to their significant
others. Practitioners know this is in the best interests of their clients. Just as it is the

case with 'normal' citizens, just as it is true for practitioners, so it is also important that those practitioners work for are affectionately embedded in their networks.

This hard-nosed logic accepted, it is a common professional assumption to act as if some, perhaps many, clients are too sensitive to, or are incapable of performing, close attachments. Despite an 'espoused theory' that celebrates the importance of relationships it is possible that the 'theory in use' (Argyris and Schon, 1975) often acts to qualify the applicability of this general principle. Exceptions are expected, reservations held – at times relating to whole classes of clients.

For example, many clients are said to suffer from more or less profound attachment issues (O'Connor and Zeanah, 2003). Damaged by their experiences as infants, they are thought to have such problems with 'interpersonal cognition' that they lack the capacity to safely and reciprocally relate to others (Baldwin, 2005). Adults who have a problem with their 'mental representations' – their internalized images – of their early significant others are understood to, at least in some circumstances, benefit from clinicians with specialist training, yet are unable to manage the intense feelings that are generated in everyday encounters with intimates and strangers without their emotions becoming deregulated.

This general point stated, there are radical complications in and around matters of definition, prevalence, and treatment effectiveness with respect to attachment disorders. For example, one heavily cited text reported that 'No 'gold standard' exists for assessing attachment disorders' and that 'No treatment method has been shown to be effective with attachment disorders' (O'Connor and Zeanah, 2003, p 233). Wanting to avoid being hijacked by the ambiguities and uncertainties in this contested sub-field, the question for the current text is this: how broadly is the diagnostic net 'attachment disorder' to be cast?

It has to be acknowledged that there are a good number of clients who, at least from time to time, find what happens in their current relationships powerfully evokes their problematic early life experiences, that what is happening currently stirs up the past's dark parts. Yet, for the current purpose, what is essential is that this idea is not over-valued or over-generalized. A small minority of clients may be especially vulnerable, but it is important not to be paternalistic or to over-indulge in diagnoses that totalize the client's whole self as disordered. You could take a contrary view and say that it is normal, absolutely to be expected, that the here-and-now of relationships will recall what has occurred in the past, so we should not allow ourselves to pathologize this phenomenon.

This is an important theoretical position to hold as reservations, even outright pessimism, concerning the relational prospects of particular clients is not uncommonly felt by practitioners. In agency kitchens, or over after-hours drinks, informal small talk can echo with what is privately voiced in the mind of practitioners: *doesn't it bring out the worst in X, and many others who are vulnerable and easily led, when they get into groups?* Instances of the validity of this suspicion are easily found: *it's trouble when young women with anorexia connect on the net* (or, when people with substance abuse problems hang out in groups, when people who are anxious and suspicious are banded together, when ex-prisoners consort). *Look out when there are negative group dynamics!*

The thinking is that such ensembles risk encouraging, even exacerbating, the exact problems for which professional help was originally sought or imposed. The young anorexic women may swap unhealthy tips on weight reduction; ex-junkies may fall back into evocative, and then suggestive, talk of old scores and great highs; men who are schooled to violence could arouse and aggravate each other in escalating, unstable 'pissing contests'. These kinds of concerns appear to give very legitimate grounds for limiting the universality of social connectedness as a professional objective. As a theoretical maxim it may be clear that clients are better off having a stock of intimate connections, but in reality, certain constraints should be acknowledged in the application of this principle.

Based on the ideas in the preceding chapters, this chapter invites these (and other) reservations to be reviewed. At the most direct level this argument is advanced because the research on the importance of interpersonal relationships has not, so far, adequately filtered into the thinking and activities of many who work in the industry's consulting rooms and outreach services. Quite likely, non-clinical, as well as some therapeutic, practitioners will be aware of the material aspects of this research: that inequalities with respect to class and gender, location, and ethnicity, are involved in the reproduction of health and social problems. Yet many practitioners are less familiar with the findings from social epidemiology that 'the locally social' is also crucial, and therefore do not tend to positively use these findings to inform their practice. This research has concluded that 'network enhancement', to use one of many phrases that have a similar meaning, is a common good for those who are vulnerable, yet so far there seems little indication that the good sense in this research has been translated into a change in the generic goals that are articulated for practice. Mostly, the drum continues to pound the old signals of empowerment and independence.

Knowledge transmission issues to one side, an even more troubling question is present: can it be assumed that the current work of practitioners has the outcome of helping clients be more attached to their significant others and to their larger networks? Even if 'network enhancement', 'interpersonal embedding', 'building the client's relational base', and so on, is not a formal goal of practice, can it be assumed that the current work of counselors and therapists, doctors and nurses, case managers and outreach workers builds rather than erodes the client's capacity for connection? For example, might the effect of some professional practices be that the client is incited to be more self-interested and less accountable? If this is the case, a by-product of intervention will be the promotion of insecure attachments because self-regard is being taught more than a regard for others.

However awkward it might be to consider, it is possible that some of the most revered professional norms have the effect of undermining the client's capacity for affiliation. It will sound discourteous to hear, but an inadvertent byproduct of conventional practice could be that practitioners are ignoring, attenuating, or even antagonizing the social relations their clients have with their intimates.

A point of entry to this task is to reflect on the professional and organizational attitudes that are present in the practice field. Is it the case that there is a casual, albeit disavowed, disrespect to the client's relationships present in some, or even many, practice settings?

Agents of connection or separation?

That practitioners might inadvertently disturb the client's prospects for secure attachment deserves an unsentimental investigation. Given the material presented in the preceding chapter, what is of particular interest is whether the values and practices of counselors, case managers, youth workers, all those who make up that larger groups of professionals who work in health and human services, aligns with, or contests, the atomizing effects of individualization. If the net effect of what takes place between the practitioner and the client acts to resist the process of individualization, this will develop the client's interdependencies – an outcome that will build the client's awareness of others and their repertoire for enabling social interaction. On the other hand, if professional practices are consistent with, or actually promote, the process of individualization, this will diminish the client's interpersonal accountability and their capacity for sustainable personal relations. A vignette is introduced here to illustrate this point.

VIGNETTE 1: NICK

Following his annual performance review Nick, a 27-year-old man of Greek descent, was advised by a psychologist in his employer's human resources department to seek treatment. "You might think," this woman told him, "there is nothing really wrong with you, but I can tell you there are features in your presentation consistent with mild to moderate depression, in addition to some associated anxiety symptoms."

Nick had not been feeling positive and thought this advice sounded authoritative. Several weeks later he met Murray, an experienced private practitioner with an initial background in cognitive behavioral therapy (CBT) who had more recently become interested in experiential approaches, particularly *Gestalt* therapy. Nick told Murray he was over-stressed, yet somehow dissatisfied, with his work in IT. He also said he and his wife Leila were not getting on and that he was playing computer games late into the night, not only because he slept poorly, but also because "it is *my* thing, it's what really challenges me and gives me a buzz." He also said he had recently stopped playing basketball, a game he had played since he was very young, and that his parents, along with his wife, "are on my back to get started with having children and are at me telling me to 'get going with your career so you can make some real money' and make us all happy."

Murray suspected that Nick was playing computer games as an escape and was, more generally, under-achieving not just in a career sense but also in an existential sense – just as many of his other clients exhibited an absence of vitality in their constricting dilemmas and emotional cut-outs. Rather than seeing Nick in primarily clinical terms, as someone who was suffering the symptoms of depression, Murray viewed Nick as being "at a cross-road, a place where he has to work out what is most important to him: self-actualization or stagnation. That is his real dilemma." After asking Nick many questions, and listening closely to his answers, at the end of the second session Murray came to a point of decision. He reasoned what was important was "to stir the young man in him who wants to get out and challenge the old man in him he is pretending to be. He is not really the prematurely grey figure he seems to be, a young man who is trussed up and put down. I can identify with him: like all who have the courage to really be, he should be on the road less traveled."

In their third session Murray asked Nick if he was sexually fulfilled with his wife. Somewhat taken aback, Nick said "no, not completely." Murray then held the silence until Nick eventually said "no, not much at all. It's pretty much no good and hasn't been for a while. She used to want to please me. This is very hard to talk about, but she doesn't want to do much that I want these days." Later, Murray asked how he responded when his parents communicated their disappointment with him and their ideas about what he should be doing. Again, Nick was surprised to be asked about this matter so directly and said somewhat embarrassedly "I just try to keep strum and ignore them, to do the right thing and not fight them about their old world ideas."

In their discussions Murray often asked Nick "What are your options?" At one point he asked Nick: "What would you like to say to these people, to anyone, who says they care about you, but who *you know* do not understand your point of view or what is most important to you?" Although he sensed the old flash of guilt at this prompt, what galvanized Nick was that, at last, with Murray there was someone who was really on his wavelength. "Not since I was a kid has someone, maybe not even then, has someone who is important been so strongly on my side. He really understands me, he's in my corner!"

Aware he had been planting seeds in being quietly, but persistently provocative, Murray formulated his approach in terms of daring Nick to claim his entitlement to be in charge of his life. Satisfied with how the process was playing, Murray said to himself: "I am like a coach, an older male mentor. My message to him is an existential truth: 'you want excitement, you have to cast off your old habits of mind, your fear and to take what it is that is really important to you. And, I am living this code: I am not stringing this therapy along, not stretching out my income stream, I am going for it too.'"

In the above, Murray was clear to himself that he did not, and could not ever, direct his client. "Whatever he does, it will always be his own decision, not mine. It is the client who carries the responsibility for his own self-determination."

Of course, in one sense this is true as practitioners never have unilateral control over their clients. Yet Murray is painting himself out of the picture if he reckons he is not an active agent. Practitioners often play an influential role in reforming and socializing their clients and for Murray to deny this is also to deny the pride he experienced at his protégée's engagement with the momentum that the therapeutic process generated. Claiming neutrality when one is trying to be of positive use to the client is to be disingenuous. And it is a position that was debunked many years ago (Foucault, 1967, 1972; Pentony, 1981). Unfortunately, this stance continues to be held by many.

In the above example there is a direction to the influence exerted by the therapist. That is, particular effects were entrained, if not absolutely engineered, by the nature of Murray's discourse, his way of framing the discussion, and his method for setting out the terms of the engagement. Over time, Nick may have come to 'kick back' against the momentum of the dialogue within which he found himself participating, but unless he did, where would this dialogue lead him? Was it towards the balancing of his interests with the valuing of the interests of his significant others? Was it to engage with the issue of personal accountability and towards a critical discussion of his fantasies?

Most likely, the effect of his engagement with his therapist was to incline him towards a more self-enclosed reverie and to incite him towards a greater intoxication with himself and his interests. By privileging the language of choice, by enthusiastically siding with the client, by pitting the therapist's unambiguous championing of his client's desires against those who, it was alleged, had failed to understand him and were pressuring him – by these and many other tactics – the practitioner constructed the client as a 'sovereign self' (Davidson and Rees-Mogg, 1997) rather than an accountable social being. According to Murray, the 'normal-as-healthy' subject is a free-standing island of interest rather than an interdependent being.

In taking up this invitation Nick would, of course, be doing what Murray was expecting of him. As such, both Nick and his mentor are working to the values of autonomy and self-determination, respecting confidentiality and promoting personal choice. These are exactly the imperatives in the texts and ethics of all professions in the field. More pragmatically, Murray had set out, as all practitioners must, to forge what is variously termed a 'therapeutic alliance' or 'working engagement'. This linkage is regarded as the precondition for successful practice: you have to get the client signed up to work with you. This can be a sensitive matter as it is often a sophisticated dance to find a form of relating that 'neither collides nor colludes' (Furlong, 2002).

Certainly, it is necessary to 'engage the client, that is, draw favorable attention to the proposed work' (Hartman and Laird, 1983, p 133). Central to this initial set-up work is the generation of sufficient trust and a coordination of meanings to 'get the job started'. In this engagement process there is a degree of ambiguity necessarily in play. In this encounter there is a mix of elements: there is the business end of the contact, the instrumental aspects of a commercial exchange, which involves vendors and customers, goals and agreements, bargaining, and so forth. And, there is also a dimension of respect, behaviors that resemble friendship, even of a kind of love. Putting the business and the personal aspects together is a sensitive, even contradictory, matter. To some degree it is useful, even necessary, to have the client take the view that there is an 'us' – the trustworthy dyad that is exclusively made up of the client and the practitioner – as there is a 'them' – the others that do not understand and who trouble the client. In Nick's case, Murray was successful in embedding this perception. But was he too successful in setting the terms of the exchange in a way that acted to estrange Nick from his friends and family?

It is exactly this kind of 'either you are on my side or theirs' definition of engagement success that I believe is problematic. The positioning 'I'm on your side – and they are against you' reflects core norms that are both problematic and also at the heart of professional and agency cultures. These norms relate to an over-valuing of self-determination, client choice, confidentiality, autonomy, and a narrow configuration of personal and professional boundaries. Of course, not all the norms and purposes that support current practices are antithetical to the prospects for the client's personal relationships. Speech therapists have to assist individuals in communicating more clearly; victims need to be de-briefed; children who have been abused need to be believed; the severe problems of living experienced by so many need to be witnessed, and so on. Such work is honorable and, if completed well, is likely to improve the chances clients have to form and maintain good quality interpersonal relationships.

Mindful of the needs many clients have for individual support and professional succor, the issue that should not be forgotten is that practitioners are, almost always, only visitors in the lives of their clients. Rather than valorizing their own expertise in being able to listen, understand and help the client as if we are their ideal life companion, a primary goal of professional practice can be to assist clients to look to their own backyard for their support. In one sense a special relationship with a skilled practitioner is worryingly unnatural: such an experience can build up the expectation that an asymmetric relationship – a pattern where one party, exclusively, is present to tune into what is important for the other, so that the other gets what they supposedly need and deserve. Here, one person talks while the other listens, nods understandingly, and says 'tell me more.' There is nothing fair or sustainable in such a division of labor.

Once this nectar is supped, more equitable arrangements can seem, somehow, less than satisfactory. Rather than glamorizing their own attractiveness as experts, practitioners can creatively sabotage this expectation in order to encourage, and also better equip, their clients to have strong relationships with their own peers, their friends, and their relatives. Peer-to-peer linkages can be sustaining and self-affirming for the client beyond the time when the practitioner, who the social researcher Mackay (2002, p 14) describes as 'an intimate rent-a-friend', is long gone.

In certain quarters it is thought that the outcome of a successful course of therapy is that the client will be able to relate more fully. This is assumed to be a secondary outcome, an effect that is downstream of the fact that the graduated client is now more complete, self-accepting, less neurotic, and so forth. I make no attempt to dispute this assumption. At a theoretical and practical level there is always the possibility that the newly healthy client will be more fully able to relate to others. What the reader is asked to consider is that this is a 'best case' outcome, one that gives a good alibi to all practitioners but which may not be the most accurate generalization. For example, Bauman (2003, p 57) suggests psychotherapy tends to have a negative affect on the client's prospects for relationship in that the process:

> … advises more self-appreciation, self-concern and self care, more attention to their … inner ability for pleasure and satisfaction – as well as less 'dependence' on others and less attention to other's demands for attention and care. Clients who diligently learned the lessons and followed the advice faithfully should from now on ask themselves more often the question 'what's in it for me?'

In so far as there is truth in this argument, the connection between clients and their significant others will be compromised as clients will be socialized into this cognitive pattern. This possibility is examined in some detail in what follows.

Problematic professional norms

The professional project is conceptualized in similar ways across the disciplines: the client will be assisted to become more autonomous and self-reliant. Autonomy and self-reliance are not understood as contingent and/or controversial values; on the contrary, they are assumed to be unproblematic and to sit together high up, above the fray, as a kind of independent variable. To want the client to be separate, to encourage the client to take up their right and duty to independence, is so taken for granted as to further a cultural program that is invisible.

This program executes a 'specification' for health and normality (Rose, 1989, 1999), which includes the following elements. The client should demonstrate:

- enterprise, entrepreneurship and ambition
- secure personal boundaries
- an internal locus of control
- personal agency
- self-determination
- assertiveness
- rationality and calculation.

This specification for normality reflects a particular design for the self that is consistent with a psychology of separation far more than a norm of interdependence. Such a design may feel natural, but it has the signature of a specific cultural and historic location. Critics, such as Duberman (2002, p 461), consider this design a 'regime of the normal'. Of particular note is that what is celebrated as the elements inherent to the healthy self implicitly traces an outline of its mirror image, of what will be seen as abnormal and unhealthy: dependency, emotionality, mutuality, guilt, and so forth. That is, the shadow side of the Western, 'male-stream' image of the rational and agentic self is that which is devalued (O'Brien, 1981).

Adjusting clients so they better conform to the ideal of autonomy is generally understood as a kind of value-free practice: "my work is not problematic. I am neutral and my practice is client-directed" (as Murray argued in Vignette 1). This is problematic in the sense that practitioners are change agents in so far as they seek to have clients better conform with, or to contest, the accepted design for personhood. Practitioners who reproduce the professional status quo cannot help but be ideological actors, even de facto warriors, in promoting a form of personhood that privileges separation and self-determination. Practitioners can never be 'non-judgmental' as there is always an agenda, whether this is declared or remains implicit. At the very least practitioners want their clients to do better, to benefit from their contact with practitioners. How else could practitioners legitimate their practice and their income?

Self-actualization

Most health and community-based practitioners are not psychotherapists, yet the image and the culture, the customs and the values of the therapies have been influential in shaping professional practice in its many expressions. Irrespective of differences in the profession of origin, in key ways all practitioners are heirs to a conceptual vocabulary and a set of norms that have been derived from the established therapies. Mixed with elements of psychological speculation (see below), this heritage includes much of what is taken as fact in relation to human development, personality, and the details of, and the relationship between, definitions of normality and pathology. And conventions concerning professional behavior, such as how the issue of confidentiality should be understood and managed, have, to a large extent, been derived from the same sources. The following brief account analyses this common heritage. At times this account is unavoidably more than a little demanding, but a short story might kick-start this investigation.

Maslow's (1943, 1970) 'hierarchy of human needs' is a schema that is familiar to nearly every practitioner irrespective of their discipline (as it is to those who have studied psychology in secondary education). To those familiar with this schema, self-actualization is understood as the highest form of human need (see Figure 4.1). Those that attain this status, such as (it is quoted) Mahatma Gandhi, Mother Theresa and Martin Luther King, have satisfied all their more basic needs and have been able to realize a higher level of functioning. No longer needing food or shelter, having satisfied all bodily requirements, and having also ascended beyond an interest in such mid-level requirements as being loved and having a sense of belonging, the self-actualized person can get on with being the best they can be. Such exemplars have been freed from, it is surmised, the constraints of being hungry or of worrying about their reputation.

Figure 4.1: Maslow's hierarchy of needs

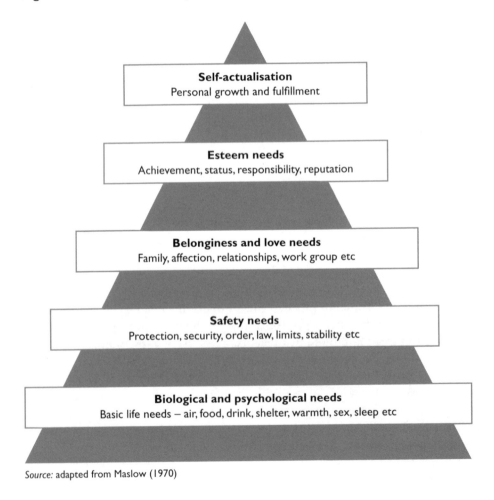

Source: adapted from Maslow (1970)

In terms of the theory every need rated below self-actualization is categorized as a 'deficit need' (Maslow, 1970). Relegated to a subsistence status, deficit needs are appetites that have a base nature compared to the more elevated aspects of the unbounded self. But is this the only way this story might run?

Having risen above the worry about how they are seen by others, it is possible that a truly unfettered individual might act less like Mahatma Gandhi and more like the mythical Gordon Gecko of Wall Street; less like Mother Theresa and more like the plotting Bernard Madoff who scalped billions of dollars from those that invested in his bogus financial schemes. If a person is materially secure, and if they are indifferent to their reputation, it is as or more likely that this person will act as a sexual opportunist or power monger more than as a progressive social reformer or devoted philanthropist. Yet, this possibility is far from the only problem with Maslow's hierarchy. Not least of these worrying issues is that neither Maslow, nor those who reproduce his schema, supply any evidence for their propositions. Were any randomized, double-blind trials conducted? Were rigorously constructed qualitative studies undertaken of samples of a meaningful scale or depth? On what basis was the initial schema of five needs (Maslow, 1943) changed to six, then seven and now, posthumous to his death, to eight? It seems no respected methodology was ever used to discover the truths that Maslow in actual fact invented.

Maslow's schema is speculative, even metaphysical. Nonetheless, it continues to be popular and to be reproduced in a realm that exists beyond the reach of critique. This reproduction is occasioned in many standard psychological reference texts (Westen, 2008; Burton et al, 2009) that purport to represent scientifically verified facts. This undetected non-science has resulted in a template for human development and, in the longer term, a definition of healthy normality being circulated without this specification having empirical validity.

How is it possible that Maslow's creation continues to be circulated in reputable texts without any reservations or review? Simple critical reflection identifies that Maslow's ideas were anything but random. Rather, they fitted precisely with the assumptions that were developing in a particular time and place. In this context, the ideal of autonomy so deeply embedded in Maslow's conjectures appeared valid simply because they were wonderfully in tune with the incoming cultural norms of the 1950s, 1960s and 1970s – patterns of thought that are now accepted at face value. Maslow's framing makes so much sense to those who now read his work that their contingency is invisible: as the fish cannot see the sea, so self-actualization seems indisputable.

Maslow's work on self-actualization has become part of professionals' shared inheritance. As an illustration of this status, each of the case managers and private psychotherapists in a recent study, a cohort of 24 multidisciplinary practitioners with between two and thirty years' practice experience post-graduation, professed a clear knowledge of self-actualization as the highest expression of human need. In this qualitative study not one participant volunteered a critique of the construct, and though all were familiar, and apparently enthusiastic, about the highest of

Maslow's needs, only a few of the interviewees were able to name all the hierarchy's less important needs (Furlong, 2008a). That so many professionals accept the story that self-actualization amounts to the pinnacle of human development is, as argued shortly, only the tip of the iceberg. More generally, professionals are heirs to a legacy of received, but highly dubious, strands of knowledge that each idealize autonomy. Woven closely into a dense pattern, these threads constitute a psychology of separation. Before re-entering the non-therapeutic practice realm, one further element that professionals in the field more generally have received from the psychotherapies should be examined.

The common denominator in therapeutic theory

At first glance there are many differences between the different schools and traditions of psychotherapy and psychology. Emotion-centered approaches privilege feelings; the cognitive tradition regards thoughts and attitudes as the proper axis of attention; psychodynamic theory concentrates on internal, mostly unconscious, processes; psychobiological theories stress physiological development and neurological processes, and so on. Moreover, different approaches also frame the purpose of the therapeutic exercise in different ways, as the pursuit of 'adjustment', 'understanding', 'empowerment', 'maximizing rational choice', and so forth. The defining metaphors of the psychotherapeutic project seem to vary considerably. In some schools it is for the client to be in charge of their life whereas in others it is to renounce, let go of, fantasies, to feel more entitled, and so on.

Beyond these differences that distinguish between traditions a recent analysis suggested that there is one common theme that unites all the major contenders: each brand assumes that the client, the person, is bounded by their skin and is a being with an identity and set of interests that are sheared from their environment – a context that is not merely one of geographical place but that also comprises the client's important others (Furlong, 2008a). Irrespective of whether the specific school is located within the cognitive, psychodynamic, or humanistic tradition, it is understood that the self will be understood as a free-standing, self-interested, and amoral actor.

This is more obviously the case in some traditions. For example, in rational-emotive theory, a close relative of CBT, 'rational' thinking is the mode of thought that is assumed to properly advance the individual's benefit:

> [W]hen Ellis advocates the abolition of irrational beliefs, he cannot be seen as appealing to some transcendental, ultimate standard by which all thought and action can be evaluated. Rather, he is advancing a value position that advocates the most expedient pursuit of happiness, a happiness defined totally in terms of a personal hedonic calculus. (Woolfolk and Saas, 1989, p 26)

Albert Ellis openly espoused a belief that 'short term hedonism' (Ellis quoted in Woolfolk and Saas, 1989, p 209) is the wellspring for human action and, more broadly, that the healthy self *needs to be* amorally active in realizing this aim.

Humanistic, so-called 'third force' approaches, such as *Gestalt* therapy, are almost as open about their standpoint: the individual is understood as, and is encouraged to be, self-interested and opportunistic. Romantic attachment and sexual attraction are, according to writers like *Gestalt* therapy's Fritz Perls, *beautiful* if they happen, but only in so far as these exist, with a *if it works for me* caveat.

There are non-mainstream exceptions to this contention, especially with respect to some threads within the psychodynamic tradition – the notion of 'kinship libido' (Jung, 1946), as introduced in the previous chapter, for example. Similarly, some recent post-structural and feminist formulations seek to construct a more relational understanding of the self (Mitchell, 1988). This acknowledged, a 'hatred of dependence' (Hoggett, 2001) and a tendency to pathologize relationships are established themes in the psychodynamic tradition. For example, what is termed 'object choice' – who a person is inclined to pair up with – is never understood as a positive matter. We are all, more or less, said to be neurotic in each of our romances. An old psychoanalytic aphorism puts this tartly: *We seek the jaws that fit our wounds.*

The narrative tradition also offers a counterpoint to the generalization that therapeutic theories are antagonistic to relational responsibility. This is evident in how the theme of personal accountability is emphasized in narrative work (White, 2002, 2004, 2007). Logically, it should be also be expected that systems ideas would have a contrary, and potentially constructive, position with respect to the premise of reciprocal influence. Sadly, just as mainstream therapies do, it is mostly assumed that the purpose of therapy is to enhance individual client choice. The systems thinker von Foerster (1984, p 60) says this emphatically in his epithet: "The ethical imperative: [is that the therapist should] Act always so as to increase the number of [client] choices."

Marginal exceptions noted, there is nothing in any of the standard approaches to psychotherapy that privilege the centrality of cooperation and interdependence; nor is there any mention, let alone argument, of the importance of interpersonal fairness and accountability. In so far as 'the other' is mentioned, this is in terms of whether the client is getting what they want from friends, lovers, and relations. And the so-called negative emotions, particularly guilt and shame, are pathologized. The sovereign self is assumed to be an autonomous, amoral, status-seeking, consumer-producer. Troublingly, that which might connect the person with the common good, such as the experience of guilt and shame, is understood as a problem to be solved as it represents a restraint to free trade. In such ways the Western psychology of separation is a descent down the "spiral staircase of the self" (de Montaigne, as cited in DiNicola, 1997, p 199).

This psychology of separation is present in a range of accepted frameworks, such as the account of the life cycle developed by Erik Erikson (1980). This account suffers from the same credibility issue as Maslow's hierarchy of human needs.

That there has been a suspension of disbelief about both of these theories can be read through a feminist lens: these accounts are machismo fantasies, parables that reflect and propagate a hegemonic account. This template casts the relational into a disowned shadow world. If the focus is on the therapeutic market leader, this argument can be made even clearer.

Cognitive behavioral therapy

The most popular brand of psychotherapy is cognitive behavioral therapy (CBT). This method presents a particularly troubling conjunction with respect to relational practice. It uses a vocabulary directly taken from the marketplace, specifically one that closely resembles the neoliberal ideal of micro-economic reform. In both cases the task is constructed by the repetitive use of notions of efficiency, effectiveness, focus, priorities, management by objectives, performance, and so forth. This common method is attractive as it involves a set of pseudo-technical terms and a logic that precisely mirrors the amoral pragmatism of commercial utility.

For this reason CBT is not difficult to understand or find credible. Its applicability seems self-evident as its logic is so familiar as to have been naturalized. Just as it is sensible to analyze the performance of ports or the function of airports in terms of their effectiveness in meeting service targets, so it is logical to measure and adjust the person so this unit meets 'its' rational goals. This protocol has been contested by critics (Pilgrim, 2011), but it is exactly this individualistic and amoral nature that makes CBT so attractive. Just as the sociologist Max Weber ([1906] 2002) proposed that the process of rationalization was characteristic of modernity, according to the mantra of CBT, the modern subject is to be improved in their ability to calculate and administer their own self and its interests.

In this sense CBT is only worse in degree with respect to other therapeutic approaches. Across all the regular approaches to psychotherapy the subject is expected to be an entity that acts upon their location like a profit and loss-driven corporation (if not as an outright predator). The rational thinking process that is to guide the person is not just benignly neglectful of 'the other', whether this person is a partner or a stranger. Rather, the other is not posited at all except as some kind of uninhabited site to be mined or, even worse, as an obstruction that requires manipulation or even removal. Just as Giddens (1992) proposed the modern citizen needs to a 'reflexive strategizer', the therapeutically well-adjusted person is the independent variable, a mobile entity who *strategizes* the other and makes rational, self-serving choices in pursuit of what is presumed to be entitlement or advantage. Even the softer, more progressive brands, such as the emotional intelligence school whose advocates seek to be at the more humane end of the spectrum, encourage the client to be other-oriented only as a tactical step towards the better accomplishment of the client's goals.

The premise that the self is one's own, that 'I am the boss of me', opaquely yet powerfully shapes how normality and wellbeing, pathology, and dysfunction, have come to be constructed in these traditions. The well-adjusted are expected to be differentiated, individuated, and self-determining, while the poorly adjusted are said to be undifferentiated, fused, dependent, and so forth. What is crucial to recognize here is that the placing of autonomy as the key specification for selfhood has the effect of disqualifying the importance of relationships and context in the construction, maintenance, and evolution of identity.

And the valorization of autonomy sanctifies allied values, particularly self-determination, control, and choice, which are themselves antagonistic to the workings of secure, equitable relationships. This is the case because strong personal relationships are forms of partnership that require a degree of surrender from their participants. Rather than understood as the sensible, even enlivening, operations of interdependency, even the partial loss of control that partnerships entail feels horrifying to the advocates of free choice: the very qualifying of the ideal that individuals have unilateral power blasphemes the holy ideal of independence. In effect, the privileging of autonomy produces a hatred of dependence that is likely to be played out, using the client as a proxy.

The above may sound abstract, yet as with all narratives, there are material consequences. If practitioners accept there is an autonomous unitary self, and this premise is set up as the axle around which the actions of the professional disciplines turn, it follows that practitioners will tend to socialize clients into conforming to this design. For example, if practitioners set up as opposites the rights of 'the patient' with the interests of that person's 'significant others', this will encourage their clients to do the same. Nikolas Rose put it this way:

> [T]he psychotherapies embody ... a whole way of seeing and understanding ourselves in modern societies. The words of the psychotherapies, their explanations, their types of judgment, their categories of pathology and normality, actually shape, have a proactive role in shaping, the subjectivity of those who would be their consumers. (Rose, 1999, p 43)

If therapeutic formations say nothing about fairness, about being reasonable to others, about personal accountability, if they equate health and wellbeing with assertion and acquisition, and they equate non-adjustment with dependence and quietude, these bodies of opinion will play an important role in forging the subjectivity of their consumers and, in turn, with formulating the larger cultural narrative. Practitioners are, after all, both acculturated citizens as well as agents of cultural reproduction.

How is this so? Expert knowledge about the non-biological aspects of human health is represented as objective data. This data is said to have been derived from the consulting room (clinical knowledge) and from the laboratory (research knowledge). This scientifically discovered knowledge is held to be of a different order from that of everyday experience – an indeterminate realm made up of custom and belief, impression and event. Unlike the realm of the laboratory and the microscope, in the everyday world the ideological and the political is encountered, as is the emotional and the random. Down there in the everyday world politicians representing both conservative, centre and left parties tell the population that what is most important is 'self reliance'. Relying on this same logic, psychological scientists stress the same premise: see Chapter 3.

Could it really be coincidence that 'personal autonomy' features so prominently across these purportedly different realms? It seems more likely that the norms present in these two fields have a common, if disavowed, base. Most likely, the value accorded to self-reliance and autonomy is mutually reinforced in that it is always being echoed from an apparently different quarter – neoliberal enthusiasts find legitimation for their beliefs in the individualistic theories advanced by high status scientists operating in health and human services, such as expert therapists and researchers. In parallel, direct clients of, and the watching public to, the human sciences find that the individualistic explanations advanced by the experts in this field 'make good sense' as the language used is essentially the same as that with which they have been socialized to accept by political commentators.

In his text on artistic judgment, Bourdieu (1984, p 7) argued that 'art and cultural consumption are predisposed, consciously and deliberately or not, to fulfill a social function of legitimating social difference.' With some transposition, the line of argument expressed in this statement can apply just as well to the above argument about the ideological role psychology and psychotherapy play in contemporary society. That is, psychology and psychotherapy tend to undertake the specific social function of promoting and legitimating the belief that each person is autonomous.

Practice wisdom and the culture of practitioners

A particular, and particularly odd, custom woven into the culture of the psychotherapies is worth noting here. This custom concerns the embedded idea that it is the role of the practitioner to 'rescue the patient' from damaging relationships. To take up this topic is to engage with something that is awkward to raise and which is also difficult to document, as the notion of rescuing is opaque as it mostly concerns the oral culture of the professions more than anything that can be identified in formal texts and professional case notes. It also connects with the wellspring of mission, the noble aspirations, that underwrite professional practice. And it is controversial to critique the 'I should rescue my client from the baddies' custom as it is a fact that there are some clients who really are being, or have been, victimized by those who should be trustworthy and caring. This is an especially evocative matter in child-centered and aged care settings where there is a crucial difference between client safety and the possibility that practitioners might be culturally programmed to be critical of their clients' significant others.

This acknowledged, it is a practical problem if practitioners begin with the assumption that a client needs to be rescued because this pre-disposes them to be suspicious of the client's significant others. Mindful that examples of abuse and neglect are encountered, it is unreasonable to expect that 'my client' is generally being disadvantaged by members of their network. However statistically improbable, this is nonetheless the position that is produced when the principles of humanistic counseling, such as being 'non-judgmental' and offering 'uncritical positive regard', form the attitudinal base of the professional project. This is not to argue that it is wrong for a practitioner to be empathic and to find themselves emotionally responding to a client's hurt and distress, but it is to suggest that relying on a single source of information can lead to unbalanced, even systematically misleading, conclusions.

The practitioner and the client's others

Put yourself into the shoes of Melissa, a case manager, who meets regularly with John, a man who is struggling with a bipolar disorder. Melissa is attuned to where John is at and finds the following thought resonant: "John's situation is really tough. Despite his best efforts, John feels the ache of not being supported by his partner." In this scenario it is likely that Melissa is not only aligned with John, but is also less than sympathetic, perhaps is even suspicious of his partner: "John is really battling with his illness," she says "and I know he could do so much better if only he was to have good reliable support at home."

This specific example can be recomposed as a general proposition. If 'any named significant other' (friend, roommate, father, etc) is substituted for 'John's partner' and the accusation 'I am not being supported' is replaced by any of the other possibilities clients present as their concern ('I am not being listened to', 'I am not sexually satisfied', 'I get no encouragement', etc), the dynamic between Melissa and John can be represented as a generic equation: the practitioner is subjected to, aligns with, and then tends to become shut up within, a single account. In so far as the practitioner becomes cocooned within their client's perspective, this acts as a constraint to open-minded relationship building, a purpose that inevitably involves at least a degree of challenge to the client's ideas and patterns of behavior. Being empathic to the client's hurt – no doubt, John feels lonely and uncared for – does not mean there is only one side to John, or almost any other client's, relational world.

Interpersonal life has ambiguity, even paradox, and it is naive and unhelpful that the practitioner has their understanding captured by a single perspective. What if the seats were swapped and it was this not good enough meaningful other (from client one's perspective) who then became the practitioner's next client? Would the practitioner have the same reaction to client two if this person told them that "I am not being supported by John." Would the practitioner say to themselves "oh, this unfortunate person is not being well treated", or would the practitioner want to shut themselves off from empathizing with client two and persist in being an advocate for John, their number one client? In work that seeks to deepen the client's relational base it is important to be able to sustain an engagement with multiple people and their perspectives. This more inclusive approach has been termed a 'multipartial alliance' (Cecchin, 1987, p 411), and is discussed as a technical skill in Chapter 8.

The assumption that the client's significant others are inadequate, and/or are failing in their responsibility to the client, exists as a hidden fact, a norm that is kept within the walls that make one-on-one practice a secret, or at least semi-secret, ceremony. Where the bias towards overly siding with 'my client' is externalized is when the practitioner actually has to have direct contact with their client's important others. For example, in conjoint discharge planning sessions that precede a patient leaving rehabilitation, relatives and carers often report they have found professionals unsympathetic, even hostile (Hatfield, 1982; Harborne et al, 2004; Askey et al, 2009). In these, and many other meetings, practitioners can too readily tend to brand the client's significant others as uncooperative and resistant if these people do not immediately agree with the practitioner (Furlong, 2001). This disposition is unhelpful as it acts to erode the prospects for working well with those who are, or might be, important to the client.

A respondent in a recent research program, a dedicated professional who worked with those with long-term psychiatric illness, said that, "If it wasn't for me, they would have nobody." This woman was compassionate and generous, yet seemed unable to see that if her clients could value the relationship they had with her, it was also possible that these clients could value a relationship with a peer or relative.

To say 'they only have me' can be read another way: 'They can't have someone else because I am the only one who has the skills to relate well enough with someone who is such a troubled person'. In perceiving the situation in this way, the worker then finds him or herself powerfully invited to take up the role of rescuer, as the only one who can supply the right kind of support or, even more therapo-centric, is the only one who can offer the 'corrective emotional experience' (Alexander and French, 1946, p 294). Such a stance precludes imagining other possibilities.

If the client's others are generally *assumed* to be inadequate or unhelpful, this puts the professional into an unsustainable position by placing an unrealistic burden on them. In turn, this produces further unfortunate results as it encourages, however paradoxical this might seem, the professional to become emotionally 'split off' from the cumulative distress of clients (Menzies, 1961) or to experience unstable reactions. For example, when feeling overwhelmed, rather than seeing the client as a victim, and imaging oneself as the rescuer, these roles can be de-regulated so that the client is experienced as the persecutor whilst the practitioner feels like the victim.

In intense and impossible to sustain emotional circumstances attributions can become unstable. Here, the roles of victim, persecutor, and rescuer can become fractious. When this occurs the practitioner – who has been thinking of themselves as the rescuer – can find themselves re-cast as the victim (or the persecutor) as the victim seems to take up the role as persecutor (or rescuer), and so on. This is the famous Karpman triangle (Berne, 1975). Being over-aligned with the client tends to leave the practitioner feeling that it is their responsibility to save this person. Unfortunately, such a disposition bundles together a measure of righteousness and resentment. No practitioner can, or should try to, single-handedly save those on their caseload because there is nearly always a potential for a broader network.

6
The practitioner's context

The organizational constraints to relationally focused practice |
Conflicts between the cultures of clients and professionals | Every
client has a culture | Accessing complex interpersonal data

The organizational constraints to relationally focused practice

If assumptions at the axis of professional practice can create difficulties, so too can the material context of practice. Core features of agency-based practice, and also the funding arrangements that support private practice, often commit a casual violence to the client's relational prospects. Like the negative effects of accepted practice theory, there are aspects of the 'system' that are inadvertently biased against what might keep clients connected and included. A simple example illustrates this point. This brief story is in the form of a third person account and introduces a blind spot in the funding model that configures the material operation of many health and community services.

VIGNETTE 2: FELIX

Felix is an 87-year-old Second World War veteran living on his own since his partner died in 1999. Having recovered from two serious heart operations, during most of these years he was relatively self-sufficient, at least until the last few years. Over this time his son, Mark, had been happy to be the key carer. Felix and Mark got on well and, as there were no longer any other immediate family members alive, this made the support role easier in one sense and more difficult in another.

Although Felix has become more physically infirm and cognitively impaired in his later years, his general practitioner (GP) – Dr C – remains convinced that it would be in Felix's best interest to live in the family home, as Felix did not wish to move in with Mark, his partner and two young adults. Felix prefers to live "at home" in an area he knows very well, and all agreed this arrangement was best for as long as it could be stretched out. Dr C and Mark know there are risks but it seems the better policy than imposing guardianship and residential care.

Dr C has been Felix's doctor for several decades and had been consistently attentive. Although Felix generally meets Dr C alone, over the years Mark would sometimes be present. Such 'group of three' conjoint meetings had happened, perhaps a dozen times.

In mid-2010 Felix was unwell and said he did not feel up to attending a scheduled conjoint meeting. Felix knew there was nothing urgent to discuss and that it would be hard for Mark to schedule in another time in the coming weeks. The appointment had been planned to discuss the usual agenda: to openly hear from each 'stakeholder', and then to confer about what was to be done about Felix's deteriorating condition. Dr C explicitly acknowledged Mark's role and, when consulted, suggested that Mark and he should meet, although Felix would not be present. Dr C and Mark did meet and agreed it had been a positive discussion.

After concluding the consultation, Mark then made another appointment for his father with the receptionist. In what Mark took to be a somewhat embarrassed tone, the receptionist, who he had come to know reasonably well over many years, then said he would have to register himself as a new patient and be given an account for a first consultation. Taken aback, Mark replied this was not appropriate as he had not consulted with Dr C about himself at all. On the contrary, he said, he had only talked about what Dr C, his father, and himself all agreed was the common goal: to keep his father at home for as long as possible. This woman said she knew this was the case but there was no capacity within the federally organized data gathering and funding system to code for a 'carer-without-patient' meeting.

Mark then registered as a new patient, tried not to be upset, but still fumed: "My commitment to, my years of doing, practical and emotional support work for my father has just been formally made invisible. Nobody might have planned it, but my role has just been blanked out."

The above is an example of the 'individual patient, first and only' structure that is at the center of health services (albeit this was a minor example in which no material damage was caused). What it does serve to point out is how the role of the client's meaningful others can be unseen by the machinery that organizes the practice context. There is a problem because:

•   the business of the practitioner is normally expected to be exclusively concerned with 'the patient' (or 'the client', the 'service user', etc), yet
•   the research is increasingly clear that the interests of patients are inseparable from their interpersonal ecology, their set of interdependencies.

The latter linkages tend not to be acknowledged by the funding system that supports and organizes the practitioner and to whom the practitioner is held accountable. This tension generates a specific contradiction, a condition that can produce in its more extreme forms a kind of checkmate. Far more than an abstract, merely academic issue, this difficulty has material consequences whose roots deserve some examination. How might this contradiction be understood?

Whether practitioners are employed in a public, private or not-for-profit setting each works within a set of conditions and stipulations that significantly structure their action. Whatever their job role (case manager, therapist, outreach worker, social worker, etc), the practitioner:

- operates within referral and accountability protocols premised on the assumption that the individual client is the concrete business of, and is the indivisible unit of currency within, the service sector;
- uses individual case files within which the personal case notes for specific clients are written. That is, it is legally not possible to have 'family files' or 'group files' as freedom of information laws, or the possibility of case notes, and/or professionals, being subpoenaed, etc, are understood to negate any possibility of an alternative form of case recording. This, in turn, makes it more difficult to organize thought concerning 'ensembles of common interest';
- is subject to case allocation procedures that place case management responsibility to a single professional;
- if located within the public health or community care system, is in a context where the funding formulae allocates resources on a 'per person' basis. And in the health system this formula is diagnostically coded so that funding is on the basis of 'per patient/per day/per typical treatment for disorder X', all of which is tied to a unit record management system that has as its axis 'individual X';
- has been socialized to accept customs and laws that cast professional practice in terms of a restrictive understanding of confidentiality – patterns that anchor and shape significant aspects of practice;
- has been professionally acculturated to accept the premise that all service users have the right to self-determination.

Such features of the practice context enact a robust reality that is lived by each professional day in, day out. Each client is structurally understood as a free-standing island, a theory of the self that interpenetrates, and is reproduced within, the experience of the professional's practice. In effect, this theory tends to determine how each service provider, and how each service user, understands their respective roles and responsibilities.

These protocols not only have an effect on the 'look' of practice, but are also instrumental in how outcomes are construed and pursued. Outcome is articulated to conform to the assumption that the healthy self is a bounded, discrete being. It follows that only a narrow band of categories will be appraised: to what extent is the client symptom free? Can the client assert him or herself? Will the client reoffend? Can the client make the right choices? This vision privileges independent living skills and tends to accord to the matter of interdependencies a status that approximates non-existence.

Idea of professional habitus

Health and human service activities, such as those that take place in aged care or psychotherapeutic settings, take place within a local 'habitus' (Bourdieu, 1977). Recognizing there are local and national variations, one aspect of this taken-for-granted cultural location is often the assumption that 'professionals know best.' This paternalism is naturalized, albeit inadvertent, and results in the views of the client, and the client's current and prospective significant others, being discounted or even disqualified.

As much of what occurs within a given *habitus* goes without saying, dimensions of the context become invisible to the participants. This is not to disparage practitioners and managers; this is a characteristic of all highly acculturated locations such as are found in the armed forces or the legal system. In such places the active participants share an informal citizenship in a given, grown-up field to such an extent that there is the likelihood of a kind of group-think. This happens, for example, amongst surgeons and members of the police force, and, in a similar way, amongst those who are chronically marginalized on the basis of 'race'. In such ensembles group members tend to share a culture and a similar outlook.

This kind of *habitus* is concerned with the processes and enduring effects of the secondary socialization that occurs when a person is inducted into, and remains a member of, a given cadre. Here, members share manners, tastes, codes of dress, and schema of thought. This generates common strategies of action. Examples of this group-think include the unspoken agreements that are characteristic of occupational groups so that these "systems of dispositions ... become like second nature" (Emirbayer and Williams, 2005, p 694). Habitus consists of both formal and embedded factors, whether they are structural, legal, organizational, or cultural or, more likely, represent an amalgam of these dimensions. For each human service practitioner, as for each service user, it is taken for granted that the 'self is bounded by the skin.' This assumption does not reflect a take-it-or-leave-it theory. It is not a contingent or rarefied idea in relation to which an individual practitioner may, or may not, take a fancy. This assumption lives in, and reproduces itself in, the more or less local customs that exist within the sites professionals ply their trade.

The well-circulated aphorism that "attitudes inform practice" (Branson and Miller, 1992, p 39), attributed to Pierre Bourdieu, makes particular sense if it is interpreted within this notion of habitus (Hillier and Rooksby, 2002). In the everyday sites of practice the dispositions that seem to be *natural* are the product of embedded attitudes so that schemas of representation are taken as 'the facts'. In this same way, practitioners tend to take up a particular model and mix it with the actual territory of action. A shared *habitus* is characteristic of belonging to a specific 'field', a location where agreements, attachments, and deeply ingrained ways of apprehending are learned, regularly performed, and livingly reproduced: *here we share a knowledge of the world through the map we make.'*

For example, Barrett (1991), an anthropologist and psychiatrist, proposed that psychiatric service settings can be understood as a worksite within which people (patients in this case) become naturalized as objects that are theorized and/or directly processed. Across this worksite, each professional category takes as their appropriate territory a dimension, an aspect of the client; for example, the client's neuro-transmitters are a medical province; that which relates to the activities of daily living belong to occupational therapists; that it is the brief of psychologists to shape the client's attitudes, and so forth. Attempts at boundary spanning, for example, in care management, seek to be interstitial and contextual in scope – an aspiration that may include the client's network. This exception noted, those professional groups who have not been registered as having an exclusive practice right to a nominated sphere in the life of the client tend to have little status and claim to authority.

Compartmentalization has the effect of, at best, marginalizing the matter of intimate relationships. More likely, in so far as this attitude to 'my patient' is in force, the relationships that this person has, has had, or might have in the future are de-animated. Rather than seeing relationships as reciprocal, accountable, and bi-lateral, the vision of relationships is one that stipulates only a unilateral action: 'Does relationship X help, or hinder, my patient?' Bourdieu (as quoted in Branson and Miller, 1992, p 40) once observed, 'it is all too easy to slip from your model of reality into the reality of your model.' As the structures of practice present a model of personhood, so this model tends to structure the reality of interpersonal practice.

Conflicts between the cultures of clients and professionals

Having reflected on the way accepted professional practices and agency norms can limit the capacity of practitioners to engage in relationship-oriented practice, a third kind of constraint arises. This constraint is itself a relational matter: that there sometimes tends to be a disjuncture between two cultures – the culture the client represents and the culture of those the client encounters which structures the client–professional exchange.

This clash is most obvious when the client is from a collectivist culture, such as is present with Eritrean or Chinese people, where a client is likely to have an identity and mode of living that is overtly relational (Triandis, 1995). Less obviously, but still quite powerfully, there is also a degree of tension that is often present in the match between mainstream 'Anglo' populations and the culture of professional groups and agencies that tend to have a protocol that is rigidly individualistic (see earlier).

Initially, more raw and more direct mismatch between collectivist cultures and professionals will be introduced before attention is given to the less obviously expressions of this dynamic. Generalizations will be made to present a broad argument, propositions that will subsequently be qualified. For now, the reader is asked to consider one sweeping statement: it is the received culture that practitioners represent that is aberrant when it comes to acknowledging the importance of personal relationships.

Professional understanding of confidentially as a cross-cultural test site

As discussed earlier, it is only those in the West that have granted independence an officially ascendant position. This status is not understood as anomalous by its 'natives', although, if you step back, it should be understood as a 'false universal' (Said, 2001). In all other cultural locations, such as Australian aboriginal or Latin American anthropologies, the emphasis is, more or less, on the balancing of the interests of the individual and the interests of the collective (see, for example, Triandis, 1995). This collective may take many forms: the extended family, the clan, the ancestral group, the sub-region, and so forth. Although this ensemble may be variably named and conducted, there is often a vigor in this identification that mediates how selfhood and behavior are understood. The issue of confidentiality brings this into focus.

In cross-cultural practice encounters between those who are from a collectivist background and practitioners who represent individualistic Western values, confidentiality can become something of a hot zone. In these intercultural meetings it can be difficult for those involved to coordinate meanings between anthropologies that have apparently contradictory priorities and sparks can be generated in these exchanges (Owusu-Bempah, 1999).

VIGNETTE 3: NEE

Nee is a 16-year-old Year 11 Cambodian student who has been staying with his older married brother (John) for the last week after a verbal, and to some extent physical, clash with his father. After failing to persuade Nee to return home John has taken him to the local community health service where you are the duty worker.

Although Nee is less than direct in his communication, in this first intake meeting he tells you he does not want to return home. He also seems to be saying that he will not, or cannot, guarantee he will not hurt himself. After speaking with Nee, you have spoken briefly to John, his brother, who has told you Nee cannot stay with him "very much longer."

It seems Nee finds it hard to talk to you, but he does seem clear on one point: he does not want to talk to you with John present, nor does he want you to talk to John any further.

- A key assessment issue for any practitioner in this situation is to estimate the matter of risk: to what extent is child safety the key question? It is therefore possible that Nee's safety is the prevailing issue. The practitioner must decide the scale and nature of the presenting problem and decide if it is best responded to as a child protection, mental health, or family casework issue. Moreover, a decision needs to be made as to whether a short-term response, such as referring Nee to a youth refuge center, might have the advantage of resolving the immediate issue of safety, but where this option might risk the longer-term consequence that tensions between Nee and his relatives will be antagonized. Placing Nee in a refuge might inadvertently have the effect of distancing, even alienating, Nee's family from the services that are involved, and perhaps even inflame Nee's relationship with his kin. His family might interpret Nee being moved into a refuge as a slight, as a symbolic dishonoring of their status, and as representing a disinterest from the professionals in understanding their views. Clearly, more information and a cool head is required.

In this case Nee is unfortunately saying very little. One thing he is saying is that he wants the practitioner to have no further contact with his brother John and, by implication, with any other family member.

 Do issues of confidentiality and self-determination present so powerfully that the practitioner has to draw a hard boundary around their relationship with Nee and to agree to exclude John?

From a 'respecting and building the client's network' position, as well as from a culturally respectful perspective, the recommended principle of decision is to seek to engage Nee's brother, and possibly other members of his extended family, even if this is to take up a course of action with which Nee does not immediately agree. (Practical, positive suggestions about how this can be done with the least possible disruption are presented in Chapter 8). For now, the intention is to make the general case that the material advantages of including the brother, and/or another significant other, are likely to be so great as make this course of action by far the preferable option. The advantages of this option include the likelihood that John is:

* able to provide key background data;
* a core element of Nee's current and longer-term ecology;
* an enduring resource who it is useful, even necessary, to involve in composing a viable longer-term solution;
* someone who has an important status in Nee's family;
* able to act as an ambassador or go-between between the two 'cultures'.

In a time of tension these are obvious, if only theoretical, benefits from the practitioner's point of view. Such advantages sound logical but what jumps up at the well-socialized practitioner is this: the action of involving Nee's

> brother conflicts with the concrete and philosophical priority that 'Nee has said to me he doesn't want the practitioner to talk to his relatives. This means I would lose the chance to engage with Nee if I ignored his views on this issue.' When it comes to confidentiality, when the immediate issue is 'with whom will the practitioner communicate?', to advocate a position that involves denying a client their stated preference courts a powerful controversy. In the culture of the professions, confidentiality has a totemic status for a very good reason: confidentiality has long been associated with the core value of trust.

Attributed to the George Schultz, a now deceased former US foreign secretary, 'trust is the coin of the realm.' In making this comment he was referring to international affairs, but his aphorism makes perfect sense to field-based professionals: if there is no trust, there can be no working relationship. If the commitment is to work well with clients, it is necessary to build a relationship with the client that is trustworthy, as many texts cogently describe (Perlman, 1979; Rogers, 1969; Trevithick, 2003). This applies whether it is casework or therapy, case management or protective practice: rapport and partnership depend on trust. This is usually interpreted to mean that the practitioner has to show the client that their ears and allegiances are aligned in only one direction.

This raises a dilemma if the intention is to be a network builder. To have a single alignment is not likely to be practical as this is associated with the practitioner inflaming tensions and alienating significant players. If this occurred, over time the primary client's longer-term interests would be compromised.

To take this position is not to discount the importance of trust. On the contrary, it is essential to be trustworthy and it is not recommended, for example, to approach John for a secret talk without Nee knowing this is being done. It is almost never right to go behind the client's back. Almost certainly, Nee should be told in advance if the decision is to speak to his brother further. Put in a more abstract manner, trustworthiness should not be equated with agreement. The practitioner can demonstrate that they are reliable and honest, that is, deserving of trust, without acceding to what the client prefers when it comes to with whom the practitioner will speak. The practitioner can genuinely negotiate with the client to agree what topics they can discuss with John (or other members of Nee's family) whilst still reserving the right to make the decision with whom it is best to communicate.

The decision to speak to this person, or that person, in the client's network should be determined by the higher order matter of what is judged the path that is most likely to further the client's long-term interests. Being direct about an allegiance to the long term with clients and their significant others is likely to help these people see the practitioner as a fair broker, as a straight talker, with whom it is possible to develop a robust confidence. Over time, clients and their 'tribes' can learn to respect that the practitioner can disagree with them and still be of service. In many cases it can be containing for the people practitioners meet with if they know their practitioners are prepared to be independent decision makers.

In terms of the above vignette, a decision was made to include John in the process of gathering further information (and to signal to him he was invited to be a voice in subsequent negotiations about decisions). As a consequence of including John, the practitioner was able to clarify the following:

VIGNETTE 3: NEE (PART 2)

Background to the clash
- Prior to the last month or so, Nee had been performing reasonably well at school.
- The clash with his father was the result of tensions that had built up about around three issues: (i) whether Nee was applying himself sufficiently to his school work; (ii) Nee's provocative statements to his father that he would like an 'Anglo' girlfriend; and (iii) Nee's sometimes bad language and attitude at home.

Family background
- Nee knows, but it is not discussed openly, that his parents arrived as a couple as "refos" in the early 1980s.
- The extended family have suffered many traumas.
- Nee's older brother and sisters are doing "well".
- The family speak Khmer at home.

In the light of this information, and after a number of intense discussions, communications that involved John speaking to his father and to an uncle, it was decided that Nee would remain with his brother for a further two weeks. During this period a caseworker liaised closely with Nee and brokered several meetings with different 'sub-sets' of Nee's extended family as well as with an informal cultural consultant. Although it was far from a storybook process, for example, the period where Nee stayed with his brother was twice extended, Nee eventually returned to his immediate family. In a review meeting with his caseworker some months later he reported: "Yeah, no way it's all good but I guess it's OK. One thing has got clearer to me. Even if I have a job and earn some money I'm never going to feel good about myself, about my life, if I am not part of my family. They are all a bit mad, but so am I. My mum, my sisters, my brother, my one uncle and even my dad, they will always be important to me."

Between cultures, between the customs and beliefs that give meaning to Nee's struggles and those the practitioner represents, there are often tensions. For each the issue of confidentiality can emerge from the fog as the tip of an iceberg, a sharp and dangerous hazard upon which good intentions can quickly founder.

Below sight, there is a submerged mass that gives a weighty base to this sharp tip for clients and professionals alike.

Every client has a culture

Although it is most obvious with those who are culturally and linguistically diverse, practitioners know there are cultural dimensions in play in every practice episode. What complicates this knowledge is that it is hard to get to grips with culture – with respect to the culture of the client, that of the professional and, even more elusive, the dynamic that occurs between these two cultures. Culture is notoriously slippery, opaque, and refracted. Stereotyping is always a danger and it is never appropriate to essentialize or 'other' difference. Practitioners accept it is necessary to make the commitment to honor the importance of culture and cultural difference. On the other hand, it is not appropriate to assume any specific client, for example, someone who the practitioner knows has a Maori background, will have the same values and worldview that is considered typical of those who 'belong' to this diverse cultural group.

And even those with equally perfect 'Anglo' backgrounds express diverse cultural characteristics. This variability in an apparently 'same-same' culture is due to the mix of many ingredients, for example, class and neighborhood, occupation, and (level of) aspiration. These external, easy to see dimensions noted, there is also that which is more personal and more opaque. A client, or a practitioner, may identify with particular elements of their own family culture they are happy to carry: a particular kind of humor, the 'right' attitude to misfortune, love of sports, whatever. More complex still are those elements of personal biography that the client, or the practitioner, is amnesic of, or is kicking back against. The latter are an especially interesting class of responses where, to paraphrase Freud, we seem to be about as attached to those we obey as to those against whom we rebel.

All of us, clients and professionals alike, have been subject to, and interpenetrated by, local family customs and biographies. We wrestle with old ghosts and look up to past heroes and remain loyal to, or try to reject (whether we know it or not) family scripts related to values, gender roles, and how close we are to others, such as our siblings. Every person, including each practitioner, exists within a specific, multigenerational tribe biographically, if not in terms of their day-to-day geography. In this way culture can have a big 'C', as in Irish or Puerto-Rican peoples, or it can have a little 'c', as in one's local family culture. For example, I am happy to acknowledge in fair part that I am a product of a mixed culture having a working-class father of Irish extraction and a strong and eccentric middle-class mother. Nominally Catholic, anti-establishment and sports mad, my local tribe is close, in some ways conflicted, and would be judged by old-school family therapists as 'enmeshed' (Minuchin, 1974).

Given my mother and father were more or less constantly at war throughout my childhood, early in my professional life I overly identified with the child-young adult who I assumed had been triangulated between their parents. That said, my tribe's attitude to connection – that it is best to have and give affection – stays with me, as does a conviction that women can, and usually are, strong in themselves as well as being the axle around which many families turn. However much reflection I have been prompted into, this tribal inheritance has transacted, and continues to transact, a powerful input in, and beyond, my professional life.

Such local anthropologies may have no apparent CALD status (culturally and linguistically diverse) given Anglo-Celtic culture is not considered sufficiently exotic, but this is not the present issue. The point is that everybody has a culture, and even the most technical of professionals act out this input in their practice to a significant degree. Sadly, this history is often played out in practitioners, like Murray, in Vignette 1 (Chapter 5), siding with his client against this person's significant others, even if this is not in the client's long-term interest.

Whether culture is big 'C' or little 'c' (mindful it is always a combination of the two), it always has a degree of power. Culture can offer a complete design for living (Cox, 1989) or have a less commanding influence. At the very least, culture inserts reference points in relation to which, even against which, dispositions form and life decisions are taken. Anthropologists, such as Clifford Geertz, agree that culture provides the programming that goes beyond the obvious, for example, a person's tastes in food, clothing, and housing. At a deeper level culture inscribes in its members how problems of living will be understood and processed, and the manner in which the fundamental questions of existence, such as how the person is to be understood, will be constructed.

This latter question, which has a key relevance to the current exercise, has evoked radically different historical and cultural formulations. The self may be said to be autonomous and rational, interdependent, fundamentally unconscious yet defended, and so forth. In resolving such higher matters, there will always be at least a degree of contest and at a particular point in time these deliberations will engender a national discussion (Trompenaars and Hampden-Turner, 2002).

Economic development and the question of cultural hierarchy

Western citizens assume their societies are more generally advanced than less affluent countries. It follows that those in nations such as Germany and the US, Sweden and New Zealand, will assume their laws and social norms are superior to those found in 'developing' or 'third world' nations. This bias is entirely consistent with the convention that divides countries into categories based on their economic status. A nation is either advanced, that is 'first world', developing or third world in its prestige. A strong expenditure on health, the presence of good roads, and having a modern legal system, for example, are regarded as central to this classification. It is understood that such markers may be important indicators of social status yet cross-cultural researchers, such as Wilkinson and Pickett (2009), have proven that individual and collective wellbeing does not necessarily hinge on the presence of such material 'advances'. Beyond the capacity to satisfy basic material needs, there is no necessary correlation between affluence and wellbeing.

This may be logically true, yet it is only Bhutan that has set out to offer a formal challenge to the practice of conflating economic status with a nation's social wellbeing. This small Asian nation, despite its absolute poverty, has gained a degree of international respect for promoting a National Happiness Index (Centre for Bhutan Studies, 2011). This index is a uniquely composed measure of material, spiritual, and relational wellbeing in preference to an assessment of a nation's status that is based on the calculation of material prosperity. Beyond the satisfaction of material needs, it may be that those from more 'backward' nations enjoy a sounder social condition than many from nations with far higher per capita incomes.

The expectation that Western economic superiority equates with a generalized superiority represents a clear example of chauvinism. Where this hubris has a particular relevance in the current exercise is that 'Anglo' institutions and professional knowledge tend to assume the values that hum at the center of their practice are self-evidently correct and are therefore above culture and critique. Rather than viewing, for example, personal autonomy and self-determination as contingent values, these *ideological preferences* are understood as absolute values. This is incorrect as the deification of independence and personal choice in post-industrial Western societies is, in fact, culturally and historically anomalous (Heelas and Lock, 1981). It is only in this period, and in specific 'advanced' nations, that the individual has been conferred the status of a sovereign, unrestrained entity. Due to the process of individualization (see Chapter 2), each citizen has been cut adrift as each person has been condemned to be free (Rose, 1989).

For Anglo-Celtic grandparents, for a Japanese businessman, for an immigrant from Somalia – for everyone except the idealized free agent in the contemporary West – lived experience has long been anchored in moral and practical interdependence rather than amoral and impractical isolation. In this particular instance it is the West that can be considered wrong-headed, off-course and unscientific in steering to the myth that individuals can, and should, be autonomous.

Western textbooks on child development, personality, and psychopathology have enshrined an ideal of separateness as if a flight from relatedness is the precondition for progress (Furlong and Wright, 2011). Despite the availability of alternative accounts of human development (Morss, 1996; Sommer, 1989), unscientific speculations, such as those put forward by figures such as Abraham Maslow and Erik Erikson, concerning the nature of personhood, continue to be reproduced. As Gilligan de-centered the sexism that animated Kohlberg's (until then) well accepted theory that female moral development was inferior to that of the male (Gilligan, 1982; Longres, 2000), it is necessary to interrogate the norms that govern professional practice given their current acceptance may mask the possibility that these protocols are not only culturally chauvinistic but also promote anomie.

In being able to positively practice cross-culturally, one key demand is that the practitioner is critically reflective. Rather than trying to learn objective facts about 'them' – the Bangladeshis, the Nigerians, the Italians – authors such as Dean (2001, p 623) urge practitioners to be 'not knowing', that is, to be curious and courteous rather than the expert. Colloquially, this can be understood as seeking to be a good host, as Furman and Ahola (1995) have discussed. It is also necessary to make a commitment to identifying and critiquing your own professional knowledge, cultural location, and personal biography. It is not much use becoming an armchair expert on other cultures: better by far to paint yourself into the picture.

Given the focus in this text in on what practitioners might do, or avoid doing, that assists clients deepen their relational base, a consideration of culture reveals two major points. First, a number of established professional norms create difficulties for cross-cultural practice as they do not align with the values and practices of those who identify with 'non-Anglo' cultures. Second, it is possible, even likely, that those practitioners who have been acculturated within the Western technical canon might learn much from exchanges with cultural difference. This latter possibility cannot be explored in the current project, however worthy it may be, but the former will be briefly introduced.

To conclude this section on culture, an 'Anglo' example might be useful. This troubling vignette focuses on the oddness, even the barbarity, of received practitioner culture when it comes to the over-privileging of autonomy.

VIGNETTE 4: BEN AND JOHN

Two voluntary in-patients, Ben and John, wished to sign themselves out of a psychiatric facility and approached one of the ward staff with this purpose. This person – Alyssa – advised the two patients not to do this as it was clear their course of treatment was incomplete. And Alyssa knew that there were particular concerns about Ben as he was considered at real risk of self-harm. Both young men had been living with their respective parents prior to their admissions and said they would be returning to the same addresses when discharged. Nonetheless, both were voluntary patients and Alyssa thought it important to preserve the sense of respect that goes with securing the therapeutic relationship by not making a fuss about discharge arrangements.

Alyssa asked Ben and John if she could contact their respective parents to let them know that they were being discharged. Both men replied they did not agree with this idea. After consulting a more senior colleague, Alyssa agreed not to do this because both these men were adults and also because to do so would be in breach of client confidentiality.

The next day the parents of one of the men discovered that their son had been discharged when they rang the ward. The other set of parents only found out when contacted by the police several days later with news of a multiple suicide. Although the coroner did not attribute the cause of death to any kind of negligence, the report did make clear that client confidentiality should never be understood by professionals as an absolute right.

> Ben and John's parents had been doing their best to look after their sons and had been put through an exceedingly tough time doing so. It had been more difficult because they thought that the service system did not honor the sense of interdependence that was part of their roles as parent-carers. For them, the dream of independence was a distracting myth that was overvalued by the professionals.
>
> At the core of many professional texts is a consensus that 'the individual' is an ideal, a dream, or even a romance. Practices based on promoting this romance can be seen in an alternative way, that is, as a 'regime of the normal' (Duberman, 2002, p 461). This vision denigrates dependency, emotionality, and other-orientedness and has as one of its primary effects the elevation of self-centeredness. If this circumstance is regarded as unfortunate, even as cultural illness, there is little point looking to the conventional psychotherapies for help. Rather, these practice formations tend to be vectors for the spread of the disease that is individualization.

Accessing complex interpersonal data

In terms of professional norms a final concern relates to that of information: how much does the practitioner know of the interactional, rather than the phenomenological, reality of their clients' lives?

Professionals' personal knowledge of relationships

Students and practitioners know an extensive amount about personal relationships from their own biographical experience. Each practitioner has a knowledge base that is founded on their current interactions and the private contacts they have previously experienced. Practitioners also know a considerable amount about their direct relationships with clients. They also have a direct experience of relationships with colleagues, managers, referrers, and so forth. This knowledge is a formidable asset yet it is also highly partial. Practitioners have never been privy to the 'kitchen talk' their clients participate in or have unobserved, up-close access to what happens in the schoolyard or workplace. In other words, they do not know how their clients behave with their significant others and have only a slight, usually inferred, knowledge of how these significant others experience their clients.

Some practitioners have a depth of experience meeting conjointly with clients and their significant others in family meetings, meetings in the home, ongoing work with couples, group work, and so forth. For those who meet almost exclusively with individual clients, there is only mediated knowledge – the self-reports – of the relationships the client has with their significant others as these contacts take place outside the consulting room. Because the majority of practitioners meet with individual clients alone, the professional usually only has access to, and will therefore tend to privilege, the client's account of their relations with others.

This is an empirical matter related to access to partial information. Unfortunately, this partiality tends to reinforce the effect of professional norms around 'unconditional positive regard', amongst a larger set of important professional customs and values. For the present purpose, the template of the one-on-one relationship places a set of blinkers on the professional's perceptions. Some practitioners, particularly those of a psychoanalytic persuasion, believe the patterns that occur in the practitioner–client relationship present a template for the relationships the client 'sets up' in their associations beyond the consulting room. There is at least some truth in this belief, but this does not contradict the claim that practitioners who work exclusively with single clients have no direct knowledge of how their clients behave beyond the consulting room.

In a strictly dyadic setting the professional receives the client's self-reports. This limited data set includes the account the client gives of their experience of relationships. Given there is no observational or outcome data available, this means there is almost no multipartial information. What is heard is anecdotal and in a particular sense 'third hand gossip' with respect to its observational, if not experiential, validity. What is heard is, with only minor exceptions, the client's experience – their perceptions. This is as it should be but it is important to note that being totally reliant on a single information trail leaves the practitioner vulnerable to systematically partial data, deeply felt but necessarily biased accounts of the client's relationships.

In the context of this current exercise, this is an important point as clients – and practitioners – are far from reliable witnesses. In a series of well-known studies, Hochschild (1990, 2003) investigated the relative contribution of women and men to domestic tasks. When she compared the participants' self-reports with the results obtained from the cameras that had been installed in the households being studied, it was apparent that the majority of men, and a smaller but still large proportion of women, misperceived and/or reported incorrectly. If the former conclusion is preferred – that participants innocently miscalculated, rather than were actively duplicitous (the participants all knew they were being filmed) – this illustrates what many studies have also found before and since Hochschild's study: humans can be unreliable witnesses even when they try to be accurate.

If self-reports do not align with direct observation when the matter is behaviorally distinct ('How often do you wash the dishes?', 'Who takes out the rubbish?'), it is likely that the degree of misrepresentation will increase when it comes to interpretive, meaning-laden matters. When a young client says, for example, 'I am not being supported or listened to by my mother', this feels true but it is not likely to be the whole story. That is, opaque categories of action, like issues that are deeply subjective, rarely achieve a coordination of meanings between participants. This is especially the case if the context of the appraisal

– the meeting between an unhappy client and a I-am-here-to-understand-and-help-you professional – is one where 'problems' are intrinsic to the *mis-en-scène*.

Questions or prompts to think around themes may be used when talking with clients, such as:

- 'Do you feel your partner really understands your feelings?'
- 'Do you get a fair deal from your friends?'
- 'Were you adequately acknowledged by your mum when you were young?'
- 'Have you got talents and desires that X (your boss, lover, best friend, father, son, etc) is not allowing you to realize?'

The prompted response to these questions tends to represent only one side of the story. If the other party/parties involved had a voice, it is likely that the practitioner would receive a counter-pointing input. For instance, the practitioner might be told that what had been said was misleading, inaccurate, unreasonable, unrepresentative, unfair, or just plain crazy.

Two additional points are relevant here. First, the context, as well as many of the questions and/or themes explored, in the professional–client exchange act in such a way as to lead the client to disparage, be unsatisfied about, find fault with, and so on, the relationships they have, or have had, with their significant others. Second, the culture of the practitioner–client exchange tends to mobilize a 'what about me!' disposition, a tone where the client is allowed to, is even abetted in, claiming an asymmetric entitlement and non-accountability with respect to their larger milieu, including their significant others. In so far as the practitioner is an unknowing vector for the process of individualization, the client is constructed to be a sovereign but hardly-done-by entity (Furlong, 2010b). This proposition sets the stage for the practice material that is to follow.

7
Attitudes determine practice

Introduction

This chapter is concerned with the attitudes and conceptual skills that support relationship-building practices. In contrast to the professional norms that were identified as problematic in the previous chapter, the intention here is to focus on, and then to mobilize, patterns of thought that appreciate and encourage interdependencies. When externalized into professional actions, these patterns generate positive possibilities: get the line of thinking right, get the imagination into a different aesthetic, and the process tends to look after itself.

To achieve this generally requires a degree of re-patterning. Seriously playing with ways of thinking that de-individualize, that look for the network and not just the node, can be exciting and satisfying, but it can also be uncomfortable. The way to proceed is to roll into the new, little by little. You might be surprised by the spark and the counter-intuitive invitation you encounter and, hopefully, it will not be too slow moving. More specifically technical material, what might be termed 'applications and executive skills', is presented in the following two chapters, where applications and concrete examples are described.

In relation to this, at first glance the material presented here might feel like it has a more preliminary energy. In one sense this is true, but this view risks judging attitudes, values, and theory as less important than, or even separate to, professional action. Although scenarios are not elaborated, throughout this current chapter a range of reflective exercises and practice vignettes are used to animate the approach. As you bring your own biography into an engagement with this material you are likely to experience at least a degree of frisson. Even if not immediately concerned with practice actions, hopefully what is set out here will feel robust and challenging. What is at issue is the vital matter of attitudes and the conceptual competencies. These elements need to be aligned – harmonized – so they can become a general disposition. Far from an abstract, academic matter, it is this disposition that expresses a *practicing for relationship* agenda when it is implemented.

The chapter consists of three sections:

- Attitudes inform practice: three reflective exercises are introduced that seek to identify helpful and unhelpful attitudes to relationship-building practice. They are designed to be provocative and engaging.
- Decision points: a review of the relationship-building possibilities which are present in situations that have differing durations of contact is set out. For example, if the contact with the client is designed to be short term, even perhaps a single exchange, there are different possibilities than if the role involves a longer, perhaps even a long-term, relationship.
- An informal relational assessment process is outlined where the practitioner scales for strengths and gaps in what can be understood as the two complementary aspects to selfhood: the autonomous and the relational self.

There is a strong logic to the flow between these sections. That said, each is relatively independent and could be approached as a distinct module. This might be a good way to proceed as there is, at least at times, a measure of obsessiveness in what follows. For example, in the discussion of the different durations client–practitioner contact might consist of – one-off, short, medium, or long term – I try to detail how this difference in the quantum of contact tends to produce variations in what might appropriately be attempted. Despite the many vignettes that are used to illustrate this account, if you are in a role that involves an extended contact with your clients you are unlikely to be motivated to closely read what is put forward about, say, those in one-off roles. Comprehensiveness comes at a cost.

Attitudes inform practice: thinking relationally

Being able to practice relationally is not about learning a set of rehearsed techniques. Well-learned behaviors can be applied across diverse presenting situations, but a one-size-fits-all approach is like a shake-and-bake, packaged cooking product: good for some occasions but not for all. What is more useful is to be able to de-code each presentation through a lens that is appreciatively relational. Particular skills do need to be mastered, such as how to effectively address the question of confidentiality (see Chapter 6), yet more important than learning how to use specific skills is to have the attitudes and values that put human relatedness into a high point of professional focus.

A coherent set of attitudes and values aggregate to form an interpretative framework or, to put this more directly, a consistent mindset. Such a schema processes the information at hand so that specific judgments, calibrated responses, can be made rather than triggering a one-size-fits-all reaction. The interest here is to find a mindset that orients practitioners towards thinking and acting relationally. This is far more complex than it might appear.

Argyris and Schon (1975) long ago demonstrated that there is often a distinction between a practitioner's 'espoused theory' and their 'theory in use'. In their view a professional's 'espoused theory' is composed of the ideas the practitioner thinks they should be doing, which is generally what they understand they *are* doing, whilst the practitioner's 'theory-in-use' is what it is they are actually doing. For example, practitioners can genuinely say to themselves: 'I am being empowering', and an observer might say: 'By being so ready to respond to small crises, the practitioner is inadvertently creating dependence.' That there is often a difference, even a contradiction, between these two viewpoints does not reflect an absence of care or education. Rather, this reflects the simple truth that we humans are partisans, participant-observers, who frequently are not intuitively able to move seamlessly between the insider and the outsider perspective.

The result of this everyday limitation is that there is likely to be a degree of tension, even of conflict, between what I think I should be doing and what I am actually transacting. This distinction between 'espoused theory' and 'theory in use' has been taken up as a fundamental concept in the development of reflective practice and critical reflection (Fook and Gardiner, 2007) where, like Argyris and Schon (1975), it is argued that professional practice will be (far) more effective if there is a good-enough alignment between the domains of thinking and action. However understandable and human it is to have inconsistencies between what is said and what is done, it is far better if there is little or no variance between professionals' action and their thinking.

This is especially relevant to the current purpose as almost every practitioner would say 'Of course I want my client to have good relationships with others.' Unfortunately, this positive sentiment does not always reconcile with what is actually done and worked for. Towards aligning a positive sentiment with what is professionally performed it is useful to interrogate one's assumptions and habits of mind. This is especially important as relationships between thought and action are the product of a professional and cultural socialization that privileges the value of autonomy and self-determination. Unless there is a genuinely positive attitude to the possibilities of personal relationship – not a mindlessly positive attitude but a constructively balanced orientation – it is likely that the practitioner will inadvertently reproduce the bias towards autonomy that is characteristic of the professional and cultural codes within which we have trained and lived (see Chapters 4 and 5).

For this reason, before engaging with the specific skills material it makes sense to engage in a process of critical reflection. Below, the reader is asked to consider two brief exercises.

Reflective exercise 1: Clarifying your values

As a thought experiment, consider how you review your priorities in life. There are many ways this can be done. Set out below is a prompt that presents three different classes of criteria. In a pencil-and-paper review, consider the different criteria you might use to review your priorities and measure your worth using a rough-and-ready Leichhardt scale where 1 represents 'not at all' and 5 represents 'most valued'.

1. Achievement and possession: How do you think you add up in relation to the following:

- What is your level of success in relation to work, education, and income?
- Regarding your material assets: do you own a house, a car, good clothes, fine furniture? Do you own what you want and need?
- Have you traveled extensively?
- What other personal achievements and possessions are of value to you? Are you on the way to securing these items?

2. Subjective concerns: How do you add up in relation to the following:

- Are you happy?
- Do you feel good about yourself?
- Are you making the most of your talents and opportunities?
- Are you getting what you want out of life?
- What other personal considerations are of value to you? Do you think are you on the way to securing a good score on these judgments?

3. Relational matters: how important are the following criteria in your estimation of your life and your self-worth, that is, what weight do you give to:

- Your reputation: do you think your significant others see you as loyal or as a user, as friendly or as self-interested, as predictable or as unreliable?
- What have you done to another that has shamed or embarrassed you; what have you done to another/others that is a source of pride?
- How much do you care how you are viewed by your workmates, friends, siblings, neighbors, regulars at your local X (pub, gym, athletic club, yoga group, etc), fellow students, parents, grandparents, children, boss?

- Whether you are loved and cared for, respected and acknowledged?
- Being loving and caring – feeling like you are making a contribution?
- Seeing yourself as fair and accountable?

After allowing a considered opportunity to review these three sets of questions, what is your conclusion? All three categories have their attractions and, of course, different respondents will allocate their preferences differentially.

Those that have taken part in this review mostly say they seek to find a balance between the claims that arise in each of these domains. And a number who have undertaken this reflection have noted that to participate in this exercise is, on the one hand, to engage in an important process of values clarification yet, on the other, it is to feel manipulated. Quite upset, one student wrote, '[T]he game was a set up. Not even the worst psychopath or most stuck-up narcissist would ignore the items in the last group! (that is, "3: Relational matters") Hermits way out in the desert, even losers and freaks, all want to think someone they look up to, a higher someone somewhere, respects them for what they are doing or might do.'

On both counts this student was right. No one likes to feel they have been pushed into a loaded experiment, and I apologize if this was your response too. That is not a good feeling and, yes, the exercise was rigged, but it was done this way for a reason: even if it is self-evident that each of us is a social being with needs of an interpersonal nature, there is a heap of dust in the air and it is not always clear that this is so.

One of the factors that obscures this knowledge is that humans tend to allocate a subjectively different weighting to the items in the above three categories at particular stages in the life cycle. For example, it is a comic strip cliché that young adults will tend to rate peer relationships more highly than their relationships with parents and extended family whilst those in a hospice tend to want to make their peace with their immediate, and often biological, kin. This said, given the right kind of reflective stimulus it is possible that these clichés are misleading. For example, in a recent in-depth qualitative study of what young, often homeless, drug users rated as 'What is most important to you?', the most common response was 'My relationships with my friends, family and professionals' (Green et al, 2012). It seems likely that nearly every citizen considers that the relational – the broad category of attention which is the focus here – is of decisive importance to them if the issue is introduced in an engaging way.

Professionals, like the larger population from which practitioners are drawn, highly value the relational dimensions of their life. Like everybody else, they value their reputation, that they are acknowledged and respected, loved and cared for, demonstrate a care for others, and are considered by others, and themselves, as loyal. Personal wellbeing, even a sense of self, is contingent on the state of personal relationships with work colleagues, parents, partners, children, friends and, in general, with that rich and diverse range of people with whom we have meaningful associations. And professionals also know how stressful, preoccupying, and debilitating it is when *even one of these relationships* is conflictual. They know what occurs to their inner life when they experience a separation, even when they think there might in the future be a separation from someone they deeply care about. They know how perturbing it is when someone they are close to is unwell or is dying, and how distressing it is if a person they are close to becomes terminally ill. And most have had at least some experience of loneliness and its consequences and know how aversive it is to feel isolated and unconnected. Nearly every professional is able to recognize the impact of the relational world on their own mood and wellbeing, quality of life, and self-esteem.

Despite this deep knowledge it seems there is often a cut-out, something of a dividing practice (Dreyfus and Rabinow, 1982), when it comes to acknowledging that this same priority is present in the lives of clients. An 'us and them' division is understandable as the received vision of the professional mission distracts their attention from a focus on the relational and entrusts them with an abiding concern for the client as a silo of exclusive interest and concern. This missionary vision has long been narrated using the nomenclature of autonomy: that the business of practitioners is to develop the client's self-reliance, empower the client to have choices, to consolidate their sense of entitlement, to improve their capacity to focus on and then get, more of what they want, and so forth. In the main the professional project has been constructed to be about the 'I, me, my, and mine' of the client rather than to be fundamentally concerned with the need to balance this priority with the client's shadow side – their interest in having relationships and reciprocity, fairness, and living in a group. Mathews (1995) and Paterson (1996), amongst a range of theorists and researchers, argue that practitioners are wise to see that clients, and practitioners, are beings who have both a relational and an autonomous aspect to their selfhood and that too much of either leads to imbalance.

Priming this bias towards autonomy is the ready empathy practitioners feel for the difficulties clients so frequently have had in their early life, in their immediate past relationships, or even in a current relationship. Many clients have suffered from poor, even disastrous, parenting; many report that their partner does not understand them or inadequately supports them and/or that they have been, or are being, bullied by their friendship or work groups. In these circumstances the professional feels it is a proper, even righteous, role to be an uncritical witness, to offer unconditional positive regard, and to attempt to ameliorate the damage that has been inflicted. As discussed in Chapter 6, practitioners often feel like they have an obligation to rescue clients from their suffering and victimization. Unfortunately, offering unconditional positive regard or, more generally, building up the client's autonomous self by stimulating their sense of independence and control, does not result in an impact that is positive and sustainable with respect to the quality of their relatedness. If someone wants good-enough relationships, this has to be learned and earned: *on reflection, it is clear that it is me who has to act generously if I am to earn the love I seek. It will not be given to me because I am entitled to it. If I want a just and respecting connection I have to earn it. Similarly, it is me who has to consistently do what will build the reputation and respect I want to receive*. In the majority of cases, it is exactly this same logic that applies to clients.

In the past many professionals, including myself, have tended to 'other' the client, to have one rule for 'us' and another for 'them'. I used to think disparaging thoughts about many of my client's friends and partners, found myself critical of my client's families and workmates, and was judgmental of others in their group homes or even of other professionals: *Damn them. If they would only look after my client better then s/he would be all right.* Bonded with my client I failed to see that almost always everyone in the client's ecology was doing the best they could, and that if this client wanted to be more liked and respected, this could not be given to them on a plate.

If professionals want to practice relationally there is a common rule: positive relationships have to be learned and earned. If this is true for you, there is no reason to think it is different for anybody else. Unlike the naive statements expressed in some health promotion reports, for example, that vulnerable people have the right to 'access' supportive relationships (VicHealth, 2005), neither planners nor practitioners can ever write out prescriptions or entitlement cards that dispense positive relationships. Unlike a financial benefit, subsidized housing, or a travel pass, supportive relationships cannot be impersonally delivered or guaranteed. There is no reason for pessimism in this assessment, however: the relational future is unwritten and you, me, and every client practitioners work with is in the process of change.

Just as each professional has the potential to make new friends and to deepen their networks over the life course, so, too, this is true for clients. Because in the past someone has been damaged, given an unfair, even outrageous, deal, and/or has learned to become defensively hostile does not mean that practitioners should not be ambitious in prompting 'this woman' or 'this man' towards tackling a course that is designed to achieve a good-enough degree of social connection. There would need to be a very compelling set of circumstances to argue that there is no possibility that even very damaged and limited clients cannot earn at least one positive future relationship if pragmatic conditions can be prompted that effectively facilitate this goal.

As mentioned in the last chapter, in a research project investigating staff attitudes to the place of interpersonal relationships in clients' lives, a mental health case manager told me:

> '[I]t is satisfying work, the person that I told the good story about [in the interview], she came up to me and said "I love you" and it was great but it was also really sad. These people only have us [the staff]. They usually don't have families or friends.'

An admirable compassion animated this statement yet, between the lines, it is also possible to see a degree of hubris and something of a self-fulfilling prophecy in and around these words.

Even as the case manager knows 'John' is suffering from schizophrenia, a condition the professional may believe has no cure, in so far as John is capable of valuing the relationship he has with his case manager, and there is no reason to disbelieve the case manager when she says John does value and depend on her, the source of this appreciation is John's human capacity to register and to value interpersonal warmth and positive regard. In this circumstance, how much more benefit would John derive if he received a degree of earned care and affection within an openly reciprocal relationship, albeit one where this was present in a more give-and-take, rough-and-ready way? Interacting within a peer-to-peer exchange, a dynamic that surely contrasts with his unfortunately one-down position as a passive recipient of a bought-in professional affection, would have many positive dimensions. Not least of these benefits can be likened to a respect dividend where John would likely feel he has warranted the affection he has had and was receiving, and would hold this as a matter of pride and dignity.

To a material extent professional values create the conditions that optimize or diminish the prospects for developing the client's social relations. We can back away from the hurly-burly of stimulating clients to hop into the relational world, saying to ourselves *they might become too stressed if they get too close to someone* or *they will decompensate if they are rejected.* Such worries have to be taken seriously, yet if they become an overriding concern, this has the effect of establishing alibis for why we should not agitate, albeit safely and slowly, for change. Reservations are motivated by the need to be protective of the client's interests and, of course, this is important to acknowledge. This recognized, at times a pessimistic attitude to the prospects of client sociality acts to co-create and maintain the social disability from which many clients suffer.

A second reflective exercise might be useful in helping externalize your 'between the lines' image of the prospects for improving the client's social relations, which follows after Vignette 5.

VIGNETTE 5: LENNIE

Lennie is a 27-year-old unemployed man with schizophrenia who lives 'rough' when he is not in emergency shelters or other short-term places. He has problems with his thinking and behavior, has no understanding of his illness, and is socially isolated. He sometimes uses marijuana and alcohol and, although this occasional substance abuse further disturbs his mood and thinking, his problems have much more of a mental health than a substance abuse profile. You are a case manger in an outreach mental health service. Although you find him friendly enough and generally well spoken, you have been struggling to engage him in the (off and on) times he has been on your caseload over the last three years. Mostly, his attitude tells you 'I just want to be left alone.'

According to his case file, Lennie had an unproblematic, although somewhat isolated, childhood and schooling. He wanted to leave school at the age of 16 to work in a relative's building company and was employed in the stores area there for several years. Whilst still living at home and working, at 19 he became more and more withdrawn and was observed to have become withdrawn and bizarre in his thinking. After a number of consultations with his family doctor, he was referred to an Italian-speaking private psychiatrist (his family are Italian and he is bi-lingual), and he was given a diagnosis of schizophrenia. Lennie did not accept this diagnosis at that time and he still continues to deny he has an illness.

For the next five years Lennie continued to reside at home with his parents and three siblings (two who are older and one who is younger), where he was reported to be alternatively withdrawn and accusatory. During this period there were many stressful incidents. These included frequent, and often intimidating, arguments between Lennie and his father and older brother. On a number of occasions these conflicts resulted in Lennie disappearing unexpectedly or being involuntarily hospitalized. Three years ago family relations deteriorated to such a degree that Lennie was told to leave by his father and elder bother. Since that time he has been of 'no fixed address'. Despite his view that he is not psychiatrically ill, Lennie receives a disability pension, a benefit he has received since he was deemed eligible at the age of 22.

Since his first psychotic episode, Lennie has had more than a dozen hospital admissions. Although he generally appears to be friendly and to have at least a degree of social competence, he is regarded as having little or no insight or self-management capacity. As is stated frequently in his (multiple) files, he is 'treatment-resistant', 'lacks motivation' and is typical of those with the 'negative symptoms of schizophrenia'.

Reflective exercise 2: Thinking about Lennie

If you had a magic wand, what *practice goals* would you suggest are appropriate in Lennie's vignette? And what do you think are Lennie's needs? These goals and needs should be categorized into those that are short, medium and longer term.

Don't worry if you repeat a goal or need across these time divisions; for example, you might nominate 'safe housing' in more than one section. And do not be concerned about limited access to resources. Rather, try to develop what you think is the ideal for the client.

Because it is quite complex, take some time to review the scenario. Then, when it feels bedded down, write up an informal paper-and-pencil formulation of the practice goals you think might be appropriate. Also consider what you think are Lennie's needs, and in a rough-and-ready way, try to write these up. There is no set way to do this, but the following could help (Table 7.1):

Table 7.1: One possible statement of Lennie's goals and needs

	Practice goals	Lennie's needs
Short term	1. Re-commence outreach work in order to begin to engage Lennie and to learn how he understands his situation and what he says he wants 2. Gather more information by reading his case notes and by speaking to other professionals with whom he has had contact	He has immediate needs relating to securing shelter, food, and safety
Medium term	1. Seek to form a meaningful engagement with Lennie as his worker 2. Seek to persuade Lennie to take regular medication in order to stabilize his symptoms	As above; in addition he needs to learn how to self-manage, for example, to be able to budget
Longer term	1. Develop insight into his condition 2. Secure stable accommodation	As above, plus find paid or unpaid employment, find self-acceptance

When you have thought through your responses, compare them with the commentary text below.

As part of a recent research project Lennie's vignette was presented to a sample of 22 mental health case managers and private psychotherapists. (Most likely, this sample was more or less 'representative' of mainstream practitioners, even if this assertion cannot be definitively confirmed.) This qualification noted, the study produced a clear finding: interviewees had very little to say about possible practice goals or personal needs that related to Lennie's relationships with other people, except for his contact with professionals. Nearly every respondent stated, mostly more than once, that a practice goal was to engage with Lennie and that he had a need to have a regular care coordinator or professional case manager.

In these responses Lennie was not presented as a social being with relational needs but as an autonomous agent whose capacity for independence and self-determination was at least temporarily impaired. In other words, almost nothing was said about the importance of the locally social, about relationships with friends and family, in how the respondents formulated the case material or constructed professional goals (Furlong, 2008a). This was a curious, even worrying, finding that was important to understand.

Interviewees were given this vignette in writing and then asked to take some time to read over it. After clarifying their questions or uncertainties, the interviewer then verbally emphasized two particular features that were also stated in the written case vignette that interviewees were given:

- 'There are no indications Lennie presents any immediate risk to himself or to others.'
- 'In formulating your practice goals you are not limited by any resource constraints. Please develop these goals as ideal statements, as if you have a magic wand.'

In being asked to respond to this vignette in a matter of moments, interviewees were being given a steep challenge. The degree of difficulty involved was high given how demanding it is to assimilate so much information quickly, and then to formulate a complex, layered response presenting short-, medium-, and long-term ideas about both goals and needs. Making this even more challenging was that this task was being done with a stranger who was audio-recording what was said. These difficulties noted, every interviewee took care to respond at considerable length to the vignette, and typically offered a commentary that was at least a page in length when transcribed.

Many different kinds of goals were suggested and the interviewees detailed their reflections with respect to the challenges with which their practice with Lennie would have to engage. There was a great variety in the structure of these commentaries. Some interviewees formally offered short-, medium-, and longer-term ideas whilst others put forward ideas of a more anecdotal nature.

In coding these interviews it was clear that even with a very inclusive reading of what might be described as statements 'concerned with the relational', the extent of this content was strikingly modest: 13 out of 22 offered at least a brief mention; 9 said nothing at all. This was especially the case with respect to 'social ties', the non-familial aspects of the relational dimension, where only 3 mentioned this dimension at all. Overall, a content analysis found that just less than 10 per cent of the interviewees' responses were associated with 'the relational' if this category of content was broadly defined.

At the risk of dramatizing, it does not seem unfair to say that the material interest in the relational dimension that was presented was scrappy, if it existed at all. Whether such ideas were associated with statements about goals, or whether they arose as part of an informal conversational commentary, there was not much there. And with respect to the instances where a relational consciousness was articulated, of the 9 instances where attention was paid to the matter of Lennie's family, and of the possibility/prospects for contact, there was a troubling tone to a number of the comments. Mindful that nearly half of the respondents had nothing at all to say about 'family and social ties' in relation to goals and needs – a finding that is especially disturbing given the fact that it is impossible to think that 'recovery' can be achieved in a social vacuum – it should be acknowledged that a number of the comments that were offered appeared to be both compassionate and culturally sensitive. Yet, others who commented on 'family and social ties' did so in ways that were not only naive and 'Lennie-centric', but were also judgmental.

For example, one interviewee stated: "He did have his connection with the family [until] the family kicked him out." To say this is more than a little family-blaming given Lennie had been actively ill for some or all of the five years between diagnosis and leaving home. In this context, it is more than likely he had been difficult to live with. (It was stated in the outline he had been accusatory and could well have been experienced as threatening, even dangerous, to family members over this significant length of time.) This possibility makes it likely that the pejorative statement he was 'kicked out' is more than a little unfair in relation to how this interviewee's sympathies were dispersed. What of the chance his relatives, most likely his aging parents, were very unsettled, burdened, and/or worn out by the time they told him to leave? A fairer response is probably to assume his parents and siblings had been supportive and tolerant over five years in very difficult circumstances.

Analyzing this matter further, the term 'need', as well as the term 'goal', was featured with respect to introducing the interviewees to their task with the vignette. As well as asking the interviewees to consider their goals for Lennie, the written material, as well as the verbal introduction, given to the interviewees specifically cited the term 'need' ('What does he need?') as well as the reference to practice goals. This distinction between the 'goals of practice' and 'the needs' of the client having been made, a clear result was present: amongst the many dozens of declarations concerned with needs and goals, not one interviewee stated at any point, even informally, that 'Lennie might enjoy a mate or two', that 'He needs to be valued' or 'Like the rest of us, what Lennie needs is everyday care and affection.'

And even if there was no mention of Lennie having a need for connection, there was also no mention of a quieter, less declarative expression of Lennie's humanity. Not one interviewee said (anything like) 'He'd be likely to benefit from having a friend' or 'Being accepted by people he cares about.' No one volunteered the idea it would be good for Lennie 'to get some respect from key people in his life.' Nearly every interviewee used the word 'need', or its equivalent ('requires', 'has got to have', etc), and did so frequently – 'He needs a safe place to live', 'What he really needs is assertive outreach', 'A CTO [Community Treatment Order] might be required', and so forth. Yet these claims were not complemented by similarly phrased invocations of the importance of friendship, respect, or affection.

Locating your responses

It is reasonable to conclude that the received responses were not well informed by current research and policy emphasizing the importance of social inclusion, especially as this concerns supportive relationships. In addition, there were also a number of other patterns, albeit not directly relevant to the concerns of the current enquiry, that arose with respect to the interviewees' responses to the vignette. Given that Lennie was bi-lingual, that he initially saw an Italian-speaking psychiatrist, and that most people, including presumably those in the sample, assume Italian families are close, there was a noteworthy dearth of attention to the cultural dimensions of Lennie's situation.

In considering how you responded to the vignette, an important step is to reflect on the thinking that went on behind the answers that you came up with. For example, what assumptions did you make about Lennie and his past, current, and prospective social relations? Did you assume that:

- Lennie does not currently have friendly relationships with anyone?
- Lennie is unambiguous in his attitude of wanting to remain isolated?
- Lennie has no need for social and/or more intimate attachments or to see himself as worthy of respect?
- Lennie does not see, or receive any support from, any member of his family even as he is 'on the street'?
- his family was, or still are, somehow at fault?
- a positive outcome could be found without some kind of reconciliation/ regularization of his contacts with one or more siblings, parents, or extended family?

How might relational issues have been considered for Lennie?

Within the case details there are a number of cues to the possibilities for longer-term significant other relationships. Most obviously these can be seen where 'family' and 'culture' intersect. That is, Lennie is of Italian background, initially saw an Italian-speaking psychiatrist, and gained his first paid work via a family connection where he worked for several years. And he lived at home for five years after his initial diagnosis of schizophrenia, a fact that probably shows he has strong, albeit perhaps conflictual, connections with his parents as well as with his older siblings and younger sister. These family members are likely to be interested in his welfare and, one supposes, if the dust settles, he will be interested in theirs. One or more of his parents or siblings might currently be offering support and, if they are not, they might be encouraged to do so in the future. There is also the chance that Lennie has, or might in the future, have positive contact with his extended family.

Whilst family-centered possibilities were signaled in the vignette, Lennie's isolation was also a cue to the relational dimension receiving attention in less conventional ways. That is, Lennie's marginal position offers an open canvas for ideas that address his social exclusion. Given there was (in the vernacular of mental health) 'no risk to self or others', and that there were no restrictions on resources, this vignette invites the practitioner's interest in the full spectrum of possible non–familial significant other relationships as *one* of the dimensions that might warrant attention.

Mindful that there was no acute danger to Lennie, or to other people, and that you were given the clear advice there was no need to be concerned with resource issues, your response to the scenario provides important feedback on where you are coming from with respect to attitudes and values around relational health. Specific to the current purpose, the scenario puts forward a kind of Rorschach test, a blank canvas onto which your responses provide an outline of your current relational disposition. Amongst a larger set of inferences, your responses provide an indication of how important you think it is for clients to have a sense of belonging, and how necessary you think it is that clients are able to give and receive affection as active participants in mutually supportive relationships.

In the vignette, as in actual practice, an interest in the relational dimension can be envisaged and realized in a score of different ways. The first step in responding to this, or any other practice scenario, is *to stimulate the process of imagining*. For the moment, put the question of 'how realistic is this idea' and 'how might this, or that, goal be realized' to one side. Broadly, the suite of possibilities that might be imagined for Lennie is composed of the many colorful refractions that express human sociality. More concretely, the palette from which ideas and goals can be painted directly reflects the diversity of forms that significant other ensembles can take. These forms include associations that might be fostered around:

- Club-like or special interest collectivities: has Lennie an interest in, or might he be encouraged to develop an interest in, one or more forms of music, in movies, food, language, gardening, social action around rights, formal or informal study, etc?
- Mateship that can grow, that can be catalyzed, in terms of paid or unpaid employment-related activities?
- The activation, or re-activation, of specific contacts with one or more family members from his 'first circle' – siblings or parents – or with one or more members of his extended family – cousins, aunts, or uncles – or by a combination of these two domains?
- The activation, or re-activation, of contact with current or old associates; with those he has met when he worked, when he was in hospital or hostels, or with whom he had met on the street; with ex-neighbors, old school friends he has lost touch with (which could be done via his informal network or using social media such as Facebook)?

No matter where Lennie might live – even if he stayed on the street for the time being, or even indefinitely – if just one of the above possibilities came through, this would be likely to make a great difference to Lennie's prospects. Any mutual relationship he might form would give him a degree of attachment and interpersonal embeddedness. Such a link would be a great prize as it would open up a dynamic space, a mobile context and transfer frame, which could act as a wellspring for the generation of a greater degree of allegiance and identification.

In the above the assumption had been that the interviewee cohort would be more or less aware of the relevant social policies and research findings that emphasize the importance of social attachment. Given this premise, it followed that Lennie's vignette would be a blank canvas upon which a reasonably fertile imagining of the intimate might be projected. That such an imagining did not generally occur says much about the hegemony of the old ways that stipulate the autonomous over the relational. Yet, if one stands back and looks beyond the orthodox professional responses, the box that equates professional action with the augmenting of the client's capacity for self-reliance, it becomes clear that it is impossible to imagine a positive long-term solution for Lennie that does not see him cared for and, at least to a degree, caring for others. How else might it be possible for him to have a quantum of self-respect as someone who is contributing to his own wellbeing and to the welfare of those he values?

The question for the reader is: as well as being able to identify what was immediately important for Lennie (that an appropriate goal was to 'stabilize his symptoms', 'engage with a worker', and so forth), were you also able to identify longer-term goals and needs related to attachment and inclusion? To become practiced in thinking relationally is to engage in a paradigm shift – the imagination that stimulates this practice is quite discontinuous with received practices as the current paradigm is largely based on a psychology of separation. That this regressive psychology has got such a hold on professional thinking presents health and human service workers with a galvanizing challenge. Below, a brief 'self-assessment' exercise might assist you in locating your preferences concerning the values of connection and separation.

Reflective exercise 3: Separation and connection

Separation

- Do you approach your clients as people who need to be autonomous and self-determining?
- Do you want to help your clients to become more self-reliant and in charge of their lives?
- In your practice do you find yourself particularly attracted to client-centered goals such as empowerment, differentiation, and self-actualization?

- Do you often experience yourself as a person who advocates for your client against those who do not understand your client's needs and point of view as much as you do?
- Those that should care for my clients often fail to adequately understand, acknowledge, and support them.
- In their early years my clients did not receive the care and respect they deserved from those closest to them.
- I try and help clients be more assertive, goal-directed, and in charge.
- In their current relationships my clients are not receiving the care they deserve from those closest to them.
- I am empathic with my client's feelings and point of view.
- Because it is important to develop a positive, trusting alliance with the client I am not inclined to establish relationships with my client's significant others.

Connection

- I am concerned, even empathic, towards my client's significant others.
- My clients are moral agents who sometimes act unfairly to those they are close to, or might become close to: my clients could often act with greater consideration to others.
- My clients are often insensitive to, even ignorant of, the feelings and interests of those to whom they relate.
- My clients often lack the skills and attitudes upon which good quality relationships depend.
- Do you address your clients as relational beings who have connections with, and responsibilities to, their significant others?
- Successful long-term client outcomes depend on the client feeling loved and respected.
- Successful long-term client outcomes depend on the client regarding themselves as accountable in their dealings with others.
- Do you address your clients as people who need to feel they make contributions at least equal to what they receive?
- I try to establish good quality relationships with my client's significant others.

It is likely that a method could be developed to quantify responses to the above, but that is not the point. What is central to the purpose of this current exercise is to invite you to open-mindedly check in, and reflect on, your responses and to ask: do I think there is a quality of balance to the weighting I give to the values of connection and separation in my practice?

Decision points in relationally oriented practice

The above exercises were designed to assist in identifying values and attitudes with respect to relationally oriented practice. Below, the aim is to outline several of the key conceptual skills that underlie an approach that seeks to see the possibilities in positive connection. This task could be approached in a number of ways. In its current form, what is offered works in a linear manner, asking 'What are the first points of decision?' in seeking to practice relationally. Alternatively, you could dip in and out of the material depending on your interests and role.

Professional practices, such as referral making, are often described as no more than *delivering basic occasions of service*. This is not merely a de-personalizing over-simplification; it is a counter-articulate description as it renders the professional–client exchange unilateral rather than interactional. Even the most humbly titled professional activities are sophisticated exchanges. A reasoned analysis of these exercises will identify that each requires dynamic decision making and the negotiation of complex actions. As a part-acknowledgment of this reality, many agencies and professional bodies seek to guide practitioners by developing practice frameworks and procedural protocols.

Mindful that professionals should not ever be regarded as autonomous – agencies, funding bodies, and professional associations must have the right to hold practitioners accountable – it is necessary that practitioners reserve the right to claim at least a degree of discretion in each and every practice episode. Even if a service is reputedly standardized, as is the case in evidence-based methods such as cognitive behavioral therapy (CBT), or in situations where agencies have developed detailed practice manuals and online record-keeping protocols, there is a mediated freedom in how the practitioner chooses to proceed (Lipsky, 1980; Jones and May, 1995). This question of discretion is vitally important here. For example, it is possible to undertake the process of making a referral or constructing a case history in ways that either augment or diminish the prospects for client embeddedness and attachment.

If such opportunities for relationship building are to be realized, practitioners need to be imaginative enough to identify them and vital enough to chase them. As discussed in this and the following chapters, it is sometimes possible to activate a powerful relational potential if the practitioner can discern important preconditions within the rush of everyday circumstance. This can be said metaphorically as being able 'to smell the spring on a smoggy wind' (McColl, 1948). Senior professionals and specialist practitioners have no monopoly on this intuition; far from it. Rather, enthusiasm and acting in ways that align with relationally based practice is about having the correct mindset.

VIGNETTE 6: KYLIE

Kylie was a 14-year-old girl with a terminal illness admitted to a metropolitan children's hospital for an improbable last set of treatments. During this admission Kylie's social worker overheard a discussion in the nursing station between the unit manager and Kylie's key nurse about Kylie being offered an appointment with a visiting hairdresser. Bern, the ward social worker, interrupted this discussion to say she was about to ring Kylie's mum – Trish – to talk over several matters and would like to let her know that staff were considering offering Kylie a hairdressing appointment.

Bern subsequently rang Trish to discuss the questions she had intended to speak to her about, and in this conversation Bern mentioned the haircut. Trish did not seem to give this idea much attention and replied immediately: "Of course, whatever you [people at the hospital] think best is fine with us."

Kylie died several months later despite the hospital's best efforts. About a month after the funeral Bern was not surprised to receive a call from Trish where she asked him to have a conjoint appointment with both her and her partner. In such circumstances these kinds of meetings were not unusual as parents were always invited to request follow-up contact. In the course of this meeting Kylie's father – Tim – told Bern that Trish had told him of the telephone call she had made to Trish where the possibility of Kylie having a haircut in the ward had been mentioned.

Tim went on the say: "It might seem a little thing that you did but we were so turned around by it. The hospital, all of the staff, you'd been fantastic, quite wonderful, and it seemed we had nothing more we could do for Kylie. We were and felt lost. We didn't have qualifications. We didn't even have Kylie at home where we could cook and clean for her. We felt like we were nothing, could do nothing. And your [telephone] call somehow got us off our backsides. You spoke to Trish as Kylie's mother, as her parent, and when Bern told me about this it stopped me in my tracks. It reminded us, got us thinking, that we were still important to our daughter even if we were not doctors or nurses. It challenged us. It changed the way we were relating to what was happening."

Bern's contact with Trish was not a professional intervention as the term is normally used. Rather, it could be seen as no more than a nicety, a kind of courtesy call, much more than it was a high-powered, evidence-based action. Nonetheless, what Bern set out to do had a powerful impact. How could this be explained?

One way to theorize this exchange is to look to the tradition in sociology known as 'symbolic interactionism' (Blumer, 1986). This school of thought is founded on the idea that humans are social beings who are particularly sensitive to the dynamics that occur in group interactions. We are, these theorists say, always monitoring and interpreting how others are seeing us and are therefore subliminally, if not always consciously, creatures of the herd. Being wired into these loops of awareness and response over the last 100,000 years has a set of consequences. According to symbolic interactionist theory, not least of these consequences is that humans tend to become, to grow into, what they are treated to be – *identity and subjectivity are not only determined by what I tell myself I am as who I am also develops in relation to what others say about me.*

If we take this understanding to the exchange between Trish and Bern, it is possible to see Bern telephoning Trish as the enactment of a particular, implicitly formal, form of 'hailing' – of being summoned to be a certain kind of subject – which in this case is that of a parent (Jarre, 2011; this idea is further developed in Chapter 8). Bern rang Trish to seek her participation in a ritual that concerned decision making. The meaning in this form of address in this context was telling as it re-invoked Trish's status as a parent, as Kylie's mother, and also as a spouse: as Bern was conferring with Trish as Kylie's mother so, in turn, Bern was obliged to (at least) inform her partner about this issue. In terms of timing this was a signal event as it occurred within a period in which the couple were experiencing themselves as powerlessness given they felt they had handed over responsibility for the care of their daughter to the hospital staff. The experts were, in fact, also powerless to save Kylie, but it was agreed that the competent authorities had to try everything that was technically possible.

The action of symbolically delegating responsibility for their daughter to the hospital was not in any sense blame worthy. It was not a cop-out. Rather, it was sanctioned and proper. Nonetheless, once Kylie was re-admitted to the care of the hospital authorities an inadvertent consequence settled in: the established roles and responsibilities parents normally undertake were disrupted. Given the trauma and anticipatory grief that so suffused this context, the timelessness and entrancement that had so overtaken the parents, Bern's action was to prickle them into resuming a not-to-be-subordinated status.

This vignette is not recycled to suggest there are always elegant solutions to complex problems. Mostly, relationship building is about steady work done with modesty and patience. Individual practitioners should not set out to and not judge themselves in relation to achieving heroic outcomes. Nonetheless, like Bern, if we can keep our eyes and ears open to possibilities for relationship building, and if we are prepared to take these opportunities in how we go about the everyday work that is given to us, this can make a difference. Little things can be done with a certain inflection, simple things can sometimes be undertaken in thoughtfully alternative ways, and this can be game changing for clients. Taking up this attitude can also make a difference to practitioners as a commitment to relationship building can become a flag to which their allegiance feels energizing and worthy.

As mentioned earlier, in even the most tightly coupled organizations practitioners are never completely controlled and always have a considerable, if never absolute, capacity for discretion. In using this discretion one option is to set out to positively stimulate a more positive relational status. Sometimes this aim is furthered by our manner as much or more as it is by our formal task, skills, or theory base. The *way* we go about what our role has us pursue can be decisive in relationship building even if the primary task is one that has been pre-ordained. A key question is this: am I being inclusive in my process? A second is: does my tone honor the client's many relational faces? Everybody can be addressed as having connections, as being a social being. This honors, and acts to further augment, human affinity.

In what follows a number of decision points in relationally orientated practice are examined. These points particularly concern *considering your role* and *the duration of contact with the client*. Each are discussed in turn, mindful that the process of decision making is not linear in the actual work practitioners do. In practice, different kinds of decisions often have to be made concurrently, not serially. This noted, the attempt is made to isolate specific instances in the process of contact where it is routinely useful to think into assessment decision making.

Considering your role

Whether the contact has been voluntary or involuntary, the great majority of professional practice involves individual practitioners meeting with individual clients who present on their own. As examined in Chapter 6, this expectation is buttressed by funding models, cultural and professional customs and, in general, by the everyday observation that is the business of the well-qualified professional to be the expert, the 'gun', who secures for the client the outcome that is right for them. Unless there is a problem of developmental or mental capacity, for example, where the presentation involves young children or impaired older people, it is *just the way it is* that a single professional meets alone with a single client to advance that client's private interests. This stipulation structures the practice of lawyers – just as it does physiotherapists and podiatrists, pharmacists and medical specialists, radiologists and speech therapists in the larger medical field.

This stipulation presents as a problem if the professional comes to believe that all people are practically interdependent. If any practitioner understands that the interests of single clients are not independent of, cannot be filleted from, the interests of those that comprise this person's vital interpersonal ecology, this has powerful implications. In contrast to this heretical view, the traditional view assumes it is the professional's role to advance the client's cause, in effect to be their advocate, as if the client is a standalone island. For example, what can the professional do if a man presents complaining his partner is not supportive, is not satisfying him sexually, and is causing him stress which is worsening his asthma (his stutter, his back pain, etc)?

Even if the professional finds the man's position unreasonable, even to a degree psychopathic, in so far as this professional is locked into the old paradigm, their focal concern is with 'my patient'. And if this person seems unfair or unreasonable in their attitude to their partner, the least distasteful option is to keep quiet. In the event the professional retains their neutrality; most likely the client will take this as silent ascent, as tacit affirmation, that 'Yes, my expert, the professional who takes my side, agrees it is my partner who is the problem because she is not looking after me adequately.' Everybody knows, including the client, that the professional has no choice but to be on the client's side in this case.

This is not the logic in the relational paradigm. As is commonsensical in every culture except in the West, if practical interdependence is assumed *at least in many instances* practitioners definitely have the chance to interact with their clients in ways that promote personal accountability and which acknowledge, hold up, or even enhance the relationships their clients have with their current and prospective significant others. This opportunity is present even though the current pattern – that individual practitioners will continue to meet with individual clients – is certain to persist. That this pattern will continue means that the 'what' of practice will be held constant, even as some aspects of practice technology, the 'how' of the work, might be modified in the service of better supporting client interdependencies. That is, some matters of professional custom, of received etiquette, can be adapted without disrupting the basic nature of the task.

This might be done in unexpected ways. A pharmacist might ask an aging client if there is a friend, partner, or adult offspring who could be 'a helpful part of our conversations as I would like to be as confident as possible I have all the information that is needed for me to do my job thoroughly.' A podiatrist might suggest 'it could be good if I show X [a partner, daughter, neighbor, etc] how to judge whether your gait is again becoming unaligned.' This kind of invitation might sound unconventional, but it really reflects a commonsense attitude to maximizing effectiveness – once the cultural fetish about independence and the professional pre-occupation with one-on-one meetings is disrupted.

Although it can be enormously beneficial for practitioners to meet with significant other groupings – what can be termed conjoint meetings or, following the narrative nomenclature, as 'witnessing circles' (see Chapter 8) – many practitioners experience multiparty contacts as difficult. At least initially, working with more than one person can feel awkward, even unnatural. This makes sense as most professionals have been socialized to assume the work concerns only the client, the whole client, and nothing but the client. For this reason, if a professional wants to advance the relational agenda, this has to be done within the accepted pattern of being one-on-one with the client. Whilst retaining this pattern, a relational agenda can be furthered in many ways. In the conversations between the practitioner and the client, the relationship-strengthening agenda can be furthered:

- by the tone of voice the practitioner uses to dignify the importance of relationship;
- by invoking, literally calling forth, the names and ethical presence of those who are the key participants and stakeholders in the ecology of the client's life;
- by introducing different points of view: 'Who in your circle sees it the same way you do, and who doesn't?';
- by introducing the theme of accountability: 'Who has some stake in you acting fairly?';
- in the micro-transactions, manners, and non-verbal behaviors – what is sometimes called the non-specifics of practice – that are a key dimension in the professional's conduct.

For example, using a caring tone, a physiotherapist might ask an aging client 'Given you and your daughter are not getting on so well, if you could be patient, is there anyone else who you could learn to be comfortable with helping you put on and take off your [back] brace? Is there another option?'

In the latter example, the physiotherapist, who we will call 'Philippa' here, might have heard, perhaps many times, Julia, the client, say 'Jim [her partner] is useless. He just gets grumpy when I tell him my back is killing me' (see Vignette 7). How might Philippa respond when Julia again complains about her partner? It is necessary, of course, that each professional has to listen and support the client and, over time, earn the client's trust. To do this each client has to learn to understand that their position and feelings, their individuality and history, is recognized by their practitioner. This absolutely understood, from time to time simply agreeing, or being seen to agree, with the client that X – their best friend, eldest child, neighbor, or spouse – is the problem is not helpful as it is homeostatic or, even worse, tacitly inflammatory. Like hairdressers, practitioners get to hear the most intimate of complaints. In these exchanges they have a considerable discretion in how they position themselves in relation to this information.

Being exposed to complaints invites the listener to stop hearing, even to become indirectly vengeful, so there are risks in Philippa's situation. Mindful of the need to remain reflective, Philippa has the option of a more ambitious, systemic response to Julia's distress. She might say, even begin a dialogue around, the following: 'Julia, we have talked about the idea your back is going to stay painful, hopefully less so, but that it is unlikely you will ever be totally pain free. Given you and I, at least from time to time, agree about this is so from my perspective a good question then comes up. In terms of getting the kind of support you would like to have in the future can we talk about ideas you might have that, with some time and patience, might be useful in engaging Jim in being more supportive and sympathetic?'

Rather than forming an alliance with the client that tends towards the unhelpfully collusive (*it must be awful that your partner is not on your side – unlike me!*), in some circumstances it can be more productive to toggle the client's position. Such a perturbing has to be compassionate and sincere. It is in the client's interest to explore the chance that their significant others are beings with whom they might come to relate with differently over time (mindful these others have their own sensitivities). Of course, it is the case that sometimes clients suffer from being exploited or victimized, and it is not always best to remain tied up in connections that are troubling. This noted, the option of the client leaving a relationship that is, in part, troubling is often neither practical nor should it ever be the practitioner's default thought.

> ## VIGNETTE 7: JULIA
>
> In the above example Philippa, a physiotherapist, has heard Julia, her client, describe Jim (Julia's husband) as not merely of no practical help, but as part of the problem emotionally and interpersonally. This complaint has not been voiced once, but has become a feature of the course of contact. That is, Philippa has heard Julia complain many times that 'Jim is useless. He just gets angry when I tell him my back is killing me. How bad is that?'
>
> Sometimes Julia seems to say this as a simple statement of fact. At other times her complaint is elaborated and/or is quite colourfully described. At these times Philippa feels invited, even expected, to agree with Julia that Jim is 'the problem.' Philippa finds this uncomfortable and experiences this side-with-me demand as awkward, even irritating. Without meaning to, Philippa has recently found herself feeling negative about Julia and, as this pattern has persisted, thinking that 'Julia is playing the victim: she is not motivated to do the best she can; she is not organizing herself around getting on with what she can do.'

Conjoint meetings

Whilst it may seem more obviously the case that those professionals who have a clear potential to, or already have, some everyday contact with their client's significant others can work to a relationship-honoring agenda, this goal is a realistic aspiration in all professional practice settings. With greater ease some professional groups can have direct contact with the client's significant others. These professional groups include community nurses and youth workers, general practitioners and aged case assessment team members, psychologists and crisis workers, social workers and occupational therapists, as well as general therapists and counselors. In relation to working systemically, what is at issue is not who the professional meets but how the practice is conceptualized and conducted.

Practitioners can meet with the client's significant others and see their role as that of a host, as someone who is genuinely courteous and welcoming (Furman and Ahola, 1995). This is both the ethical and the practical option.

It is the professional who has (most) of the power in this context; that is, the professional tends to set and modify the agenda, determines when the session starts and finishes and decides if further contact is called for – is 'appropriate', is 'indicated.' In this sense it is the professional who writes the rules and owns the game when an 'extra' is invited into a session.

Even if a practitioner has the intention of being inclusive and caring, conjoint meetings can be difficult. As many have experienced, putting people together is not necessarily positive, and these meetings can become prickly, even antagonistic, in their atmosphere and interaction. Although tensions can be present, practitioners should remain thoughtful hosts who are attentive and interested, curious, and welcoming. Yet, if a meeting is to work well they also need to ensure a containing milieu is established. Being able to play the steady bobby or traffic cop is at times a necessity.

It is naive to put people together thinking that open communication, or some such cliché, will be helpful when in fact uncontained encounters are often counter-productive: they can be like putting out a fire with gasoline. (More detailed pointers for convening and conducting conjoint meetings are presented in Chapter 8.) As with all practice that is designed to be relationship building, it is not just who you meet with but how this contact is conducted that is telling. Good intentions are important, but are seldom sufficient. Even with positive intentions, a practitioner can meet with the client and one or more of this person's significant others and inadvertently have the effect of disrupting linkages between these people. This is often done in case conferences and discharge planning meetings when the practitioner, or even a team of practitioners, do not see the client's significant others as having their own biography, perspectives, and needs. This is a touchy subject as 'we' professionals pride ourselves on being client-centered as well as believing we have the right to be the legitimate and exclusive advocate for 'my client'.

Unfortunately, such a positioning tends to set up an adversary dynamic between the professional and the client's significant others. At its worst this dynamic can result in a dance where the professional, high on their sense of expertise and righteously pursuing what their self-perceived role is as the client's advocate, rounds on those present as if these significant others' total purpose in life is to serve the practitioner's definition of the client's needs. It follows that it is not surprising that many 'guests' feel misunderstood, even 'bashed up', after meeting with professionals. This kind of event reflects the grim sequelae of the old paradigm. Such dynamics stem from the assumption that it is proper for the practitioner to represent 'my client, right or wrong', and to simply transpose this allegiance into conjoint meetings beyond the practitioner–client dyad.

Of course, the opposite can also be undertaken. That is, a professional can meet with a single client and take up a systemic perspective, a mindset that understands the centrality of interdependence and the importance of the biographies, perspectives, and needs of those with whom their client is associated. It is not who we meet but how we understand and go about the work that is crucial. As discussed earlier, a physiotherapist or a podiatrist might take up a relational disposition just as a psychologist or a community nurse might. It is not about training; no professional group has a monopoly on thinking contextually.

In summary, a practitioner's role actualizes their point of contact with the client. This role also organizes the practitioner's point of contact with the client's significant others as it does for other professionals in, and beyond, the practitioner's place of practice – if you are an outreach worker in a position funded to assist young people who are, or are at risk of, homelessness, this role structures the way in which you see, and are seen by, the client.

The key point is to examine your role in a tough-minded way so both opportunities and the constraints in its design are identified. For example, in some roles there is a degree of authority and prestige, almost a lordliness, where a quiet word might have a ripple effect. Although it still remains surprising to those practitioners who wish to be heirs to the non-directive counseling tradition, many clients seek advice and guidance (Mayer and Timms, 1970; Silver, 1991). In other roles the degree of intimacy and continuity is so high that an ongoing focus on interpersonal relationships and personal accountability may be possible. In roles involving, for example, grief work or in intense youth outreach, it may be possible to have more indirect discussions, perhaps even philosophical debates, around personhood and connection that could be useful in planting a seed. Once the analysis of the role's possibilities and limits is done, the task is to work creatively, yet realistically, based on this analysis.

Even family court lawyers can seek to practice with a degree of allegiance to the relational aesthetic. Rather than working to the old principle that their exclusive aim is to be a dedicated advocate for 'this wo/man's' material interests, a calculus that acts to inflame tensions and to antagonize a separating couple's relational prospects, practitioners might choose to hold against too zealous an advocacy. Unless the practitioner reaches the view that their role might be productively redesigned, working in clear relation to the possibilities and drawbacks is all that can practically be done. If the professional, perhaps in concert with their colleagues, does decide that a more general reconfiguration is preferable, this requires a complex consideration of the developmental tactics that are relevant to such a renegotiation. Although this issue can be of crucial importance, a consideration of role and workplace reform is beyond what is presently being attempted.

Further reflections on the variations in professional role

Some practitioners work with clients briefly and others over a longer term. In each case there are possibilities and constraints to working with a relationship-building agenda. Before considering the effect duration and frequency of contact has on the prospects for this work, it is clear there are other variables. Amongst a broader set, these include:

- Whether contact with the professional was initiated by the client or a third party: where is the contact situated on the continuum between voluntary or involuntary encounter?

- Has the role a focus on the here and now, such as crisis work, or does it have a developmental, even consultative, character?
- What is the nature of the role: is the focus on medical matters (GPs, nurses), rehabilitation (physiotherapists, case managers), immediate practical problems (housing workers, vocational counselors), advocacy (social workers, lawyers), therapeutic work (private therapists, counselors, psychologists), interpersonal issues (group workers, couple counselors), or a broader, more generic action (pastoral care counselors, mentors, life skills coaches)?
- Is the service private or public in its funding and location?
- In relation to the tone of the professional–client interaction is there a quality of formality and hierarchy, informality and equality, or a mixture between the two? That is, has the role the character of being an expert, a support person, an advisor, or a companion?

Given the enormous variation in the nature of roles, and the further complication that different clients, and other stakeholders, tend to personalize and refract their definitions of these roles in ways that might differ from the official definition, it is not possible to firmly generalize across and between professional groups. Even if a generalization represents an accepted trend line – for example, that doctors have a greater prestige than nurses – this expectation will not hold in every instance.

How is this relevant to the subject of relationally based practice? It is important because it is crucial to create space for a diverse range of practitioners to have the ambition to mainstream the relational agenda. For example, whilst it is statistically true that podiatrists and pastoral care counselors generally have a differentiated capacity to affect the relational base of their clients, it does not follow that 'this podiatrist' may not be more effective than 'that pastoral care counselor' in facilitating this purpose. Moreover, a fine-grained analysis of any particular role is almost certain to reveal that this role is multidimensional. A given role – for example, a police officer or a manager – is composed of a mix of core and more marginal components. More problematically, in many roles there is a tension, even a conflict, between the component elements that make up the role. This is powerfully the case in the tension present between the care and control dimensions in therapeutic and protective work (Pentony, 1981; Furlong, 2002). Another example of friction is the tension that can be present between a professional's commitment to practice neutrally – to not be directive, intrusive, or overbearing – and their duty of care obligations to, and beyond, the client (McMahon, 1992).

Reconciling such divergences generates much of the satisfaction, and sometimes the frustration, that is at the heart of professional practice. Put colloquially, you have to be able to ride two horses at once if you want to work in a circus. There is always complexity, as it is also the case that there will be at least a degree of discretion in how the work is undertaken. The matter of discretion is crucial as, at a distance, it seems that it is only certain roles that have the purchase and the legitimacy to pursue the relational agenda. Despite conventions and ordinary appearances, for each discipline and in each role this agenda can be accorded *at least* with the status of a marginal priority. As such, it is not responsible that this agenda should be owned or antagonized by any professional or professional group. Given its importance, some attempt to further the quality of the client's social connectedness warrants at least a degree of attention from all practitioners irrespective of the nature of their role and whether it is enacted in a short-, medium-, or long-term involvement.

Duration of contact with the client

In terms of their nature, duration, and frequency, different practice roles produce varying patterns of contact with clients. In some positions the practitioner may predominately undertake home visits while in other contexts communication with the client is exclusively by telephone or via the internet. Mindful such variations determine the form practice will take, and that in each form there are possibilities for, and constraints to, relationally based professional action, it is the duration and frequency of contact that is the concern here (ICT-based contacts are discussed later, in Chapter 9). Given a decision has been made to work to a relationship-building agenda, the aim of the following material is to assist the reader in identifying what is possible in a specific local role.

In some roles a single contact is mandated, as occurs in many aged care assessments or single session consultations. At the opposite end of the scale there are roles that require very long-term contact as is the case in some disability program areas, or where a case management service is offered to those with an acquired brain injury. Between these extremes there is a diverse set of possibilities in terms of the duration and frequency of contact. Some providers have a fixed limit to the number of contacts, say between six and twelve, whereas others have periodic, but not frequent, contact in a pattern that resembles the way GPs function.

Jumbling up the picture further, naming conventions are inconsistent as what may be framed as 'short term' in one context may be termed or 'intensive' or 'long term' in another. For example, in one major Australian city a public therapeutic center has been established to offer psychodynamic therapy to hard-to-reach clients. This service describes itself as providing 'short- to medium-term therapy', that is, a contact of up to 50 sessions. Yet anything over 12 sessions would be termed long term in CBT.

Whatever the description, when it comes to strengthening the client's relational base the rule is to take the opportunities that are presented in the role as it is, mindful of one qualification: even if there is some chance to engage in relationally oriented practice it is important not to over-reach one's warrant. Without discounting the value of having a relationship-strengthening ambition it is necessary to acknowledge that the structure of a position, its particular configuration of core and marginal functions, has to be respected. Put simply, and using the most common definitions of the terms, case managers should not try and be group facilitators and speech therapists should not attempt to act as couple counselors.

Good practice entails practitioners doing what they can to acknowledge, support, and build the client's relationships with their significant others. This established, it is important to closely monitor to what extent you have the legitimation to devote attention to building the client's relational base. Mindful of this concern, a respectable relational ambition can be built into the actions of all practitioners.

One-off sessions

Often professionals do not know if contact with a client will be restricted to one visit: about one third of those who consult a therapist only attend once even when there is the option of having further contact. This possibility to one side, in the circumstances the professional does know there will only be a single contact, that this meeting can either be a planned or an unplanned exchange, and it is the ordinary nature of the business to meet with a client once in many settings. These planned one-off meetings include:

- when a representative, or representatives, of an aged care service have a scheduled assessment appointment with an older person and, perhaps, one or more of this person's carers and relatives;
- when an immediate single session consultation is offered to a family on a waiting list for therapy where participation in this session depends on an agreement to complete a protocol of 'before' and 'after' questionnaires; or
- when there is a scheduled intake meeting which has a specific assessment and/ or gate-keeping function.

In terms of unplanned meetings there is an enormous diversity of types. Amongst a larger set, these include exchanges where a person presents urgently for emergency relief without an appointment, encounters with a health professional of an emergency/crisis nature, or where there is opportunistic contact initiated by one or both parties, for example, in outreach work. Whether planned or unplanned, single session meetings with clients are rarely labeled as consultations, yet for the current purpose the suggestion is that this framing offers many advantages. In this way the practitioner can consider themselves a change agent in even informal meetings. Just as a consultation is expected to be purposive, so many one-off interactions between a practitioner and a client can be richly purposive in seeding relational improvements.

If the professional knows it is a one-off meeting, it is easier to have their radar on alert for relational spaces and constructive impacts, but at times these can also be identified in unplanned meetings. In all these contacts the questions that are asked and the statements that are made can, at least from time to time, bring the matter of relationships into the foreground:

- a nurse in an A&E department might make a professional commitment to being inclusive and acknowledging of the significant others of their patients;

- an assessor in aged care may make a special point of summoning up important support figures out of the shadows by being committed to asking clients 'Who is the most important to you amongst your informal network?' given non-biological and non-legal connections easily fall off the horizon. Follow-ups from this kind of querying could include: 'Does your X [the most formal carer] know how important Z is, and how they might be contacted?'

It may feel awkward, but weaving links between the informal and the formal elements in the client–professional interaction can contribute enormously to a tied-in network.

Once the relational has been raised into awareness, more or less nuanced attempts can be made to honor, revive, imagine, or hold up this dimension. This can be done in a number of ways, including by:

- using the actual names of a person, or persons, in the client's network: 'You've told me about your friend X. Have you let her know where you are at?'
- making enquiries with respect to categories of relationship: 'Have you any cousins (siblings, old workmates, etc) who might want to have a role?'
- introducing themes that have a specifically relational dimension: 'This might sound like a tough question, but how do you think a man of respect would deal with what is in before you right now?' (These ideas are developed further in Chapter 9.)

As well as asking questions and making statements, if the preconditions have been secured it may also be possible to undertake specific actions: telephone calls and visits can be made that introduce and reassure, that help build bridges, and restore connections.

Whilst it is easier to organize one's mindset towards the purpose of promoting client embeddedness in a planned single session, there is likely to be some potential for advancing this aim in unscheduled cases. For example, in an informal meeting with a young homeless person, an outreach worker might say, 'Down the track, when all this crap and drama has settled down, do you think it would be better if you can look back and say to yourself "I'm proud I did nothing when I was down and out that really buggered my self-respect and reputation."' If the practitioner felt it might have more sway, the same idea might be put in a different form, which is truer to where I encountered this idea.

In the vignette below, an experienced outreach worker related a conversation he had recently had with one of the young people he was in contact with in his current role.

VIGNETTE 8: JACK

"I found myself telling Jack (a homeless young man of 19) that I had run into an old client about a week earlier. This guy, who I'll call Greg, is not really that young these days, maybe 23, but I'd met and worked with him six or seven years before when he was really skidding around. Greg was then homeless and had been knocked around before he left home, as well as properly roughed up out on the street. [I told Jack] Greg had done all the shit and drama that you've got going now: the stand over or be stood over shit, the round-and-round troubles with the law, every kind of dope there is. The whole banana.

"He eventually got through it and when we met we had a cuppa and a yarn. He ended up telling me something I reckon is pretty wise. He said 'I don't know how I did it, but I'm proud I can look back on my time on the streets and know I never did anything that really buggered my self-respect and my reputation. Sure, I did heaps of dodgy and illegal things, you had to, but I never started a blue and never hurt anyone more than I had to. I never pimped or hit my women and I reckon I tried to be fair. And, this is not just my story as those who knew me, well, that'd say so too.'

"And I said to this young guy Jack I'm working with now: what do you think, do you reckon he might be onto something?"

The outreach worker who related this story was a tough operator. He had the 'weight' to be this kind of messenger and, one imagines, also had the sense of timing to know what he was doing. I asked him if Jack heard what he had said. He said "I've no idea, but you never know. Sometimes, you plant a seed but it can't start growing until there is a bit of spring around. Who knows, that may or may not ever be there for Jack. Or, Jack might not be around when it gets warmer out there."

It is unlikely that any kind of short, sharp shock will be relationally developmental. It is almost always about patience, about saying to oneself 'What am I trying to build here?' and staying in first gear. From time to time a rich opportunity may arise, as occurred in the vignette about Kylie mentioned earlier in this chapter (Vignette 6). Mostly, it is about being a stubborn outpost that persists in holding up a light for the relational when it looks hopeless and dark. This is not about being a jock–hero, about breaking through, pushing hard, or even chipping away. A feminine sensibility informs relational practice. It is about nursing a possibility, planting a seed, keeping a dream nourished.

Short-term practice

Contact that is designed to be short term, say between three and six sessions, is in many ways similar to infrequent contacts that might occur over longer periods. In these interactions the same kind of possibilities exist that are present in one-off contacts, but there is also more of a chance to prepare the ground, at least to some degree. A practitioner might be a youth worker ('Jingo') who meets young people on the street and has the chance, developed over years but with frequent interruptions, to become something of a constant figure to a particular young woman ('Bebe', see Vignette 9).

VIGNETTE 9: BEBE

An experienced youth worker ('Jeff') in his mid-20s has contact with out-of-home young people on the inner urban streets of a large city. Developing over several years, Jeff has become something of a constant figure to a Bebe, a 17 year old young woman, although this contact has occurred randomly usually with many months separation each exchange.

Initially, Bebe was suspicious of Jeff. And, on one occasion, she openly accused him of being 'Just another John. I bet you get off on girls. You're all the same you men.' Perhaps influenced by the good word she'd heard about him from another young person who'd had contact with him, or because he had once secured her a much needed crisis over-nighter or, ore generally, that he 'could keep it together' Bebe found herself almost comfortable when, once more, she'd run out of options.

Vulnerable young people tend to put adult workers 'on probation'. Over time, if Jingo has been able to demonstrate his reliability in times when the tension has been high, he may have been able to build some symbolic trust (even if this belies the fact that these participants have only had a relatively small number of hours in each other's company). In this context, if and when the timing is right, the practitioner is in a privileged position to push a line that concerns how this young person might be able to do better relationally: 'No shit, you were lucky to pull through with that one. I don't know but maybe it might it be the time to think about getting in touch with that sister you talked about a while ago, you know the one out west?' The message is, of course, the question: 'Do you think it might be possible to build a bridge?' There are classes of interventive question, to use Tomm's (1988) initial nomenclature, which can be used to embed the assumption that change is possible with relationships no matter how stung and scared the client might feel.

   The worker might ask, 'If you had a mind to, who's the one, the two, and the three who you most want to tell that you are still out here alive and kicking?'

Getting some kind of agenda going, one that might be picked up the following time (or time after) when the parties next meet, is a form of intervention. Depending on the timing, the worker might raise an interim, more decisive, query: 'Do you want to do make this contact, or might it be better if I did? If you want me to do it, should I ring, drop in or write?' Bebe and Jeff might then be able to have a discussion around this question and, perhaps, about the hopes and dreams Bebe has around relationships more generally. In its form, if not in its intention, this recycles the original Milan group's notion of 'circular questioning' (Selvini-Palozzoli et al, 1980) – of using questions that ask the client to speculate about the relationships that can or might exist between significant-others in their own local ecology.

Such discussions offer the chance to bring into greater brightness the particularities of individuals and the relationships – however dimmed or untended they may be – that make up the client's symbolic and practical ecology. 'Bebe, what is the difference between your mum and your sister's reasoning about how they go about getting on with your brother?' These kinds of conversations may be discontinuous but also thematic. They also seek to ride the waves of the client's mixed feelings. And if such dialogues are emotionally attuned, they can both externalize and witness, bring into the fresh air and light of day, what would otherwise remain internalized and yet still be in play. You don't responsibly dig up what cannot be emotionally managed, yet to name and acknowledge, if not necessarily make a theme of, past and future relational intimacies, can be powerfully settling.

Medium-term contact

In contacts with clients that have significant duration, or when contact is not continuous in its pacing but in its cast of participants, the practitioner often has a good chance to embed a theme around the worth of, and the possibilities for, relationship building. In this kind of contact there can be persistent opportunities to construct case formulation and goal setting in such a manner as to be inclusive of this agenda, even as the formal business of the work is unlikely to be couched in these terms. The work of practitioners is mostly designed and documented without any mention of relationship building at all.

The role may have its fundamental concern with rehabilitation, as in maximizing recovery from a work accident, or in the securing of employment for those who have been retrenched; the role may focus on trauma, for example, with veterans of military service, or with those who are experiencing profound grief. These, and many other, presenting situations offer interested practitioners a milieu within which practice can be informed by the broadly based research on the social determinants of health, summarized in Chapter 2. This inspiration may also be found in the field-specific research that is becoming available which almost universally aligns positive outcomes with the quality of a client's social connectedness. (There is emerging research across specialist settings such as mental health, aged care, and the treatment of chronic illness that is applicable here.) Nominate a specialist area and there will be research that supports the importance of interpersonal support.

In terms of case formulation and goal setting, in the last section of this chapter a generic, and relatively informal, assessment framework is introduced that can be imported into any given practice setting. Using this, or another, device helps externalize possibilities related to the adequacy of the client's relational base and the status of the client's relational skills. For now, a different kind of idea is examined, particularly for its relevance to medium-term work. A brief vignette introduces this idea.

Imagine you are a professional, 'Stella', who has the demanding task of supervising child access visits in the context of a contested child protection order and a refractory family court dispute. Whist seeking to be cordial and low key, in this difficult circumstance you have a clear focus on the interests of the children involved, yet you also know that their longer-term interests are not advanced by the continuation, let alone the escalation, of the dispute between the parents. To effectively undertake your role it is necessary to be transparently and scrupulously neutral whilst retaining a clear authority to be clear about, and to police limits on, parenting behavior vis-à-vis the children.

You observe patterns over some months that you see as unhelpful, yet you keep these perceptions to yourself. You make a note to yourself of what you understand is at issue, but unless a breach of accepted standards occurs, you remain 'buttoned up'. Your role is to regulate the hours of contact, organize transport, monitor who is present, ensure there is no alcohol or other drugs, guard against violence, and so forth. Yet, regulating these variables will not, as you know, improve the context of the dispute that is the defining condition in terms of the longer-term outlook for these children. It is not in the nature of your role to be the case manager, the mediator, or the separation counselor. You are not a therapist for either of the adults. Many times you hold against saying what you think might be helpful in order to preserve your position as a neutral protective agent.

However much you are seen as an official, as a regulator, over the months you sense your impartial, though compassionate, companionship has been accepted as a welcome, if not as a directly acknowledged, element for all concerned. The same patterns are still there, for example, you have noticed how the children always become hyped up before and after contact visits, a problem for which each parent blames the other. You've noted this, seen it so many times, and still have to hear each parent disparage the other: 'She stirs them up before you bring them to my place' says dad whilst mum says 'As fucking usual, they let me know with their behavior they are scared of him.'

One day, months down the track, when the mood seems right, you offer this out-of-formation comment to the father (and plan to say the same thing to the mother).

VIGNETTE 10: STELLA

"It might be hard to hear it but they love you both. They want to prove how loyal they are to you – and then they will want to do the same to their mum. It just figures the kids can't help but get both anxious and excited before and after changeovers.

"I see it happen with lots of families, including those goody-good types who have never had anything to do with child protection. It's not about her or your fault. Get over it. Your shittiness with her disturbs them further. And I am going to tell your ex the same thing when I see her later today.

"I am not going to say anything else, and I hope I haven't upset the good way we've been working together. I'll be taking the kids back to their mum at the usual time. If you want to respond to what I've said, I'm more than happy to do this, but can we do this a little later?"

The above is child-centered and you might have good reason to expect, if you have read the wind right, that saying this now is more likely to have a positive impact than if it had been said months earlier. Rather than continuing to keep this thought to yourself, which is always option one, in saying what you did at this point you selected option two, which was to make a brief comment, offer an observation, and then to move the conversation on. Commenting, and moving on, can be done in many situations where you want to let the other person know you have registered their distress, wish to honor a feeling by naming it outright, or want to state an idea, but do not wish to dwell on this. The use of this naming-and-then-moving-on option can be both containing and acknowledging, but it has risks, as does every choice.

There is always another option, which is to make a theme of an issue, a feeling, or a principle. In practice, situations that extend into contacts that have medium-term duration can also present practical possibilities. Making the relational a continuing, if rarely an exclusive, theme fits very well with many examples of professional practice: 'How are you going with what we spoke about last time, with working out who you would like to get on better with?' This approach is not necessarily about trying to reorganize a client's interpretative framework. Rather, it can be both behavioral and cumulative. In the next section the focus is on longer-term practice and it is here that belief change may be usefully attempted.

Extended term practice

When practitioners have the chance to work long term, and it is a chance that is less and less available, it is often possible to pursue a relational agenda with consistency.

For example, over months, even years, in the role of case manager a practitioner might occasionally drive a client with severe disabilities to appointments with specialists. Such an extended companionship offers the chance for the casual, but somehow quite special, intimacy that is occasioned when two people are alongside each other rather than staring at each other across a desk in an office.

For many clients this kind of informal closeness is preferable to the ultra-private exchanges many professionals have naturalized as at the center of their work. (Professionals tend to assume that these intimate ceremonies are what genuine professional practice is about, even as many clients find this configuration overly intense.) Whilst driving, and in other not so formal meetings such as sharing a bus trip, it is possible to have the importance of, and the intrinsic difficulties that are presented by, close relationships boomerang in and out of the exchange. In these discussions practitioners can make a point of sharing some of their own ideas and experiences and to not shy away from the question of values. If it is introduced in the right way, there are few clients who are not able to be reflective, even philosophical, in their own style, and this material can be returned to over and over. *Do you think affection and respect are important in your life? Are these values important enough to have you investing time and effort in doing the right things – even if liking, maybe even loving, someone has the potential to leave you feeling hurt?* If the client comes to the point of wanting to take up a new opportunity, or to revive an older contact, there is the possibility of undertaking some relationship coaching (see Chapter 9).

In other situations it is not possible to develop a theme consistently. As explored in Chapter 3, many clients have been seared by their past experiences in relationships and insist that their drawbridge stays up. Although the practitioner might be clear that the client is, in effect, cutting off their nose to spite their face in remaining locked away from others, charging at this fortress will most likely only harden its defenses. There is no assured tactic in such situations, but patience is likely to be a precondition for progress. A longer vignette might be useful here.

VIGNETTE 11: ROUGA

A gay woman in her early seventies has had no contact with her two adult children for nearly 10 years. This woman – Rouga – now lives alone in a set of semi-independent units where she is popular and has been happy for the last five years. Following complications with recent open heart surgery, she has recently lost a good deal of her mobility, her general sense of robustness, and, in general, her positive health prognosis. Rouga's GP – Dr Quine – knows her well and they enjoy a good relationship.

Dr Quine has been Rouga's GP for many years and, over time, has built up a clear understanding of Rouga's background. She knows that Rouga is a strong and intelligent woman who had an unusual, and quite successful, quasi-military career. She knows Rouga took the tough decision to leave her husband to live as a gay woman when her children were in their early teens, that she was castigated by her large family for doing this, and that shortly after this separation she moved in with Ruth whom she lived with until Ruth died six years ago.

Dr Quine also knows that Rouga kept in contact with her children, who her ex-husband brought up during their teenage years, until they had what she calls a "falling out" when these children were well into their adult lives. When Rouga told Dr Quine about this history some years ago, she was adamant in saying, "I've divorced them and they have divorced me. End of story." Dr Quine initially brought up, and tried to discuss, this 'divorce' with the view that it was an issue that Rouga might benefit from re-examining. Despite this, Rouga remained insistent that she was not prepared to talk further about it.

Rouga's recent health scare, and her deteriorating health status, prompted Dr Quine to again think of re-raising the issue: 'What,' Dr Quine reflected to herself, 'is the ethical thing to do? I do not think it is in my patient's interests, or her children's, or their children's, to have Rouga become more ill, and eventually die, without me again seeking to explore the possibility of some kind of reconciliation. Yet, if I bring this up again Rouga will feel she is being besieged. And, if she feels under attack, she is likely to dig in further.' If Dr Quine decided to take this matter up, is there some way that she might do this so as to avoid, or at least minimize the chance that it will cause the outcome she seeks to be pushed further way? Rather than setting up a siege–repel dynamic, how could Dr Quine seek to prompt a new dynamic, one that was more likely to be cooperative than antagonistic?

Dr Quine is not in a classic double bind, a trap that cannot be stated out loud. Hers is an overt dilemma, a simple bind, that is better being given the light of day. Based on the premise that it is likely Rouga has mixed feelings, that she does not want to, and yet she does want to, have some sense of contact with her grandchildren, if not necessarily her adult children, Dr Quine prepared the following letter:

Dear Rouga

I am in a dilemma, a really unhappy state. You've told me you have divorced your children and I have heard and respected this point of view until now. Your recent health problems have given me cause to reflect further.

In brief, in my heart and in my head I believe your stand-off with your children is not good for your health and wellbeing, nor is it likely to be good for theirs. And, all adult interests to one side – you adults can be expected to be knowing – what about your grandkids? How old are they now? What about their interests?

On the present course they are likely to come into adulthood, and beyond, not knowing about you. This will be far from good as having some contact with, some knowledge of, where they have come from is grounding. For example, times have changed and they ought to know and be proud of how independent you have been right through your life, that you were so game you were prepared to be ostracized in order to be true to live in a way that was true to yourself.

Yet, to raise this with you risks having an independent woman, and a stubborn one, be pushed into a corner. I do not want to do that. This dilemma is so real to me that I am going to ask you to do something really tough. What I'd ask you to do is to write me up an opinion, one that canvasses all the choices fully and with the emotional and the practical costs and benefits set out. Can you agree to do that?

This is the territory the anthropologist Gregory Bateson described in terms of symmetrical and complementary patterns (Simon et al, 1985). For Bateson the former occurs in arm wrestles and arms races, as it can also be present within relationships when, for example, a father does not feel respected by his son while the son feels his father is not listening to him. For both, the experience is of the other being the problem and of your own actions being inevitable given the provocation you are experiencing.

Standing back, it is of course the dance, the dynamic, that is problematic. For Bateson what is required is to insert – genuinely, and not as a trick – a little of the opposite kind of exchange. He termed these 'complementary processes' where the dominant characteristic is that participants exchange *exactly the opposite behaviors*: the more I pursue, the more you recede, the more you insist you are in charge, the more I seek your direction; the more you challenge me, the more I submit. In his analysis Bateson argued that any pattern that is too symmetrical requires one participant to do what is unexpected: to offer an honestly complementary response that will interrupt the cycle of escalation and misunderstanding. And if the pattern is too complementary, the introduction of a genuinely different response can act as a circuit breaker to this one-up/one-down pattern.

As Dr Quine was aware, in her long-term work with Rouga it would be disastrous to allow an overly symmetrical (or complementary) pattern to exist. She knew that if she was experienced by Rouga as overbearing, this would lead to a vicious circle that would cause blow-back, a reaction that would have the opposite effect of opening up the new space she was interested in developing. She wanted to find a form of engagement that neither colluded nor collided (Furlong, 2002). This reasoning is exactly why Steve de Shazer, the pioneer of the solutions focused practice school, was adamant it was counter-productive if practitioners pathologized clients – called them 'resistant' (de Shazer, 1984) or, more broadly, 'in denial', 'insightless' or 'uncooperative' – if the client had a different opinion to that of the professional.

Longer-term work, like work of any duration, requires the practitioner to be able to dance in a number of styles. Finding ways to invite the client to engage in, and stay engaged with, building their relationships with others is an art, but it is not art for art's sake.

The assessment process

As discussed earlier, supportive relationships cannot be dispensed to clients; no adult gets a voucher entitling them to one good-enough portion of love and respect. Apart from a lucky few, relationships have to be earned and learned, and it is no small challenge to turn it around if there is an insufficient quality of affiliation in someone's life. This is especially true if a person has learned to be defensive, even to a degree phobic, about the vulnerability relationships occasion (see Chapter 3). Believing in the importance of relationships the practitioner can make a good, even convincing, case to their clients that their happiness and wellbeing would be likely to improve if they felt connected, loved, and respected, but where does this get you? If the timing is misplaced, such a discussion can be like distributing menu cards in a famine (to again repurpose one of Freud's tart quotes).

If the timing and attunement are right, if the dialogue coincides with a reflective moment, the client might agree with you. This agreement could be expressed strongly – 'For sure, what do you think! Of course I'd like to get on better with people.' Or you might hear something wistful – 'It would be great to feel someone liked and valued me, but it's never been like that so I don't' think so.' With some clients you get to hear what is both poignant and defiant: 'Yeah, fat chance. Who'd want a loser like me got me for a partner? In your dreams fella.' Even some who are well motivated and materially well resourced are not able to simply 'pull their socks up' or 'lift their game' when it comes to relating to others. Attempting to relate well for those who have not learned to do so can be as frustrating as trying to do Chinese algebra. Realizing the goal of bettering connectedness will not automatically advance from a wish or even an intention, but it is often a good start.

It is impossible, of course, for the practitioner to wave a magic wand so that a client immediately acquires the values, attitudes, and skills that equip them to engage in and sustain respectful relationships. Positive outcomes cannot be conferred. As with any other professional goal, such as empowerment, this aspiration can only be approached by way of the participants joining together in a process where the desired endpoint is reached only after there has been a beginning and, most often, a cloudy and extended middle phase.

In this process an early, if not initial, point is for the practitioner to make a relational assessment optimally, but not necessarily, in concert with the client. This sub-process involves checking in for a sense of the client's relational strengths and the areas that might require further support and development. A simple, all-purpose and innovative way to do this is to build a picture using the following categories:

- the balance between the autonomous and the relational self;
- the client's actual relational context.

The relational context is the material network within which the client is located. This dimension is empirical and has a specific geography that can be externalized using established formats such as eco-maps, sociograms, and genograms. The balance between the autonomous and the relational self is where the original take on assessment resides, and its meaning needs to be briefly elaborated before proceeding.

Freya Mathews, a feminist philosopher, proposed in her book *The ecological self* (1995) that each person can be considered to have an *autonomous* and a *relational* aspect to their selfhood. Introduced in Chapter 1, this formulation is fundamental to this current project. The proposition is that each of us is composed of these two reciprocally related, dynamically opposed, and yet hopefully well-balanced aspects of the self. As developed for practitioners by Paterson (1996), neither aspect should dominate: too much of the autonomous leads to isolation and the tendency to ignore or even exploit the other; too much of the relational and there is an insufficient degree of self-determination and a tendency to be overly other-oriented, to interpersonal fusion, and to experience poor self-regard. According to Paterson, each client (and each professional or citizen more generally) has a characteristic profile with respect to these aspects and their relationship with each other. Each of us can be characterized in our autonomous/relational patterning; each of us has our attributes and limits (Furlong, 2003a).

The regulative assumption in this formulation is that health and wellbeing depend on there being an energizing dynamo between the autonomous and the relational poles of being. Too much charge at one pole compared to the other and there will be an asymmetry, a lack of balance between the rival contentions. Such an imbalance preempts the generative synthesis that is optimal for the holistic functioning of the self and social relations.

This is story making, but it is a fiction that can be used to serve an ethical and a practical purpose. Using this metaphor as a frame, the suggestion being put forward is that practitioners, hopefully in collaboration with their clients, can use criteria associated with autonomy and criteria that are associated with relationality to develop and write up a kind of scorecard. This informal assessment can then be used to externalize where the client is at with respect to the question of balance.

The balance between the autonomous self and the relational self

What is required to make a relationship tick? Many authors and researchers have examined this question. There is a publishing industry that has developed with respect to romance and marriage (see, for example, Schmitz and Schmitz, 2010), but there is also an abundant literature around workplace relationships (Rosier, 2001), friendships (Gallagher, 2005), and so on. For the current purpose a simple claim is put forward: the values, attitudes, and skills required to conduct good quality personal relations are based on participants having a good-enough balance between their 'autonomous' and their 'relational' selves. This is obviously a very crude claim yet, in the context of the larger argument, it is being used as a 'regulative fiction', a frame that can hold the picture together (Khan, 1971). Hopefully, the reader will come to agree that there is an intuitive appeal in the idea that there should be a quality of balance between the *autonomous* and *the relational self*. There is an ethical and a practical sense in there being a generator, a dynamo that has two contradictory poles, in the action of these elements.

In what follows, an outline of a broad-brush approach to assessment is presented which is grounded on the premise that a balance between the autonomous and the relational is associated with health and wellbeing. It is acknowledged that this is an unproven, and quite possibly untestable, proposition. The absence of scientific warrant noted, the premise that is advanced here has the advantage of a firm grounding in feminist, systems, and ethical theory.

An analogy might be helpful. Walking is a deceptively complex undertaking as what is required biomechanically is the achievement of what has been termed 'dynamic balance'. Dynamic balance is a highly sophisticated accomplishment as a functional, two-legged gait requires a tremendous degree of neurological and musculo-skeletal coordination: think how ungainly even the most advanced two-legged robots are. To be in a relationship requires a similar, if presumably far greater, degree of difficulty. Relationships (and there are so many different kinds) require participants to be able to establish and maintain a dynamic balance within an almost unimaginable set of possible conditions.

At one pole of this dynamo each participant has to be able to maintain an independent position and point of view: how do I feel? What do I want? How do I understand this situation? Have I a preferred choice? This point is never a stand-alone entity, even if you or I think it is. Your internal narrative and experience may be organized on the basis that 'I am autonomous and distinct from all others and the environment I live within', but in fact, this is not true as indigenous cultures, feminist scholarship, systems theory, and ecological ethics tells us. No one is independent as humans are social, interdependent begins who are inevitably open rather than closed systems. Closed systems are not living systems; living systems have to have a coordination of inputs and outputs, sustainable exchanges, with their environment, otherwise they cannot function well (or they simply die).

If these exchanges are relatively unbalanced, are asymmetric, but to a degree that is not deadly, the organism will survive, but will do so with its quality of life compromised. What enables a single person to have exchanges that are sustainable, even optimal? What is required is a quality interface, a set of boundary conditions that are appropriate, if there is to be a reasonable degree of fit between organism and environment. When it comes to the interpersonal, rather than the crudely physical, aspects of life, it is the *relational self* that acts as this interface. In contrast to the *autonomous self's* inward-looking agenda, the relational self is concerned with looking out, with others, with empathy, with accountability, with negotiation, and so forth, in order to ensure there is a quality of fit with the milieu.

In this formulation the *relational self* finds its dialectical opposite in the *autonomous self*. Between the two there is endless tension, a clash, and a conflict, which generates rather than destroys. Rather than either/or, there is the dynamo of difference where the one sparks the other. Yet, if there is too much power in the one, there is less vitality in the whole. If there is too much energy in the relational self, for example, there is a tendency towards unsustainable self-sacrifice. If there is too much energy in the *autonomous self*, there will be a different set of non-sustainable asymmetries such as the phenomena of loneliness, self-preoccupation, and the unethical exploitation of others.

Why is this story being introduced? Imagine you are beginning to work with a client. Perhaps it is your practice, or your agency's, to administer a standardized diagnostic or functional assessment. Whether you do this or not, if you are interested in experimenting with developing the client's relational base, a constructive step can be to schematically give a value to each of the skills and attitudes required for a vigorous *autonomous self*. Key criteria are listed in Table 7.2. Although it is not recommended for the current purpose, each of these criteria could be annotated with respect to the literature, for example, being able to 'identify and regulate feelings' could be referenced to Goleman's (1997) notion of 'emotional intelligence' or Orbach's (1999) of 'emotional literacy'.

Table 7.2: Elements of the autonomous self

- Confidence and self-entitlement
- Assertiveness, both in terms of self-projection and self-protection
- Self-management: self-determination, independence, self-reliance, personal agency
- Awareness of own desires, interests, and thoughts
- Internal locus of control, choose goals, make choices
- The capacity to identify and regulate feelings

Rather than getting into detail it is possible to use the above criteria to quickly build an impression, a broad-brush appreciation, of the robustness of a client's *autonomous self*. For example, if person X presents as particularly shy, and/or tells you that they feel unworthy, it means they are unlikely to rate highly on 'confidence and entitlement'. This gives the practitioner, and the client, a possible goal with respect to the *autonomous self* to work on: unless a person has a reasonable degree of self-worth they will tend to avoid, or be exploited in, relationships. If the other dimensions of the autonomous self are considered, it is possible to thicken this description. Vignette 12 is a case in point.

VIGNETTE 12: JARVIS

Jarvis is a well-spoken man in his early thirties, attending a fee-for-service psychotherapy practice on the gentrified edge of a large Australian city. As he put it, he had been "nudged" to attend by his ex-partner Seher: "She told me, 'You've stalled, fallen in a hole. Maybe you're depressed or something else. Go and see someone, it can't hurt. See this woman Rose.'"

Rose asked the standard assessment questions and Jarvis answered simply, without much elaboration, over the first half of the 50-minute interview.

"Yes, I am embarrassed, for sure," he said, about finding himself a client of a professional therapist; no, he was not sleeping or eating well; no, he had no history of emotional or psychiatric problems (nor did anyone in his family); yes, his mood, energy level, and libido were lower than normal; "Yes, I am going over things, and going over things – over and over again" and, "No, I am not thinking of killing myself." A little later he returned to the question of self-harm and repeated, "No, really, I've no plan to do that. [But] yes, I am really sick of all this. It's like I've got the handbrake full on – and I'm trying to drive my life somewhere! I'm going only half-pace, less, and I'm going as hard as I can. Worse, I'm not even heading in a straight line!"

During this briefing Jarvis appeared both disheartened and agitated. Speaking more intensely, he said he had lost "pretty much all I used to own – the value of my shares, the equity I had in my [inner city] unit, my pied-à-terre I used to call it, my bolt hole, my cave – it's all gone, down the gurgler. Like my confidence: shot."

In this statement Jarvis seemed to exhibit a degree of narcissism, but Rose did not believe this was the best formulation for his presentation. He was not manipulative, nor was he uncaring, at least in the abstract, and he was, to some degree likeable, albeit feckless.

Although there is little information here, it could be surmised that Jarvis is reasonably confident and has a fair to strong sense of his own entitlement. He is able to be assertive and can make decisions for himself; yet, on the other hand, he seems somewhat unreflective and out of touch with his feelings. Such a broad-brush outline provides a glimpse of Jarvis' strengths and, as the Jungians say, his shadow side. Respectfully, and in a provisional way, practitioners can discuss the impression they have built up with their client. Hopefully, this dialogue will be the seed for a collaborative plan.

Since the publication of Robert Alberti's *Your perfect right: A guide to assertive behavior* (1970) and Manuel Smith's *When I say no, I feel guilty: How to cope using the skills of systematic assertiveness therapy* (1975), the behavioral end of the above has been the object of 'social skills' and 'assertion training' programs for some decades. In such programs clients are introduced to the importance of, and are invited to rehearse, certain behaviors: the making 'I-statements'; the use of repetition as a technique for getting what they want, for example, if a product or a service is faulty; and basic negotiation tactics. Generally, the principle is to educate clients towards a competence in behaviors that maximize choice and minimize the chance of being walked over. The emphasis is on the assertion of personal rights.

Given the immediate focus concerns the establishment and maintenance of relationships, it follows that a rehearsing of, and some mastery over, such behaviors contribute an important building block: if a relationship is to be successful and healthy, each party should be heard, not be used by the other, should know what they want and be able to ask for it, and so forth. As advocates for their clients, it follows that service providers will prioritize this kind of approach as it concerns maximizing client rights and choices. This is a goal that is obviously important for those who have frequently been disenfranchised and practically disempowered.

This line of approach is familiar and comfortable to practitioners yet, more broadly, it has a strong cultural logic to Western citizens. This broader resonance is occasioned as the above specifications – to be able to speak up, to be self-managing, etc – are drawn from a language all citizens have learned and are expected to speak: the vocabulary and grammar of individualization. They are about her, or him, or me, getting on with it, about the assertion of rights, the promotion of individual interests, feelings and desires, and so forth. The focus is on the individual rather than on their relationships.

In contrast to the assumption that relationships come naturally, the skills and attitudes required for relational health are anything but spontaneous. Yet even if they are not automatic, they may be learned. What makes for a strong relational self consists of a suite of more abstract and complex operations. Towards an approximation of this set, the following criteria – noting they are increasingly complex – could be the subject of a focused attention.

Clients can rate themselves on each of these criteria. The effect of such a process is not simply bibliometric. Rather, to be engaged with this appraisal is itself interventive as it is an analogue activity that itself begins to bring the relational into focus. If the first of these criteria is taken up, a practitioner might ask a client to consider their aptitude and attitude to 'warmth and sincerity'.

This could be done in more or less direct ways. One low-key option is to ask Jarvis, or any other client who seems socially disconnected, to consider and discuss with you the following statement: 'Years ago a satirist named Groucho Marx said "The secret to life is honesty and fair dealing. If you can fake that, you've got it made. What do you think?"' Jarvis might laugh; he might say 'He got that right', or he might just be confused. Although the statement may sound frivolous, like many who find the dance of social relating difficult, if not mysteriously alienating,

Jarvis might struggle with the concept of genuineness. How, he might wonder, can one take up different social roles and still be both authentic and polite? 'You can only be rude or lonely' he might assume. Engaging him around the theme of warmth and sincerity could, after all, stimulate an enquiry into what is an inherent thread within interpersonal relations. Much more will be examined in how relational themes can be incorporated into everyday practice, especially in Chapters 8 and 9. For now, the focus remains on assessment rather than the processes of professional action.

Returning to the Jarvis vignette, preferably with Jarvis' direct involvement the practitioner can direct attention to one or more of the other criteria relevant to the functioning of the *relational self*. That is, it is possible to take a reading of his capacity with respect to each of these criteria: how does he rate himself, and how do think he is going, with respect to 'empathy', his interest in, and aptitude for, 'fairness and accountability', his 'awareness of others', and so forth.

For the sake of argument, let's say he and you both reach the view that his aggregate of relational values, attitudes, and skills is less developed than those of his *autonomous self*. Around this view, a plan could nominate areas for further development with respect to:

• his capacity to identify and regulate his emotions, a capacity that is absolutely tied in to being in relationships, which relates to his *autonomous self*; and
• his function with respect to 'empathy' and 'fairness and accountability' which is associated with his *relational self*.

Without underestimating how difficult it can be to modify existing patterns, simply putting these goals into focus is itself an intervention that lifts into awareness categories of attention that had previously been in the background. This can be likened to what happens in a yoga class where the teacher may frequently direct the participant's attention to, say, the alignment of the head and the torso. Over time, this kind of instruction tends to be internalized, a development that embeds a different dynamic between bodily elements than had previously been present.

Similarly, if Jarvis came to engage in a genuine process of values clarification about fairness and accountability, this focus could become a theme, an adult learning transfer frame, that has the real prospect of shifting the relationship that had existed between his actions and his attitudes in his previous dealings with others; see Table 7.3 for a beginning list of the elements that are central to the relational self.

More generally, engaging in the exercise of considering the elements in, and the balance between, the relational and the autonomous self can give the practitioner and the client something of a map. Such an externalized representation can serve as an aid in both navigation and the gauging of movement. In so far as this occurs, this can be wonderfully orienting.

Table 7.3: Elements of the relational self

- Warmth and sincerity
- Empathy
- Fairness and accountability
- Social skills: assertiveness; ability to ask, answer, and be silent; initiate and maintain contact; negotiation skills; use of self-discourse
- Awareness of others: sufficient access to 'the generalized other'/'theory of mind' to be thoughtful of others
- Interpersonal literacy: being able to read and make judgments about social relations; to be able to modulate distance
- The capacity to be (relatively) intimate: to be able to coordinate meanings with another

Relational context

Having outlined the relative strengths and insufficiencies of the client's autonomous and relational self, a complementary step is to develop at least a broad-scale map of the client's actual interpersonal environment. This may sound a straightforward task, and a simple grid for undertaking this task will be introduced shortly. This said, in the current literature there is no consensus about how the interpersonally social is best depicted.

There are hundreds, if not thousands, of recognized methods for the diagnostic and functional assessment of individuals. Although the classification of individuals is an easier and more popular pastime, it comes as no surprise that there are also many frameworks for analyzing the client's relational space. One high-profile schema is the Global Assessment of Relational Functioning Scale (Mottarella et al, 2001). This is a standardized instrument that has achieved a degree of popularity in the mental health field to depict the patient's relational context. Like any instrument, however, it has both strengths and difficulties.

For example, given the mental health field tends towards hyper-individualizing, its use can be argued to be progressive; yet, this protocol can be critiqued as its construction exclusively privileges the connections individuals have with their nuclear family, a feature that is highly problematic in so far as the interest is in the overall *Gestalt* of relationships. That is, this instrument ignores, in effect pushes into an unseen background, extended family contacts and the broader class of social relations clients have, or might have, with the broader world of friendships, work, neighborhood, and leisure. Although it has the advantage of being validated, the scale therefore presents with a very substantial deficit given the narrowness of its scope. (Never believe it when the definite article is put before the term 'assessment': there are always multiple assessments that could be done so. Although a given assessment protocol can have distinct, even decisive, advantages in relation to a given purpose, it is not possible any single schema is comprehensive in the human and social sciences.)

The question of scope, of what social relations are included and excluded, is a crucial issue when it comes to relational assessment protocols. The two best-known schemas for mapping social relations are 'genograms', a form of assessment most often associated with family therapy practice (McGoldrick, 2011), and 'eco-maps', a harder-to-pin-down device that is regularly part of the 'person in environment' assessment process in the functional social work tradition (Snyder, 1997; Green and McDermott, 2010). Each schema has its strengths and its drawbacks, but it is important to note each shares a common goal, albeit more accentuated with the eco-map: to systematically trace out the actors in, the levels of, the relationships between, and the problems within, the client's relational ecology. It is not possible to formally present each of these schemas as this would be an extended task. For the current purpose a simple, one-paragraph summary is set out below which provides a brief conceptual introduction to each. Additionally, Figures 7.1 and 7.2 are presented as examples of how a simplified eco-map and genogram were used in a real situation: as a component in the process of assessment that a couple underwent in order to be considered for an adoption program.

Something like a Russian doll, in their basic form eco-maps place the client at the center of a set of concentric circles. The nearest of these is the 'micro-system' which is the realm of the client's immediate social contacts. Here, friends, associates, and family are specified as equally weighted players. Next is the 'meso-system' that consists of those formal sub-systems that are relevant to the client: employment, church, neighborhood, and so forth. The next is the 'macro-system' that comprises the institutional and cultural components that are relevant to the client, such as the legal and social security systems. (In some versions the broader layer of social structure, such as culture and ideology, is also presented.) The key idea with this schema is to work out where there is a mis-match, an 'absence of fit', between the needs of the client and the resources that are available to the client from their environment, and to identify whether this mis-match is caused by dysfunctions in relationship between component sub-systems (for example, a single mother might be in a dispute with her children's school) or are due to gaps or deficits in what is available to the client from the meso-, micro-, or macro systems.

Unlike the functionalist traditions in sociology that inform the making of eco-maps, genograms are derived from quite different sources. At their most basic they resemble the humble family trees where at least two, but far better three or more, generations are represented. Relationships are generally described using the conceptual vocabulary of structural family therapy (Minuchin, 1974). This vocabulary is highly normative and describes relationships between family members (as close, conflictual, etc), with respect to generational boundaries (rigid, porous, etc), and in relation to alliances, feuds and cut-offs. In its more complex forms, a clear effort is made to identify (usually thought to be problematic) intergenerational family patterns and traditions such as so-called 'unfinished business' of the past that is thought to be causing difficulties in the present for the 'indexed patient': the person who is the bearer of what is unresolved.

What are the respective benefits and drawbacks of eco-maps and genograms as methods for representing the relational world? Table 7.4 attempts to summarize this difficult calculus.

Figure 7.1: Using an eco-map in an adoption context: the 'first circle'

Of particular interest is that eco-maps, which are a supposedly systems-based schema, are actually individualistic in their operation: unlike genograms, eco-maps put the client, not social relations, at the visual center. This is interesting to a degree, even paradoxical. Nonetheless, in an ideal world there are definite advantages in practitioners constructing both an eco-map and a genogram. Such niceties noted, there is a good argument that it is often preferable to proceed in a more direct manner by asking the client about, and by then systematically building a picture that traces, 'the relational places' of strength and tension and where there might be a potential for a relationship be renovated or invented.

Figure 7.2: Using a genogram in an adoption context: representing four generations

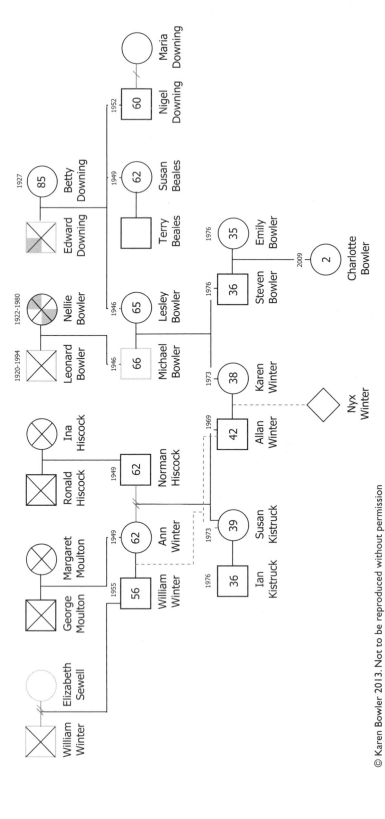

Table 7.4: Comparing genograms and eco-maps

	Genogram	Eco-map
Advantages	1. Puts the client into a relational context, albeit a limited one 2. Stresses legal, biological, and romantic linkages 3. Many workers, and some clients, see this representation as familiar and sensible 4. Acknowledges historical dimensions	1. Includes family as well as friends 2. Totally in the 'here and now' 3. Inclusive of complex levels of context
Disadvantages	1. Privileges traditional affiliations in that informal linkages are ignored, for example, friends, neighbors 2. Tends to be backward-looking, that is, past-oriented 3. Tends to pathologize families	1. Gives a flat, even unrealistic, relational picture as the different types of relationship are accorded an equal value 2. Has no sense of history 3. Is not an intuitive or familiar schema 4. Cannot be seen as an organization of data that has a systems logic as a single person (the client) is placed as the center of attention 5. Is conservatively functional in emphasizing adaptation

Using relational assessments in practice

Because the interpersonal is intimate, clients may find this realm, at least initially, difficult to discuss. In addition to being very personal, this area of life can seem abstract and opaque and many clients seem more comfortable talking about problems or, to put it baldly, the 'her', the 'him' and the 'me'. Action and event – 'he did this', 'she said that' – is what tends to be recounted. For this reason simple open questions are useful: 'Who do you think respects you most?' 'Who is most important to you?'

This style of approach can be complemented by closed questions that give the client a clear referent in composing their response: 'Is X the person you are most wanting to be closer to?' 'In terms of your extended family what relationship, or relationships, have strength for you?' 'Can you think of a relationship in your old friendship group where there has been conflict but where there might be some kind of chance this relationship could be renovated, renewed, or even remodeled?' The use of structured questions can be powerful as they serve as triggers to awareness.

This use of leading questions can be further elaborated by delineating between classes of relationship. For example, the practitioner might say something like this:

'There are many different kinds of connection. All of these different types of contact can be important. I can think of ten different kinds, different types, of relationship, and I know we have talked about some already. But, getting down to it, if I am going to understand your position so we can work out where to go first I would really like to build up my understanding of where you sit in relation to each, or at least most of, these ten different types of connection.

'We can do this over a few meetings if you prefer, and we can do this without this hassling you. Please, you take change by making sure you tell me if you think you are getting upset, or if it seems like I'm pushing you or boxing you in. Can you to tell me about where you are in relation to whether you are getting and giving love and respect in relation to…?'

Guiding the practitioner can be a set of the different kinds of social connections that attention can be drawn to. This set is not a copyrighted secret and can be given to the client so they can go through it at their convenience. This list of possible relationship types is broader than many expect it to be, a characteristic that has the potential to open up the horizon of possibilities, to stimulate a sense of new space, to the client. Remembering it often only takes one positive change to the stock of relationship to make a positive impact on the client's wellbeing and degree of optimism, seeing there are so many different kinds of possible relationships can itself be mobilizing.

This informal, interim list consists of the following types of relationship:

- Romance
- Friendship
- Inter-sibling connections
- Extended family: cousins, aunts, and uncles
- Parent–child connections
- Neighbors: old and current
- Leisure activities, more or less formal clubs, common interest groups
- The constructed environment: workplace relations; others in the group home; fellow students, teachers, etc
- Regularly met others such as shopkeepers, those who serve in bars, other regular customers where the person shops, eats, or drinks
- Contact with professionals, such as GPs, teachers, support workers, etc

In working through (or across) this list of possible domains for action there are a heap of nuances and mini-steps that can be taken along the way. The practitioner could ask, amongst a thousand possibilities, 'Have we left anyone out? Or 'Can you think of anyone else that is, has been or could be important to you?' Mindful it is necessary to proceed with an active concern to develop a genuinely collaborative process, in assessment-related work the more the practitioner embeds a focus on the relational in the regular dialogue between the practitioner and the client, the more this arena of concern is mainstreamed. In itself, this pattern constitutes a process of interventive questioning (Tomm, 1988).

Summary

What has been suggested is that the following guidelines are observed. Ask the client and yourself the following questions:

- Where do relational strengths currently present? Identify the positive relationships that exist right now.
- What relational conflicts currently exist? Identify the relationships where there is tension.
- Are there any current relationships that could be improved? Mindful that not all 'under-performing' or 'conflictual' relationships can be improved, what relational sites could be the subject of an attempt to be remodeled or revived?
- In what, if any domain of relationship, are there gaps? Nominate one, or more, categories of relationship that are currently missing.

Engaging clients in these kinds of dialogues can be highly evocative. Yet, if these conversations are conducted thoughtfully, their overall effect is much more likely to be associated with the mobilization of hopefulness than the essaying of regret and bitterness. There is naturally the potential for memories and feelings to be unsettled as the relational field is brought into focus, but this is not necessarily a negative by-product. It is important that the practitioner is both acknowledging and containing as it is to proceed with the positive, forward-looking spirit that is associated with narrative, strengths, and solution- focused approaches. Over the longer haul, emotionality and a positive tone tend to forge knowing partnerships.

Lastly, in most situations there is no point in making a fuss about, let alone fetishizing, the assessment process. An assessment is a formation, a mobile construction, which is only useful if it generates possibilities. If it helps clients and practitioners externalize their assumptions and their thinking, this is a creative practice. Once we have stepped back from a position, put it 'out there' so to speak, it is possible to walk around and inspect this thinking from different angles. This is the opposite of practices where so-called scientific assessments are used as labels, paralyzing descriptions that can 'become the cornerstone of an emergent identity' (Saleebey, 2003). In some settings there is an instrumental necessity to assess where the rule in operation is that a particular diagnosis has to made in order to access a service. For example, in many services potential clients have to be assessed as suffering from a mental illness or as having experienced trauma to be eligible for assistance.

Rather than assessment being understood as a 'this box must be ticked' procedure, in what has been ventured above the purpose has been to assess as in explore: to offer leads, ideas that can be investigated, with respect to the relational agenda.

Assessments, like record keeping in general, can be undertaken in ways that are defensive as well as in a manner that stimulates problem solving (Pawsey and Firestone, 1983). If a practitioner in their own practice or, even better, with the agency or broader service with which they are affiliated, is successful in having a relational component included in the design of assessment and record-keeping protocols, this can have a multiplier effect on how practice is conducted.

8
Relationship-building skills

Getting started | Addressing the client as a relational being |
Working systemically with individuals | Bringing in others: conjoint
work and its variations | Being creative with confidentiality
| Advanced relational work | Role of planners, managers, and
supervisors

Getting started

The task of this chapter is to present examples and concrete applications of a relationship-building approach. Based on the assumption that the right attitudes and values are in play, six distinct categories of action are discussed. The account begins with a core behavior, an action so simple it could be mistaken for an inconsequential formality. From this point the reader is asked to engage with descriptions of increasingly sophisticated activities before a final section discusses the role supervisors, planners, and managers can play in contributing to the relationship-building agenda. Material is presented on the following:

- The pragmatic importance of *addressing the client as a relational being*. Rather than talking to clients as autonomous beings, speaking to clients as social beings brings into focus what tends to be consigned into an opaque, if not invisible, background: the client's existence within an ongoing landscape of relationships.
- *The theme of working systemically with individuals:* this investigates how acting on behalf of the client tends to be detrimental to the prospects of improving the quality of the client's interdependencies. The focus of this material is to develop the conceptual skills associated with systemic practice, with taking up an inclusive and multilateral perspective rather than acting as if you were the client's unilateral agent.
- *Bringing in others: practicing with more than one person.* Practical ideas are introduced here that are relevant to those situations where it is preferable, or simply necessary, to have contact with one or more, of the client's significant others. These ideas are organized around two activities: how to 'convene' and how to 'conduct' multiparty sessions.
- *Approaching the issue of confidentiality creatively.* Following the initial discussion of confidentiality in Chapter 4, this more detailed sub-section presents concrete ideas practitioners can use to deal with confidentiality pro-actively. These

ideas concern beginning work with new clients, and also how arraignments with established clients might be reorganized. It is argued that a negotiated degree of information exchange with one of more important others in the client's ecology can be reconciled with preserving, even consolidating, the trust between the practitioner and the client.

- Examples of *advanced relational work:* as reference points for further enquiry, three advanced examples are outlined – the narrative tradition's development of witnessing; group practice with men who are violent; and family group conferencing within a restorative justice framework.
- As a coda, the chapter concludes with a discussion of how planners, managers, and supervisors can play a tertiary role in furthering a relationship-building agenda.

Each of these sub-sections is relatively extended. Taken as a whole this makes the chapter substantial, but each of the components is more or less independent and can be approached as a specific unit.

When it is initially encountered, some of what follows may feel unfamiliar, even a little awkward. What is important is for the practitioner to remain confident that the theoretical foundations that inform the approach are strong and legitimate. Being clear that the theory that drives relationship-building practice is well grounded will strengthen your resilience when you begin to experiment with the applications that express this commitment. At first, you are likely to be aware, perhaps even over-aware, that you feel uncertain as you think into, and begin to try out, the new actions that are discussed. Expect a few bumps and minor skirmishes. What makes this introduction easier to manage, what helps with the anxiety that always accompanies engagement with the new, is the knowledge that your efforts stand on attitudes and values you are prepared, even proud, to be identified with.

What will happen, and which can happen surprisingly quickly, is that those who identify with the logic of the approach inevitably become more sure-footed and clearer in their orientation. In turn, this comes across to others as having a confidently easy manner – having an appreciative attitude to the possibilities of relationships facilitates that combination of lightness and sure-footedness that optimizes the client's engagement with the introduction of a relational agenda. This claim is not made in order to be a product booster, a marketer of a pseudo-technical solution. It is made because being values-driven generates energy and daring. Given practice is an exercise in applied ethics (Paterson, 1996), taking up the relational agenda drives practice development far more authentically than the search for purely technical solutions. The quest for the quick-fix, for the magic bullet, might have colossal organizational and cultural allure, but what is low-tech and interpersonally real advances the long view with greater substance.

Addressing the client as a relational being

The material in this chapter proceeds from the less to the more complex in conceptualization and application. Starting right at the beginning, in its simplest expression the practice of deepening the client's relational base begins when the practitioner names and gives voice to the relational dimensions of the client's everyday life (Furlong, 2010b). This can be done in two different ways: literally and analogously.

First, and most obviously, it can be promoted by conversing with the client about, and bringing into the light, the significant others who are, or might be, in the client's orbit as real and active figures, talking to the client about the individuals who are part of their network, people who have their own names, unique biographies, interests, feelings, and perspectives, those who 'hail' the client as a social being (Jarre, 2011). Second, the relational nature of the client's existence can be summoned indirectly by way of discussing themes such as reputation and accountability, shame and pride, in conversations with the client. Each of these themes is predicated on the fact that every client is a socially embedded entity rather than an exclusively autonomous being. These two allied approaches are now examined in turn.

Talking with the client about the individuals who are part of their network can be understood as 'small talk', as little more than the preliminary chatting that proceeds getting down to the real business of focusing on what the client needs, wants, feels, or thinks. Rather than assuming the client's 'me, myself, I' should be the staple diet of each session, being interested in the client's real, or possible, others should not be dismissed as numb courtesy.

Everyone is familiar with those throwaway formalities, the 'how are the grandkids?' kind of inquiry, that expect only a nominal response. In contrast to these arid courtesies, actively naming and discussing the important individuals who comprise the client's network, getting a dialogue happening about the specifics of the client's connections with these unique others, has the function of constructing the client as a social being (Furlong, 2010b). Similarly, if the client reports they have few, if any, meaningful contacts, this invites an interest in, for example, a discussion of who the client would like to have as a partner or friend, mentor or colleague, neighbor or companion. In this theatre a premise is embedded: the autonomous self finds its healthy sibling in its interactions with an active relational self.

If the practitioner has a traditional, office-sited role, this kind of exchange can be begun in the pre-session chit-chat and then laced through the remainder of the meeting when this becomes a good option in terms of timing and content. If the practitioner has a less traditional role, such as a hands-on support worker, there are likely to be richly diverse opportunities to have relationally oriented conversations in the everyday moments of intimacy that take place along the way. These can pop up in the more casual moments when you are driving a client to an appointment, helping this person move their furniture, or simply hanging out in a residential unit playing table tennis. Although it might seem odd at first glance, the idea of constructing the client as a social being can be described generically.

VIGNETTE 13: JACINTA

Imagine you are meeting with Jacinta to work on a specific presenting problem. In different contexts this problem (which we will call 'P') could be an intensively practical concern, such as an acute financial issue or the need to secure accommodation. In a different presentation 'P' might be a problem of living that has a less immediate, more reflective status. For example, 'P' might be Jacinta's concern that she is experiencing a mid-life crisis and has to develop an alternative set of criteria for defining her identity in order to feel she is more than a shadow of her more vital, younger self. In another context 'P' might be Jacinta's long standing anger management issue.

However 'P' is composed, the practitioner's role is clear: to focus on 'P.' Whatever the presenting problem may be, the following claim is put forward: when it comes to talking about, and acting on, 'P' there will always be some scope to acknowledge and animate Jacinta's interpersonal ecology. A minimal attention to this dimension can be realized in simple questions and statements that address Jacinta as a relational being. For example, in a tone that is respectful and inclusive, the practitioner can ask Jacinta to name another who is important to her with respect to her problem (and/or more generally). 'Who do you talk to about P? Is there someone special?' If Jacinta nominates someone, or perhaps names several people, you have honored and acknowledged Jacinta's intimate social relations and the interpersonally social nature of her life.

This idea can be theorized within several different traditions. Social constructivists and narrative practitioners explicitly acknowledge the power of language and, from a somewhat different point of view, symbolic interaction theory has a sympathetic position. What is wanted are forms of address that signify the client as having a relational ontology given the transactional nature of everyday life. In a very particular way this is exactly what occurred when the worker spoke to Kylie's mother, summoned her, to act as an actual guardian rather than nominal mother (see Vignette 6, Chapter 7, p 131).

Symbolic interactionalists contend that humans become what they are treated to be: if I am denigrated, I tend to see myself as stupid; if I am treated as a opportunist robber-baron, that is how I will tend to act (Blummer, 1986). Within the terminology of critical theory, choosing to refer to the client as a relational being is an 'interpolation' (Althusser, 2006; Jarre, 2011), albeit in such a way as to deliberately repurpose its initial usage. That is, speaking to the client as a relational being hails – calls out to, even summons – the client in such a way as to imply, even impose, a particular form of personhood. In the current usage the intention is to construct the client as an ethical and interdependent being. If this lineage sounds grandiose, the principle is a simple one, and its implementation offers a sharp contrast to a pattern of communication that speaks to Jacinta as if she was simply an autonomous being who is at odds with 'them' – those others who are not on her side.

Once the client's *nested-ness* has been named, the practitioner can begin to find out more about, and to get on with the thickening and diversifying of, these connections: 'Does Joey see it the same way you do? Do you talk to him as much about it as you'd like? What do you think of the statement "a problem talked about is a problem halved?"' Relationally threaded discussions are in symbolic and practical contrast to recycling the received cultural and professional premise that 'P' should be understood as a private trouble.

If Jacinta cannot, or is not readily prepared to, name a person or persons who are involved, if not helpful, this provides the practitioner with information that is not definitive but which refines the set of possibilities that might warrant further enquiry and attention. Especially early on, it is not likely to be useful to push Jacinta about her contacts, but if the tone is at the caring end of light, if the practitioner can be both playful and engaged, more information can be sought at the same time as the practitioner embeds a quiet point: 'Wow, Jacinta, it seems to me someone as [organized, bright, tough, well-mannered, etc] as you has to have at least someone in your corner. I'd be really surprised, and a bit worried, if there is nobody who gives a toss, but maybe I'm wrong.' Whether the client immediately follows up with the answer 'Nope, there is no one,' the idea that the client does not perceive she has personal support offers the practitioner an initial, albeit tentative, entry to the assessment category 'significant other network'. As examined in Chapter 7, knowledge of the content of this category is required for a contextual assessment.

Asking a client about who offers them back up – 'Who keeps the air in your tyres?' – can be understood as a particular kind of 'support question' within the strengths-based practice tradition (Saleebey, 2003). Often, the practitioner has to be nimble in these inquiries and to be careful not to gloss over, or to overly dramatize, the sense of loneliness, even betrayal, many clients experience. Clients might claim to be indifferent, or even proud, about being alone, and this position should not be initially challenged, yet over time, it is good to give some air to the disappointments and hurts this person feels they have suffered from others. Unlike the 'lets all be positive' ideology (Ehrenreich, 2010), there is no advantage in the reflex to move the focus from what has been painful. This noted, as Saleebey has discussed, it is rare that there is no one in the client's life who offers a degree of contact and support, even if the perception of isolation is the client's dominant experience.

If the client tells you no one comes to mind, this can be part of an 'I have reason to feel aggrieved' attitude to life. For many years a client may have felt let down, isolated, hard-done-by. In this circumstance, if the timing and tone is sensitive, practitioners often have the chance to gently perturb such generalizations. Without becoming wedged into taking up an 'always look on the bright side' speech that

Pollyanna would use – it almost never pays to get into an arm wrestle – a curious and persistent environmental scan is likely to identify the odd exception. There may be the shopkeeper with whom a friendly word is sometimes shared, the neighbor who keeps an eye on the client's aging mum, the aunt who keeps in touch. There will nearly always be figures the client endows with a degree of grace, even if these figures are kept deep in the background or have passed on. Looking for exceptions is a form of appreciative enquiry. Results from these informally conducted studies add information and awareness that is of vital interest to both client and practitioner. Relational gaps, as well as what might be termed assets, are important to recognize mindful that relationships should not be commodified.

These informal discussions are termed 'yarning' in the Australian vernacular. In these dialogues it is important not to dig up and agitate what might prove too disturbing. Your antennae have to be on alert as it is not responsible to leave clients vulnerably undefended. Nonetheless, being attuned to this possibility, and yet holding to the specific purpose of your role, more risky enquiries can sometimes be constructively made: 'You've told me you do not have anyone who is there to look after you. Was there ever someone, someone who is no longer with you, who used to have this special role?'

If the client says 'Yes,' you can ask 'Has that person gone away, that is, have they separated from you, or are they no longer alive?' In either case you could follow up by asking, 'What was their name?', maybe even going so far as to say 'What do you think, Jacinta, what might this person want to say to you if they were still with you?' This is consistent with the narrative therapy idea it can be good to say hello to, rather than to let go of, those who have been special to us who are no longer alive (White, 1988). As well as cueing sad feelings, everyday conversations can also summon up memories endowed with affection and affirmation – 'good objects' in the parlance of psychoanalysis – if the practitioner is not shy or scared. As Kay Redfield Jamison, a noted professor of psychiatry, sufferer of bipolar disorder and autobiographer of grief, recently noted, we humans never lose the loved people who are no longer physically with us. Rather, we change the kind of relationship we have with these people (Jamison, 2009).

In naturalizing the habit of addressing clients as relational beings, practitioners act to contest the bias of the larger culture that is to solicit the autonomous self. When addressed as a 'person who values others' or as 'someone who feels isolated and hungry for more closeness', it is a social being that is being hailed. This form of address can easily be extended, for example, in talking with the client about wanting 'to be a true friend', 'a caring brother', 'an engaged colleague', and so forth. Such discussions narrate clients as relational and ethical agents rather than as self-interested, needy entities. Get the right mood and momentum going, it can also be possible to ask questions such as 'How is X faring: is she doing OK? You've mentioned she has had a bad run.' To ask about another, or others, introduces the power of thoughtfulness and perspective taking, and encourages ethical thinking.

A second method of introducing the relational is to pick up on, even raise, themes that are embedded in this dimension. The client might mention (more or less in passing) being keen to be respected or feeling upset about not being respected. Like many other key social themes, respect is a public phenomena, a matter that is concerned with the person's relationship with their primary audiences, whether these are material, such as the living and named people with whom the client works or lives, or with audiences that are internalized, such as grandparents. Asking about, and perhaps coming back to, questions of respect – or reputation and honor, purpose and accountability, shame and face, and so forth – enlivens and exercises the relational self. There is no end to the possibilities for challenging the sovereignty of the self as a supposedly free-standing republic.

As argued in Chapter 4, practitioner habits that concern being neutral and non-judgmental have sometimes been conflated with the goal of encouraging clients to be independent. This slippage was based on an odd, even unaccountable, notion of independence as it was assumed that client autonomy, and the practitioner's advocacy of this attribute, was an incontestably ethical stance rather than representing a debatable ideological position. Practice is inevitably partial and not neutral; this cannot be avoided. The question is: in the applied ethics of practice, what kind of being is being called forth?

Accountability and altruism

Relationally oriented conversations with clients can take many forms. For example, rather than taking the position that guilt is necessarily a negative emotion, a feeling that is neither useful nor progressive, it is possible to weave into the practice dialogue connections between altruism and personal accountability. Traditionally, the therapeutic habit has been to say that guilt and shame are ugly and inhibiting and are aversive to the empowered self.

A contrary view is to say that delivering on our responsibility to others is conducive to feeling good about ourselves. If the timing of the discussion is right, it is rare to find someone who would not acknowledge that 'doing good' for another – their cousin, their friend, their neighbor – is not an honorable behavior as it contributes to both fair relationships and a pride in oneself. This theme can be voiced in terms of building a positive internal and external reputation in how you behave with others. Without being stipulative or moralistic, it is possible to discuss conscience and interpersonal ethics as spokes in the relational wheel.

For example, you might say to Jacinta: 'You've told me it was [the now deceased] Aunt Edie who often had a ready smile and a friendly word for you, and you felt good about yourself when this happened. This support meant heaps to you didn't it? Knowing what this meant to you, is there anyone special who you are trying to have the same effect on?' Taking this theme further, it is possible a supportive challenge might be soldered together: 'Could you manage a compliment or two for X [someone Jacinta has named]? If you are not that type, or you don't know now how to do that, how else might you let X know that you appreciate her efforts and intentions? Can we talk about how this could be done in a way that would be likely to work for X, and also for you? What do you think: would a nod, a pat on the back, a thumbs up or a big smile be the way to let her know you are in her corner? What are your thoughts?'

It is not necessary to use the old *Gestalt* therapy technique of placing empty chairs in the consulting room, and having the client give each of these names, to allow third parties to have a symbolic presence. (This practice was generally used to give the client the chance to 'vent', to sound off at, significant others, whilst the present purpose is quite different.) However it is done, finding ways to externalize the interiorized other can bring Jacinta's important others to life in your mind and, more importantly, in hers. This can be done in relation to those the client is currently in contact with, and, if the practitioner is thoughtful and agile, also those who are no longer proximal or who may no longer be alive.

A thread in discussions about accountability is the theme of empathy (see Chapter 4). Empathy, a compassion for others, is associated with fairness and can be practiced. This can be especially important for those who feel besieged. When a person is on guard they tend to become self-referential which, in turn, leads to the loss of the imaginative connection with the feelings, interests, and points of view of others. Goleman (2006) and Szalavitz and Perry (2010), for example, regard empathy as a core element in interpersonal literacy and everyday discussions that invite clients to perspective-take, to put themselves into the shoes of others, can be cumulatively interventive: 'If X doesn't see it the same as you do, where might she be coming from? Might she also have had experiences that have taught her to be defensive, to be cut-off, from your needs and the feelings of others?'

Being able to summon up, and then to be able to dance with, the emotions and views of imagined others is about practitioners chatting with clients in the service of what could be interpersonally practical. If the practitioner wishes to introduce the relational, and this dimension is not obviously central to the task with which the client and the practitioner are engaged, this should be not be done in a way that distracts from, or is felt to trump, the core business; nor should this interlacing of the relational with the everyday work of practice feel like it is overbearing or an interrogation. Best if one remains light on one's feet, and interpersonally intuitive, in trying to blend the relational into one's everyday work. Mostly, this is about being an active listener, being on alert for the implicitly relational spaces which can be traced out in the process of everyday discussion. This sensibility is not expressed in being centre-stage as the expert, the star, who intervenes with aplomb. Rather, it is expressed in asking oneself what kinds of possibilities, what kinds of attitudes, values and behaviors, am I trying to co-create here?

In one particular sense 'yarning' with the client about their current, past, and future relationships is simply to observe a carefully chosen professional aesthetic. If the expressions of this sensibility are considered collectively, they make up the most basic element in the execution of a practice that is relationally oriented. In such a practice the next level of conception and action is to seek to undertake work in ways that act in relation to specific interdependencies within which the client lives. This can be framed in terms of 'systemic work with individuals' and is the focus of the next section.

Working systemically with individuals

What is systemic work with individuals? Theoretically expressed it is the idea that practice should be organized to align with the principle that each client is an interdependent being who is embedded within a dynamic set of personal relationships. Two examples might clarify this idea: 'Vicky', an elderly woman with an intellectual disability, lives in an established group home. Those who know her noticed long ago that her moods seem to correlate with the happenings and atmosphere in this household. A second example is more complex, but is based on the same principle. 'Clare', an educated alternative thinking young woman, made a commitment to living in an alternative community many years ago. Despite going into this communal arrangement with "my eyes open", she reports she has been surprised at the degree to which her sense of wellbeing is responsive to the dynamics in the group.

What is apparent to an observer, if not necessarily to Vicky or Clare, is that the direction of causation is not linear in either case: Vicky and Clare's moods, beliefs, and behaviors also have an impact on the functioning of their context. As is the case with any ensemble, the whole affects the parts as the action of the parts effects the whole. In the language of systems theory, this co-varying quality has been termed 'co-regulation' (Simon et al, 1985). It follows that working well with, and for, Vicky or Clare, involves acting in ways that are mindful of their membership of their particular local ecologies.

The phrase 'systemic work with individuals' is likely to have arisen within the family therapy tradition even if its exact genealogy is debatable (see, for example, see Weakland, 1983). Whatever its origins, the logic of the approach has a purchase that is far broader than any reference to 'family' might imply, and a number of texts have explored this larger ambit more or less extensively (Boscolo and Bertrando, 1996; Hedges, 2005). Mindful that 'systemic work with individuals' is a frame with a potentially broader application than to work with families, a good illustration of what it involves can be seen in the work of an old-fashioned solo general practice. Imagine you are in such a role and work in an isolated rural setting.

Over many years in this role you will have contact with every member of each family that is on the practice's books: mothers, sons, grandparents. And you will come to know about, and most likely meet with, some of this family's in-laws, cousins, and broader extended family. Over the years you are likely to develop relationships with, and acquire a reasonably detailed knowledge of, each of these people. Even if you are not much interested, you are inevitably likely to learn a great deal about this group itself: its history, vicissitudes, achievements, and culture. As with the other families you work with, you will come to know what affects one person in a family, for example, if a father has a serious farm accident, that such event will have consequences that ricochet through the lives of other family members. You will also be aware that all who are in this orbit will be affected if there are long-term sequelae from this accident as these consequences can reverberate loudly over an extended period, perhaps even across generations. You know it is simply not possible for any single member of a tribe to be an island.

In this context your key role is to treat individuals for any medical issues that are presented to you. Along the way, you will inevitably also be told much that is interpersonal in its nature. Mothers will communicate to you, sometimes indirectly but still poignantly, how hard it is, maybe even how impossible it is, for them to carry the practical and emotional care of children, partners, and aging parents. If not in so many words, men will tell you they are depressed because of the mounting farm debt, the impact of extreme weather events, or the fighting that is occurring between soon-to-be adult children about who will take over the family farm; one partner may have told you it is so bad they think they might go mad if they do not separate from their spouse. In embarrassed tones, perhaps a daughter will tell you there are double standards when it comes to how sexuality is understood by their parents, or one of the sons might let slip he has done something transgressively he is feeling guilty about. Like many aspects of general practice, these matters are at the interface of medicine, psychotherapy, and family counseling.

Do you simply hear out those who bring up non-medical issues, or do you discuss these awkward complications with the individual in front of you? Of course, you keep confidences as you have a duty of care to each individual patient. In this context, at the back of your mind, might you say something like this to yourself?

> 'Each of my patients is a member of a group. This ensemble is a set of reciprocally influential parts, a collective of mutual interest. What I think, say, and do has to be informed by this knowledge. I should respond to the person in front of me – this particular family member – in relation to the knowledge I have of their context and the part they play in this cast of characters. I want to act holistically, but not moralistically. This seems the ethical imperative, the bigger mission, that goes beyond simply not breaching my professional code of ethics.'

In so far as the above makes sense, you have the mindset of a systemic practitioner. Broadening the reference out from 'family' to 'social group', informed by this same aesthetic you will understand it is impossible that each of your individuals ever live in, nor can they find meaning in, a vacuum.

This can be imagined visually. Humans are social beings who interact with each other, rather like elements in a child's mobile. Imagine and think how this works. Cause one element to experience a change in its speed or the direction of its rotation and this will perturb the cluster it is part of. As one cluster in the mobile experiences a change in momentum, so the whole ensemble is prompted to function in a changed way – a collateral change of status that then affects each cluster, and each element, in the general whole. Such patterns of reciprocal influence do not proceed in a linear manner. Rather, a transitional event occurring at one node can sometimes stimulate contrary, even unexpected, changes in direction and energy status elsewhere in the system.

Just like the relationship between element, cluster, and whole in a mobile, individuals do cartwheels in and through, across and over, the lives of their significant others. Beyond traditional doctoring, in a best-case scenario this perspective has long been understood in the work of other local authority figures such as Parish clergy. Mindful that persistent sexism, and other regressive attitudes, has been evident in how these traditional authority figures have often gone about their business in the past, in the ideal case these figures possess a similarly systemic mindset. They know how important it is to be able to reconcile the interests of the one with the whole.

In therapeutic circles the idea a practitioner could work systemically with individuals was first formalized in the 1980s. This idea had a very specific context when it was introduced. This meaning relates to, but is also quite different to, the way this term is currently being defined. The interest here is to repurpose the original use so that its meaning aligns with the idea of a practitioner who is mindful of human interdependence and who wishes to practice in ways that respect and enhance the quality of relational reciprocities. Before developing the usage that is preferred here, it is important to contrast this with how the construct was initially understood and deployed.

The idea of systemic practice with individuals was initially put forward in order to offer family therapists an 'in', a way to proceed, when it was not practicable, or it was not possible to persuade whole family groups to attend. That is, up until that point the premise was that the family therapist had to, as Napier and Whitaker (1978) proposed, win the battle for structure and control so as to convene whole family meetings. This was thought necessary as it was believed that individual problems persisted due to the homeostatic tendency displayed by the family as a kind of closed system – movements towards positive change, so the theory went, would be evened out by a reassertion of the problematic patterns of relations. This tendency of systems to maintain a 'steady state' meant that the symptoms experienced by the so-called 'indexed patient' would then tend to persist until a qualitative change in the organization of the system was prompted (Simon et al, 1985). On this basis, having whole families present was essential so that charismatic therapists, like Salvador Minuchin, could properly analyze, and then work in the here-and-now with, all members to enact new and more functional patterns.

Before narrative, strengths, and solutions ideas became prominent, the orthodox view held that it was these behavioral repetitions – the 'pattern that connects' (Bateson, 1973) – that were the real problem. It followed that it was these patterns that ought to be the proper target for intervention. To change the dance, the fixed rules that organized the conduct of the ensemble required the therapist to meet with all those involved in order to interrupt ('perturb') this pattern. There was, and still is, a degree of logic in this understanding, but it was pushed much too far as it entailed a universalized view that it was the family that was the unit of pathology. The problem was not the problem, it was 'them'.

The idea that it was possible to work systemically with single individuals remained true to this received epistemology but differed in its tactics. Rather than having to meet with all concerned, in this revision it was suggested that if one person could be prompted to reposition themselves in the dance, and if this change could be maintained despite the (sometimes dramatic) events that tended to reform the old pattern, then the rules of the game would come to be reorganized. Patterns tended to be stubborn, but they were fungible. As Gregory Bateson, in so many ways the key conceptualist informing this approach, was said to have remarked 'the ripple that lasts longest lasts longer than the ripple that doesn't last as long.'

At the time the premise was that every individual who presented with a problem was thought of as the 'indexed patient', the 'symptom bearer'. Irrespective of whether it was the young man with schizophrenia, a woman who was depressed, a child who was refusing to attend school, this was the mindset. In other words, it was *never* the presenting issue itself that was understood as the real problem. That one person happened to be experiencing a difficulty was understood to be a signal, a metaphor, that pointed to the underlying problem that was, at its core, family dysfunction. That one person was suffering was certainly unfortunate, yet it was assumed this was a signal that had the potential benefit of bringing the family into an engagement with the bone fide expert who could really help. What was assumed was that the family itself – its dynamics and customs, its beliefs and its communicational sequences – were the root of the real problem. In effect, it was believed that the person with the problem was a kind of victim. This person could, it was thought, be rescued from this role when a new and more functional pattern of interaction was prompted.

This theorizing took place in very different days . At that time it was assumed every symptom had a function. This disrespectful principle held there was a secondary gain to the family from the son's schizophrenia, that the woman's depression was a symptom disguising the problems with the parent's marriage, or that the child's refusal to attend school allowed a homeostasis which preserved the family, and so on. It is now well recognized that this amounts to an institutionalized form of family-blaming. Yet, it would be unfair to single out family therapists as the sole exponents of this dark but persistent practice (see Endnote 3).

Whilst in the past some practitioners sought to manipulate families so that they might become better environments for their patient, there is now a consensus that in almost all cases families, indeed everyone in a significant other grouping, is doing the best they can. There is no reason to attempt to trick those with whom the client is, or might be, embedded. As the solution-focused tradition says, the problem is the problem (de Shazer, 1984). There are, of course, exceptions as some friends do bully their 'mates', some adults do exploit, bash, or steal from their aged parents, some men are dangerous to their partners and offspring, and some young people are violent to their siblings. That such injustices do occur does not mean that these transgressions are the norm. In the great majority of situations it is not a constructive starting point if practitioners are suspicious of the client's significant others.

What distinguishes current systemic practice from its outdated predecessor, what juxtaposes the premises of, for example, the infamous double-blind theory of schizophrenia (Bateson et al, 1956) to the relational building practices of today is that the practitioner does not assume it is their mission to rescue 'their' patient from the predations of others. On the contrary, the mission of those who work systemically is to think and act in ways that support the client's relationships with others. In the sense that the term 'systemic work with individuals' is currently being used, it is to make the point that it is essential for practitioners to know about the client's key networks, and to act in relation to the client's embededdness in these groupings. Broadly, the principle is to promote good quality partnerships within these linkages.

This is a nuanced position. It is definitely more complex than seeing oneself as the hard-charging advocate who assertively acts on behalf of a single client in relation to those who have an involvement with this person. In most situations, to simplistically act as the client's advocate to those with whom the client is engaged simply causes blow-back: it makes things worse as it enrages and alienates the client's others to have some come-lately professional be a blaming know-all. To act as a unilateral advocate is to assume the client is a standalone entity and, in effect, to believe it is right to shear off the client's interests from the interests of those with whom the client is connected. Working systemically is based on the premise of interdependence. Rather than seeing the client's others, such as that person's friend, carer, or partner, or, more broadly, the larger group of significant others who form the client's vital network, as either positively serving the interests of the client, or as 'a problem', is unhelpful as it causes the professional to take up a black and white, either/or attitude. It is preferable to understand those with whom the client is involved are *both* actual or potential resources to the client *and* are entities who have rights and interests that overlap with, but are not the same as, those of the client. Immanuel Kant's famous categorical imperative says never treat others as a means to an end. Similarly, relationships are an irreducible end and should not be understood as a means to serve the purposes of any one person.

At times clients do suffer abuse and victimization, exploitation and neglect, and if this is the case, being able to thoughtfully advocate on this person's behalf is a professional necessity. These anomalies are mostly outlier phenomena, and the simple effect of encouraging clients to set themselves and their interests in opposition to those with whom they are connected is counter-productive as it gets everyone into an 'us versus them' battle. A simple example not drawn from the practice domain might make this point clearer.

VIGNETTE 14: PETA AND CHARLOTTE

Peta is helping her friend Charlotte move her furniture into a new flat. At one point Peta and Charlotte are struggling to move a heavy desk and drawer unit. Charlotte has hold of the front of this unit and Peta has the weightier rear side. In the middle of this awkwardness Charlotte says: "Arrrh, my hand is jammed in the desk drawer!" Charlotte's tone is full of fright and pain, and her only thought is to get Peta to help her.

Peta reacts quickly and immediately drops her end, assuming this is what Charlotte wants her to do. Unfortunately, this is the opposite of what Charlotte hopes for because this puts an increased pressure on the edge of the drawer that is jamming Charlotte's fingers. Charlotte yells out: "Stop it, it's killing me. My hand's getting squeezed even tighter. Get it off me *please*."

Feeling like Charlotte is unfairly blaming her, Peta retorts "Stop yelling at me. I never intended to hurt you!" Charlotte, very much in pain, yells back "It's not about you! It's my hand that's jammed!" With a rising tide of indignation and impotence Peta loudly lets Charlotte know "I am only here to help" whilst saying under her breath, "This is so unfair, I'm out of here." Somehow, in a willy-nilly of effort by both women, Charlotte is able to get her hand free.

Charlotte is relieved, albeit still in pain and suffering a degree of shock. Peta is indignant and tells Charlotte "You were so unfair yelling at me. Surely you know I was not trying to hurt you!" Charlotte can't believe what she is hearing. Before she can think it over she says "Peta you are being a complete baby. What do you want me to do – to apologize to you because I was in pain?"

At this point Peta sees she only has two choices. She says to herself 'I can either walk out right now or I can be unfairly silenced in being forced to swallow my feelings. Both of these are shitty options.'

Obviously, in this case Peta is not accountable for the outcome that Charlotte suffered, but it is also not reasonable that Peta feels blamed. It could be said that Peta is being overly self-referential, but the same could also be said of Charlotte. A systemic attitude sees the 'pattern that connects' (Bateson, 1980, p 8) and holds up a frame of attention that eschews linear causation. Analogously, the practitioner should try to understand, and be aligned with, multiple points of view. As Lynne Hoffman (1985, p 384), a well-known systems thinker, says: 'There is no first horse on the merry-go-round.'

Imagine Peta and Charlotte were a couple who have had the kind of tussle mentioned above many times. What would be likely to happen if one of this pair presented to an individually oriented practitioner? This professional would tend to focus on their client's 'point of view'. An attitude of unconditional positive regard, of being non-judgmental, even a tactical 'I'll have to appear to be on her side', would result in the message to the client being something like 'It's no good that this happens with your partner. You've not felt supported or understood.' This message would tend to deepen, even inflame, the falling out that had occurred, and to embed the disappointments and misgivings that are present in any relationship. The effect of this would be to play up one side of the mixed feelings that are present, and to encourage a dynamic that diminishes the stock of optimism and affection that is available to each participant. In contrast, to work systemically with individuals is to act towards bettering social relations and to reach towards a multipartial understudying of the context of the presentation. Interactions in the interpersonal realm are dynamic and non-linear and it is rare that one party deserves to be totally righteous whilst another is judged perfectly guilty.

Working systemically with individual clients means being holistic in your attention and in the purposes of your actions. Given the majority of practitioners meet with the single person who is presented to them, this idea can be used as an organizing principle around which everyday relationship-building practice can turn. In health settings, in substance abuse settings, in most community, therapeutic, and specialist roles, whether in private practice or in agency-based service, this is the case as it is the pattern of meeting with a single person – 'my client' – that persists as the common design for the delivery of services. A series of specific exercises are presented in the next chapter that can be used to further this agenda when the contact is necessarily with a single client.

Bringing in others: conjoint work and its variations

As an adjunct to work with single clients, not infrequently practitioners sometimes find themselves having contact with one or more of their client's significant others. This contact with carers, neighbors, partners, Parish priests – the list of possible significant others is very broad – can be undertaken for many purposes. Sometimes these contacts are apparently simple, such as when there is a joint meeting to take a history, to discuss medication, or to relay details of diagnosis and/or prognosis. Other contacts are more complex in nature as they might involve the intricacies of care planning, discharge arrangements, or coordination issues around chronic illness and rehabilitation.

In these contacts the other, or others, are part of the client's more or less intimate network, but they are not recognized, nor should they be, as clients in their own right. Into this tricky context arises an extra, and quite sticky, complication: many practitioners feel uncomfortable in meetings with more than one person. This feeling fades with the experience that meetings with more than one person can be not only productive but also enlightening and energizing. Like surfing, if the conditions are right, such meetings can be like riding a wave. (This uncomfortable feeling will not fade if problematic attitudes and values are present which act to set up an 'us and them' configuration between the professional and the client's significant others: see Chapter 6)

Often described as conjoint work if it becomes an ongoing pattern for meetings, work that involves contact with more than one person is the next area of relationship-oriented practice to be examined. This consideration will not be extensive and is not designed to consider specialized forms of conjoint practice, such as 'spouse-aided therapy' (Hafner et al, 1993). Two core aspects of practice with 'client-plus-one-or-more' are reviewed:

- the issue of 'convening': getting the right people involved in a meeting; and
- how sessions with more than one person should be conducted.

Further ideas about conjoint work are examined in relation to the issue of confidentiality in the following section. The decision to tease out dilemmas and possibilities that arise around confidentiality has been taken as it is here that there can be a perceived conflict between the practitioner's allegiance to client-centeredness and their interest in promoting relationality. Before focusing on this intersection, basic attention to convening and conducting multiparty sessions is offered.

Convening: getting the right people involved

As well as meeting face to face with your client, it is often the case that there is another person, or people, with whom it makes sense to have contact. For example, in work with very young or very old clients it is obvious that at least some communication should occur with this client's relatives and significant others. In other practice contexts it is a matter of considerable sensitivity to identify, and find the right way to be in touch with, the person or people who it is best to have involved. A high degree of professionalism can be required in many situations when it comes to 'convening', that is, to have the right people engaged in the right kind of way, as Carpenter and Treacher (1983) set out in their classic paper.

A rule of thumb is for the practitioner to carefully identify, and then to actively consider directly involving, whoever the client perceives as central to their most subjectively meaningful relationships. This caste is often quite dissimilar to those an outsider, such as a professional, might assume. Closeness is a subjective phenomenon, a quality that cannot be predicted by convention or legal expectation, by proximity, or frequency of contact.

This is not to discount the importance of formal relationships and legal reasoning; nor is it to ignore the fact that in many practice contexts, such as child protection and in-patient medicine, there are protocols about who is to be involved, who is defined as the next of kin, the legal guardian, etc. High quality convening has to respect such generational and legal prerogatives but will also operate to be thoughtfully inclusive of alternative forms of affinity. Given a reasonable relational assessment has been undertaken, decisions about who *ought* to be involved are likely to be relatively straightforward. (Knowing at a theoretical level who it is best to have involved will not automatically clarify how this involvement is best secured: more on this shortly.)

If it is clear who to meet with, the next decision concerns whether it is best to meet with the significant other separate to, or conjointly with, the client. Flexibility is necessary as it is can be important to agree with, say, a partner's request to meet alone to discuss how they are coping since the client suffered a serious injury. It is also possible that the practitioner might have reasons to solicit a meeting with a significant other even if this has not been requested by that person. Mindful that the issue of confidentiality has been clarified (see the following section), such meetings have an important place. That said, it is generally preferable *not* to develop a pattern where two or more people – the client and one or more of that person's significant others – are having parallel rather than conjoint discussions with the professional. Of course, it is theoretically possible for the one practitioner to be thinking and acting systemically in relation to each of a number of serial inputs, but unless safety is the abiding concern, it is generally preferable to work towards a situation where those involved are able to communicate directly.

Without doubt there is an essential place for private communication. For example, if it is necessary, or if the practitioner decides it could be constructive, to meet with one or more of the client's significant others, it is highly likely that it is worth spending a considerable amount of time talking on the telephone, or in person, to this person before any conjoint meeting actually takes place. This action might not appear in how the organization records practitioner statistics, or be funded for private practitioners in terms of billable hours, but the good sense in being pro-active was recognized many years ago because pre-session contact can be crucial in engendering engagement (Carpenter and Treacher, 1983). More recently, those from the solutions tradition have been particularly active in emphasizing the importance of pre-session contact, for example, Berg (2007). Unless there is positive pre-session contact, those who are invited to attend for a session when the practitioner already has an established relationship with the client have reason to feel at least 'one out', if not actually set up, anxious, and defensive.

There are a range of other questions: what should be done if the client is an in-between age and is developmentally and chronologically neither an adult nor a child? What if the client is cognitively impaired or psychiatrically disturbed? In such cases there may be some reasons why they should not be invited to, say, a case conference in child protection or a discharge planning meeting at the rehabilitation center. For example, what if the client is an aged person who will be grumpy, even angry, if they think their relatives and the professionals are set on interfering with their autonomy? In this kind of difficult terrain it is apparently easier, perhaps even necessary, to exclude the person with the problem. If it is absolutely necessary, so be it, but this judgment is one of last resort as it is a principle of decision to be inclusive and for the practitioner (or the service) to take responsibility to ensure that each and every meeting is conducted so as to be structured and safe for every party who attends (discussed in the following section). Clearly, there is much to decide in terms of convening: where to meet? With whom? At what time? With what kind of facilitative preparation?

If an assessment indicates that there are relationship possibilities that might be important to catalyze, there is a considerable scope for inventiveness when it comes to convening. For example, if well worked up, old contacts that have faded can be renewed by a thoughtfully managed invitation. With a view to taking a beginning step in remodeling relationships that have been unsatisfactory in the past, there is sometimes a potential to reconvene a contact with someone where there has been conflict or avoidance if this is done with due care and planning (see Vignette 11 on p 149). Thinking into the future, a forward-thinking practitioner might seed new possibilities by the selective recruitment of one (or more) people with whom the primary client could interact. In this new contact the client may not passively benefit from the receipt of a helpful relationship (as in the premise of the client having 'access to a supportive relationship'). Rather, the client and a new other might forge a mutually advantageous alliance.

Such options noted, it is naive and often irresponsible to simply put people together. Getting the right people together is not an end in itself as this contact has to be positively conducted. Often a preparatory meeting with a client's partner, neighbor, priest, or imam can be a good way to build a containing degree of trust and understanding prior to having a conjoint session. This is often very useful if there is a prospect that simply bringing people together will escalate into an unpleasant encounter. Assuming that free and open communication will be productive is not a sound premise.

Conducting multiperson sessions

Attitudes inform practice. It follows that if the practitioner's attitudes are well aligned with the principles of relational practice, decisions will be made that intuitively establish multiparty exchanges as collaborative spaces. If the practitioner really is interested in different points of view, if the message is maintained that agreement is a preferred endpoint and is not the necessary starting place, if good intentions are expected from those present, if the practitioner genuinely comes across as acknowledging that everyone is doing the best they can, then there are sound preconditions for successful meetings.

As with work with a single client, at the level of operations there are several behaviors that are important to practice. Rather than the practitioner quickly 'getting out of the spotlight' and throwing the focus onto the visitor by immediately asking questions, it is generally the better option to become comfortable being, at least temporarily, the center of attention. This is not about dominating or lecturing but signaling that you are at ease and know what it is to be a reliable host. Be clear to those present how long you have, about the context of the meeting, about what you know about the person, or persons, who have come in, and acknowledge that coming in is a sign of commitment and good will. Being able to take some time to allow the significant other/s to settle in means you have to be able to feel comfortable enough in being the initial focus. This can be containing for your guests and is the opposite of rushing to the lower profile, but often implicitly powerful, position of being the listener–observer. Let the other(s) be the judge for a few moments before turning the tables. There are no hard rules here, but taking responsibility to set up a positive beginning, and also later making sure there is a clear ending, is the host's task. You have the role of being the conductor, the person who sets up and maintains the context. This includes keeping an eye on the time and how the agenda is being managed.

There are two central imperatives. First, as noted earlier, the professional is the host (Furman and Ahola, 1995), and it is essential to be welcoming and friendly, and to take some time to ensure introductions are fully and patiently undertaken. The guest(s) is likely to be uncertain about your role as initially they will be strangers in an alien setting. They are also likely to be unclear what is expected of them and to have expectations that are colored by fantasy or the earlier experiences they have had with other professionals and services. After carefully explaining your role and the purpose of the meeting, ask if there are questions or ideas that the visitor thinks it may be important to express.

The second imperative is to keep the session structured and safe. Taking responsibility for the environment, ensuring it is personable and yet reasonably orderly, is the opposite of allowing the discussion to regress into uncontained venting or a pattern where one person's feelings and opinions take over. As with most kinds of group work or individual work, in conjoint sessions the aim is to be an active facilitator rather than a passive observer. If the session goes flat or blows up, it is not proper to act as the bystander who thinks, 'Oh god, look at them: how bad is this!' Taking responsibility to ensure there is a sense of structure, a frame, to the flow of communication is like acting as an old-fashioned police officer at an intersection, someone who is both interested and fair. Like this guardian, the task is to be multipartial. No one avenue into the intersection should be favored or neglected, but this single image conveys only one technical aspect of the role. Far from looking out at 'them' from the refuge of your vantage point, the broader task is to be involved so as to establish the conditions within which collaboration can be realized.

If practitioners are particularly nervous about a conjoint meeting, whether they are newcomers or old hands, if they raise the dust and then complain they can't see, they tend to get exactly what they fear. For example, if they do not insert enough structure because they worry this will be provocative, this can stimulate the very dynamic that is feared as a lack of structure can engender conflict. Similarly, if they are concerned that there will be silence and insufficient interaction, they can work very hard to have an agenda and a set of norms only to find that there is too much niceness and too little real exchange. There is not a formula, or fool-proof bluff, that ensures such meeting will be productive. All they can do is to put themselves into the shoes of those who will be present and be guided by what this tells them. A vignette might help illustrate this issue.

VIGNETTE 15: SHAUNA

Imagine you have something of an established relationship with Shauna, an unemployed 16-year-old who has committed a number of offences, has drug problems, and a likely mental health issue. You work for juvenile justice where, once again, you have begun work with Shauna following another court order. She is meant to be living with her single-parent mother, Tracy, who Shauna tells you she gets on poorly with. You think it likely that Tracy has had a difficult past herself.

Without any elaboration of the case details, if you try to think where Tracy might be coming from in relation to meeting with you, what do you come up with? What do you think this woman might expect? Might she expect you are a partisan, someone who has already got a closed mind to her side of the story? Might she be likely to expect you will be captive to, and will see yourself as the advocate for, Shauna's point of view about what kind of mother she is? Might she worry she will be blamed, be asked to take more responsibility, or be asked to step back and take less? Alternatively, would she expect to be acknowledged for taking the time and effort to attend, for her persistence, for her positive intentions? Would she expect that you would be open to, really interested in, her point of view and wellbeing? More likely, Tracy would expect she would be viewed suspiciously, maybe even blamed, in her contact with the practitioner.

To offer the latter in your attitude and action is not about currying favor, about pretending to be caring for the strategic purpose this might be seen to further. If they have been around the health and welfare system, clients and their significant others have a finely tuned radar for the inauthentic. You honor those you come into contact with because it is right to do so, not because it is a means to an end. Practitioners will go a long way towards earning credibility and trust – with Tracy, with any of the client's others – if their conduct in this first meeting signals both competence and interest. Even if the practitioner has already said this to Tracy in a pre-session telephone contact that was made to arrange the meeting, it is often appropriate to take the floor and to say very early in the first meeting, something like:

> 'Tracy, one of the key things this meeting is for is to hear how you see Shauna's situation. Right now, I really don't know what you think and it is important for me to learn about, and to learn from, your point of view. The meeting is not about blaming you, or about trying to push you around. I've spoken to Shauna and she has told me how she sees the situation, or at least I've heard some of what she is thinking and feeling, but I have no idea how you see his situation.

'What I do know is that you have ideas and you have a commitment to her, and of this I can be sure.

'Often when a parent, partner or a friend comes in to meet with me as an X [a probation worker, a counselor, etc] about someone they care about, they expect to be blamed and not to be given a fair hearing. What do you think? Have you had experiences, like watching TV or having contact with other professionals, that have you thinking that this meeting might not go well for you?'

After hearing Tracy's response, and (most likely) discussing this response with her, it could be worthwhile a little later to come back to this in a more applied fashion:

'In terms of our meeting today, what do you want us to do? And, almost as important, what do you not want to see happen?'

Of course, if practitioners put themselves into Shauna's situation, a different set of scenarios can be imagined. Shauna could suspect you might betray her, get together with her mother and gang up on her. She might expect you will give her mother a good telling-off. As discussed earlier, if at all possible, it is good to prepare the client before the first conjoint meeting by telling them that you want to have a positive, trustworthy relationship with their important others, as well as to deepen, to honour and maintain the relationship with the client. How you advance both these goals, how you develop and maintain the confidence of all those involved, leads to the consideration of trust, of how and what information will be exchanged between the practitioner and the different stakeholders. This is exactly why the issue of confidentiality is so powerful (see the following section).

Balancing the different demands – that meetings should be structured and yet curious, cordial yet business-like, open yet safe – is something of an art. Different practitioners develop different personal styles that are equally able to achieve this balance. Some may be more chatty at the beginning and end of sessions whilst others appear less expressive and more distant. There is no template, and great diversity can be seen in the forms engagement can take. As long as there is a reasonable degree of balance between the competing demands, it will be fine. It is about evolving your own style mindful of the salient principles. This can be fulfilling as it involves the practitioner stimulating and experimenting with a mixture of what professional and personal growth is about.

This brief introduction to conjoint work has not addressed all the important variables that need to be considered. There has been, for example, no mention of the impact that home visiting has on the dynamics of conjoint work, or how different cultures have distinct norms regarding how hosts should behave, or how quickly, if at all, it is appropriate to 'get down to business' and engage in direct and open discussion. With confidence, what can be said is that it is now established across a variety of practice contexts, albeit referred to in different terms, that the practitioner has to be able to initiate and maintain 'multipartial alliances' so as to be on positive terms with more than one party (Couture, 2007).

In the initial engagement process there are a number of items that need to be mutually understood, if not always mutually agreed to, by the client (Turnell and Edwards, 1999). Crucial amongst these is the definition of the rules that regulate the exchange of information. Clarity, if not necessarily agreement, has to be reached as to what can be said conjointly and what is to be kept private within the multiple relationships that are transacted between the client, their significant others, and the practitioner. This is a crucial issue and is discussed at some length below.

Being creative with confidentiality

The following discussion on confidentiality does not seek to speak to the broader issue of privacy, for example, how the value of personal privacy might be reconciled with the demands of public safety with respect to, say, infection control, mandatory reporting in child protection, or the larger concern with the integrity of electronic data storage. What is addressed is limited to the issue of practice-based communications between a practitioner, a specific client, and that person's significant others. Within this narrower sub-class two conditions that service a relational approach are examined:

- how the practitioner can positively set up the terms of information exchange when meeting with new clients; and
- how understandings of information exchange can be renegotiated with clients who have become accustomed to a tight dyadic boundary being drawn around communications between the client and the practitioner.

First, it pays to have a reflective and creative approach to confidentiality if the practitioner decides to, or simply just has to, have contact with a person, or people, in addition to their client. Unless this thoughtfulness is present, meetings will tend to be trussed with unworkable expectations about what can, and cannot, be said. Unless all concerned are clear about the rules of information exchange, communication will be tentative or transgressive, and this will have a negative impact on the development of a trustworthy working alliance. That is, if a client and/or their significant others feel the rules are unclear, or are not being honored, if it feels like there *might* be leaks or lies, trust will be compromised. Trust is based on the professional being reliable, genuine, and competent more than it is based on being in a permanent state of agreement with the other by promising anyone absolute confidentiality. In reality, it is never possible to guarantee complete confidentiality, and there are clear reasons for arguing that promising, or implying, such a commitment is not only inappropriate but is also undesirable.

There are always written case notes, records of sessions, and client histories that remain indefinitely on file. This material can always be subpoenaed. And it is also likely that formal and informal discussions will take place about particular cases with colleagues and supervisors: clients are 'handed over', referrals made, and possible referrals discussed. Clients are registered, and mostly diagnostically coded. In some form this data is communicated to external authorities for funding and accountability purposes. Because such boundary conditions are to a degree porous, it is never true that there can be an absolute boundary around what occurs between the client and the practitioner. As discussed earlier (see Chapter 6), this means that many practitioners find they face a dilemma with respect to confidentiality. On the one hand, they must assure the client that discussions are confidential, yet on the other, they know the reality is that they are not in a position where they can guarantee this condition will be honored.

Rather than accepting the view that the issue of confidentiality presents an unavoidable dilemma, a more optimistic position can be taken – it is possible to understand that pro-actively dealing with the question of confidentiality offers the practitioner a crucial opportunity to build secure alliances that are based on transparent and honored foundations. If this opportunity is well grasped and based on realistic expectations, a shared understanding can be forged through points of clarity that are stated up front. Such an understanding should clarify which specific classes of information will, and will not, be exchanged between the practitioner, the client, and the other key people in that person's network. In developing this understanding, attention should be given to particular circumstances that would trigger different levels of information exchange; for example, if circumstances of actual, or potential, self-harm are to signal shifts in the pattern of exchange.

How confidentiality is handled is therefore a signal issue. In traditional practice confidentiality tends to be considered simply: hold in confidence what the client tells you unless there is (the very rare) disruption that is present when an issue of third party safety is so compelling as to override regular operations (McMahon, 1992). Regular technical transgressions *do* occur with respect to the actual practice of confidentiality, exceptions that are not concerned with third party safety (such as client data being recorded in files or discussed with colleagues and supervisors), but it seems the majority of practitioners assume these breaches constitute no more than understandable, even necessary, minor infractions which do not compromise an allegiance to the basic principle. Within the professional community, and based on this specific understanding, client confidentiality enjoys an esteemed position. This status is translated into the belief that client confidentiality should be held as an abiding, even ascendant, professional value.

In part, this view reflects the idea that communications between adult clients and practitioners have a degree of legal privilege. This being understood as a general, if not absolutely, delineated condition, it is the association between confidentiality and trust that strikes the most vital chord with practitioners: 'I can effectively serve my clients [patients, consumers, service users, etc] on condition that they know they can trust me.' This belief generates the commitment professionals have to ensuring there is an apparently rigid boundary around their relationship with, and their knowledge of, their clients. Unfortunately, such a hard boundary can have inadvertent consequences, for example, when the practitioner–client relationship comes to resemble an enclave or an expression of monocultural chauvinism. For example, Owusu–Bembah (1999) clearly describes how African societies do not share the Western premise that there is privatized, non-accountable realm.

In many cases an exclusive coupling between practitioner and client has the potential to diminish, perhaps even antagonize, the prospects for the client developing a broadened and secure affinity. Practitioners can find themselves troubled when this happens as there is a kind of claustrophobia present in the relationship when 'me and my client' find ourselves driving into a cul-de-sac. However awkward it can feel to be too closely paired with your client, once an awareness arises that there is too much closeness, perhaps even collusiveness, it is often unclear how this situation might be resolved. 'I feel snookered', you might say to yourself, 'it would not only bugger my relationship with my client to include contact with the client's others; anyway, to do so is legally barred.' Yet, it can feel that, on the other hand, 'My working alliance with the client is currently so inward-looking and exclusive that this is not really in the client's actual longer-term interest.' A particular contention is put forward: if the practitioner is not able to communicate positively with anyone other than their primary client, in many instances this will diminish the practitioner's capacity to serve the client well.

VIGNETTE 16: LYLE

Lyle is an 80-year-old man currently being assessed by an aged care assessment service. Although his wife died some years ago, Lyle has lived in the same house for nearly 50 years. He has adult male children, and half a dozen grandchildren, to whom he is attached and who he sees regularly. Over time, Lyle's adult children have come to fear for his safety and now believe it is dangerous for him to continue living alone.

Lyle says he 'does not want to cause a fuss' and early in life learned 'you have to take the good with the bad.' Lyle's 'old mate' Bert, his close friend since their days in the infantry in the Second World War, also lives alone, just around the corner from Lyle, in an inner northern Melbourne suburb. Bert is more robust than Lyle, particularly with respect to Lyle's cognitive functioning, a capacity that has deteriorated in recent years.

In case planning discussions it was deemed "inappropriate," "not really what we are meant to do," to speak to Bert as client confidentiality had to be respected, client self-determination encouraged, and so forth. Clearly, Bert did not have the status of immediate family, let alone was he 'next-of-kin'; in fact, it was clear he was not a relative at all. This was unfortunate as Bert was the person with the most reliable information about, and the resources able to offer the greatest support to, Lyle.

These advantages were not observable to the professionals as Bert was, in effect, invisible. After Lyle was moved into supported accommodation his functioning deteriorated, as did Bert's, who felt both guilty and isolated after Lyle moved away.

Consider:

- your response to this vignette;
- the reasons why Bert was not considered a 'significant other' to Lyle;
- in terms of assumptions, laws and conventions, what, if any, constraints are present that prevent the team from including Bert into a consideration of Lyle's best interests?

In the above, and more broadly, it is far better if practitioners do not assume the issue of confidentiality is an intransient problem. There are two reasons for this. First, and in a sense less importantly, it is probable that what the law will support is any reasonable practice that is guided by contemporary principles and research. In most jurisdictions expectations about confidentially have an implicit basis in common law rather than being dictated by stipulations in the actual statues. That is, the assumption that 'there is a legal bar' to broadening the circle of communication is incorrect if, and only if, the practitioner acts respectfully in relation to what has been said in confidence, and acts in such ways as to be reasonably guided by judgments that the practitioner has made about what is in the client's best interests. Clearly, in a given jurisdiction there may be specific statutes in play, such as a mental health act, as there may be agency and/or profession-specific ethical codes.

Mindful of the local legal context, a second factor offers a less defensive, more proactive consideration. When practitioners thoughtfully negotiate the issue of confidentiality directly with clients, this creates opportunities to develop a 'no bullshit' connection with clients. Good quality, even robust relationships with your primary client – and also with those significant others that form, or might form in the future, the milieu that is a sustaining ecology for the client – can be forged by 'talking when the talking is tough' (Miller et al, 2004a, p 377). By initiating, and by sticking with, a discussion about what will and will not be shared with others, practitioners demonstrate an integrity that generates trust.

Most clients, certainly all those who are experienced service users, know practitioners talk about them behind their back even when there is a veneer of confidentiality. These people suspect, and practitioners know, there is talk between immediate colleagues about clients as there is with supervisors and students. To a degree the client knows that the professional will write case notes, fill in intake and review forms, provide information about diagnosis and progress to managers, to funding bodies, and so forth. And the client also knows that case notes can be accessed by staff other than the person they are seeing, can potentially be subpoenaed by courts, move from one setting to the next (for example, from in-patient to out-patient settings), and can be summarized for the purpose of writing referral and/or interagency case planning. There is never a hard boundary, only the pretence of one, so why not call it for what it is?

Alongside the intrinsic sense in 'telling it like it is' there is an additional reason to talk to the client about including one, or more, significant others. Practitioners are only visitors in the client's life and it is better to be clear to themselves, and to the client, that this is so. If this can be stated it gives a context for the discussion of who else might also be important to include, and within what particular conditions. That practitioners might have contact with more than one person as part of their work with the primary client is an extension of the idea of systemic work with individuals and is based on the importance of multipartial alliances (Couture, 2007), that is, to have change-directed concurrent relationships with multiple stakeholders.

This idea is broadened in what follows. The priority here is to challenge practices that misuse or over-generalize confidentiality. This being clear, there are complexities and sensitivities that have to be acknowledged and thoughtfully addressed if the question of confidentiality is to be constructively managed.

Teasing out the issue of confidentiality

It has been understood for some time that in each national jurisdiction no client ever has a right to total confidentiality (Marshall and Soloman, 2000; Andrew et al, 2009). The assumption of confidentiality is always mediated rather than absolute. For example, in contemporary practice with complex clients it is now unusual, and usually inappropriate, for a single practitioner to have an exclusive relationship with a client (Keene and Li, 2005). The multiple needs of clients are increasingly recognized by a service system with multiple components. Given that multiple linkages are necessary, two questions arise:

- Given it is necessary that some information needs to be exchanged, what classes of information will be exchanged and within what specific circumstances will this be done?
- What kind of relationship does the practitioner wish to build, with whom, and to what ends are these relationships designed to serve? Put another way, is information to be exchanged in an ad hoc manner, secretly, and reticently, or will it be communicated directly and pro-actively?

If the intention is to build collaborative and robust relationships with clients and with their significant others, trust will develop when what is said by the practitioner is what is done by the practitioner. If practitioners operate honestly with their clients, the relationship becomes endowed with trust. Being real with clients is not associated with implying there is a degree of confidentiality that is greater than what can legitimately or sensibly be promised.

With respect to working with significant others, it is often more constructive to work towards clients expecting there will be particular kinds of information that will be exchanged with one of more or their significant others, a limited but normalized interchange of opinions and feelings that is consistent with a negotiated degree of openness and accountability. Such a pattern will not be without boundaries and protocols. It might be agreed that, for example, where a client is to live, their diagnosis and prognosis, and what medications are being used will be discussed by the practitioner with a client's siblings, but that the client's difficulties with their employer, their romances, or plans for the future will not.

Understandings must be regulated but it is not useful to embed an overly privatized set of expectations if the practitioner is seeking to acknowledge and develop the client's relational base and needs for emotional and practical support. There are often different stakeholders and there can be different, as well as common, interests to be honored. Given attitudes determine practice, the key variable is for service providers to develop a sensibility that offers a positive attitude towards the client's social network, including the client's family. Such a frame assists practitioners in flexibly responding to the different decision points that arise:

- as the process of contact with the client takes its specific course;
- between different clients and their significant others, such as friends and relatives.

Practitioners and agencies that have developed a positive attitude to these networks are less likely to experience problems with confidentiality because the decision points that inevitably arise are not formulated in oppositional terms. It is rarely an 'us against them' circumstance. Over the longer period, a duration that usually outlasts the contact that a practitioner has with a particular client, it is preferable to expect that 'this client and their network are of the same ecology' more than to assume that 'my client's interests are in fundamental conflict with those of their significant others.'

To a marked extent decisions about what kind of information is to be exchanged, and in what circumstances (conjoint meetings, in parallel discussions, etc) should be taken with respect to the broader issue of 'what kind of relationships am I trying to promote?' Consideration of this broader issue helps orient practitioners to think within a longer-term perspective. For example, a key person in a HIV care team, someone who has been a lifetime friend of an ill person, might request a one-on-one meeting with a clinician in the same way that a client may want particular details kept from their partner. Being able to flexibly respond to these requests, mindful of a longer-term interest in developing collaborative relationships, is not assisted by the presence of hard and fast rules about confidentiality. Being clear that professionals must reserve the right to make careful decisions, pragmatic ideas are set out below that relate to two specific scenarios:

- initially setting up understandings around information exchange with a new client; and

- renegotiating understandings of information exchange when a client has developed the expectation there will be a rigid boundary around what is said between them and their practitioner.

Each of these scenarios are now discussed in turn.

When a practitioner encounters a new client

In the first contact it is necessary to establish the local context of practice. This entails establishing an understanding of what the respective roles and responsibilities of each participant will be, and to clarify what rules are involved in determining, and subsequently changing, these respective roles and responsibilities.

For example, if an elderly patient is unable to manage their finances, a guardian may have to be appointed. And if the question of personal competence is a broader concern, decisions may have to be made for this person in relation to housing, hospitalization, and medication. In this case the 'rule' being observed in the allocation of respective roles and responsibilities amongst the participants is one that respects the functional needs of the elderly, infirm person. When this person regains their cognitive function, or is in the process of attempting to resume this capacity, the 'rule' governing the allocation of responsibilities will be varied in order to maximize this person's capacity for self-management. In this latter case, the roles and responsibilities of carers and service providers are significantly less like parent and child.

Discussions about rules and responsibilities can themselves be therapeutic as the metaphorical issue for the client is always the developmental tension between dependence and independence. The issue of confidentiality can therefore be used as a context for considering themes of relatedness and internal/external control. A good option is for the practitioner to say to the client at the outset of their contact is something to this effect:

> 'The way I prefer to work ['It is my philosophy' or 'It is this service's standard practice'] is to see the key people in your network as important to your health and longer-term welfare. Maybe, in your network it is your mates, or your sisters – it could be anyone – that can play an important part in you being able to achieve the best outcome.
>
> 'Often these people can have a role in providing me with information, being consulted about some questions, or just have a need to be kept informed about one or more of the things that we might talk about. In fact, this is my [or agency or profession's] clear preference, something like a policy. This might be a sensitive issue for you, so it is necessary for us to talk this through, and perhaps to do so slowly and with care. For starters, does this general principle make some sense to you?'

This sentiment could also be stated in information brochures given to new clients, as it could be displayed in waiting rooms and included in official documentation, such as mission statements and policy and practice frameworks (see later in this chapter).

Over time, an inclusive attitude to working collaboratively with the client's significant others can become an accepted norm for individual practitioners (as it can for agencies: see the conclusion of this chapter). In so far as the practitioner naturalizes a thoughtfully inclusive attitude, it follows that the set of practices that align with this attitude will tend to be naturalized by the client. That said, the issue of confidentiality remains sensitive, even talismanic, given its unstable location at the interface of autonomy and relatedness. This symbolic endowment means practitioners will often be required to have direct and detailed discussions with clients about the specifics of this issue and the meanings that these pragmatics turn on. Such conversations offer a broadly therapeutic theme as 'working the loop' (Wender, 1968) between autonomy and relatedness, considering how the patterns of connection have to evolve over the life course, is always a site of energy and growth.

Even if an agreement appears to have been reached, or an understanding more or less happily settled on, being prepared to take up this issue multiple times is frequently appropriate. For example, if 'Imogen', a young homeless person who is 15 and normatively spiky about her independence, reluctantly comes to understand the practitioner will have a degree of contact with her single mum – the minimal stipulation may be to let this parent know her daughter is safe – this limited contact can be extensively rehearsed between the client and the practitioner (Vignette 15). What the practitioner seeks to do is to demonstrate reliability, practical trustworthiness, within an allegiance to inclusiveness and the relational agenda. Almost certainly, it is best to discuss with Imogen exactly what one proposes to say to her mother, what one would prefer to say if the mother asks the expected questions – 'Where is Imogen now? Is she on drugs?' – and to indicate clearly to Imogen what the practitioner will be guided by in terms of the client's wishes and what they are not prepared to negotiate about: 'You've got things you are sensitive about, maybe things you might not want me to say to your mum. Before I contact her, we need to be clear about what is closed off because it is confidential to you and the other areas that I know I will have to talk about.'

Such discussions require a high level of focus in the initial engagement stage. Putting to one side matters of abuse, what is essential is not to allow the early stage of engagement to devolve into a permanent injunction against exchanges with the client's significant others. Understandings of practice that assume a rigid boundary around the practitioner–client dyad are generally contra-indicated. Put simply, the traditional psychoanalytic understanding that there must be a primacy in the relationship between the therapist and the patient (the 'analysand') is not an appropriate template in many situations. A privatized relationship between professional and client does not transpose into settings where good outcomes are facilitated by having the practitioner develop multiple linkages with those people, both lay and professional, who are central to the client's ecology.

It is important to be informed by the analytic tradition's expertise in theorizing the significance of personal boundaries, and this can be done without reifying the practice model that is associated with this tradition. For example, child protection workers can be psychoanalytically informed about, for example, what it means to a parent to have a worker unexpectedly knock on their door, and to then have to proceed with whatever action is mandated. This can be done mindful that this amounts to a breach of confidentiality – but one that will be conducted sensitively yet unambiguously. Some actions, such as telling Imogen you will have limited contact with her mother or being up front with a parent that a notification has been received, have to be done. If these actions are done openly, initially (and sometimes continuously), clients may not like this but, over time, will generally come to respect the practitioner's independence and trustworthiness. Significant others are, in crucial ways, a well-considered part of the team, and each relationship within the service network requires sensitive attention.

In establishing and maintaining complex relationships care is needed in order that information given is, in fact, actually understood. Because there are often intense feelings present, it can be useful to state and restate what is being communicated. Carers, for example, can be so besieged and overwhelmed that statements may need to be simplified, repeated, and then checked that they have in fact been understood. As with clients, friends, and relatives can be 'in shock' and their thoughts and feelings can be in an intense state of turbulence. In attempting to establish the context of practice, which is difficult even in stable practice situations, it is necessary to check that information sent is actually information received.

In situations where the client is not new

Many clients have been led to expect that what they discuss with 'their' practitioner will be kept totally confidential. Many clients have learned, have become accustomed, to think there will be a hard boundary between what is said between the practitioner and themselves and what the practitioner can communicate with members of their network. Whilst a good number of experienced clients are aware this expectation is far from iron-clad, this expectation continues to be endowed with great symbolic force. Clients who have been acculturated to hold this view know that their practitioner has to be polite to their friends and relatives, but they assume confidentiality is such a powerful rule as to prevent their practitioner, or practitioners, from having good quality relationships with members of their network. Courtesies to one side, meaningful information exchange is just 'not on'. If it was otherwise, so the client assumes, this would be disloyal.

In so far as a client has this expectation, it is a barrier to many practices that seek to develop the client's relational base. That said, the significance of the symbolism involved means that any effort to renegotiate this understanding has to be approached with the greatest sensitivity. It is possible to modify expectations, but this can only be achieved with care and thoughtfulness (De Jong and Berg, 2001). Being genuine, and advancing a clear set of reasons, is part of what is required. At the heart of these reasons is the genuine belief that it is in the client's best interest to be treated as a social being whose longer-term interests are promoted by positive personal relationships with people who have a different status to those who are paid to relate to them. At some level this makes intuitive sense to everyone, including the most bruised and defensive of clients, yet finding a path to access this understanding is often challenging.

Towards re-establishing a context of practice that is relationship building, five lines of approach are suggested below (Furlong and Leggatt, 1996). These can be considered as more or less cumulative steps in such a process:

- The practitioner can raise the issue with the client. For example, they could say 'I am worrying I have not been helping you as much as I should have if I can have no real communications with those that care for you and know most about you. This might be a shock to you, but I want to say I have become uncomfortable with this worry.'
- Aligned with the above, a stronger from of expression could be used: 'I am in the process of revising [or, 'I have revised'] my policy about being in touch with those who are the significant others of my clients. I am clearer and clearer it is best to have at least some degree of meaningful contact with those who are important to the people I work for and with. This makes much more sense than pretending that everyone is isolated. What do you think about this: is this change of policy a shock?'
- The practitioner can suggest there is a problem: 'I am in a dilemma as a professional: if I speak to the people who you are close to, which you are likely to feel is disloyal, you might give me the flick. On the other hand, if I do not speak to those who are important to you I'm probably being part of the problem between you and them.'
- Alternatively, the practitioner might say, 'Over the long haul your interests and those of your friends [or siblings, relatives, etc] have a lot in common – but the way it has been arranged so far, it as if you are all enemies where there can be no communications, no go-betweens, between all of you.' This is a stronger intervention than simply raising the issue, and may be useful in seeding the idea there is a need for change.
- Lastly, the practitioner can say to the client that information exchange between them and one or more members of their network is currently not good enough and that this problem needs to be addressed. Without blaming anyone, and with the greatest care, a clear position can be taken: 'The situation has to change, but I am committed to doing this in a way which preserves what it is that you really need to keep private whilst also allowing me to work well with your partner [sister, daughter, etc].'

The practitioner can then engage the client in participating in how this change process is to be undertaken. For example, 'Could you tell X, will I tell X, or will we do it together?' The classes of information that are to be exchanged and not exchanged need to be clearly identified: 'We will all need to talk about where you will live after leaving rehab, but no one except you and I will know about the mixed feelings you are having about your sexuality.' In the context of no choice (Overton, 1954), the practitioner invites the client to be part of the process of working through how the change can be best accomplished: 'Given there needs to be better communication, what do you think are the better and worse options in how this might be achieved?'

To the extent that the client's understanding has been based on the assumption that 'my practitioner and I have an exclusive relationship', the process of re-assembling expectations can be difficult. In a managed sequence, all five of the above ideas might need to be worked through as transition issues can be persistent. Such transitioning problems are less frequent than might be anticipated as a good number of clients already know intuitively, if not pragmatically, that a rigid boundary never really worked well for them: at some level of awareness many clients have long known that confidentiality was not only a sham but was actually unhelpful. For these it can be a relief, even a tonic, to have clear rules for regulating and normalizing information exchange towards a pattern that is sensibly inclusive. Making these rules transparent can be a challenge for practitioners as it presses them to be able to articulate, and then to negotiate with, their clients as to exactly what information will, and will not, be exchanged, and to be clear within which circumstances such exchanges will occur.

Being up front with the matter of confidentiality transforms a problem into an energizing opportunity for partnership building. In such a process boundaries can be clarified and realistic levels of trust earned and secured. Once mutual agreement about confidentiality has been achieved, an understanding that neither colludes nor collides (Furlong, 2002), there is a creative space within which inclusive, information-generating and, on occasions, decisive transformations can take place.

Advanced relational work

There are more complex examples that work to the same set of principles. A thorough account of these innovative practices is not feasible given that the aim of this present exercise is to acknowledge, celebrate, and develop what can be achieved by practitioners in grass-roots roles who do not have specialist training or high status roles. What is attempted in the following is to annotate several 'out there' examples in order to point to the range and ambition that can be located within the ambit of relationally oriented practice. Hopefully, this material will feel positively suggestive, even to a degree inspiring, rather than being seen as so advanced as to be discouraging or overbearing. What is at issue in these examples is the vitality and creativity that can be found across a suite of allied approaches.

Interested readers may choose to explore the examples further if this is relevant to their actual role or future interests.

The existence of this set of innovations can be read as evidence that relationship-building work is not a fringe or fly-by-night anomaly. In fact, in many fields and disciplinary traditions there are signs of an emerging convergence in the development of practices that have a common premise: clients, like the rest of us, are social beings who should not be exclusively rendered as autonomous entities. Given these innovative examples have arisen out of differing traditions and practice contexts, it is not surprising that they have not been categorized as examples of 'relationship-building practice' in the professional literature. That said, the rationale for bracketing these practices as examples of a similar practice sensibility is so powerful that once put together, their connection is apparent.

Witnessing circles

Narrative practitioners value interdependence and personal accountability and do not see clients as independent entities (Parton and O'Byrne, 2006). Taken as core values within this tradition it follows that these principles are translated into how practice is actually conducted. This has led to a suite of innovative ways to embed, even ceremonialize, the social self of clients. This is especially seen in the stimulation of small gatherings of significant others – *witnessing circles* – around the client, the discussion of their problems, and the process of change (Denborough, 2008).

Narrative practitioners initially tended to the view that it was preferable to work with whoever happened to attend rather than seek to organize who was to be present. Subsequently, pioneering figures such as Michael White and David Epstein discussed and experimented with the notion of 'recruiting an audience' to the client's emerging new story. This notion referenced, but also sought to critique, the maxim attributed to Carl Whitaker that the family therapist had 'to win the battle for structure and control', that is, determine who was to attend sessions before the 'real therapy' could begin. Eschewing the coercion associated with this idea – that clients and their others can, and should, be herded – narrative-based practitioners have gone on to evolve a set of authentically novel practices designed to tease out the description of problems and to embed what has been termed 'preferred' identities as the therapeutic process progresses.

These practices reject the received clinical and therapeutic convention that has practitioners concentrate on the diagnosis and treatment of individuals. Rather, the view is taken to privilege the potential of specially convened small groups to challenge the burdening personal narratives clients tend to experience. This role is based on the sociological and anthropological premise that the self is a social being which is alive to the influence of that local ensemble to which the client endows with a deep significance. In the language of narrative practice this collective of significant others is termed a 'witnessing circle'. These are one-off, or serial meetings that are convened and conducted with the purpose of re-authoring, and then settling in, new forms of client self-understanding.

How are these rituals of transition theorized? For narrative practitioners it is understood that selfhood and identity are dynamic, performative, and social:

> If the stories that we have about our lives are negotiated and distributed within communities of persons, then it makes a great deal of sense to engage communities of persons in the renegotiation of identity. So, regardless as to whether I am meeting with an individual, a couple or a family, I am thinking about possible audiences to the unfolding developments of therapy, and thinking about how this audience might be invited to play a part in the authentication of the preferred claims that are emerging in the process of therapy. (White, 1994, p 78)

What follows from this theorizing is that different participants – those who might have been or could now be the client's significant others – can be invited to be engaged in a group process that 'witnesses' and 'scaffolds' alternative accounts of the client's identity. The narrative use of such a practical anthropology is both potent and highly original, but it is not unique. The development of 'witnessing circles' has much in common with family group conferencing and restorative justice (see below), perspectives that are also centered on the imperative that a relational understanding of personhood should inform practice.

Family group conferencing and restorative justice

The restorative justice movement in general, and the practice of family group conferencing that it is part of, represent an outstanding example of an approach that is based on the principle that humans are essentially social beings. Rather than perpetrators being summarily punished, an outcome that is often associated with degradation and social ostracism, this approach speaks to the nobler and more practical idea that several allied purposes can be served by a holistic response: victims have a need to experience justice but, interdependent with this goal, perpetrators should be held accountable for their wrongdoings in such a way as to facilitate the possibility of atonement and social inclusion. It is possible to design responses to crime that balance the rights of the victim with the interests of the offender. The following brief account concentrates on perpetrators, yet a similar logic also applies to the position of those who have suffered an offence.

Family group conferencing was initially developed in New Zealand with the Maori population (Griffiths, 2001). Inspired by this example, but with the clear understanding that different local circumstances warrant extensive customizing, programs based on the use of family group conferencing specifically, and restorative justice more generally, are now found in many national jurisdictions such as New Zealand and the US.

In brief, in family group conferencing a specially selected ensemble of those with whom the offender has practical and symbolic ties is convened. This grouping can include elders, cultural, and religious authority figures, relatives, and peers: in other words, a thoughtfully composed set of significant others. These meetings may also, but will not necessarily, have the victim or their representative present. This group acts as a reference and processing body to 'hear' the details of the offence and to develop a more or less formal disposition. In some instances, particularly in juvenile justice contexts, this process is mandated by the courts. In other contexts, for example, if the setting is less official and more therapeutic in its design, the same kind of gathering can be organized without a formal court auspice. Koori Courts, legally authorized panels specifically designed to deal with crimes committed by Australian aboriginals, are one such example of a particular local variation (Borowski, 2011).

Such assemblies cannot be set up without a great deal of planning and an appropriate formal and/or informal auspice. Who is to be invited requires high level judgments predicated on considerable local expertise; there is no blueprint as to which parties should be represented. And decisions about the design of the meetings – how a particular group, or class of groups, should be conducted, who is to act as chair, the proper order of business, and so forth – calls for judgments that are as sensitive as they are sophisticated.

In the quest to achieve a dual aim – for victims to secure a quality of reparation and for perpetrators a degree of atonement and social integration – there are considerable risks. One of the key elements in this equation is shame. On the one hand, if intense shame is experienced by the perpetrator as a result of a capricious or sadistic process, this can overwhelm and capsize the person, a disastrous outcome that is likely to lead to a worsening of their trajectory. Therapeutic jurisprudence is a high-wire act that, if it to be effective, has to be grounded in a set of meanings and outcomes that are authentic to those concerned. Even if the structure and the outcome are perceived as legitimate, the nature of such rituals remains tense. As in all rituals of transformation there is a quality of liminality that is an inevitable part of the process where the individual's identity is initially disturbed prior to it being reconstituted in its preferred new form (Rapaport and Overing, 2000). In the uncertain middle phase of this transition there is therefore the potential for what is counter-productive to occur. Uncontained, destructive experiences of shame can lead to unintended and exclusory consequences.

On the other hand, shame is inherently entwined with the theme of personal accountability. For this reason its experience can have a constructively pro-social action (Furlong, 2010c). Shame is a social emotion, a subjective but publicly generated feeling whose presence can have beneficial effects. And as a social emotion, shame tends to regulate human behavior. Being an aversive sensation, it can serve a positive social purpose: given particular actions are regarded as shameful, the individual's membership within the larger unit will be endangered if these behaviors are committed. Within a properly auspiced and conducted process, a carefully modulated experience of shame can therefore play an intrinsic role in animating, or re-animating, ties with the larger unit represented by the group conference. In this context if a perpetrator experiences, and is seen to experience, the sense of shame that is commensurate with the offence, this can play an important role within a ritual of inclusion. That humans are part of many groups, and that human wellbeing is correlated with the quality of this belonging, introduces group work as a mode of relationally oriented practice.

Group work

Many kinds of group work directly advance the relationship-building agenda. In the following the initial focus is to introduce an advanced, highly specialized example. This is presented prior to a brief overview which advocates for the important place of more general examples of group work, examples that less specialized professionals can undertake, which can make a real difference in relationship-building practice.

In terms of advanced practice narrative-based group work with men who have been violent is a stand-up example of a relationally grounded program. As practiced by Wirtz and Schweitzer (2003), the model consists of an open group that meets weekly in the evening and is located within a local community health service. Referrals to the group are mostly non-statutory in nature, but not necessarily. Upon receiving a referral, there is an initial interview where the protocols of the group are outlined and the suitability of the person is broadly assessed. Given it is an open, rather than a closed, fixed-duration group, the norms of the group, its culture and patterns, are designed in large measure to be maintained by the participants themselves; as these norms are so particular, it is essential to formally introduce the possible new member to these rules prior to this person agreeing to attend. Unlike some programs for offenders, 'insight' and an open and full acknowledgment of wrongdoing are not pre-requisites as these sentiments are understood as preferred outcomes of the process rather than as pre-conditions or starting points. This all said, what is so particular about the structure and rules of this group?

What is unusual, and what is so constructive, is that group discussions do not have the expected boundaries. Rather, what is said in the group is understood by all to be available to the women who have been the victims of the men's violence. Symbolized by the possibility that one, or more, of these women may be hearing in real time what is said in the group – sessions are 'miked' to a room which is out of view to the men – the group leader makes it clear that they will inform a partner, or ex-partner, if what is said indicates the possibility that the victim is not safe. In this design, accountability, not collusion, is the norm that is embedded. This provocative approach turns the traditional use of confidentiality on its head by having groups of men who attend sign up to an understanding that what is said in their group is not confidential if it relates to issues of safety – the group and its discussions sit within a larger circle of accountability to the women and children who have been abused. Reunion with the partner who has been abused, which is often high on the men's agenda, is never promised or traded in any form. All that is offered is the chance for each man to reflect on their own values with their peers in a structured setting. This setting has a clear policy: accountability is expected and any sense of entitlement contested.

Studying this creative, progressive, and durable model – one Melbourne-based group has been successfully running for more than 10 years – brings into focus the themes presented earlier, but also across the whole book. That is, Helen Wirtz and Robert Schweitzer's approach (2003) advances the relational agenda in several decisive ways. First, in its design and in its operations this form of group work embeds the theme of personal accountability; second, in pioneering a non-conventional, and creative, use of confidentiality the interconnectedness between people is made clear and etched in more firmly.

This example clearly points to the possibilities of professional practices that are based on an interpersonal understanding of identity and dysfunction, of wellbeing and interdependence. Practitioners like Wirtz and Schweitzer may be exceptionally committed and highly skilled, yet they may not have this profile to make meaningful degrees of difference. To this end there are an immense number of important ways to add to the client's relational base and you do not have to be in a senior position, have a specialist role, or have made a long-term commitment to advancing your skills to play this kind of role. Being able to prompt small steps, such as a specific client developing (just) one friendship or deciding that you value your reputation more than your power, can make a huge difference.

Advanced examples of group work noted, the relationship-building agenda can also be advanced by many far less specialized and demanding groups. Such groups may be designed to enjoy ongoing professional leadership or, perhaps, were initially 'seeded' by practitioners but which continue to self-manage without external leadership. Support groups, activity groups, informal groups based on common interests or a shared residence, these and many other varieties of groups can play a telling role in promoting interpersonal skills and deepening connection. (A concrete example of residents in a hostel developing a common approach to how they wish to collectively relate is outlined in Chapter 9, on p 218.)

For the current purpose, from amongst this rich larger set those groups that align with the mutual aid tradition deserve a particular acknowledgment (Steinberg, 2010). Without discounting the skills that dedicated group work practitioners commit themselves to developing, and mindful that many consider group work a specialist practice, the kind of peer support and learning that is available in groups based on a mutual aid ethos have a mighty potential. Much that is positive can be achieved without a group being tagged 'therapeutic', or where the practitioner has no high level of group work training. Such groups can, in some circumstances, be catalyzed by sharp-eyed practitioners in more basic roles. Necessarily, the practitioner has to take responsibility that there is sufficient structure to ensure safety, just as this has to be ensured in any form of conjoint practice. As noted earlier, it is naive and possibly even dangerous to lump people together thinking that 'open communication' or a vapid form of 'group facilitation' will ensure a positive process.

One of the key conditions that either encourages or constrains the possibility of stimulating good quality basic group work, and relationally sensitive work more generally, relates to the actual conditions within which the practitioner operates. These conditions are determined, at least to a large degree, by the actions of planners, managers, and supervisors. They tend to stimulate 'communities of practice' (Wenger, 1999) that support practitioners deepening the client's relational base, or they undermine this possibility. The following examines how planners, managers, and supervisors can achieve the former.

Role of planners, managers, and supervisors

The majority of health and human service practice takes place within settings that focus on individuals (as examined in Chapter 4). This practical emphasis can sometimes be so exclusive as to marginalize, even disqualify, the importance of the relational aspects of the client's life. For example, in high-profile expressions of intent, such as mission statements and public brochures, it is not unusual to find statements that identify a service (or a profession) with the exclusive purpose of advancing the client's capacity for self-reliance and autonomy. In effect, these policy statements are flags of allegiance that publicly announce that independence (whatever that really means) trumps the achievement of interdependence and the quality of a person's connectedness. There is not even a nod to the importance of intimacy and relatedness, accountability and other-orientedness, on these mastheads. Presumably, those who read or hear these policies find the veneration of independence unremarkable as it is so familiar. It is a cultural slogan that autonomy equates with wellbeing.

This anti-relational bias can be expressed in informal, as well as formal, ways, as the following vignette illustrates. Representing Gay and Lesbian Victoria, the story was told by Anne Mitchell, an activist and researcher, at a public health forum in 2008.

VIGNETTE 17: ANNE

As a new patient, Anne attended a chiropractic appointment and was given a clinic registration form by the receptionist to complete whilst she sat in the clinic waiting room. Mid-way through completing this form, she was confronted with the choice 'married' or 'single'. Anne decided to leave this blank and to fill in the remainder of the form.

She then returned the form to the receptionist. Clearly audible to all in the waiting room, Anne was then asked "Well, are you single or married?" Ann said "Neither." The receptionist replied, "You must be de facto then" and over-wrote this onto the form.

In a forthright voice the receptionist then asked "What is your partner's name?" Anne replied with the name of her female partner. Surprised the name she heard was not an obviously male name, but assuming it had to be the name of a man, the receptionist raised her voice and said "That's a strange name. How do you spell it?" Anne clarified the spelling in a to-and-fro exercise that eventually reached a clear resolution. To the relief of all who took part in this embarrassing exercise, the apparently simple task of patient registration was then completed.

The above vignette is a casual, yet telling, example of institutionalized homophobia, yet it also illustrates how the many flowerings of affiliation can be rendered invisible by convention. Usually without intent or malice, alternative examples of intimate sociality can be discouraged and marginalized, sometimes even vandalized, in the more or less subtle acts that are performed by professionals and those who more broadly act on behalf of agencies and institutions. The relational may have no vote or voice yet, like any form of life, it has to be recognized if it is to be sustained. Given the purposes, and within the limits of this current exercise, several possibilities are raised that speak to the importance of this recognition. These involve a selection of summary points, prompts that might be elaborated into formal and/or informal steps that might be of interest to planners, managers, and supervisors who wish to advance the relational agenda.

Formal documentation

It is possible for organizations to formalize mission statements and associated documentation, such as statements of objectives and policy and individual position descriptions, so this material is inclusive of the relational dimensions of client welfare. Material should be vetted for a possible bias towards 'independence', 'autonomy', 'self-determination', and so forth. This appraisal can be linked to efforts to balance these values with the priority that is publicly given to the relational self and its workings: to interdependence, personal accountability, relationship-building skills, and relational quality.

Given that the latter terms sound awkward compared to the streamlined, bullet-like appeal of established 'sound bites', it may be useful to mainstream an allegiance to a relational flag by way of another referent, such as 'social capital', 'recovery', or 'social inclusion'. For example: 'Our mission at [say] UK Pathways is to promote recovery and social inclusion, outcomes that cannot be achieved without consumers having what professionals already have: good quality personal relationships where there is both love and accountability.' Some services, such as Mind Australia, decided some time ago to abandon the fetish around independence, and now feature an official allegiance to interdependence and relationality in their public documentation. Service brochures, and other outward-looking documents, can be worded to declare this allegiance: 'In our service we seek to appreciate, listen to and work closely with all those with whom the client has, or wishes to have, good relationships.'

Record keeping

A similarly themed audit of record keeping can also take place. These arrangements are never neutral and most current iterations tend to construct the client as an almost exclusively separate site. In so far as this is so, this amounts to a de facto policy which relegates the importance of the relational to, at best, a marginal status – the minimal 'Who is the next of kin who will be contacted when the patient needs transport' kind of role. In contrast to their traditionally individualistic form, record-keeping formats can be set up that draw attention to, and then formally document, informal as well as traditional connections. As in the hetero-sexist vignette above, even basic client registration formats are important to check for their inclusiveness.

A start can be made in eliciting subjectively defined connections, including non-conventional linkages such as same-sex relationships and other non-biological and non-legal significant other relations, by standardized formats that have professionals regularly ask clients questions such as 'Who are you close to?' or 'Who would you like us to keep informed?' And in line with a positive policy, and supported by circulated advice-to-client material, such as agency brochures, practitioners can be expected to say to prospective or incoming clients something to the effect that, 'Here at UK Pathways we believe that good quality relationships are good for the health and wellbeing. For this reason we want to have a trusting alliance with each of our clients *and* we also want to develop a positive connection with those who are important to each client.'

Assessment and history taking

Tied to the task of ensuring that record keeping is sensitive to the relational is the matter of the protocols that are used for assessment and history taking. These can be organized so as to prompt practitioners to seek out and to acknowledge the relational, or they can effect an opposite outcome. For example,

- eco-maps and genograms can be included in standard hard copy and electronic templates;
- an expectation that interviews with at least one significant other will be undertaken as a normal element of history taking;
- significant others can be regularly asked 'What has been your experience of helping services such as ours and others with whom you have had contact?' and/or 'How could we learn more about your views and ideas?'

Several particular classes of action that draw attention to the relational base of clients are set out below.

Practice frameworks and customs related to case formulation, goal setting, and service review

An old maxim says 'As the twig is bent, so the tree aligns.' If the prevailing culture is one that favors social connectedness, it will mean that case formulation, goal setting, and outcome review will be conducted so as to place a positive focus on intimate social relations; if the wind blows in the opposite direction, the converse will tend to be present.

For example, if it is the prevailing custom, if not the official policy, with a particular aged care service to be suspicious of the adult children of elderly patients, then case presentations will tend to approached in a manner that is insensitive to the client's relatives. This may simply represent a habit, an apparently unremarkable pattern, more than it expresses a serious values issue. Yet if an actual antipathy to relatives is present, this will be expressed in the service's 'theory in use' (Argyris and Schon, 1975) – in the manner cases are formulated, goals are set, and case reviews conducted. Perhaps the appropriate ambition, therefore, is to re-visit or to develop an agency-wide practice framework that is sensitive to friends and relatives.

Over time, the aim is to incorporate, even feature, the relational agenda as a core theme within the official practice framework or relevant practice manual. In part, this purpose is advanced if appropriate practices relating to case formulation, goal setting, and service review are stipulated in this documentation. Ensuring the presence of specific details is important, even crucial, yet the inclusion of a commitment to the importance of strengthening the client's relational base is invaluable in itself as such formal expressions of agency have a richly symbolic character. Like an agency's culture, a practice framework has a totality that is more than the sum of its parts: it has an iconic status. Stripped back from the technical language that such frameworks tend to be couched in, what is really at issue is the 'practical ethics' that will be demonstrated (Paterson, 1996). These ethics are influenced by, but cannot be completely identified with, what is set out in official documents.

Workforce planning and professional development

Those charged with directing the development of agencies are in a unique position to influence the attitude and skill set of employees. Mindful this is not a 'monkey-see-monkey-do' exercise – staff are not robots and may kick back against unwelcome change – over time those with control of workforce planning and the design of programs tend to be influential. Decisions about the direction of workforce planning and professional development will either enhance or diminish the possibility of practitioners being able to effectively develop their client's relationship-building capacity by their actions in giving this approach to practice a high point of focus or letting it slide off the radar.

Like developing cultural awareness, the promotion of attitudes and skills that build the client's relational base can be undertaken in more or less meaningful ways. If a program of development is to be initiated, especially if this is seen to mirror emerging agency policy and objectives, this is welcome even as it risks giving practitioners the message that what they are currently doing, what they endow with immense meaning – their practice – is being disregarded, put down, and not respected. Organizational change agents are well aware of this dynamic and know it is better to spend time establishing the legitimacy of any new direction prior to an attempt at implementation. Fortunately, it is hard to be remain cynical that there is not a decency and everyday sense in the aim that 'We should improve our capacity to strengthen the client's relational base.' That said, it can take time and creativity to set up the conditions within which this good sense will take root. Establishing 'circles of learning' (Wenger, 1999), and other collective aids to reflective practice, can play a key role in generating the kind of solidarity that embeds relationally oriented practice.

Professional supervision

As well as having an important role in quality assurance functions, supervisors play a large role in developing and maintaining professional customs. Whether acting as line managers and case allocation monitors, or when employed at a distance as third party consultants who have a role in the professional development of the practitioner's role, supervisors are culture bearers. They themselves will be aligned with the relationship-building project, or they will not. This quality translates directly into how the supervisory process is conducted.

The theoretical model of the supervision is important, but this is less likely to be a factor than the disposition that is formed by the supervisor's implicit values, their attitudes, and their 'buttons'. Relationship–oriented practice sits well with, or does not, some dispositions: think of Vignette 1 (see p 84). Murray, a very experienced practitioner, could be expected to be qualified to deliver good quality external supervision except that he is caught up in the old score: to liberate clients from those who would hold them back. This disposition is antithetical to an appreciation of inclusion and tends to reproduce exactly the psychology of separation that has produced so much damage. Supervisors who are appreciative of the possibilities of relationships are a necessary investment.

An atmosphere and philosophy that is sensitive to the role of friends and family

Do friends and family feel comfortable contacting the practitioner? This is a prime indicator of the sensitivity of the practitioner and the agency to the client's others. In effect, the answer to this question tends to be the mirror image of what is 'comfortable' for practitioners. Putting the issue of confidentiality to one side, it is clear that funding models and rebate systems in private practice, along with statistical record keeping in public settings which are predicated on a narrow definition of 'occasions of service', act to discourage practitioners from devoting attention to, and spending time with, those that the larger system does not make an official priority.

Mindful of this larger tide, friends and relatives will be happy to be involved if they are treated in a courteous and welcoming manner. This is the 'low-tech' highway to relationally sensitive practice: significant others will feel welcome if they experience attitudes and structures that are positive about their involvement. Developing a culture that is appreciative of the client's others is the key attribute and the presence, or the absence, of this culture can be assessed in many ways. For example, 'friends and families' focus groups can be convened, and senior practitioners and supervisors can keep their ear to the ground for the way practitioners informally talk about the client's significant others. There may be a sub-text of appreciation or denigration in these unofficial, but telling, 'around-the-coffee urn' conversations. Perhaps a relationally oriented consultant could be commissioned to develop an opinion. Over time, by way of decisions about professional culture, or, if it concerns organizations, of agency policy, recruitment priorities, workforce planning, and professional development, a more positive attitude can be promoted.

The promotion of a positive attitude can, in some circumstances, be difficult to achieve. Sometimes this is due to a residual bias against relatives or a view that relationships, particularly romances, are too dangerous for many clients. A range of other factors could also be constraining, including the possibility that there is a structural problem. For example, very stressed practitioners often think it is better if they keep it simple and say to themselves 'My business is my client [or patient, service user, customer, etc].' This is an issue as an appetite for, and a capacity to positively deal with, complexity is a sine qua non for good relationship-centered work. That said, over time practitioners can be encouraged to act more like systemic thinkers and multilateral actors. Even if a little rough and ready, this kind of practitioner approaches their work wanting to do what is decent and sensible, not what is hubristic and precious. Relationally oriented practitioners know it makes sense to be inclusive and to appreciate that the client will only do well in the long term if they are, as social planners say, 'joined-up'.

Planners, managers, and supervisors have a key role in normalizing this message by encouraging practitioners, and the services for which they are responsible, to be aligned with the commonsensical belief that each client is better off if there is a good-enough quality of affection and accountability in their lives. If this message is put simply, and is furthered with ingenuity and persistence, by those with more say and status, this will result in practitioners tending to buy in to this well-intended project.

Particular professional associations, such as those that represent occupational therapists and nurses, psychologists and medical specialists, can also make a telling contribution.

Although it is beyond this current exercise to detail how these professional bodies can advance the relational agenda, one obvious step is to examine the official documentation that governs professional ethics, training, and the delineation of practice standards. To this end the selective revision of existing codes of practice, schedules of accreditation, and programs of professional development could play a decisive role in fostering a professional culture within each of the disciplines that is more positive about, and more organized around, the practitioner's responsibility to promote vitality in the relational base of their clients. It is currently not unfair to say that this priority has a very minor status within training academies and across the varied fields of professional practice.

9
Learning to act well relationally

Building on the core competencies outlined in Chapter 8, included in this current chapter is a substantial volume of practice-focused material. This is varied in its focus and has been condensed from many years' practicing, supervising, teaching, and consulting across a broad spectrum of disciplines and fields. The theoretical and case material that has been integrated from these sources has been designed to have a direct application to the diverse, yet often almost discrete, networks within which health and human service professionals practice. Innovative ideas from this store can be selectively incorporated into daily practice with presenting individuals mindful of the demands of particular settings.

With some adjustment, these ideas and applications can be used to strengthen the client's relational base irrespective of the specific role that is, or might in the future be, undertaken. As emphasized in Chapter 1, the material is not primarily designed for senior practitioners or those in specialist couple, family, or group work positions. Rather, the emphasis has been to offer input to those in non-specialized graduate positions and in the senior years of undergraduate preparation.

This chapter explicitly aligns directly with the conceptual framework that forms the spine of the text. This backbone is elaborated and increasingly concretized in what follows so that a coherent theory–practice dialogue is present. This dialogue is used to substantiate, animate, and enact a relational approach to casework and clinical practice. The material is presented as follows:

- Using a purposive relational theme – 'working up an etiquette' – to develop relationship-building values, attitudes, and skills with individual clients and small groups, for example, residential units or more loosely affiliated networks
- An illustration of the approach in a simple case example
- How practitioners can 'coach for relationships'
- The description of five specific exercises where one or more can be incorporated into everyday practice to promote the relationship-building agenda

- The use of mediated forms of communication such as social networking and online gaming to facilitate relationship building with those who are isolated and socially anxious
- A more detailed illustration of the approach in an unusually difficult, closed-off practice context

In one sense some of this material may seem somewhat more 'out there'. This strangeness is not due to the theoretical complexity. Rather, it may appear initially unfamiliar as it has been derived from a diverse selection of traditions, not all of which are associated with health and community practice.

At times, these sources are less than mainstream. For example, techniques are cited from the emerging, if somewhat esoteric, field of 'philosophical consultation' (Colgate, 2004). Other ideas have been borrowed from more recognized traditions of practice, such as Narrative Therapy (White 2004; 2007) and Action and Commitment Therapy (Blackledge et al, 2009). What is common to these sources is the stress that is put on mobilizing the client's capacity for relational agency and personal ethics. This bias is grounded on an ontology that understands personhood as relational and dynamic rather than as unitary and unchanging. This theoretical practice is in sharp contrast to approaches that concentrate on the formal assessment of deficit and the diagnosis of personality. At the core of all the sources mined in this chapter is an allegiance to the former, rather than the latter, prejudice.

It only takes one new, or one improved, relationship to make a great deal of difference to the quality of a client's life. Dip in and out of the exercises discussed in this chapter: the material should be considered as a resource that can be selectively mined.

Working up an etiquette

It is generally assumed that relationships 'just happen'. This expectation holds that personal relationships are spontaneous products, connections that take their particular form as naturally occurring events where people 'just click' or there is 'a clash of personalities'. You either like someone or you don't. We have all heard it said that 'Wendy and Pete have fallen in love' or that 'Mary and John just don't get on.'

This description is so familiar as to be experienced as unremarkable, even self-evident. Positive relationships, it is said, occur as examples of natural alchemy (*you just get on with some people*) just as poor relationships reflect bad chemistry: *you can't get on with everyone*. Rather than understanding the relational domain performs according to choice and attitude, skills and philosophy, this standard account uses a language that is passively deterministic: 'John and his business partner just fell out 18 months ago' or 'May and Louie were immediately taken with each other.' This language practice depicts a vestigial domain, a realm that is beyond ordinary human agency.

Of course, there are thought to be the occasional contrary examples, exceptions where the notion of choice is acknowledged. Whether someone is familiar with the pseudo-technical term 'strategic friendship' (Pierce, 1996) or not, we are all familiar with the idea that in some situations *you have to get on with people you don't like* for reasons of manners or self-interest. Yet, such interactions are taken to be merely a sideshow, a theatre, and their existence does not disturb the expectation that it is chemistry that really determines the nature and operation of real relationships.

This is an unhelpful assumption. Being able to relate well and, more generally, to perform competently across the spectrum of associations that are required in life's varied domains is far from a natural faculty. On the contrary, being able to get on with people is an astonishingly sophisticated, highly learned accomplishment. Whilst this capacity seems natural, it is, in fact, the capacity to play an opaque game that has no transparent and fixed rules. For example, in situations where there is humor and irony present there are multiple and opposing levels of meaning that, if you don't just intuitively 'get it', the social game is experienced as a confusing, even alienating, drama. (Think of the clunky cross-cultural experiences you have had with humor and irony.) A parallel might make this clearer.

According to Tim Page, a person with a self-declared diagnosis of Asperger syndrome, people with an autism spectrum disorder find social interactions random and un-patterned, puzzling to the point where they tend to become cut-off or alarmed (Page, 2007). In a high-profile essay in the *New Yorker*, Page recounted how in his early adult life he had found the higgledy-piggledy of the social dance so distancing he could not find a way in, no matter how hard he tried. Unlike those he referred to as 'neuro-typicals', that is, everyone else, those who were normal, who did not have an autism spectrum disorder, he only found disorder in everyday interactions. Interestingly, Page reported that later in life he found it was very useful to read, and to then to try to employ, what he had memorized from classic books on manners, such as Debrett's *Modern Etiquette and Modern Manners*. He said these texts gave him a code that he was able to use to orient him through the unpredictable drama of social interactions.

That Page found guidance in concrete rules is not to say others who have difficulties with relationships could or should take the same route. The difficulties in relating associated with who are said to be 'on the spectrum' are not the same as the difficulties that are the result of ostracism or a person learning to be defensive; nor are they of the same order as the relationship issues associated with, for example, those who have a diagnosis of schizophrenia. Rather, what is being illustrated is that relationships – our capacity to initiate, maintain, and exit from interpersonal relations – should not be understood as a competence that is natural and effortless. In so far as this is so, relational competence can be worked on and improved. Building up this competence by engaging in discussions about the values and skills, attitudes, and behaviors, which can be helpful in relating, as well as the errors and accidents that are not helpful, can offer a high point of focus, a theme, in professional work that seeks to be build the client's capacity for relationships. The following exercise broadly introduces this possibility.

Reflective exercise 4: Leading questions

Clients who are lonely sometimes say to their practitioner 'I wish I had friends, even one friend.' Or, they might say 'It'd be great to have a partner [boy/girlfriend, to get on better with my siblings, those in my group home, my kids, cousin, aunt, etc].' In this circumstance it can be useful to discuss questions of interpersonal conduct with them. This is not to imply professionals should tell clients there are rules or commandments. Rather, might it be useful to discuss specific examples that could be brought up by the client (or the worker) and to use the idea of etiquette as a focus for review?

There are many items that might be raised with the client in this kind of dialogue. From a many-colored palette the scenarios that might be painted include thought experiments such as asking the client:

- 'Do you like it when X [your roommate, the guy who makes your coffee, your sister, etc] shows an interest in your mood, activities, clothing, health, or hopes?'
- 'Do you think showing an interest in the kind of day someone is having might be a friendly gesture and a positive step in relationship making if you do this genuinely?'
- 'Who should make the first statement/ask the first question when people meet?'
- 'If you agree it is good to be thoughtful about others, what exactly does thoughtfulness consist of – what does it actually look like?'
- 'Is an essential part of relating being fair?'

In visiting different countries, travelers often find local social conventions differ from those with which they are familiar. Similarly, if you visit a community of deaf people, a different suite of manners is in play. For example, a person who wishes to communicate knocks sharply, which creates vibrations, in order to draw attention to the fact they have something to say. Residents in this setting have naturalized the sense in this practice whilst outsiders can find this jarring. In other new environments, such as the internet, it is not self-evident how we are to conduct ourselves. A Melbourne social worker, Jaime Power, facilitates 'net etiquette' groups for people with a mental illness who are trying to learn how to use this mode of communication in a cooperative manner. These groups are not about reading from a rule book so much as acting as centers for collective reflection.

Such discussions can be useful in two ways. First, it is possible for someone to learn, as Tim Page mentioned, a guiding convention, something that clarifies the 'regulatory fictions' that make life easier (Khan, 1971). More importantly, such attention can contribute to the development of an agenda, a particular kind of figure and ground effect, which brings the matter of the interpersonal into focus. In the same way a group work program could set out to have clients develop their own cookbook of easy recipes, a focus on compiling a 'How to get on with others' discussion page, even codebook, offers an action learning process that embeds an ongoing attention to that which oils the mechanics of relating.

It is well established that a client's friends, workmates, informal associations, and relatives are important, but so is the quality of everyday contacts; for example, if someone is regularly 'dissed' on the street, this injures not only their pride, it prejudices their prospects for health (Wilkinson and Pickett, 2009). In light of this knowledge, conversations the practitioner has with the client can refract, but be informed by, Tim Page's idea of learning the rule book of sociality. A reflective theme can be forged: *can you, can we, work out how a person should conduct themselves in order to get on well with others?* Dialogues on and around this theme have a tremendous capacity to be both emotionally evocative and also constructively challenging.

Western citizens know more about, and have more of a language to describe, the individual than interpersonal processes or social contexts. What is known about the attitudes and skills associated with relationships tends to be implicit, what has been referred to as representing a kind of 'tacit knowledge' (Argyris and Schon, 1975). This kind of intuitive information is relatively inaccessible and does not represent as strong a form of knowledge as that which is conscious. The following seeks to make the relational more conscious.

Biological and social learning models

It is understood that people with schizophrenia, and other serious mental illnesses, have fewer social ties than the population as a whole (Burgess et al, 2010). This finding is usually explained in terms of the interplay between 'negative symptoms' and 'neuro-cognitive deficits' (Lewis and Ronan, 2010; Schizophrenia.com, 2011). Typically, it is said that those with a long-term mental illness have deficits in social cognition as a consequence of the interplay between neurological impairment and the negative symptoms of their illness.

The elements of social cognition said to be especially at issue include impairments in affect recognition, theory of mind, and insight. This explanation has considerable research support, yet might this view represent an overly deterministic summary and a rationale for pessimism? Given it is accepted that:

- the research has proven people with schizophrenia are 'in deficit' when it comes to being able to relate well, and
- the practice wisdom in the mental health field holds that consumers tend to become over-stressed by close relationships

might the result of these views be that practitioners have learned to lack optimism when it comes to promoting the social connectedness of their clients?

Rather than 'other' consumers – to say *I need my connections, but those with a serious mental illness are somehow different* – it is more consistent with the goal of social inclusion and recovery to expect the same for 'them'. That is, rather than recycle biological explanations, is it possible to look through another lens and to think of what has been learned by those with a diagnosis of serious mental illness and, by implication, by those who been pilloried and ostracized, blamed, and castigated? As discussed in Chapter 3, many service users:

- are so frightened, so intensely suspicious, that this static wards off others;
- do not offer the interpersonal initiatives that start up conversations (the 'anticipatory postures'), or, if they do, their initial moves will seem odd and inappropriate;
- trust far too little, or way too much;
- do not often offer the 'free information' that assists conversations, and therefore relationships, to build;
- do not readily declare attachment;
- do not respond reciprocally when another presents the start-up gestures that have the role of signaling an openness to exchange;
- seem to be resolutely concrete in remaining 'where they are at' to the extent that they appear to lack empathy and therefore lose track of where the other is;
- will 'get in first' and exit (a class or meeting, a new associate, a budding friendship, a romance) so as to avoid the possibility that they will be hurt again.

In so far as this is the lived experience of many clients, it follows that an active approach to assisting these people have a facilitated access to the skills, knowledge, and values that promote positive relating becomes a high priority.

Skills for conducting more or less intimate personal relations

As discussed earlier, getting along with others is an astonishingly complex business. Unlike the naming and defining of elements – think of the precision in the periodic table as to the definition of carbon or iron – there remains an intrinsic uncertainty in the naming and defining of social categories, including the relational. One approach to 'How do we get along with, or not get along with, others' is to talk about 'social intelligence'. This construct was first proposed in the 1920s (Goleman, 2006, p 83) and has its own advantages and controversies. For example, Goleman's own description of the dimensions, and the relationship between these aspects, of social intelligence has not been rigorously tested, as he notes himself (Goleman, 2006, p 355).

Putting aside questions of hierarchy and categorization, any listing of the elements of 'social intelligence' has to be extensive. How eye contact should be undertaken, personal distance regulated, introductions made, gestures interpreted:

there are an almost infinite number of elements and levels. Nonetheless, there are many schemas that have been constructed for presenting the competencies involved in relationships – it is relatively easy to locate guidance. (This text put forward its own limited contribution in nominating the need for balance between the autonomous self and the relational self: see the discussion in Chapter 7 .) More or less formal scholarship acknowledged, it is not necessary for practitioners to rely on any particular schema.

The goal of assisting clients to relate well can be approached from any number of angles and often arises organically in contact with clients. It can also be the product of a deliberate attempt. For example, a client ('Jodie') might say to you 'I just don't know what to say when Jack ignores me!' Rather than simply expressing your empathy once again, at a certain point you might say 'What do you think your options are?' Jodie might say, 'I can just tell him to get fucked or I can grin and bear it.' After following through with the pros and cons of each option, you might ask 'Have you thought there might be other possibilities, other tactics? For example, have you seen anybody apparently getting on with someone they don't click with without either pretending or being silenced?'

Assisting clients undertake a thoughtful scan in order to generate different ways forward can be achieved in many ways. You could ask Jodie to consider questions like 'Have you ever been watching two people having a hassle and thought one, or both, might usefully try something other than the "stuff you" or "suck it up" idea you came up with?' A dialogue can be started, a themed interaction, that can be as creative as it is practical. You might ask Jodie to do some research between now and the next meeting, to take a note or two from her favorite television shows, to review how her mother and father, or most successful aunt and uncle, did things.

There are many ways forward. As long as it is not a form of colonialism, the practitioner might even venture an idea or two:

> 'I'm no role model, but sometimes I think it's better to dance around a little, to not go straight to how I feel or see it. Sometimes it seems to work better when I tell myself to slow it down and to make a point of asking the other person "What's happening for you: how do you see it?" You know, really work hard at listening before I jump in or just go quiet. Might it sometimes pay to be curious and to dance around a little first? What do you think?'

An act of self-disclosure that has been carefully reflected upon can be useful. At times, examples taken from the actual process of the interactions between the practitioner and the client can also be profitably explored – if it is the right time, the right kind of relationship, and the client will not see it as 'smart arse'. For example, the practitioner might say 'This might seem an odd thing to say but I've found myself thinking you are very careful not to hurt my feelings. Do you sometimes find yourself pulling your punches given you are an older, worldlier person and I am a young practitioner. Is that how it is sometimes?'

If a client is apparently lonely and wanting more social contact, but this isolation has not been presented directly by the client as a problem, this can be raised by the practitioner in a casual way as a possible issue. For example: 'Jodie, do you think you sometimes keep potential friends away, at least in part, because you have learned to get in first and reject others so you don't get hurt?' Starting a dialogue with this kind of enquiry, or re-inserting it in subsequent contacts, is not about Jodie needing a rule book. Rather, she is in the driver's seat and remains the expert on her situation so that the intermittent dialogue that takes place between her and the practitioner on the topic of relationships is as discontinuous as it might also be thematic. However zigzagging these discussions may be, if the practitioner remains emotionally attuned, the effect is likely to be both cumulative and optimistic.

In addition to ongoing conversations with a single client, a focus on 'How do you think it best to get on with others?' can be used in a group program, like a social skills group, or in regular meetings in a share house with the aim of developing a 'culture', a shared set of norms and expectations. This can be a galvanizing and dynamic theme in constructed environments such as group homes, hostels, work teams, or day centers. The following is a composite account of how this was undertaken in a residential setting.

VIGNETTE 18: THE RESIDENTIAL UNIT

Twelve people with a long history of mental health difficulties live in a small block of flats auspiced by a non-government psychiatric disability and rehabilitation service. After an initial assessment, each successful candidate for residency is placed in one of six two-bedroom units where each unit has its own kitchen and small lounge. Over an extended period the aim is to assist residents in developing their independent living skills, to become more ready for paid employment, and to become more socially included. In the spirit of the sector the emphasis is less on formal diagnosis than on functional assessments. This acknowledged, each of the residents has multiple deficits where a low social skills quotient tends to be a common characteristic.

All residents have access to one common area and convene there twice a week for house meetings. These meetings are designed to plan outings, review house rules, and to resolve the practical and interpersonal issues that arise from time to time. Over the last few months the support workers attached to the unit have decided a priority is to develop a culture within the group that is more appreciative and affirming. So far, this goal has not proceeded well as there is an established group dynamic that is passive, even surly. This atmosphere seems rigidly fixed. So negative is the dynamic that attempts by staff to steer the group towards a more active and respectful attitude have produced a 'The more we push, the more they back off' interaction. Residents also resent the meetings and rounding up residents for group meetings has become a terse issue.

Following a near violent incident between two residents in the common laundry, it was expected this episode would be the focus at the next group meeting. This prospect generated a feeling of impending drama for residents and staff alike. After some serious reflecting, and some internal controversy, in an ad hoc staff meeting that preceded the house meeting it was decided not to specifically focus on the incident. Rather, two staff volunteered to try something different.

When the larger group was gathered, one of the support workers said: "We are going to have a special meeting tonight. Our only agenda item will be this: 'How are we getting on with getting on?'" Before being divided into three groups of four to come up with at least one behavior, each of the small groups said they wanted to see more of, and one less of, the larger group were told they were not to form sub-groups on the basis of friendships "It might even be better if you tried to group up with some of those you don't get on so well with." Each sub-group was asked to nominate a spokesperson, preferably someone who tended to be shy and not so comfortable talking up in the large group, and to take 15 minutes out of earshot of the other groups to think over the task.

After dividing up and leaving the common area, the support workers left the groups alone for five minutes. They then visited each group and made sure that each group had nominated a spokesperson. With only one exception, the sub-groups returned on time (the other group had to be reminded), and the support workers underlined the importance of the spokesperson not quoting any particular group member, to keep their report anonymous.

The list of 'do's' and 'don'ts' was, not surprisingly, similar: "Our group all wanted us to be more respectful", "We agreed it is not on to feel scared", and so forth. The support workers then gently challenged each group, with just a few minutes' preparation, to demonstrate in action what their particular 'do's' and 'don'ts' looked like from the outside, as a behavior. This created a set of 'funny-meets-clumsy', but good humored, role-play performances. Each sub-group was asked to see if someone in their group was prepared to write up something of their experience from the evening.

At the end of the meeting, the support workers said, "We can try and back you all up, and we will because that is our job. What we'd ask you to begin to do yourselves is to start a project: to develop a code – a set of manners, an etiquette of your own creation – of what will work for the group as a whole. What kind of flag do you want to salute when it comes to how your tribe is going to get on with each other? What values do you want to see define what you stand for? We can bug you, hassle you, but you know who has the power here, even if you often don't feel powerful."

Over the next few months, and facilitated by a subtle but containing group facilitation, a peer-driven culture began to take shape. At times it was a bumpy process, but it was vastly more exciting and infectious than anyone expected. Statements like 'I want this place to be about being accepted, and that we all believe it is good to listen' became, for example, expressions that residents said aloud, and to themselves. At different points staff, and visitors, heard it said: "When a new resident joins us, we want this person to know this is a special place. At our place prejudice and bullying aren't accepted. We know what its like to be bossed around, to have people really look down on you like you are a freak. This won't happen in this space. We want to have a reputation for cooperation and respect. It's not who talks loudest or longest who wins. It's who doesn't believe it's about winning that we care most about."

• People are proud if they have participated in building a positive culture. It is enlivening to believe in relating, in feeling a nest is growing within which those included can be happy to be held in and to identify with. Not only is there a 'buy-in' when this occurs, which is an instrumental good, participants who see themselves as standing for something worthwhile will internalize this as an ennobling aspect of their identity. Most likely, those who behave well with others will also become more popular with others. This is both a means and an ends in terms of social inclusion.

Getting on well with others is not simply about behaviors and skills; it is more about having the right attitudes and values as these internal qualities set the stage for quality relationships. Seeing the value in being fair, thoughtful, and contributing goes a long way towards being popular, but having these values also helps us feel good about ourselves.

The psychotherapies, and Western culture more generally, encourages each of us to be 'I-centered', to be focused on 'What I want, intend, think, or feel.' In effect, this acts to consign to personal accountability a minor, old-fashioned, even relic-like status. Like guilt and shame, an attention to 'what is not about me' can be inadvertently stimulated by practitioners to slip over the horizon of consciousness, just as the opposite process can also be mobilized.

As discussed earlier, 'kinship libido' (Jung, 1946) involves an appetite for connection. This appetite is always present even if it may sometimes be dormant. Given the right circumstances practitioners can fan this latent hunger into its pro-social expression. Accountability, fairness, and a concern for others is an energy that can be exercised, and when these qualities are up and about, they help form the axis for secure and positive interactions. The aim is to "strengthen the bonds of inclusive membership by trying to nurture reciprocity, sharing and small scale redistribution between individuals, household, groups (and) communities" (Parton, 2008, p 255).

A simple relating exercise

The presenting problem is rarely understood by the client, or the agency/funding body, as loneliness, under-developed relating skills, or the like. The single issue, or more probably, the complex set of presenting problems encountered by the practitioner, will mostly have a far grittier and complicated profile (Keene, 2001). Substance use, gambling, child safety, self-harm, homelessness, unstable diabetes – these are but a few of the wildly diverse problems presented to practitioners. When such compelling realities have to be the focus of attention, the question becomes: where should I start if the intention is to collaborate with the client to improve their level of connectedness?

Conscious that the presenting problem has to remain at the foreground of attention, practitioners with sufficient professional vision understand that the longer-term prospects for securing a resolution, or a substantial amelioration, of the presenting difficulty depends on the client achieving a good-enough relational status. Hopefully, this idea can be discussed with the client directly, and agreement reached that this is an important concern. At other times, for example, when the contact is brief or the client is not ready to talk about their loneliness or disastrous history of relationships, the practitioner can work in relation to this theme even if a joint agreement has not been forged. Even well-resourced, focused clients can be approached in this way. Because those who are materially advantaged have not been tarred with the marks of injustice and stigma, in so far as these clients are products of the process of individualization they will, as those who have been stigmatized, tend towards the practice of self-absorption that so injures the mutuality upon which relationships depend.

In this context, coaching for relationships begins with the client, or the practitioner, identifying:

- one current relationship whose quality might be improved, and/or
- one possible new relationship that is desired.

If only one opportunity is identified, and if this single relationship is worked up with enterprise and creativity, it is possible to make a great deal of difference to the quality of the client's life. In one sense it does not matter which kind of relationship is the subject of action as, once begun, the process of becoming more relationally adept tends to roll out into the other sub-domains of connection. A short vignette might be helpful in introducing this topic.

VIGNETTE 19: TOM

Tom is an isolated man aged 45 who receives a disability pension because of chronic respiratory and vascular problems. He also has financial difficulties, often drinks to excess, and says he has little or nothing to live for. Gemma is a caseworker employed by a not-for-profit agency funded to support clients who are likely to be high-demand users of health services. Gemma has met Tom on several occasions and they appear to get on fairly well, but it is early in the work.

In passing, during a home visit Tom mentions he was asleep on his couch one afternoon last week when he was woken by a knock on the door: "Bastards," he tells you, "they won't let you alone! I was just minding my own business and this so-and-so upset me just as I was nodding off."

Raising up her courage, Gemma says: "Yes, I bet that was annoying, but did you actually know who it was who knocked?" Tom then says, "Well, I didn't answer the door. I just wasn't feeling myself." Gemma is curious and, after some banter, decides to push him a little. Tom then says: "Yeah, I do know because I got up to look through the blinds and I saw it was a neighbor. That was Jack. He's an alright kind of bloke mostly. It was a bit awkward really. He saw me looking through the window at him. But, you know me, my life is a battle and I just was not in the right mood to talk to anyone. He must know I just wasn't feeling well. I didn't mean to snub him. You have to know I was not meaning to piss him off, to hurt his feelings. No, it was nothing like that."

In Tom's mind he had mixed up his intentions, his feelings, with the effect of his actions — as we all do, at least from time to time. It is not unusual to assume others know and can appreciate your point of view. This is a kind of benign sorcery, a form of magic thinking that is oblivious to the feelings of others and the effects our actions, however innocent we assume they are, can have. Like all of us can do, Tom forgot that 'not relating' is never an option: not talking, not answering a text, even keeping a stony face, is a form of communication.

In this situation imagine you are Tom's worker. Listen to Tom's account and make a note to yourself to remember this story. A little later, at a point when Tom and you are talking about how stressed and isolated he feels, it might be constructive to say something like this: 'I've been thinking over what you told me about Jack, your neighbor, waking you up when he knocked on the door a week or two ago. What do you think, maybe, you might feel a little embarrassed at the idea that you might have to bump into Jack again given what had happened?'

If Tom then said something like he had already met Jack at the bus stop and he was surprised Jack seemed a little colder than normal, you might say, 'Putting yourself in Jack's shoes, what do you think he might have thought when he saw you through the window after you didn't open the door to him?' If Tom did not think you were being attacking, if your relationship with him is generally positive, Tom would not have to think much before he might say: 'I guess it was a bit of a bad look, that he thought I'd blanked him. Whatever, it happened. I can't do anything about it now.'

Tom is likely to be at the discouraged end of the social continuum, to be someone at the point where it feels as if nothing can change. The voice in his head tells him 'It's the same as it ever was. Hopeless. As it was, so it will be.' Outsiders, such as professionals, are able to see it differently and will disagree with his view he 'can't do anything about it now', that it is too late to mend what had occurred between him and his neighbor. Professionals know this from a mix of personal and professional learning. Research has demonstrated that if practitioners successfully identify and address difficulties that arise along the way in the evolving practitioner–client relationship, this creates opportunities to deepen the working relationship. Similarly, rather than avoiding dealing with difficulties in everyday relationships, practitioners have learned that if problems are genuinely addressed, this can act to consolidate these connections. On this basis you might say to Tom: 'I've an idea here. I am not telling you that you should, but if you decided to make an effort at amends, at trying to build a bridge with Jack, what could you do?'

It is likely that Tom will not immediately hook up with this idea. At least initially, it is more likely he will decline the invitation to engage with anything that has the potential to underline his loser-dysfunctional pedigree. So, having planted a seed, you do not want to get into an arm wrestle, a pursuer–pursed dynamic. You could say: 'Your call. No drama. Let's leave it there.' A fortnight later when you meet again, Tom might surprise you if he told you 'On a whim, on the spur of the moment, I knocked on Jack's door with a couple of beers last week. I was breathing a bit hard but I told him what had happened, and that I felt a loaf for coming over so unfriendly to him when he came over to visit. He looked strange, like he was going to cry or deflate or something, but he opened the door and I went in and we had a good yarn. I was proud of myself. I put myself in the driver's seat and have taught myself a good lesson.'

Unlikely outcome? No doubt this probably seems like one of those fairy tale stories (even if it did really happen). If a process is begun whose purpose is to develop social connections, it will mostly not proceed so seamlessly. Rather, it will ebb and flow over a longer time period. Tom and his caseworker are more likely to turn the scenario over during a number of sessions, having it come back and forth, around and around, on a zigzagging path. Despite this probability, in some cases social relations do not act incrementally as they can jump to the new by taking up qualitatively emergent forms in what can be the blink of the eye. This is because humans have, at least to some degree, a potential to connect.

Coaching clients

There is a 'fuzzy space' between coaching and therapy (Spinelli, 2010). Definitional issues to one side, coaching has become a motif of interest in some settings. For example, the idea of 'coaching for health' has emerged as a particular type of intervention with those struggling to manage chronic disease and other complex medical difficulties (Lindner et al, 2003). Similarly, Carter and McGoldrick (1999, pp 440, 450-2) propose that professionals in counseling and case management-like roles can, if the circumstances are appropriate, set out to coach clients. This purpose may only relate to a component of the practitioner's larger brief; it may only be a marginal rather than a core role. Whether central or peripheral, if furthering relational competence is a mutually agreed, or mutually understood, goal (Turnell and Edwards, 1999), this specific purpose can be advanced if practitioners position themselves to 'coach for connection'. In taking up this purpose the focus can be on one or more of the following elements: mobilizing motivation, education, behavior change, challenging, and psychosocial support.

To reference the idea of coaching is not to imply that it is generally helpful to be directive. Yet, in so far as goals such as education, behavior change, or psychosocial support are in play, it is useful to be able to communicate directly. For example, rather than 'beating around the bush' it is good to have a repertoire that includes direct questions: 'In terms of your family and friends, who in particular would you like to get on better with?' Preferably, the names of the people who are part of the client's interpersonal environment can be used if a network assessment has been completed:

> 'Sam, you've said that Neil and Von are your mates in your group home, and that it is Hennie who you reckon is the house horror. Given you and Hennie already get on so badly, what about the wild idea of starting a campaign to get on better with her? This probably sounds like a far-out, science fiction thing – but stick with it a moment: if you could get things 10 per cent better, even 20 per cent, this would improve your life a whole heap. Are you game to give it shot? The way you tell it, you've got nothing to lose.'

In a given client contact it may even be sound useful to directly introduce the relational in a pro-active way. For example, it might be progressive to say something like, 'I'd really like to talk with you about family and friends, about where you are right now and where you might like to get to in the future. What I want to talk with you about is where you might get and give more friendship, love, and respect.' If it seemed indicated, the practitioner could turn this discussion into an up-front theme. For example, they might say something like:

> 'There are so many different kinds of relationships it is often hard to know where to start. One way to get to grips with this stuff is to take some time and do a kind of stock take. This one-page score sheet is a relationship review table that divides up, and then puts into, groups, the different kinds of relationships you have. Can I give you this checklist so you can review how you rate each of the different types of relationships you are involved with between now and the next time we meet?

'The idea is to work through this review in four steps taking as long as you like. The first step is to rate each of these relationship groups in terms of good, neutral, non-existent or conflictual. Second, make a comment on which kinds of relationship you'd like to change – and be as specific as you like: use real names if it fits. Third, say which areas you'd like to get changed in terms of what has the highest long-term priority. Fourth, and this is the hardest part, nominate one, or maybe two, relationship groups where you think there is the best chance, or where you have the strongest motivation, to work on first.'

Table 9.1 sets out a one-page checklist that the client, perhaps with the practitioner's assistance, can use to focus in on the above task. This can be customized in many ways. For example, column one could be filled in using real names in relation to the ratings of *positive, neutral, non-existent, conflictual*; a five-point Likert scale

Table 9.1: Relationship review table

		Status: positive, neutral, non-existent, conflictual	Which of these relationships would you like to change?	The highest priorities for long-term change are?	The most sensible starting point?
1	Companions and friends				
2	Romance/ partnership				
3	Sisters and brothers				
4	Extended family: aunts, cousins, etc				
5	Parent or parents				
6	Current neighbors				
7	Where there is a common interest				
8	In your workplace, school, etc				
9	Regulars where you shop, drink, eat, etc				
10	Professionals, eg doctors; support worker, etc				

could be used for column two items in order to prioritize different options; and in column three clients could be asked to rate the degree of difficulty they would see in changing particular relationships. Many variations can be used to tailor this task to the interest and capacity of the client. This externalization does, of course, also allow for time periods – T1–T2 intervals – to be set **and** self-report comparisons to be undertaken.

The use of this table enables clients to externalize their thinking, to give their inchoate inner feelings and meanings a visual form. This can be a powerful tool for reviewing personal relationships. If this domain is objectified, however fluidly, it is easier for clients to 'walk around' the issue, to find a place of outlook from which the relational world can be seen in perspective. Practitioners can take up the specifics of what is raised – the particular relationships and relationship types that are nominated as current strengths or goals for development – and use these as a focus for reflection, dialogue and action. If this is done concretely multiple practical possibilities can evolve and unfold. Delineating the sub-types of relationships, outlining them in terms of their class on this spreadsheet, holds against clients conflating their attitudes and ideas about relationships into an impenetrable stew. Giving the sub-types of relationship, visual differentiation allows for a more exact articulation of the current state of play as it also previews new space and diversified possibilities. Practitioners can take up what is raised and use this as a focus for dialogue, for multiple conversations that can evolve and unfold.

Such a collaborative approach draws on the advantages demonstrated in many of the more contemporary practice traditions. These advantages include the directness of the task approach (Marsh and Doel, 2005), the optimism of solutions approach practitioners (Berg, 2007), the self-report – 'performance metrics' – emphasis of Scott Miller and his associates (Miller et al, 2004b), and the 'can-do' of motivational interviewing (Rollnick and Miller, 1995). Key to the effectiveness of this device is the catalyzing of an active review and the pre-figuring of goals that make sense to the client. Establishing goals is certainly an important step, but the know-how to be able to participate in relationships may, to a degree, still be missing. Like Tom in Vignette 19, some particular coaching may be useful.

Five specific engagements to improve relational capacity

Although no definitive answer is available to the question 'What attitudes and skills are associated with doing well in relationships?', it is clear there are certain elements that need to be present. At least to a minimal degree, a person has to have a capacity to be considerate, respectful, to able to listen and speak, and so forth. These general capabilities noted, if the question is more closely addressed, relational competence is revealed as a complex, even contradictory, matter (as discussed earlier in this chapter around the theme of etiquette, p 212). Given there is no formula for satisfactory relating, it is therefore impossible to offer a program of rote learning. And each of us has a distinct mix of advantages and areas for further development.

This heterogeneity acknowledged, there are a number of observable patterns in many of those who have:

- suffered the depredations of isolation and exclusion, and/or
- been acculturated within the logic of individualization.

For example, those in one, or both, categories often shoot themselves in the foot in interactions with others because they paint the effects of their own actions out of the picture, as Tom did in the above vignette. Tom was so self-absorbed, so mindful of his own feelings and troubles, he defaulted to blaming others when something went wrong. Blaming, like denial, may be a primal defense, but it is counter-productive as it disempowers the blamer: blaming pre-empts the possibility of coming up with alternative forms of action. Literally, blaming the other short-circuits the possibility of active reflection and sidelines the prospects for personal agency. *She (or he) is the problem – not me!* Unless a person is able to say 'Perhaps, I might have done things differently', they have shut down their imagination of what is potentially in their power to do differently.

But blaming does have its advantages. As each of us has experienced, casting blame covers over feelings of personal failure and self-reproach. There is certainly a protective-defensive function to blame, but it is too simplistic to assume this is the fundamental explanation why we are so ready to blame others when relationships go awry.

A different interpretation is that blaming occurs when a person does not register that the other is a separate entity, with their own subjectivity, legitimate interests, and unique perspective. Shaped by the workings of disadvantage and/or the process of individualization, the modern subject can be pushed to such a degree of self-absorption that the other slips over the horizon and becomes invisible as a sentient and distinct other being. This disturbance can be related to the eclipse of what sociologists have termed the 'generalized other' by sociologists, and what developmental psychology refers to as the 'theory of mind'. In so far as this slippage occurs the capacity to imagine the other's interests, feelings and point of view can be misplaced. This has important interpersonal consequences because empathic and accountable social interaction is premised on the imaginative presence of the other. Of course, anyone can, at least from time to time, lose sight of the other, but what has to be avoided is a pattern where the reality of the other slips over the horizon into invisibility more permanently.

Each of us is able to raise the dust and then complain we can't see. Everyone can, at least at times, come across as unengaged, as spiky, as defensive, or as distant, even as we are only aware of our own intentions or feelings (as was Tom). Rather than being able to maintain a focus on the social cues we are delivering, it is human to become overly self-aware. Being self-aware is a key competence, but it is also an action that can easily merge into self-absorption. Being overly self-referential – an outcome that organizes our thinking and our perceptions into a life that is lived inside our own bubble – is always a possibility. For example, if I feel lonely, or unappreciated, or lacking in self-confidence, this can lead me to *expect* that the other person will ignore me, reject me or abuse me – that they will 'do it to me again.' This disposition, of course, then acts to set in train exactly the kind of outcomes I wish to avoid.

As discussed earlier in this chapter, an inability to identify and process social cognitions is said to be associated with certain psychiatric diagnoses. More speculatively, this apparent deficit could also be associated with developmental problems, such as autism, and personality formations such as the psychopathic, the narcissistic, and the borderline. It is also the case that those who have had adverse life events, and/or who have had unfortunate 'careers' in the health and welfare sector, are likely to find themselves maintained in a holding pattern within which 'the other' is perceived as a potential threat, if perceived at all. This is quite poignantly the case for many clients, and those potential clients identified as members of at-risk groups, for example, people who are homeless, or un/under-employed.

The larger possibility arises that there is also a pattern of self-reference built into the subjectivity of everyday citizens to the extent that they have been shaped by the process of individualization. As discussed in Chapter 2, the process of individualization demands that each citizen looks after themselves first, is an effective strategizer, knows what they want, acts opportunistically, and so forth. In so far as a person is forged by this attitude set it follows they will reference events and interpretations in relation to themselves. The consequence of this self-absorption is the loosening, even the loss of, an intuitive grip on the reality that 'the other' has their own legitimate needs, perceptions, and perspectives. Trying to put this in a seriously playful way, it seems we are being invited to be the becoming products of the process of individualization.

Against this background, five related engagements are outlined that practitioners could use as exercises in relationally oriented practice:

- Being able to separate intent from outcome
- Identifying and managing the 'me–first maneuver'
- Considering the question: 'How direct should my communications be?'
- Being able to back down
- Discussions about what is fair and right

These original engagements have been designed for use in casework that seeks to 'coach for relationships'. They are put forward as offering scenarios within which discussion and rehearsing can be undertaken. They could also be used as distinct topics – even as they are not serial in their relationship.

Being able to separate intent from outcome

From time to time each of us becomes preoccupied with our own intentions. We say to ourselves, or to another person, 'I meant well' or 'I didn't intend any harm'.

Similarly, a person might say 'I did not mean it' or 'I just couldn't help it' if the other becomes upset or a situation has not resolved well. In the same register are comments like 'I haven't done anything wrong. Can't they see I was doing the best I could?!' We often concentrate on our own inside story, our own internal theatre. This experiential base does not inform an endearing response to others. However understandable, it is not interpersonally literate to be insensitive to the consequences of our actions or to another's feelings, needs, and perceptions.

Imagine you had been badly held up in traffic and this left the person you were to meet standing about for half an hour. When you finally arrive, what is the best way to act? You could hold the silence and try to stay in tune with the other's feelings, but this option leaves many of us feeling awkward. Another option, often the easier one, is to rush into an account of your own difficulties. You might offer a perfunctory 'sorry', but you might not even do that, before launching into something like: 'I am having such as bad day and am really stressed out. The mobile had no credit, and anyway it was nearly out of charge. You know what I mean, it is such a downer when that happens! And, do you get it, it was, you know, just the worst kind of thing that had happened, is still happening, at work. I didn't mean to, you know, do the wrong thing by you. Whatever, there's no point getting stuck on it, shit happens. What will we do now, maybe take a coffee? Has to be quick mind, I've got so much on at the moment that I just need to tell you about.'

There is no acknowledgment of the other's feelings in this option – it is the statement of a person who has no guilty mind, no *mens rea*, as the law would put it: if no harm was intended, then no harm could have been done, right? No. Neutral intentions, even good intentions, can never guarantee no harm will be done. Accidents can happen, everyday unexpected events can cause injury and insult, irrespective of whether harm was or was not intended.

This slippage between intention and consequences is especially poignant in the lives of many clients. If a client is full of feelings, they are unlikely to make the distinction between their intent and the effect of their actions, between what is happening in their thoughts and feelings and the impacts of their actions (just as Tom was not able to do without a supportive prompt). Because this pattern is so frequently seen, and its impact on the prospects for relationships so profound, there is a strong rationale for practitioners introducing this distinction as a focus in conversations with clients, mindful, as they always have to be, of the importance of timing and tone.

Conceptually, it is clear that being able to make the 'intent' and 'outcome' distinction is empowering as it enables choices. Yet how might the idea of this distinction be introduced in a dialogue with the client? For some clients it might be appropriate to raise the issue directly. For example, 'I sometimes get so caught up in my own bubble I forget that I can have a shitty effect on others, even when I am not intending to. Has that ever happened between you and me? Have I ever given you a fright, maybe even put you down, when I did not mean to?' The client might pick this up and run with it, or they might say, 'I don't get it.

What you are asking?' In the latter case you might then turn it around and ask, 'Have you ever got so caught up in your own movie that you did not realize you had upset someone even though you were not intending to?' Alternatively, the practitioner might know about, and be able to use, a real world example (as Gemma did in Vignette 19).

Depending on the personal style of the practitioner, this distinction could be raised in more abstract or direct prompts. You could ask 'Have you heard that old Cockney saying "Don't' piss on my shoes and tell me it's raining." What do you think this means?' If it is done in an attuned manner, you could say to an embattled client: 'From the work I've done over the years, I've seen a common pattern when it comes to relationships. Those who feel most under attack, those people who have every reason under the sun to feel aggrieved and fed up, sometimes get out of practice at being in touch with how others feel, with how the other sees things differently to them. Do you think it is ever a little like that for you?' Once well introduced, this theme can often go a long way.

Identifying and managing the 'me-first maneuver'

If a relationship is a mutual exchange, each party has to able to communicate their position and preferences. This mostly involves being able to make 'I-statements'. Variations based on culture, gender, generational position, and organizational status mediate how direct the parties can be, but it still remains the case that finding a way to tell the other that, for example, 'I'd like to do X' or 'I'm not up to doing Z today' is a key ingredient in the negotiation of social relationships.

Some individuals become very practiced at offering 'I-statements' in their dealings with others and do so to their own advantage. For example, if an interaction is uncertainly poised, if it might be about to become awkward, it can tilt the odds if one party says 'I'm feeling really low. It is just not going my way at the moment.' When this occurs the other will find it hard not to respond within the terms that this statement recommends. If the other responds in the expected way – 'Oh, that's no good. Tell me more' (or 'What can I do? Wow, you've got it tough' etc) – the interaction is tipped towards one party's concerns and perspectives. If habituated, this leaning becomes a pattern that is naturalized as the accepted reality, as a local custom, between the players. It becomes a 'just-the-way-it-is' given. (The same inequity occurs when one party is more ready to say what they want.)

The issue is not whether an asymmetric pattern of 'I-statements', or other non-verbal signals that have the same effect, is consciously pursued. What is at issue is that the making of an 'I-statement' can be read as a move, as an interpersonal tactic, because it changes the options that are available to the relationship's other participant, or participants, as communication theorists well understand (Watzlawick et al, 1974; Cronen and Pierce, 1982). Crudely put, the *me-first maneuver* has advantages in configuring an exchange to one party's apparent benefit. Some clients, especially those who have felt undervalued, should be coached to be *more* able to use 'I-statements'. This has been much discussed in assertion training and social skills programs and has its place in practice. Without discounting the importance of such programs, the current emphasis concerns the over-use of these statements and, more specifically, how these statements can be understood and responded to by those who are less practiced in the use of the *me-first maneuver*.

Those who frequently use the *me-first maneuver* frame their position so they become a kind of independent variable. Over time, the framing of situations in this way embeds an evasion of personal accountability, a configuration that, in turn, encourages the experience of entitlement and indignation (Pease, 2010). Think how Paris Hilton, for example, or any member of an entitled class, would react if they had done, and then had been 'sprung' for doing, something unfair or inappropriate by a 'lesser' person. As the privileged have long done, rather than accepting their wrongdoing, they tend to evade responsibility using denial or feigned inattention. If this does not work they can ramp it up, saying righteously, 'Nobody told me' or 'How could I be expected to do X? I've too much going on to be concerned with that!' This person might even say, or imply, 'Just get over it: don't disappoint me with that look.' A complete listing of the iterations of the *me-first maneuver* is impossible to complete yet, for the current purpose here, what is salient is to be aware that this maneuver functions as a powerful interpersonal intervention.

When one party's 'me' has been inserted into the conversation, the other party has only two choices. They can either escalate the stakes: 'Well, you talk about how you felt, but it was you who let me down, not the other way round!' – an option that clearly risks conflict. The other option is to be silenced and to swallow your feelings by going along with the game. Unfortunately, the *me-first maneuver* seems to be becoming more common as it is frequently modeled in the media and is being relentlessly taught by the process of individualization. Poignantly, it is also often inscribed into the everyday subjectivity of clients by the narratives that structure professional practice (see Chapter 5).

It is a complex matter to analyze this tactic as it involves dynamic interactions between intra-physic, phenomenological, behavioral, and context of meaning dimensions. What is important to note here is that the *me-first maneuver* is injurious to the prospects for a relationship if too frequently employed. For example, many readers would be able to relate to the sense of dilemma that arises when someone states in a tense discussion that, 'You're just going to have to trust me on this one.' This statement pre-disposes three choices: you can either happily say 'It's over to you. I am in your good hands'; you can unhappily comply, an option that risks being (knowingly) manipulated; or it is possible to query the speaker, a decision that risks the interaction becoming darker in its emotional tone.

Towards the encouragement of personal accountability (Colgate, 2004; Jenkins, 2009), and the allied aim of helping clients learn the pragmatics of getting on with others, the *me-first maneuver* can be directly discussed with clients. Such conversations seek to 'work the loop' (Wender, 1968) between the experience of being 'inside' and 'outside' the behavior – how it feels when you are the subject of the tactic as well as the examination of how it feels when you use this practice. It is highly recommended in this exploration that the practitioner considers how the skill of 'perspective taking' might be promoted, as Goleman (2006) suggests in his work on social intelligence. Being able to put yourself in another's shoes, to go from your own position to the imagination of another, is a competence that can be practiced. (This skill is not only relevant to personal relationships; it is now also the focus of effort in corporate teamwork training and organizational development.)

The *me-first maneuver* has become so common it has become a topic comedians joke about. In a skit sending up a New York 'yuppie', a sketch that had its protagonist talking incessantly about themselves, this person said to a friend: 'Enough of all this talk about me! Let's talk about you. Now what I'd really like you to tell me is what do you think about me?' Some clients might laugh if this joke is recycled whilst others might sigh given the real sensitivity with which this matter is endowed. As one upwardly mobile young lawyer said to her therapist: "If I don't keep pumping myself up, I'm going to drown. It's a dog eat dog world out there and you have to keep putting yourself forward or you'll fall over the horizon and end up out of sight." In a dialogue with her practitioner, this woman was more than ready to tease out, to see both sides of, her dilemma, and an attention to the professional necessity of being 'up-front, even aggressive' allowed her to explore how this work-related logic was incompatible with what worked, and did not work, in her more intimate relations. Laced into many sessions this discussion became a linking thread in her therapy as it was not only central to the pragmatics of her relationships, but it was also implicated in larger questions about clarifying her values and commitments (Blackledge et al, 2009).

Not surprisingly, an exploration of the *me-first maneuver* can be emotionally evocative, even telling, given its contemporary relevance. What can also be discussed and worked up are behavioral options as to how a client might respond if they are subject to the *me-first maneuver* or if they are overly well practiced in its use. Less verbally adept clients may not be so abstract in their thinking, but almost everyone is able to reflect on what works, or does not work, for them, given the right context. One simple distinction that can be embedded is between 'reacting' and 'responding' to situations: 'OK, so your partner [again] starts to talk about the work stress he's under, you've told me you react by either switching off or going at him for being a whiner. Just for fun, what are some of the other ways you might deal with this? If you were in his shoes, is there something he could do, or say, that would let you know you've really been heard without putting you on the throne as the only important person at home?'

Turned over, if the focus is on a client's tendency to get in first, a similar process of imagination can be initiated: 'If you held back, if you decided to do something different that disrupted the old pattern, what might you do? Could you, for example, keep a diary of your thoughts and feelings, find another way to communicate with your sister, maybe even see yourself as someone who makes space for others to grow into rather than as the needy one?' The goal is approximating a balance between the expression of the relational and the autonomous self. Towards this end being too much the listener is as much a problem as being too frequently the talker.

Considering the question: 'How direct should my communication be?'

Many who are isolated and feel they have been bullied avoid conflict. This aversion to the prospect of conflict attenuates the chance to secure attachments. Plain speaking becomes inhibited, and the giving and receiving of feedback feels risky. Similarly, those who are accustomed to using the anonymous forms characteristic of new technology tend to be averse to face-to-face disagreement.

Text or email exchanges are asynchronous – they do not happen in real time – unlike face-to-face interaction where there is far less opportunity to consider how to respond and represent yourself. In so far as it is the practice to send a 'sneaky text', to 'text in bad news' that, for example, informs your boss you will not be coming to work today, communicational indirectness has been naturalized. This sensitivity tends to cross over into how embodied relations are conducted. For those who have bought into mediated habits of interaction, as for those who have been bruised and pushed around, it seems essential 'to keep it light' and not allow the situation to become awkward, as this feels threatening.

There is, of course, some legitimate sense in this logic. Direct, to-the-point communication is not always the best option. Questions of gender, class, and context should be considered, and those from more traditional cultures have good reason to be at least somewhat oblique if generational and role distinctions are to be respected. For these, and other reasons it is not interpersonally literate to put a blunt form of honesty on a high altar. Being patient and a good listener, being able to carefully approach what is difficult to discuss, contributes to good grammar in the writing of relationships.

Mindful of these complications, the topic of directness is important to reflect on with clients if the relational agenda is being pursued. As a generalization, it is better if clients learn to have the attitude it is more effective to 'talk when the talking is tough' (Miller et al, 2004a, p 377) rather than remaining unhappily quiet or simply walking away. This is no small matter as many clients conflate the anticipatory inner experience of personal discomfort with the inevitability of actual conflict. For example, the larger proportion of clients 'catastrophize' and mistake the expression of difference with the inevitability of rejection or outright conflict. This leads many, and not just those who have been socially excluded, to panic and to exit the relationship, first running an old movie that they are about to be left or attacked.

Coaching for steadiness, for the values of patience and hopefulness, is a key priority when the client's inner experience tends toward tumult given there is little or no memory that disputes can ever be resolved. In this context the skills for dealing with discomfort, with the presence of awkwardness, become misplaced, and clients find it especially tempting to remain quiet or to try to 'keep it light'. Acknowledging that some clients can sometimes be in danger from their significant others, many more avoid what they fear might become a conflictual situation. This tactic means their feelings and points of view are not expressed and can therefore never be heard. This is disquieting, even alienating, and can lead to the silent decision that 'I'm out of here' as soon as this is practical.

What is paradoxical in this kind of dynamic is that not speaking up risks the outcome of prompting exactly what it is that is feared – not speaking up can be counter-productive as it can encourage conflict in its own strange way. This can happen as the prospect of conflict can be so aversive that the attempt to avoid it can inadvertently bring on what is feared because there can be a contradiction between what is said by the client to their current significant other and the feelings they are indirectly communicating to this person. The client might say nothing at all, just sitting as still as possible in mute silence; or they may offer a safety-first response saying, 'OK, I'm fine with that', an act which grants a kind of pseudo–assent to the other's position. Yet, in terms of non-verbal communication, what comes across contradicts this data, for example, in conveying the message 'I don't like what is going on – but I am not going to tell you that' (Mehrabian, 2007). Such mixed messages often contribute to a context that exactly encourages what is feared.

Direct communication has a constructive relationship with the minimizing of conflict and disengagement and this can be discussed. For example, conflict can be normalized, disaggregated, and scaled ('unimportant everyday differences', 'differences I can live with', 'items to be negotiated', 'things I will not compromise on'), and the skills for the clear but quiet expression of ideas and feelings rehearsed. Depending on the extent and type of contact the practitioner has with the client, decisions have to be made as to how much, and to what depth, this work should proceed. Aspects of the issue can be directly raised with some clients: 'Do you tend to get out first if you think the other person might reject you?' or 'Do you just find yourself going quiet if the temperature might be about to heat up?'

Complementing this, or perhaps as an alternative, attitudes and values might be a preferred focus: 'If you come across to X as someone who believes in cooperation and reciprocation, as a man who isn't full of his own entitlement and right to make all the big choices on your own, do you think she might feel more free to tell you what she feels and wants?'

Skills can be specifically taught if this seems appropriate. For example, it is relatively simple to coach the ground rules for giving feedback and these can be demonstrated and rehearsed. Feedback is best if it is:

- behavioral and not personal: it is fine to say 'I got confused and upset when you yelled at me just as we left the pub last night', but it is not helpful to accuse the other by making universalizing statements like 'You know you are a really angry person';
- particular and not global: it is fine to say 'When you walked out after dinner I felt rejected', but not 'You always walk out on me when it gets difficult';

- personal and not categorical: it is fine to make 'I-statements' ('I feel helpless') but not to act as the judge ('It is wrong when you make me feel bad');
- concerned with reviewing your own actions rather than exclusively concerned with telling the other what was not appreciated: 'When I told you yesterday I was angry with you I was getting mixed up. After thinking it through, it was not you I was angry with. I took it out on you rather than being clear with you it was about what had happened at work. I screwed up and am genuinely sorry';
- last, but not least, comments should more often be appreciative than critical.

You can also practice how to constructively receive feedback. This is often highly useful as comments from the client's significant others can too easily be construed as damning or bullying. It is sensible to make sure the other person is given an uninterrupted, genuine hearing and it is important to try and respond, and not react: 'Loud and clear: you've told me it's a struggle for you when I get antsy and go silent. Can I have a little time [15 minutes, a day, a week] to get back to you on this?'

Being able to back down

Interpersonal literacy has many facets. One of these is the capacity to recognize one class of interaction for what it is: an arm wrestle that can have no winner. Everybody has found themselves in such situations, such battles, where it feels there are only two courses of action. In the middle of such a contest you can either continue your defense or you can abjectly surrender. The anthropologist Gregory Bateson (1973) termed these interactions 'symmetrical processes'.

In his fieldwork in the 1930s, Bateson observed that Balinese groups sometimes became caught up in reciprocally escalating cycles of behavior. Caught up in these cycles, each party reported that it had felt forced to push harder, to raise their voices higher, to stand up for themselves more forcibly, and so forth, whilst apparently unaware that this action then acted to compel the other party to do the same, which, in turn, furthered such runaway patterns. More recently, game theorists and conflict resolution practitioners, amongst other traditions, have also identified how destructive such patterns can be. Novelists and satirists, like the US writer James Thurber, have also depicted the same phenomena in personal relationships and have graphically described the negative momentum that can be detonated in these 'my-dignity-or-bust' conflicts. (Thurber wrote about a couple who came to end their relationship at the conclusion of an argument that originated in a very minor original difference: what attitude each had to a Disney cartoon character.)

What is characteristic of a symmetrical process is that each participant insists on 'being heard', 'being right', 'being respected', 'having been wronged', or the like (see Chapter 3). Once set off, the power of this process can be phenomenal. Subjectively, no participant sees it as an interpersonal process as each individual experience is that it is the other party's behavior that is the cause of the problem:

'He made me do it', 'I had to stand up for myself', 'I would have died if I had submitted.' Such processes can be loud, but they can also be coldly conducted. Conflict does not have to be forthright to have intense meaning.

Bateson proposed that the only remedy to an escalating dispute was for one party to do the opposite of what was being 'invited' by the process. To stop defending yourself, asserting yourself or the like and to say, for example, to your roommate, 'I'm not sure I understand where you are coming from? Can we slow down a minute so you can let me know what it is I've missed that is most important to you?' According to Bateson, this introduces an element of complementarity, a process that is fundamentally the opposite of the kind of process that had been running as it involves the exchange of opposite, not identical, behaviors. If this is done genuinely, if this baring of the throat is not a cynical trick, it has the capacity to dilute the rich mixture that is fueling the runaway fire.

Anger and righteousness intoxicate. These feelings interfere with the possibility of listening, of creating a new space for the hearing of the other's point of view. Whilst it might be thought of as a sickly act, a kind of dumb turning the other cheek, being able to at least temporarily back down, to surrender, can introduce crucially important moments into a dynamic which is able to sustain an ongoing relationship. Being able to say, 'Oops, I didn't do that well' (or to listen, be patient, be curious about what X meant to you, etc) – to make and take a chance to genuinely apologize can keep the ship on a better long-term course, although this is not easy to do if the client is insecure and is tightly bound into being defensive. Practitioners can talk this through with clients and small exercises can be rehearsed before being trialed in the clients' real relationships.

It is not faux forgiveness that is wanted but the idea of patience, of clients learning to know that they have more chance to be heard and respected if the other comes to know that, over time, they will also be given this grace. Assertiveness, toughness, focus, each of the 'male-stream' (O'Brien, 1981) virtues, have a place, but so does the more vulnerable, 'open-to-the-other' aspects of what it is to be a social being. Just as there is often sadness behind anger and helplessness fueling outrage, there is a need to coach clients towards restraint and other-orientedness. In casework practice this imperative can be brought into awareness and dialogue in a similarly diverse set of ways to the three earlier described engagements.

Discussions about what is fair and right

Trained to be technical and non-judgmental, many practitioners shy away from conversing with clients about values and ethics. This is unfortunate as it is possible to have important interactions concerned with what is fair and thoughtful without being either teacher-like or judgmental. Just as it is possible to talk to clients about blame – 'How do you feel when you are blamed? – without blaming, it is possible to raise questions of relational morality without being moralistic. Similarly, it is appropriate to respond to clients if they raise a question like 'Do you think it is right, do you think it would be fair, if I left my partner?' As Goleman (2006, p

101) argues, it is not possible to "eliminate human values from social intelligence" without impoverishing the concept.

Attention to the ethical is potentially interventive if it is introduced and given attention. Putting the spotlight on fairness is to honor the matter of values as a key concern. This can be done around practical tasks such as the division of labor in the home ('Who puts out the garbage?'), around what Hochschild (2003) has termed 'emotional labor' ('Whose job is it to take responsibility for how the kids are feeling at your place?'), or it can be raised and discussed as a question of principle ('Do you think it is important to be fair?'). These kinds of discussions have a clear place in a number of less conventional approaches to practices (see, for example, the narrative therapy tradition [Jenkins, 2009], logotherapy [Frankl, 1964], acceptance and commitment therapy [Blackledge et al, 2009]), as well as in those specifically philosophical consultations that engage with the question of the ethics of personal relationships (Colgate, 2004). In contrast, the more accepted approaches to practice purport to be both ethically neutral, and, in something of a paradox, to be 'on the client's side'.

The relationship-building approach developed here proposes that the themes of reciprocity and personal accountability should be woven into the fabric of the work. This is not to say discussions with clients about personal accountability, thoughtfulness to others, and cooperation should be corrective or stipulative. On the contrary, it is important to be philosophical in the proper sense of the word – to be interested in what is good and right without being overbearing. Most clients are able to engage with these themes as they are bracing and dense with meaning, but this is not to say discussions around these themes are without tension.

Despite a practitioner's intention to engage in open-ended conversation, to be Socratic, it is almost inevitable that some clients will feel chided or admonished, shamed, or in some other way cast down when asked to reflect on choices they have made or actions they may be considering. To ask a client to consider 'What do you think it takes for a wo/man to be worth the respect of others?' or 'What do you think your [now deceased] mother would think is right?' is not to be disapproving, but a client may initially, at least, feel it is. If such questions are initially challenging, the client may later come to think that taking up these fundamental questions is less taxing that continuing to avoid them.

Given their sensitivity, it is especially important to be emotionally attuned and practically timely in raising higher order questions. That said, there are any number of ways of introducing and sustaining this talk. Less formal practice contacts (for example, if the practitioner is driving in a car with a client to an appointment, rather than sitting opposite them in a formal consulting room) can make it easier to talk about practical ethics without as much risk that this might become too intense. Alternatively, taking up the chance to write a letter to a client offers a personalized context for the articulation of relational dilemmas (the GP's letter to her client Rouga in Vignette 11, p 150, is an example).

As to the content, the actual form of words that might be used, there is no manual, but there is a wide world of possibilities. A personal favorite is to use a short quote from the long deceased, once esteemed, and now out of favor Polish novelist, Joseph Conrad, as a riff: 'An old Polish writer once wrote in one of his stories 'there is sometimes the attractive error and the stern truth.' What do you think about this idea: do you think there might be a good distinction between what Conrad called "the attractive error and the stern truth?" Many clients have apparently been able to reflect on this powerfully simple distinction to good effect.

Just as the personal is the political, the interpersonal is the ideological. Concentrating on the traditional concern for enhancing client choice, self-determination, autonomy, and privacy can be balanced with an active interest in the values of cooperation, mutuality, reciprocity, and accountability. Each of the above five engagements has this as their common premise. Getting on with others is a business, a pragmatic affair, yet as Paterson contends (1996), personal relationships are a privileged arena where practical ethics are also inevitably and continually in play.

Mediated forms of relating

ICT is now recognized as an important medium within which practice can be undertaken (Hill and Shaw, 2011). And in some quarters, enthusiasm for ICT-based services has developed to such an extent it is claimed that online services are not merely less expensive than face-to-face contact, but can be more effective in many circumstances: for example, in the treatment of social phobia (Andrews, 2009) and some forms of depression (Perine et al, 2008). These claims may or may not be exaggerated, but is indubitable that ICT has clear advantages in certain situations for some at-risk populations. For example, vulnerable young people living in conservative, perhaps even dangerously intolerant, settings who wish to explore non-mainstream sexuality can do so anonymously, and therefore more safely, on the net. Rather than having to project a faux self, the young person can "stay closer to reality in their online expressions of self" in an online environment (Huffaker and Calvert, 2005, p 1).

Mindful that the mediated world has regressive, as well as progressive, possibilities (Greenfield, 2008; Carr, 2010), the intention here is to examine one particular aspect of practice that can advantageously employ mediated communication: how ICT can be used by practitioners who are committed to developing the client's relational base. Simply put, this aim is not about encouraging clients to post on Twitter or to become intense Facebook users. Having a secure relational base is not about the frequency of a person's posts or the number of people numbered as their Facebook friends. ICT-based communication does have the advantage of being able to send messages that can be accessed instantaneously by people anywhere across the globe, but this communication can be as hollow and futile as an anonymous wave to an unseeing crowd before a loner jumps off a bridge. It is also noteworthy that the internet can be associated with diminished personal accountability and unhealthy hibition, as seen with cyberbullying and the naturalization of pornography.

Getting to grips with the new technology entails remaining aware that a double-edged sword is present when it comes to personal relationships. Put another way, the new technologies introduce an unstable equation where there are both advantages and disturbances to the prospects for accountable and reliable affiliation: it is both positive that a net user is in control and can drop out of any connection at their will, but it is also a disadvantage in terms of the stability of the personal connection that this person can do this capriciously, simply on a whim. Such problems acknowledged, ICT can facilitate the development of communities of interest which are secure and humanizing. The interest here is to examine how practitioners in everyday roles might look to new technology to improve connectedness and to address social isolation. A reasonably complex vignette is used as a focus to develop this purpose (see Vignette 20 below).

A good way to respond to this vignette is to rough-out ideas that might contribute to an intervention process, particularly as this action seeks to deepen the clients' social network. The rationale for this goal is the rationale for this whole book:

that a positive interpersonal network is

- protective of wellbeing;
- in the event a person currently experiences a problem of living, for example, a primary mental health issue such as depression or anxiety, a positive social network will facilitate resilience if not complete recovery.

The vignette that follows is based on a real example. Read it over and picture yourself as an outreach worker with an interest in ICT. Your agency is funded to do assertive casework and 'Sandra' is one of your clients.

VIGNETTE 20: SANDRA

Sandra is a 44-year-old woman who lives with her 22-year-old son who has been referred to your service to improve her 'work readiness'. You are employed in a small community-based support agency and Sandra has been contracted out to your service by the Income Support authority.

The referral paperwork notes that Sandra has been out of work for more than two years, has chronic financial difficulties, personal health problems, a stressful relationship with her own mother (who lives nearby), periodically drinks to excess, and was, until her mid-thirties, an extensive user of illegal drugs. Sandra rents a two-bedroom flat in an outlying, low socioeconomic status suburb of a large city. It is reported that she leads an isolated life with her only regular contact being with her son ('Steve') who has a diagnosis of autism. Sandra cares for Steve full time, an obligation that the referrer reports she finds burdensome.

The referring agency has suggested the reason for their referral is to 'improve Sandra's work readiness.' In addition to the above, the referral letter reports that Sandra:

- has become more overweight, withdrawn, and isolated since losing her last job two years ago;
- in the past has worked on and off in retail, data entry, and housekeeping/cleaning;
- is receiving anti-depression medication from her GP.

You decide to do a home visit where you find Sandra seemingly happy to talk. She tells you "No, I don't feel that depressed. My doctor tells me the medication is doing its job well enough and I guess she is half right." Sandra also tells you "My only really big problem is my son Steve. He doesn't talk, or at least can't talk in the usual way. He's been like that all his life. I was told when he was at school that he'll be like that. That he is wired wrong and that's a forever thing. All he does all day is play his stupid computer games. This makes him double hard to get along with."

As well as telling you Steve is a "giant downer to live with," she also tells you "Yeah, I guess I'd like to have a job and have more money. It'd be great to lose some weight, be a bit skinnier, and go out a bit to have some fun but, do you know what, who wouldn't? I've had to learn the hard way: if you mix with the fast crowd you get into dark places." Sandra does not seem to mind talking, but you doubt she sees you as someone who has much to offer her.

In relation to a relationally centered case formulation, it would seem likely from the above that Sandra:

- is structurally excluded in terms of employment, yet has a degree of social inclusion in that she has close family affiliations (with her son and her mother) that are likely to have a high degree of meaning;
- experiences these intimate relationships as stressful, even conflictual;
- appears to be otherwise isolated – she is unlikely to have immediate friendships and positive neighborhood linkages;
- does not have a current partner;
- has contacts with some professionals, such as her doctor and the Income Support authority.

There are no details concerning Sandra's contact with other members of her immediate family, such as her siblings or her son's father, or her extended family. And it seems unlikely, but possible, that Sandra has good friends and neighborly relations. This uncertainty means it is best to only gently hypothesize about these aspects of her relational situation.

The task is to develop:

- a plan 'on the back of an envelope' as to how you might try and engage Sandra, and
- with an emphasis on the use of new technology, suggest possible ideas and activities that *might* be productive.

Of course, there are many details you do not know. Responding to this vignette involves undertaking a thought experiment, a game of serious play, that calls for imagination much more than realism and appropriateness.

With no more awareness of what is known, or unknown, students in a final year social connectedness elective came up with a long list of possible practice ideas. After sketching in your own ideas, examine the ideas this group developed and review what is common with, and what is different to, the options you developed compared to their thoughts.

In terms of engagement and assessment actions, the group suggested the following:

- to speak with Sandra appreciatively about her long-term commitment to her son's welfare and to find out from her what she found positive, as well as stressful, about her relationship with her son;
- to engage in forms of address (interpellations: see p 69) that narrate Sandra as a relational being whilst finding out more about the substance and the tone of her relationships with her mother, extended family, and her neighbors;
- to co-construct with Sandra a genogram and/or an eco-map and check in with her about the attributes, gaps, and conflicts present in the relationships that these depictions bring into focus. This would include seeking information about who Sandra receives support from and with whom she would like to get on better;
- to look into the possibility of involving Sandra's mother and/or son in these initial meetings;
- to move towards constructing a set of aims that are meaningful to Sandra.

In terms of ideas that might be relevant to the process of a relational intervention, the following ideas were raised as options, mindful of the collaborative process that is involved with goal setting:

- to work out with Sandra what past relationships, if any, she would ideally like to reactivate and to discuss with her the possibility of doing this by telephone, letter, personal contact, or via social media such as Facebook;
- to work out with Sandra what, if any, current relationships she would like to remodel; and
- to work out with Sandra what possible new relationships she would ideally like to have.

This review could be done by way of asking Sandra to consider the relationship review table introduced earlier in this chapter (see Table 9.1). Being able to discriminate between categories of relationship visually allows for a greater sense of possibility in thinking. For example, in considering, and then marking up, each of the 10 categories of relationship with a specific status ('good', 'neutral', 'non-existent', or 'conflictual'), and in identifying several of these, say 'neighbors', 'romance', and those with whom there might be 'a common interest' as 'priorities' or possible 'starting points', Sandra puts herself on the brink of a strength-based appreciation. She can choose, as a practitioner might say, 'if and when you are ready', to look for a support group online or in real time for parents of adults who have an autism spectrum disorder, to scan social networking sites for former neighbors, or to think about dipping her toe into the online dating game.

In the real circumstance from which this vignette was drawn an unexpected, and highly positive process occurred. What took place, and what most facilitated change, was that Sandra developed a far closer and more convivial relationship with her son when she (after some prompting) linked up to him in the only communication medium with which he was comfortable: in an online gaming environment. In this medium he was at home, like many with his diagnosis. Here, he became the host and thrived on being, for the very first time, one-up on his mum. Sandra took a little time to become accustomed to this initially alien medium, but quickly became convinced that this arena allowed her to see her son in a completely new light. Rather than the intensity of face-to-face communication, in the mediated world they could swap ideas rather than be stuck together in the same physical space feeling awkward.

After some time sharing participation in this online world, a place where he and she could talk in a less intense and more playful way, Sandra stated that her relationship with her son had been transformed. In turn, this improved quality in their connection was associated with a shift in mood, a greater appreciation of her own dedication, and a general increase in her sense of personal agency. A little later Sandra began dating, found some part-time data entry work she could do from home, and developed a degree of optimism and self-belief that enabled her to continue to live within her limited financial situation with a far greater quality of life. Although not everything improved – Sandra stated that she was getting on worse with her own mother, for example – the improvement in her connection with her most important significant other underwrote what, on her account, was now a qualitatively more satisfactory life.

Although it is true, the above probably looks like another of those fairy tale stories. It is recycled here mindful of the cyberbullying and predatory stalking, the pornography and mind-altering violence, that is alive and well on the net. Facebook may have 800 million users but it can be, as Hodgkinson (2008) says, close to sinister in its commercialization of relationships. And Parton (2008) has warned that ICT-based record-keeping systems and their logic can be transformational in de-personalizing practice. Mediated communication can certainly erode the prospects for secure attachment in some instances, but it can also facilitate and invigorate connections in other circumstances. Thoughtfully encouraging clients to use ICT is to be aligned with its many positive possibilities, but it is not to be a mindless booster of the so-called information superhighway.

A complex example: working relationship building in a secure setting

So far, you might have found the material presented here okay but a little abstract. *Yeah, that's kind of good, but I am not sure it would work for me.* Perhaps, you've said to yourself, *but what about…?* Or thought *it's hard enough doing basic interviews, so it's a really big ask to try and be more ambitious.* Maybe it has been a struggle to imagine how you might splice more of a relationally oriented approach into your high pressure work setting: *it sounds nice enough, but I don't think so….*

If your response aligns with pragmatic doubts like these, you might be interested in Vignette 21 that follows shortly. The site of this example is the message: a secure psychiatric hospital. On any calculation this practice context makes the implementation of a relationship-building approach challenging. The account presented in this vignette describes how the relational approach was undertaken by a practitioner, Grant Burkitt, and his colleague, Lisa Wright. Over some time, they have worked up forms of relationship-building practice that can be accommodated into such a demanding workplace.

The argument is this: if a relationship-building agenda can be used in a forensic setting, selectively employing aspects of the approach can be incorporated anywhere. Before describing this example the particularity of this practice context is outline to orient the reader to this unusual setting. The following describes an example of the work undertaken by these practitioners and was written collaboratively with Grant.

Practice context

A close monitoring of patients, staff, and visitors is a fact of life in all forensic facilities. At the hospital every effort is made to generate pleasantness, for example, in the design of its friendly outdoor spaces, yet the level of supervision is more reminiscent of a progressive prison than a regular hospital. Internally, the physical arrangement and the program established in the center's six units, in conjunction with an annex unit that sits outside the walls, models the clinical pathway of patients – patients progress from the more secure initial admission unit to a less intensely gated pre-discharge unit. Mindful of the many architectural niceties, entry and exit from the facility requires passing through a high-tech screening process. As is obvious from the outside, so it is from the inside: there is a six meter wall enclosing the facility.

The purpose of the hospital is to treat patients. Although there are many nurses and other professionals present, their first priority is to protect society from the risk of harm presented by those confined, with treatment and rehabilitation following as a second line of attention. Risk is constantly monitored, calculated, and assertively managed. Hourly contacts with in-patients are frequently undertaken for this purpose.

In-patients are not formally convicted or sentenced but are placed on orders because a court has declared that their crime, or crimes, have been the result of psychiatric illness consistent with the relevant legal framework. Historically, those so confined were indefinitely detained 'at the Governor's pleasure'. This outmoded condition resulted in many patients being sequestered for periods that exceeded the length of time that would normally be given for a specific offence, say, aggravated assault, in a standard prison. More recently, this anomaly has been refined so that patients may not normally be confined beyond the period for which the maximum penalty might apply. Even though 'Governor's pleasure' is no longer the disposition, it would nonetheless be a mistake to view a forensic conviction as a soft option compared to regular goal, as discharge is contingent on patients being judged to have complied with a suite of onerous conditions. Patients have to demonstrate that they are prepared to (in their terms) play the game and be, for example, cooperative in being open to sharing their thoughts and feelings as part of their recovery. Additionally, compliance with supervisory conditions is required for a very practical reason: to be eligible to proceed along an extended period where a graduated program of progressively more open leave is granted – the successful completion of which is the precondition for discharge.

Due to complex legal and social factors forensic in-patients are subject to multiple stigmas and physical disadvantages. Custodial orders are made because patients have committed serious offences yet, at a second level of judgment, they are also confined because they have been found to have caused harm at the time of the offence due to psychiatric illness. Being labeled as both 'mad' and 'bad' creates a double whammy as their identity is negatively re-cast ('you are both crazy and dangerous') at the same time as everyday rights are withdrawn. Amongst a larger set of restrictions, this exclusion limits the chance to participate in past associations that sustain health and wellbeing within, and beyond, their confinement. For example, in-patients have no access to the internet or to mobile telephones.

Complicating the issue of social connectedness even further, a number of forensic patients have injured, or at least have placed at perceived risk, family members and significant others with whom they have had relationships. These people, in the usual life course, would normally be expected to continue to be their significant others. Even if no risk or injury occurred to the person's intimates, the nature of the offences committed, and the nature of the illnesses that are present, represents a particular challenge to friends and relatives. These significant others may experience a complicated form of grief, often with a dimension of embarrassment, about the offences that have been committed and the risks they might face when the significant other – the in-patient– is discharged.

Perhaps most evocatively, as a cohort there is a potentially high level of isolation and social exclusion present in the lives of patients residing in closed environments. They may be physically cut-off and have been officially ostracized, but their loneliness has a unique, complicating quality. Although alone, the patient is observed as if they were a principal on the set of *The Truman Show* – a movie about a man who lives as the real life centre of a reality television show he initially does not know he is the star of. This gives the experience of isolation a kinked, strangely intimate quality. As well as relief when this monitoring diminishes post-discharge, in one sense this dimension of impersonal contact, however routine, can also be missed as they no longer experience that their life is being witnessed.

Given the legislative mandate the facility authorities have been delegated (to preserve public safety), and given that there is a public media that is highly tuned to the headlines any breach of this security stimulates, politicians and administrators are not likely to see such a degree of isolation as a problem. In one sense, the authorities and the public assume it is a positive circumstance that forensic in-patients are 'walled off' from the community. This is generally their preferred option, yet there is a contradiction here. Ostracism and loneliness present as a significant safety risk if they persist post-discharge – longer-term isolation, emotional discord, and dislocation are not associated with the promotion of public safety nor the reduction in the likelihood of re-offence.

This contradictory condition is exactly the context within which practitioners have to work. The forensic hospital is not at all medieval – it is nothing like the hellhole depicted in the recent movie *Shutter Island*, for example – but it is nonetheless a highly demanding professional setting. How Grant, Lisa, and their colleagues approach the challenge of preparing patients for community integration offers a signal example of how a relational paradigm can be used in even highly contested practice settings.

In order to address this challenge practices have been developed to facilitate the relationships their clients have, or might have, in the future. This is no straightforward task as these clients are securely locked away, often for many years, prior to being discharged. The effects of this immersion can be summarized in terms of the development of a very particular form of identity – what Irving Goffman (quoted in Pilgram and Rogers, 2008: 47) termed 'patienthood' and Alcabes and Jones (1985: 49) termed 'clienthood.' This learned identity involves:

- a loss of personal power and agency;
- the perception that the environment is not only dislocating, but is also threatening;
- adjustment to feelings of despair, confusion, anger, and boredom;
- the loss of past supports, social amenities, and freedom;
- involuntary treatment where compliance is closely monitored;
- a marked degree of social disconnection in access to all relationships that are not hospital-based;
- being socialized to understand that they have a culpable 'moral career' where misbehaviors, such as swearing at a staff member, are stigmatized and considered a continuation of their 'spoiled identity' (Goffman, 1974).

A person's initial induction into life as a forensic patient can be likened to arriving raw and vulnerable in a new environment, and then learning that they must accept that personal openness is a permanent house rule.

The following vignette introduces one particular patient, Rory, and outlines some key details of his background. Having broadly outlined the effects of forensic incarceration, the focus then moves to the work that was undertaken with Rory towards community re-entry, giving a particular emphasis to the relationship-building aspects of this program.

VIGNETTE 21: RORY

Rory is an isolated 32-year-old male who has been a forensic in-patient for six years. Amongst a more complex picture, he has multiple convictions for assault and a long-standing diagnosis of schizophrenia. (Earlier diagnoses included 'drug-induced psychoses' and 'anti-social personality disorder'; he also has convictions for a diverse range of other offenses, including using and selling drugs, burglary, and affray.) He is eligible for a form of conditional discharge in the near future contingent on satisfactory assessments being made of his mental functioning, preparedness to comply with his post-discharge treatment plan, and of securing suitable accommodation.

Rory's early background was fragmented and disturbed. His mother experienced persistent substance abuse and mental health issues and suffered from domestic violence. Although Rory was informally placed with several aunts (and others) at different points, he spent the great majority of his early years in different forms of state care. He never knew his father, has five stepsisters (that he knows of), and several aunts and uncles. Since his late adolescence he has fathered four children to different partners with whom, until recently, he had no contact. Rory is far from an unintelligent man but has had no formal education and has never had a conventional job. Over the last few years in the hospital his mental health has been reasonably stable. He takes regular psychotropic medication, mostly, it seems, readily. He reports he continues to "hear voices" but that they are neither as persecutory nor as commanding as in the past.

From Rory's perspective his best years were as a small-time drug dealer and regular user. In this period he recalls having friends, confidence, money, and status. At that time he lived in a specific area – he still calls it "my hood" – and has mixed feelings about returning to this area: "For sure, if I go back I'll most likely get into trouble, maybe even get those feelings back again [of being a target, of having to hurt someone before they could hurt him]. But, it'd be great. They all know me as someone different over there [not as a 'mad' and 'bad' loser]. I could get the weight back off my shoulders, stand up straight, be able to look myself in the mirror. I know I have to stay away, to 'reside as directed', but as shit stinks, I'm going to find it hard to stay away." And he expresses a real sense of camaraderie and compassion for those whom he still "bumps into" from this milieu.

As part of a larger team, Lisa initially worked directly with Rory prior to Grant having contact with Rory over approximately 18 months. The focus for this work was his readiness for discharge, particularly in relation to developing his social skills, his contact with relatives and friends, and the interests he might pursue once he left the hospital. This focus sharpened as steps towards discharge were taken. These included a period in the hospital annex and having overnight leave. Close contact was expected to continue post-discharge until the point when it was appropriate a longer-term case management role consistent with the relevant statutory orders could be implemented.

The process of community transition

It is not possible to address in this account all of the tasks that a successful transition required (Draine et al, 2005). For example, in order to adapt to the form of patienthood required in such a closed-in psychological and social space, Rory had, like all other patients, undergone a powerful induction process. This involved learning a new identity, a pervasive and contrary identity as someone who was not a citizen but someone who was inspected and acted on. With this as background, discharge had to be staged so that Rory could learn an 'in-between' identity status. Staff also had to be satisfied that Rory had accepted he must comply with the level of self-disclosure and the restricted nature of his citizenship post-discharge, yet he was also to be a driver himself. Such a supervisory context tends to understand indiscretions, however small, as major problems.

Preparation for discharge started long before these formal last steps. Over a three-year period the team had carefully mapped Rory's family and social connections and, more generally, his attitude to relationships. This review clarified that:

- Rory had no contact with his siblings, parents, children, ex-partners, or old friends and assumed that this was simply a fact of life: as it had been in his biography, so it would always be.
- He believed attachments were not safe to have as they made him vulnerable.

Following an intensely considered process, a critically reflective exercise that did not assume 'it is all about Rory', it was decided to make contact with one ex-partner with a view to developing some contact with the child of this relationship. Proceeding in a highly mediated way, this ex-partner eventually visited the hospital because it was understood that if Rory was to have contact with his daughter, it would be necessary that her mother (Shelley) and Rory needed some common ground with respect to their daughter's interests.

For his part Rory had almost no understanding of the developmental needs of children: he initially assumed they were some kind of mini-adult peer. This noted, he was guilt-ridden as a father and had no knowledge or positive models. He had no idea what kind of father he could, or should, be. Amongst a larger set of process outcomes, Rory eventually introduced himself to his daughter by letter – he did not want this 10-year-old to ever see him in the hospital – and later bought her a birthday present. Later still, Rory received a picture of his daughter, an emblem he kept close and out of sight of his fellow patients. This is not to say matters proceeded smoothly: the above is but the barest summary. Mostly, there seemed as, or more, difficulties than there was progress, but this work had as one of its effect that Rory held out for a two-bedroom flat post-discharge, as he hoped to have his daughter visit in the future. Personally, however flickering, he now had a light on the hill and, more broadly, some positive tracings of an identity as a relational being where attachment had become less a danger than a source of energy and accountability.

Over time Rory's problematic relationship to his older social network was examined and became more understood – his idealization of his old lifestyle was identified as a persistent, and potentially de-stabilizing, factor with respect to his longer-term prospects. The power of his attraction to his old ways had to be reported to the larger treatment team: they must be trusting of, and trusted by, their colleagues who were not part of the discharge planning team. Yet, as any worker comes to be close to the fears and dreams of their clients, there is always a dance between colluding and colliding (Furlong, 2002). This is especially the case in settings where major social norms have been, or are in danger of being, breached. Mindful of the pull of his old patch – his "hood" as he put it – sustained efforts were made to imagine and activate a new base – a place where he had a sense of place. In addition to important pragmatic work with respect to case coordination, involvements in in-patient groups, and the planning of referrals to structured activities, over a considerable period a dialogue took place around where he was to live. This matter had both a symbolic and a practical substance.

In engaging Rory in a multidimensional pre-discharge process that included a concern for his relational status, there was certainly a 'it just feels right' emotional factor, but there was also a rehabilitative advantage. Meaning-generating work with Rory contested his experience that each day was 'groundhog day', another day in an institution when it was the same as ever. Working towards connections being bridged helped temporality to be re-activated, that life did not have to be permanently deferred and put on hold. A sense of progress, of movement, was advanced by orienting Rory to who he would like to be, and with whom he should be in contact. This occurred at several levels of action. Rory needed assistance with the task of resolving past, present, and temporary identities. (He even went by a different name in his old patch, a name he viewed with pride as this name recalled the status he once enjoyed) In order for him to live outside the hospital, a tribe he could belong to had to be imagined. However modest, this acted as a collectivity he wished to join or return to. This process went beyond functional rehabilitation – can a person cook, budget, and so forth? – and became meaning-based rehabilitation. Long the loner, building his relational base could be said to 'warm his bones' – to give his life meaning and some hope to live for.

'Better alone than in bad company'

Rory's sense of belonging had been associated with his use of illegal drugs. This connected him not only to a sub-culture, a way of living, but also to relationships with the people who also lived within that sub-culture. Rory still recalls fondly many people from this time, and a good proportion still live around his old patch. He had a sense of connectedness to this area and to these people, and at least in memory it was around this locus that he experienced a sense of camaraderie and compassion.

This recalls classic studies of marginalized, outsider societies, such as Irving Goffman studied in *Where the action is* (1961) and Elliot Liebow in *Tally's corner* (1967). In these milieus personal relationships are conducted in stylized, even encoded, forms. Whether on the street corner or in an institution, whether the insider/outsider boundary is determined by racial stigma or the attraction of a freely chosen rebel cachet, a highly charged attention is accorded to the character of interpersonal connections within these groups. That interactions tend to be both ritualized, yet fractious, is characteristic of these milieus as the politics of difference is the group's stock in trade. As with codes of dress and speech, the patterning of relationships is a key component in what transacts the boundary between those who are in and those who are out.

If one is 'in' – a net-based collective that views anorexia not as an illness but as a lifestyle choice, a gang who trade drugs, any group that transgresses major social norms – there is a level of acceptance that is advantageous as membership of this association can also be problematic. Positive effects can be articulated using a vocabulary that references the benefits of strong intimate connections: you can talk of 'bridging' and 'bonding' social capital (Putnam, 2000), social attachment (Maris, 1998), sustaining networks (Trevillion, 2000), and so forth. Members feel included, respected, and valued as part of the group. Identity is buttressed as the interpellations (see Chapter 8, p 169) of those around you confer a sense of self. There are also often practical benefits, like being able to access illegal drugs or get tips on how to avoid the authorities by disguising your anorexia.

This latter aspect is, of course, where membership can also be problematic. Not many groups are entirely pro-social, and not everything that happens to a person as a result of being 'in' is positive – as was the case for Rory. A large painted sign on the border between Pakistan and the tribal regions of Afghanistan expresses this possibility clearly: 'Better alone than in bad company.' The reality has to be acknowledged that there can be an unstable relationship between the advantages and disadvantages of 'company'.

10
Being an agent of cultural change

The business of practice

One new friendship will improve the quality of an isolated person's life. Similarly, if a client revives a connection with one significant other, or learns the skills to renegotiate one difficult current relationship, this will strengthen their relational base. Such examples present reasons to be optimistic about the prospects for many clients. It only takes a minor shift in relational disposition, for example, if a client takes the decision to be more curious about how others think and feel, it is likely that this action will have a considerable impact over time.

If this person can be encouraged to persist by their practitioner, most probably the dynamics of their interactions with others will turn, at least to an appreciable degree. Actions that prompt clients to venture away from established habits of thinking and behavior, patterns that were previously negative and self-referential, towards what is more interpersonally engaging and open-ended, will pay off. Positive consequences are also likely if the contact with a practitioner focuses on the issue of values rather than behavior — if a client trialled a new charter that put fairness and respect in the foreground, this would change the way their relationships were understood and conducted — modified the rules of the dance as it were — so that a person's attitudes towards others became more concerned with fairness and sensitivity. Given anything like a good prompt, 'kinship libido' (Jung, 1946) will stimulate expected and unexpected possibilities for connection. Some of these will be unstable, others will be awkward, even anti-social, but others will generate the wondrous, the lived experience of greater affection and acceptance.

It is realistic to be optimistic that clients can develop the values, attitudes, and skills that are associated with an improved capacity for relating. The trouble is that professional work which aims to be relationship building is infrequently recommended, and is almost never mandated, by those professional bodies, funding arrangements, and employing organizations. In official accounts it is not regarded as the business of practitioners to work with relationship improvement in mind.

In one presentation the role of the practitioner might be to assist this woman with her depression, or to find accommodation for that man. In another context the task might be defined as the assessment of an elderly person's suitability for nursing home care, or to minimize the disruption a client's delusions cause in their everyday life. In these, and the diverse range of scenarios practitioners encounter, judgments will be made about effectiveness with respect to one criterion: to what degree has the presenting problem been addressed? This is, of course, how it must be, but a complementary imperative might also be added. Practitioners could also be expected to undertake their primary task in such a way as to contest the process of individualization. Rather than act in a manner that, however inadvertently, supports this process by ignoring, weakening, or even antagonizing the client's relational base, practitioners could seek to do the opposite.

This is a strong contention. And it is a proposal that seems extreme when first encountered. We have been acculturated to understand that our focus should be narrow and technical. Funding bodies, councils that accredit professional programs, registration boards, as well as privately paying customers and the public at large, expect the professional's task is to deliver a bounded service rather than to think about, and interfere with, the client's relationships. Professionals are supposed to act neutrally, to be guided by proven theories and objective science. Isn't the aim of professional practice to provide an effective and minimal intervention?

This is the accepted orthodoxy, yet this understanding has become untenable. Not only is it out of date, it is no longer possible to pretend that good practice is neutral and that practitioners can wash their hands if their clients have been schooled to be less, rather than more, personally accountable and interpersonally connected. The larger social context, the big world within which the little world of practice sits, is producing atomization at such an alarming rate that the environment within which professional decisions are made, and professional actions evaluated, has been transformed.

Of course, practitioners never set out to encourage their clients to be selfish or cocooned from the feelings and interests of others. In so far as this outcome is occurring, and might be subliminally recognized, it would be dismissed as incidental and inadvertent. Professionals dedicated to helping their clients never intend to be associated with the production of loneliness and amorality, and would be insulted if this accusation was made. Nonetheless, however positive their intentions might be, there is a strong argument that much that has been done in the name of 'serving the client' has eroded the client's prospects for good quality local social relations. The client is never a standalone republic, but much of the substance of the theory and practice practitioners are heirs to functions as if this is true – that the client is an island of abiding self-interest.

What has been argued here is this: there is an over-determined amnesia concerning the importance of the client's relational base. This is because practitioners have been disciplined to privilege autonomy over connectedness, choice over obligation, monoculture over diversity. And they have been schooled to be suspicious of, even to pathologize, intimate personal relationships as they are assumed to undermine the client's capacity to be authentic and independent.

In so far as practitioners have taken up this position they have acted as representatives of the larger culture their professions have been set up to serve. They help individual clients with the often intense troubles they have; they do honorable service as they value, hold, and seek to be their agents. And, from a place of outlook that co-exists with this daily work, health and human service professionals are a vanguard group whose actions have expanded the ideological kingdom within which the value of autonomy has been given a sacred place.

The practitioner as cultural actor

Practitioners cannot be neutral when it comes to the ontology and the life practices of clients. The following vignette seeks to illustrate this point in the form of a make-believe briefing from a consulting anthropologist (Jim) to a newly graduated counselor (Jasmin).

VIGNETTE 22: JASMIN AND JIM

Jasmin: "I want a briefing about the cultural context I will enter as I begin my career. As an anthropologist, as an expert who specializes in the Western cultural field, what are the characteristics, the crucial variables, I need to know about in the social field I am about to enter?"

Jim: "You want a summary, a quick heads-up. Listen up: what is central in terms of values is that the modern world accords an ascendant status to the individual and their capacity to be self-reliant. In the developed world this is the lynch-pin value. Just about everything in the Western belief system is built on this value. Two practical ideas flow from this.

"First, in presentations where your client is *not* from the first world, such as migrants from Eritrea or China, these clients are unlikely to have been socialized into this modern belief system. They don't know, they don't understand, what is currently accepted in terms of our customs. It follows you would be sensible to proceed cautiously with these people.

"Second, this knowledge prompts you to be aware those from barely first world cultural backgrounds, such as southern Italians, Greeks, Turks, or Brazilians, are also unlikely to be respectful of the priority that should be accorded to the rights of individuals.

Jasmin: "What about indigenous people, like the first nations people of North America or Australian aboriginals?"

Jim: "These people are coming from a long way back. They have not even learned to separate person and place. For example, they can become physically ill when confronted by the inevitable externalities of progress, such as their ancestral lakes being affected by the tailings from a mine. That is, they have not been acculturated to accept that pragmatism is a necessary and esteemed aspect of modernity. More specific to your work, almost certainly these people have a collectivist understanding of personhood. You cannot assume that they are on the same page as us and you should be very patient if you wish to educate them. It will be a long process to bring them to progress given how far behind they are culturally.

"I must emphasize you should never underestimate the extent to which the thinking of these people contravenes rational sense. For example, they believe that it is us who are uncivilized and superstitious. I've heard their representatives say our reverence for autonomy and personal self-determination is a form of voodoo. They say the privileging of the individual and their rights is only found in what they term the dangerous white-fella world. In other words, rather than see themselves as deficient and wrong-headed, they go so far as to be critical of modernity. I have even heard these representatives say such misplaced things as it is us who are the idolaters in putting 'the individual' onto the high altar."

Jasmin: "I am catching on. Is it that I should be an emissary, even a soft-spoken warrior, for the benefits of progress and rational thinking? I guess I have a mission to bring others to the light of unfettered personal freedom. Yet, how big is this task? Can I really be confident that all white Anglo-Saxons and Anglo-Celtic people have accepted that the purpose of life is to maximize individual achievement?"

Jim: "You have an open and enquiring mind and the question is shrewd. It is tempting to give you the answer that would make us all sound modern, make us sound enlightened. Sadly, I cannot do this and still function as an impartial commentator.

"The fact is there are many amongst us who still persist in having a vestigial regard for the interests of others, for worrying about their so-called mates, for the honor of giving it up for the regiment, sacrificing themselves for the nation, and so forth. Such thinking is, as you well know, now understood by psychological science as totally irrational as it is derived from guilt and shame, emotions that are archaic and barbaric. These dead-but-not-quite-buried handbrakes to freedom and personal achievement are no more than that, the death rattles of that discredited and sentimental claptrap about what used to be referred to as 'the greater good.'"

Jasmin: "Yes, I know the science, but who exactly do I have to contend with?"

Jim: "Good to know you are tough-minded. I will get down to specifics. Old people are one group who act as fifth column behind our own lines. Almost always, they have *not* been brought up to see the great advantages in unrestrained freedom. For example, they are often so ancient as to view modesty and humility as virtues. They commonly do not see shyness as a defect. More, it is a sad and regrettable truth they are often so old-fashioned as to value good manners, self-sacrifice, and other-orientedness rather than see these as signs a person lacks vitality and ambition.

"Parents too, particularly mothers, are also a problem. They suffer from an attitudinal defect that is related to the syndrome that afflicts old people. These people find themselves saying uneducated, sentimental things – 'I can't be happier than my least happy child' for example. That is, they often have boundary problems. Many men have also lost their moorings. Even if your clients are white you should not assume their attitudes and values are sound.

"Young adults also present difficulties. They often suffer from idealism, which is the mirror image to the pragmatism and opportunism that is, as you know, the gold standard that Albert Ellis identified for rational thinking. Children too, but this is no surprise as they cannot be expected to have yet learned the wisdom of the marketplace."

Jasmin: "This briefing is tough to hear. I know I have to be a realist and to face the facts, but I had no idea my task would be so big. You have told me I can trust almost nobody, that I have to be on guard at all times."

Jim: "You have a mission, but you can rest assured you are not alone. You have colleagues who are also on the same mission. And you can look forward to having the comfort and the company of a warm inner glow over your own long professional life. You have the righteousness that is the forever gift of finding yourself a formal member of a missionary elite.

"Your mission is to bring the word to the natives, all natives. Your divining texts are those of Maslow and Erikson, Ellis and Beck, Rogers, and Abraham. Even if it might seem something of a surprise, your real allies are the purists of the marketplace, those economic rationalists and neo-conservatives, who see the world as Darwinian. Hard but true, the world is a place of winners and losers, robber-barons, and those who can be forgiven for being also-rans. Often, those who are unsuccessful know not what they do – but there are also willful misfits. There are none so blind as those who refuse to see.

"It will sometimes feel like a lonely job. There will be tiredness, but this is what you have signed up for. You are a member of an elite fighting force for the good that is personal freedom. You are a change agent who can make a difference. You can help bring the freedom that goes with being able to make private choices. Client by client, you can take this gift to the masses. You can be a vital agent in the process of the shapeless herd being transformed into differentiated individuals who can get on with the business of navigating their own separate paths.

> "Be assured, over time the market will confer on you gold and ermine. You will receive the prestige of being seen as a soldier, a priest, and a noble in this secular land. Believe in yourself and your mission. When your clients realize their potential for autonomy they will be set free."
>
> **Jasmin:** "You have reminded me what I stand for. My work is the work of progress."
>
> Like most practitioners Jasmin is an enthusiast, she is fired up about her work as she has been trained to believe she is on the side of the angels in wanting to build up, or restore, the autonomy of her clients. This is not an arbitrary or idiosyncratic goal; it is not an aspiration that represents a private fantasy about what people are meant to be. On the contrary, this value has a hegemonic prestige. The belief in autonomy is an incoming tide in the larger culture and it follows that this creed will also be totemic in each respected professional sub-culture.

Specialist local groups like counselors and therapists have been licensed to undertake certain functions and therefore have a remit to disseminate specific practices. Broadly, once professional socialization has been completed, members of these professional cadres tend to replicate these larger cultural values in their own internal norms. Unless a group is adversarial in their disposition, its internal worldview will tend to mirror what is accepted in its broader context – Jasmin is part of a group and is not alone in her allegiances.

Unlike members of a 'bikie' gang or a monastery, for example, people who explicitly choose to run counter to the majority, Jasmin is a professional and will tend to think and act as an insider. Whether you are an occupational therapist, a social worker, a nurse, or a psychologist; whether you are a doctor, a teacher, a counselor, or a housing worker – whatever the discipline of origin – as culture bearers practitioners will experience a chord in the term 'autonomy' that evokes an anthemic tune. Each will become fired up when they feel they are championing the autonomy of the client. Each will feel proud when they can say their client has more choices, is now empowered, is now more in charge of their own life.

As examined in Chapter 4, a powerful set of reasons is at work here. Not least of these is the fear that being 'in relationship' requires a degree of surrender. Like any real partnership, no one participant in a close relationship is really in control. This is a worrying prospect for those whose sense of independence is vulnerable. Compromise, bargaining, loss of unilateral control, and the irritations that inevitably accompany domestic living are the realities of life within every relationship that is fair and mutual. Given this compelling, if not exactly joyous, reality, the idealization of autonomy represents a longed for, albeit unattainable, dream.

Fantasized and complex autonomy

Autonomy, real autonomy, is not about separation, privacy, and a hard boundary around the self. More than a hundred years ago Karl Marx said that the self could be understood as an ensemble of social relations (Leonard, 1984), that humans are social beings rather than private entities. Although this idea probably sounds counter-intuitive, it can be articulated using the language of systems theory:

> The more a system develops its complexity, the more it can develop its autonomy and multiply its dependencies. We construct our psychological, individual and personal autonomy through the dependencies we undergo. (Morin, quoted in DiNicola, 1997, p 200)

Rather than acknowledging the primacy of human interdependence, to continue to pursue autonomy is to be in thrall to a fantasy, yet the allure of 'autonomy as independence' continues to intoxicate. Autonomy's insistent appeal lies in its association with what is treasured in contemporary culture, with what is the taken-for-granted gold of neoliberal thinking. This sensibility is captured in those mesmerizing bylines we know so well: *I must maximize my choices, take control of, and get on with, my life. I am obliged to be self-reliant, to know what I want.* These aphorisms are experienced as truths that seem impossible to resist.

The advertising industry has identified, mined, and fanned this fantasy ruthlessly. For example, high-profile campaigns to recruit students to particular Australian universities are centered on slogans such as 'Put yourself first', and 'enroll with us'. Surfing this tide, perhaps even leading the charge, another university has been running a year-on-year advertising program with a changing, but thematically consistent, slogan. The slogan initially read 'I am writing a new chapter' – an advertising pitch that tried to embed the idea that the university's good people would be there to ensure that 'you-the-canny-consumer get exactly what you want.' Before the next enrollment round this pitch evolved into 'I am not afraid of heights', with the next iteration being 'I am waiting for no one' – and then the next, and the next, 'me-me-me' incantations rolled on. These catchy appeals were embedded in state-of-the-art graphics as they were surely also grounded in sharply observed demographic research.

You are powerfully invited to identify with this story. It is a version of an old Yankee proverb that you might hail from a log cabin in the sticks but, if you want it bad enough, you can still end up in the White House. Unfortunately, the sweet-smelling well this dreaming draws from remains an underlying inspiration informing the texts and customs that remain at the base of professional practice. Of course, many clients do lack an adequate quantum of autonomy in terms of rights and resources, and the redressing of these absences is a highly proper practice aim, yet it is now well past the point when this pursuit can be allowed to totalize the whole of a practice mission.

Cross-cultural, ecological, feminist, and systems traditions offer a basis for seeing that the idealizing autonomy is a dangerous fantasy, but this allure should not be underestimated. In Western culture there are major social norms, deeply ingrained conventions related to age and stage expectations of life, that mean that in lived experience autonomy and self-determination feel sacred. This is demonstrated in the devastation that occurs to older people when a guardianship order deprives them of their right to administer their own funds, or an authority disqualifies their driving license. There are practical concerns when this happens, but there is also a symbolic blow as their independence has been officially disconfirmed.

Tony Abbott, a senior Australian politician, wrote in his book *Battlelines* that owning, and being licensed to drive, a private vehicle confers a sense of mastery. This is similar to the quip attributed to Margaret Thatcher that she looked down on any one over the age of 25 she saw waiting for a bus. To be awarded a license is to have undergone a rite of passage, and to lose this passport is to be forced to go backwards, to regress, through an altogether unwanted transformation. This process takes away the person's adult status and is often experienced as a ritual of humiliation. In Western culture full legal status is granted on reaching the age of 18; they are then granted the right to vote, to sign contracts, and to formally make their own decisions including, in many jurisdictions, the right to drink. If to be an adult is to have autonomy, to have this status voided is to become a non-adult. This is an especially troubling issue in protective settings in and beyond mental health where a range of formal procedures have the effect of disconfirming expectations of autonomy (discussed in some detail in Chapter 3).

With respect to the focus of this book, the theme of autonomy is such a central issue because relationships are sites where a person's sense of control is threatened. As with any meaningful partnership, for example, when one agency really collaborates with another, in a social relationship each party is required to give over a degree of control. This is scary as you are not really in charge: of the other, of where the relationship will go and, perhaps most worrying, of your own self and your feelings. For this reason the prospect of losing control in relationships is a problem for mental health clients, as it also is for any others who are at the bottom end of the social hierarchy.

It seems that an aversion to losing control is also becoming a problem for many beyond clients who are identified with the health and community sector. The impact of the process of individualization has made a perceived loss of control a concern about which many modern citizens struggle. (Elaine's distress at her loss of relationship control in the *Seinfeld* episode mentioned in Chapter 3 essays this neatly. Like Elaine, clients can be hungry for, and yet fearful of, connection.)

Given the professional and cultural environment it can be difficult to get a clear run at enhancing a client's relational base. Practitioners can be strong about the premise, that the interests of clients and their significant others should be understood as interdependent. They can also be confident that this understanding creates a different conceptual space within which professional practice is to be conducted than what has generally been received. They can also sense that the client intuitively knows this premise is emotionally true. All this can be grasped, and yet there is another voice, an insistent and primitive chant, that the client hears and the practitioner reacts to: 'What about me? I need to have what I want. That's what being every adult who trades in the adult marketplace is entitled to.'

If the practitioner can get both these voices into a dialogue, an engagement, there is scope for both the autonomous and the relational self to be heard and appreciated. This is hard work but it is a task that is informed by the desire to reflectively undertake an ideological as well as a technical role. This may sound heretical to those who lay claim to the preciousness of neutrality and its paradoxical relation, client self-determination. Many counselors, for example, have been coached in their training and supervision to support clients in the direction that the client is already heading: if the client has mixed feelings about their choices, but is leaning more to one option, the pragmatic course of action for the practitioner is to privilege, albeit subtly, the option that has the greater apparent momentum. This is fine if the choices are about what only involves the client, for instance, changing careers or deciding whether to talk about grief.

But it is generally not so simple as nearly every client choice has a relational impact. Deciding whether to have a secret lover, whether to tell your partner that you will leave when your youngest child turns 18, even the decision to have no further contact with a sister who you feel has been hurtful, are obvious examples of options that have a relational impact. Discussions about what seems a personal matter, such as 'wanting to be more in touch with my feelings' or 'exploring my sexuality', have relational implications, and these deserve explication in the practice encounter.

Once the view is rejected that the task of practitioners is to deliver a technical service, the result is that the professional project is recast as a process that is irrevocably ethical and ideological. It is not possible to side-step this challenge by citing the neoliberal mantra 'I am only providing options' or 'I am not in charge, it is always the client's decision.' Practitioners inevitably co-construct the decisions, as well as the subjectivity and sociality, of their clients. This is unavoidable, and it is onerous. Practitioners must choose whether to undertake practice in a way that constitutes the client as a sovereign, self-serving being, or whether to encourage the client to be an interdependent, accountable social being.

Can traditional models of practice be relationship building?

In a project that investigated the attitudes of practitioners to the relationships clients had with their significant others (Furlong, 2008a), an interviewee from the psychotherapy cohort presented an outlier opinion:

> 'Okay, well I don't know if I can answer how practice might be different if we [ie, practitioners] considered people to be embedded in their networks, but I think it definitely would. I think it's hard to imagine how that might happen because I think all this sort of psychotherapy

thought is … [pause] … it's deeply informed by a particular way of thinking about individuals which is fundamentally as these sort of independent beings, which I think is very problematic.'

This person was commenting on psychotherapy theory, particularly the cognitive behavioral therapy (CBT) and humanist approaches with which she was most familiar. What she was expressing was the opinion that the basis of all the approaches she had been taught was the same: that the client is a bounded private entity rather than a social being. For this reason the interviewee was pessimistic whether psychotherapists could ever be positive agents for a reprioritization of the relational.

There is logic in this position, but it is not a logic that has to be complexly accepted. Another view is that CBT practitioners, *Gestalt* therapists, indeed all those who follow any of the established therapeutic flags, have a real capacity to promote personal accountability and interpersonal connection without abandoning their preferred model. Practicing to the relationship-building agenda is likely to be a greater challenge if the practitioner salutes such flags than it would be if the allegiance was to, for example, a narrative or systems ethos, but it is not impossible. Conversely, practitioners can espouse a narrative or systems view and not materially privilege connection in the actuality of their practice. More broadly, those who practice with a commitment to a psychodynamic or disability perspective can be deliberately inclusive when it comes to involving their client's significant others. Whatever the theoretical allegiance, practitioners could draw attention to, for example, the importance of making a distinction between the client's intent and the effect of their actions (or any other of the relationship skills engagements detailed in Chapter 9; see p 211-252).

Beyond the counseling ambit, a relationship-building agenda can be promoted in practical, non-therapeutic roles. For example, in a material aid agency a client may appear requesting an emergency payment. Mindful there are sensitivities and risks, in this context, it may at times be possible to invoke the relational:

> 'You may be eligible to receive up to 25 euros, but before a decision is made it is our policy to understand at least the outline of your circumstances and your network. Without wanting the names and addresses of your significant others, we need to discuss the following:
>
> • Is there a person, or persons, you share your resources with?
> • Is there anyone you borrow from, or might borrow from, if you have no money prior to you receiving your next benefit?
> • Are you pressured by anyone in how you manage your food and money?
> • Do you have any debts that place you in any danger if you do not repay them?

- Have you any mates or relatives who care about the situation you are in?
- Is there anyone who might be able to put you up for a night or so?'

Based on what is now routinely asked in an outreach service for homeless people, these kinds of enquiries draw attention to the interpersonal context of clients' lives – an environment that is likely to have its dangers as well as its strengths. Lines of conversation that articulate the client's interpersonal context help professionals, and their clients, to remember, animate, and imagine what an exclusive emphasis on the individual relegates to the shadows.

As discussed in Chapter 8 , planners, managers, and supervisors can promote the same agenda in many formal and informal ways. Record keeping can be formatted to document informal connections, assessment and history-taking protocols can be established that prompt practitioners to acknowledge the relational dimensions of clients, and frameworks for goal setting can be organized to focus in on 'intimate social relations'. There are many roads that can be taken.

Summing up

To take the relationship-building path is to go against the grain. But in another sense the choice to take this path is to identify with a project that can be deeply satisfying. This different path triggers the possibilities of cooperation and mutuality, personal accountability, and interpersonal connection (Colgate, 2004; Jenkins, 2009). To choose this path is to actively decide not to promote self-entitlement and the atomization that his generates: ethically, it seems far preferable to incite solidarity and reciprocity than to advocate for a 'me-my-mine' future.

In contesting the process of individualization there is a chance to assist in developing the meaning that is summoned when fairness and hopefulness operate. To assist clients find more companionship and cooperation in their everyday associations, in maybe just one social relationship, is an ethical goal. People can change – many do, sometimes surprisingly quickly – and being a witness to a transformation where the client is more linked in is a special joy. Being with a client as they struggle with, learn to be better at, and then take up just one intimate connection offers a more lasting dividend than the 'Look at how good I am' experiences of expertise that sometimes occur in face-to-face professional practice.

Practitioners always have a difficult task. As well as being technically effective, each practitioner has to be gender-sensitive, aware of cultural issues, and thoughtful about the spiritual dimensions of their clients' lives. Additionally, if persuaded by the logic of the social inclusion argument, practitioners are aware of the structural factors that impinge on the chances of greater inclusion, that housing, employment, and stigma, as well as other factors, are implicated in what maintains exclusion. These multiple demands understood, a necessary element to achieve social inclusion and sustainable wellbeing is that clients, all people, are reciprocal players in meaningful circles of personal relationships. As argued earlier, seeking to build this quotient is a goal that can be pursued irrespective of one's formal role.

An old Arabic proverb has it that 'Men resemble their times more than their fathers.' This asserts that all humans will be shaped by the circumstances that prevail in a given place and period. A common humanity is always present, but life in Victorian or medieval times, growing up and growing old in such periods, such as working in and then migrating from Angola or Odessa, will leave its mark on the experience and conduct of the self. Life in the current conditions, a location that is increasingly both post-industrial and techno-consumerist, presents experiences that also shape, if not stamp, the selfhood of those currently participating as modern citizens.

The current milieu is associated with the presence of greater assertiveness, self-confidence, and individual freedom than was possible even a generation ago. These are progressive developments in many ways, yet, as with any example of change, there must also be losses and less desirable consequences in this evolution. The shadow side of these developments is present for all citizens even if those who are disadvantaged, those who are known to the mental health and welfare authorities, will presumably be most affected. Consequences may be iniquitously distributed but there is, perhaps, an oddly paradoxical effect that is currently in operation. Ordinary citizens, these who have been termed the 'worried well', may continue to be better off than those with less resources and opportunities, yet it may be that the more fortunate are coming to resemble those who have been diagnosed in an unexpected way.

This might seem a strange idea, but the profile of ordinary citizens now seems to be more generally resembling negative characteristics that have long been associated with the description of some developmental and personality disorders, characteristics that have previously been associated with more difficult clients. Terms like autistic, narcissistic, exhibitionistic, schizoid, and psychopathic are now being applied in descriptions of ordinary, everyday citizens more than was earlier the case. Until very recently this class of diagnosis was regarded as obdurately negative, as in the 'Oh but for the grace of god' category – like cancer. Perhaps ordinary citizens have become more self-absorbed, amoral, and isolated, but this point should not be overstated. To generalize, to draw a firmly negative conclusion about what remains contested and uncertain, is to cede far more ground than has been taken. One point is that emerging forms of selfhood may be read in unflattering ways, but it is not logical to throw our hands up in despair. Sociality, how people interact in their local small group affiliations and interpersonal relationships, will always reflect changes in the nature and understanding of selfhood, but this is not a one-way street. Causation runs both ways.

If practitioners conduct their professional practice, and their own social relations, in ways that promote fairness and encourage empathy, this contests the patterns of anomie and self-absorption many commentators assert are becoming the norm. This aim could be a key aspect of life politics, a personal-political mission. Just as it is accepted that 'The personal is the political', it also follows that 'The interpersonal is the ideological.' There is a lived politics that is expressed in the day-to-day domain of interactions and relationships, and this is a site where progressive options can be forged. In these exchanges affection and respect can become the lore, just as exploitation can be mistaken for an accepted norm. Making relational decisions a matter of clear attention, turning the focus to acts that actively choose a preferred relational ethics, has been the purpose to which this book is dedicated. It is not a fact that focusing on what one wants that selfishness pushes one towards the winner's podium whilst other-orientedness castes the carer as loser: you can't be a loser if you have friends, to recycle the punch-line from the film by Frank Capra, *It's a Wonderful Life*.

For the lonely and excluded, as well as for those who are included and resourced, relationships can be dangerous. There is always the risk of being misunderstood, not listened to, led astray, possibly even rejected. Whatever the negatives, what is the alternative? In an increasingly secular world good relationships are a wellspring in the desert, a source of sustenance that is almost spiritual in its power to revive. Where materialism has a strong hold, a friendship with another, or a secure bond with a group fastens those individuals so associated to what is larger, more meaningful, and potentially more enduring than the fragility characteristic of any single self.

Finally, the question of relationships is itself interesting for at least three reasons:

- Traditional family patterns, such as gender roles, have been challenged and are in the process of change.
- The new technologies, such as mobile phones, the internet, and assisted reproduction, are quite generally reorganizing our modes of social connectedness.
- There is now a greater acceptance of diversity with respect to sexuality and, more broadly, to the possibilities of elective community than has ever previously been the case.

These new possibilities for relationships present as a positive, as well as a challenging, landscape. To clients, indeed to each of us, this reshaped relational landscape puts into focus ethical and practical questions it is in nobody's interest to ignore. Having even one good quality relationship in a turbulent world generates a stock of existential meaning. It is also to have something of a lifeboat in a stormy sea. According to philosopher Emmanuel Levinas (1987), ethics relies on proximity, that I am only a moral human subject in my concern for, and interaction with, the other. As this is true for the practitioner and normally well citizen, so it is for clients.

Endnotes

Chapter 7

[1] The claim that good-enough personal relationships depend on there being a balance between the autonomous and relational aspects of the participants is an obvious simplification. The possibility of satisfactory personal relationships depends on a complex set of contextual factors as much or more as it relates to the presence of attributes which individuals might, or might not, exhibit. Not least of these conditions concern the presence of explicit and implicit rules that govern the conduct of relationships in a particular context. Such rules allocate, for example, respective roles and responsibilities between the participants. That is, there is always an empirical dimension in where gender, culture, and historical location, amongst a larger set of factors, are constitutive. The claim that a balance between the 'relational' and the 'autonomous' self is necessary for good quality relationships has been made in order to act as a focus in a particular discussion.

[2] That there should be a balance between the *relational self* and the *autonomous self* is itself certainly a construct, but it is not a lonely one. It has an obvious similarity with Jung's notion of the feminine and masculine aspects of the self as it has another quite different frame – the relationship between the left and right hemispheres of the brain. Each of these schemas emphasis the importance of balance, of neither aspect becoming hegemonic, so that the other is not suppressed. According to McGilchrist (2011), an energetic right hemisphere is holistic, aware of interdependencies, and reasonable whilst the left privileges the hubristic, the optimistic, and the narrowly logical. (McGilchrist contends we live in a period where the left brain has taken charge.) Jung's ideas, neuro-anatomy, and the ecological metaphor do certainly have similarities, but there are many differences, not least in the degree of abstraction employed.

Chapter 8

[3] Family blaming, a social practice that is most often a disguised form of mother blaming, remains a potent impulse. In the past it has been used to castigate mothers for a whole variety of disorders and problems. In addition to blaming mothers for young adults developing schizophrenia – the so-called 'schizophregenic mother' (Fromm-Reichman, 1948) – it has also been used for such diverse purposes as explaining why some children are autistic to excusing men who have sexually abused their children because the children's mothers have not adequately protected their offspring. Some on the left have also been active blamers, for example in holding individual families responsible for the production of sexism and inequality.

Such propaganda is now officially disallowed even if there remain persistent shadows of this superstition. For instance, the 'expressed emotion' research does not blame families for causing schizophrenia, but does hold families responsible for causing relapse: see, for example, the critique on the early 'expressed emotion' research as a disavowed form of family blaming (Hatfield et al, 1987).

References

Abbott, T. (1999) Interview, Radio National 'AM', Australian Broadcasting Commission, 20 May.

Abbott, T. (2009) Battlelines, Melbourne: Melbourne University Press.

Akst, D. (2010) 'America: land of loners', *The Wilson Quarterly: Surveying the World of Ideas* (www.wilsonquarterly.com/article.cfm?AID=1631).

Alberti, R. (1970) Your perfect right: A guide to assertive behavior.

Alcabes, A. and Jones, J. (1985) 'Structural determinants of clienthood', *Social Work*, Jan–Feb, pp 49-53.

Alexander, F. and French, T. (1946) *Psychoanalytic therapy: Principles and application*, New York: Ronald Press.

Althusser, L. (2006) *Philosophy of the encounter: Later writings, 1978-1987*, London: Verso.

Andrew, M., Farhall, J., Ong, B. and Waddell, F. (2009) 'Perceptions of mental health professionals and family caregivers about their collaborative relationships: a factor analytic study', *Australian Psychologist*, vol 44, no 2, pp 94-104.

Andrews, G. (2009) 'Online psychiatric treatment', Interview with Professor Gavin Andrews, Life Matters, Radio National, 14 January (www.abc.net.au/rn/lifematters/stories/2009/2438596.htm).

Argyris, C. and Schon, D. (1975) *Theory in practice: Increasing professional effectiveness*, San Francisco, CA: Jossey-Bass.

Askey, R., Holmshaw, J., Gamble, C. and Gray, R. (2009) 'What do carers of people with psychosis want from mental health services? Exploring the views of cares, service users and professionals', *Journal of Family Therapy*, issue 3, pp 310-31.

Atkinson, A. and Marlier, E. (2010) *Analyzing and measuring social inclusion in a global context*, New York: Department of Economic and Social Affairs, United Nations (www.un.org/esa/socdev/publications/measuring-social-inclusion.pdf).

Babiak, P. and Hare, R. (2006) *Snakes in suits: When psychopaths go to work*, New York: Harper Business.

Bageant, J. (2009) *Deer hunting with Jesus: Dispatches from America's class war*, Melbourne: Scribe.

Baldwin, M. (2005) *Interpersonal cognition*, New York: Guilford Press.

Barnes, M. (2005) *Social exclusion in Britain: An empirical investigation and comparison with the EU*, Aldershot: Ashgate.

Barrett, M. and McIntosh, M. (1982) *The anti-social family*, London: Verso.

Barrett, R. (1991) 'Psychiatric practice and the definition of schizophrenia', *Dulwich Centre Newsletter*, vol 4, pp 5-11.

Bateson, G. (1973) *Steps towards an ecology of mind*, London: Paladin.

Bateson, G. (1980) *Mind and nature: A necessary unity*, New York: Bantam Books.

Bateson, G., Jackson, D., Haley, J. and Weakland, J. (1956) 'Towards a theory of schizophrenia', *Behavioral Science*, vol 1, no 4, pp 251-64.

Baum, G. (2003) 'Still not out', *The Age*, 15 November.

Bauman, Z. (1992) 'Introduction: The re-enchantment of the world', In *Intimations of post modernity*, New York: Routledge.

Bauman, Z. (2000) 'Am I my brother's keeper?', *The European Journal of Social Work*, vol 3, pp 5–11.

Bauman, Z. (2001) *The individualized society*, Cambridge: Polity Press.

Bauman, Z. (2003) *Liquid love: On the frailty of human bonds*, Cambridge: Polity Press.

Beck, U. (1999) *Ecological enlightenment: Essays on the politics of the risk society*, Atlantic Highlands, NJ: Humanities Press.

Beck, U. and Beck-Gernsheim, E. (2002) *Individualization: Institutionalized individualism and its social and political consequences*, London: Sage Publications.

Berg, I.K. (2007) *More than miracles: The state of the art of solution-focused brief therapy*, New York: Routledge.

Berkman, L. and Glass, T. (2000) 'Social integration, social networks, social support and health', in L. Berkman and I. Kawachi (eds) *Social epidemiology*, New York: Oxford University Press, pp 137-174.

Berne, E. (1975) *What do you say after you say hello?*, London: Corgi Publishers.

Blackledge, J., Ciarrochi, J. and Deane, F. (2009) *Acceptance and commitment therapy: Contemporary theory, research and practice*, Bowen Hills, Queensland: Australian Academic Press.

Bloom, H. (1998) *Shakespeare: The invention of the human*, New York: Riverhead Books.

Bloom, H. (2003) 'The sage of Concord: on Ralph Waldo Emerson', *The Guardian*, 24 May, pp 1-9 (http://books.guardian.co.uk/review/story/0,12084,962070,00.html).

Blumer, H. (1986) *Symbolic interactionism: Perspective and method*, Berkeley, CA: University of California Press.

Borowski, A. (2011) 'In Courtroom 7: the Children's Koori Court at work: findings from an evaluation', *International Journal of Offender Therapy and Comparative Criminology*, vol 55, no 5, October.

Bos, H. (2010) 'Planned gay father families in kinship arrangements', *The Australian and New Zealand Journal of Family Therapy*, vol 31, pp 356-71.

Boscolo, L. and Bertrando, P. (1996) *Systemic therapy with individuals*, London: Karnac.

Bostrum, N. (2005) 'In defense of posthuman dignity', *Bioethics*, vol 19, no 3, pp 202-14.

Bourdieu, P. (1977) *An outline of a theory of practice*, New York: Cambridge University Press.

Bourdieu, P. (1984) *Distinction: A social critique of the judgment of taste*, Cambridge, MA: Harvard University Press.

Bourdieu, P. (1986) 'The forms of capital', in J. Richardson (ed) *Handbook of theory and research for the sociology of education*, New York: Greenwood Press, pp 241-58.

Bowlby J. (1988) A Secure Base: Clinical Applications of Attachment Theory, London: Routledge.

Branson, J. and Miller, D. (1992) 'Pierre Bourdieu', in P. Beilharz (ed) *Social theory: A guide to central thinkers*, St Leonards, New South Wales: Allen & Unwin, pp 37-45.

Brett, J. and Moran, A. (2006) *Ordinary people's politics: Australians talk about life, politics and the future of their country*, Melbourne: Pluto Australia.

Brown, G. and Harris, T. (1984) *Social origins of depression*, London: Tavistock.

Burgess, P., Pirkus, J., Coombs, T. and Rosen, A. (2010) *A review of recovery measures*, Australian Mental Health Outcomes and Classicization Network, National Mental Health Strategy, Canberra.

Burton, L., Westen, D. and Kowalski, R. (2009) *Psychology: Australian and New Zealand* (2nd edn), Milton, Queensland: John Wiley & Sons.

Cacioppo, J. T. and Patrick, W. (2008) *Loneliness: Human nature and the need for social connection*, New York: W. W. Norton.

Cacioppo, J. T., Hawkley, L. and Thisted, R. (2010) 'Perceived social isolation makes me sad: 5-year cross-lagged analyses of loneliness and depressive symptomatology in the Chicago Health, Aging, and Social Relations Study', *Psychology and Aging*, vol 25, no 2, pp 453-63.

Carpenter, J. and Treacher, A. (1983) 'On the neglected but related arts of convening and engaging families', *Journal of Family Therapy*, vol 5, pp 337-58.

Carr, N. (2010) *The shallows: How the internet is changing the way we think, read and remember*, London: Atlantic Books.

Carter, B. and McGoldrick, M. (1999) *The expanded family life cycle*, Boston, MA: Allyn & Bacon.

Castells, M. (2004) *The power of identity*, Oxford: Blackwell.

Cecchin, G. (1987) 'Hypothesizing, circularity and neutrality revisited: an invitation to curiosity', *Family Process*, vol 26, pp 405-15.

Centre for Bhutan Studies (2011) *Gross National Happiness Index* (www.grossnationalhappiness.com/).

Christakis, N. and Fowler, J. (2009) *Connected: The surprising power of our social networks*, New York: Little, Brown & Co.

Clark, A. (2003) *Natural born cyborgs*, Oxford: Oxford University Press.

Clegg, J. and Lansdall-Welfare, R. (2010) 'From autonomy to relationships: productive engagement with uncertainty', *Journal of Intellectual Disability Research*, vol 54 (supplement 1), pp 66-72.

Colgate, C. (2004) *Just between you and me: The art of ethical relationships*, Melbourne: Pan Macmillan.

Couture, S. (2007) 'Multiparty talk in family therapy: complexity breeds opportunity', *Journal of Systemic Therapies*, vol 26, March, pp 63-80.

Coyne, J. (1985) 'Towards a theory of frames and reframing: the social nature of frames', *Journal of Marital and Family Therapy*, vol 11, no 4, pp 337-44.

Cox, R.D. (1989) *Welfare practice in a multicultural society*, Sydney: Prentice-Hall of Australia

Crisp, B. (2010) 'Belong, connectedness and social exclusion', *Journal of Social Inclusion*, vol 1, no 2, pp 123-32.

Cronen, V., Pearce, K. and Lannamann, J. (1982) 'Paradoxes, double binds, and reflexive loops: an alternative theoretical perspective', *Family Process*, 20, pp 91–112.

Curtis, I., Sumner, B., Hook, S. and Morris, P. (1979) *Transmission*, Birmingham: Factory Records.

Davidson, J. and Rees-Mogg, W. (1997) *The sovereign individual*, London: Macmillan.

Dean, R. (2001) 'The myth of cross-cultural competence', *Families in Society*, vol 82, pp 623-31.

Decety, J. and Moriguchi, Y. (2007) 'The empathic brain and its dysfunction in psychiatric populations: implications for intervention across different clinical conditions', *BioPsychoSocial Medicine*, vol 1, no 22, pp 1-21.

Denborough, D. (2008) *Collective narrative practice*, Adelaide: Dulwich Centre Publications.

De Jong, P. and Berg, I. (2001) 'Co-constructing co-operation with mandated clients', *Social Work*, vol 46, pp 361-74.

de Shazer, S. (1984) 'The death of resistance', *Family Process*, vol 23, pp 11-21.

DiNicola, V. (1997) *A stranger in the family: Culture, families and therapy*, New York: W.W. Norton.

Dominelli, L. (2002) *Anti-oppressive social work theory and practice*, Basingstoke: Palgrave.

Donald, E. (Edit.) 1981. Debrett's Etiquette and Modern Manners, London: DeBrett's Peerage Ltd.

Douglas, T. (1995) *Scapegoats: Transferring blame*, London: Routledge.

Draine, J., Wolff, N., Jacoby, J.E., Hartwell, S. and Duclos, C. (2005) 'Understanding community re-entry for former prisoners with mental illness: a conceptual model to guide new research', *Behavioural Sciences and the Law*, vol 23, pp 689-707.

Dreyfus, H. and Rabinow, P. (1982) *Foucault: Beyond structuralism and hermeneutics*, Chicago, IL: University of Chicago Press.

Duberman, M. (2002) *Left out: The politics of exclusion*, New York: South End Press.

Dumont, L. (1986) *Essays on individualism: Modern ideology in anthropological perspective*, Chicago, IL: University of Chicago Press.

Durkheim, E. (1997 [1951]) *Suicide: A study in sociology*, New York: Free Press.

Dutton, K. 2012. The Wisdom of Psychopaths: What Saints, Spies, and Serial Killers Can Teach Us About Success, William Heinemann, London.

Ehrenreich, B. (2010) *Smile or die: How positive thinking fooled America and the world*, London: Granta.

Eldred, M. (2010) 'The digital dissolution of being', *Left Curve*, pp 96-121.

Elliot, A. and Lemert, C. (2006) *The new individualism: The emotional costs of globalization*, London: Routledge.

Emirbayer, M. and Williams, E. (2005) 'Bourdieu and social work', *Social Service Review*, December, pp 690-724.

Erikson, E. (1980) Identity and the life cycle, New York : Norton.

Florida, R. (2008) *Who's your city? How the creative economy is making where you live the most important decision of your life*, New York: Basic Books.

Fook, J. and Gardiner, F. (2007) *Practising critical reflection*, Maidenhead: Open University Press.

Foucault, M. (1967) *Madness and civilization*, London: Tavistock.

Foucault, M. (1972) *The archaeology of knowledge*, New York: Pantheon.

Foucault, M. (1973) *The birth of the clinic*, London: Tavistock.

Frankl, V. (1964) *Man's search for meaning: An introduction to logotherapy*, London: Hodder & Stoughton.

Frazer, N. and Gordon, L. (1994) 'A genealogy of "dependency": a keyword of the welfare state', *Journal of Women Culture and Society*, pp 309-36.

Frazer, N. and Honneth, A. (2003) *Redistribution or recognition? A political-philosophical exchange*, New York: Verso.

Fromm-Reichman, F. (1948) 'Notes on the development of treatment of schizophrenics by psychotherapy', *Psychiatry*, vol 1, pp 263-73.

Furlong, M. (1995) 'Difference, indifference and differentiation', *The Australian and New Zealand Journal of Family Therapy*, vol 16, no 1, pp 15-22.

Furlong, M. (2001) 'Constraints on family-sensitive mental health practices', *Journal of Family Studies*, vol 7, no 2, pp 217-31.

Furlong, M. (2002) 'Neither colluding nor colliding: practical ideas for engaging men', in B. Pease and P. Camilleri, *Working with men in the human services*, Melbourne: Allen & Unwin, pp 54-67.

Furlong, M. (2003b) 'Self-determination and a critical perspective in casework: promoting a balance between interdependence and autonomy', *Qualitative Social Work*, vol 2, no 2, pp 177-96.

Furlong, M. (2003c) 'Critiquing the goal of autonomy: towards strengthening the "relational self" and the quality of belonging in casework practice', *The European Journal of Social Work*, vol 6, no 1, pp 5-19.

Furlong, M. (2007) 'Emphasizing "the relational self" as a goal in casework', *Practice Reflections*, vol 2, no 1, pp 1-19.

Furlong, M. (2008a) 'Disturbing the dream of the autonomous subject', PhD thesis, Deakin University, Melbourne.

Furlong, M. (2008b) 'Captured by the game: could an allegiance to the therapeutic relationship displace a positive imagining of the client's significant-other relationships?', *The Australian and New Zealand Journal of Family Therapy*, vol 29, no 1, pp 25-33.

Furlong, M. (2009b) 'Is the vocabulary of health and well-being colonizing the "the social?"', *Arena Journal*, vol 103, pp 34-40.

Furlong, M. (2010a) 'Psychotherapy as vector for anomie and isolation', *Psychotherapy in Australia*, vol 16, no 2, pp 38-43.

Furlong, M. (2010b) 'Sovereign selves or social beings? The practitioner's role in constructing the subjectivity and sociality of the consumer', *New Paradigm*, Autumn, pp 50-7.

Furlong, M. (2010c) 'Love and shame: checking, trumping and snookering each other', *No to Violence Journal*, vol 5, no 1, pp 20-9.

Furlong, M. and Leggatt, M. (1996) 'Reconciling the patients' right to confidentiality with the families' need to know', *Australian and New Zealand Journal of Psychiatry*, vol 30, pp 614-22.

Furlong, M. and Wright, J. (2011) 'Critiquing "cultural competence", promoting "critical awareness": towards disrupting received professional knowledges', *Australian Social Work*, vol 64, no 1, p 38-54.

Furlong, M., Young, J., Perlerz, A., McLachlan, D. and Reiss, C. (1991) 'For family therapists involved in the treatment of chronic and longer term conditions', *Dulwich Review*, vol 4, pp 58-68.

Furman, B and Ahola, T. (1995) *Solutions talk: Hosting therapeutic conversations*, New York: W.W. Norton.

Gallagher, B. (2005) *Friends are everything*, New York: Barnes & Noble.

Geertz, C. (1995) *After the fact*, Cambridge, MA: Harvard University Press.

Gerdes, K., Segal, E. and Lietz, C. (2010) 'Conceptualizing and measuring empathy', *British Journal of Social Work*, vol 40, pp 2324-43.

Gergen, K. (1994) *Realities and relationships: Soundings in social construction*, Cambridge, MA: Harvard University Press.

Giddens, A. (1991) *Modernity and self-identity: Self and society in the Late Modern Age*, Cambridge: Polity Press.

Giddens, A. (1992) *The transformation of intimacy: Sexuality, love and eroticism in modern societies*, Oxford: Polity Press.

Giddens, A. (2002) *Runaway world: How globalization is re-shaping our lives*, London: Profile Books.

Gilligan, C. (1982) *In a different voice: Psychological theory and women's development*, Cambridge, MA: Harvard University Press.

Goffman, I. (1961) *Where the action is*, London: Allen Lane.

Goffman, I. (1971) *The presentation of self in everyday life*, Harmondsworth: Penguin.

Goffman, I. (1974) *Stigma: Notes on the management of spoiled identity*, Harmondsworth: Pelican.

Goleman, D. (1997) *Emotional intelligence: Why it can matter more than IQ*, New York: Bantam.

Goleman, D. (2006) *Social intelligence: The new science of social relationships*, London: Hutchinson.

Green, D. and McDermott, F. (2010) 'Social work from inside and between complex systems: perspectives on person–in–environment for today's social work', *British Journal of Social Work*, vol 40, no 8, pp 2414-30.

Green, R., Mitchell, P. and Bruun, A. (2012) 'Bonds and bridges: perspectives of service-engaged young people on the value of relationships in addressing alcohol and other drug issues', *Journal of Youth Studies*, doi: 10.1080/13676261.2012.718433.

Greenberg, J. and Mitchell, S. (1983) *Object relations and psychoanalytic theory*, Cambridge, MA: Harvard University Press.

Greenfield, S. (2008) *ID: The quest for identity in the 21st century*, London: Sceptre.

Griffiths, M. (2001) 'Restorative justice conferencing', in B. Pease and P. Camileri (eds) *Working with men in the human services*, Sydney: Allen & Unwin, pp 134-46.

Hafner, J., Badenoch, A., Fisher, D. and Swift, H. (1993) 'Spouse-aided versus individual therapy in persisting psychiatric disorders: a systematic comparison', *Family Process*, vol 22, pp 385-99.

Hall, C. (1990) *Women and identity: Value choices in a changing world*, New York: Hemisphere.

Hall, E. (2010) 'Spaces of social inclusion and belong for people with intellectual disability', *Journal of Intellectual Disability*, vol 54 (supplement 1), pp 48-57.

Harborne, A., Wolpert, M. and Clare, L. (2004) 'Making sense of ADHD: a battle for understanding? Parents' views of their children being diagnosed with ADHD', *Clinical Child Psychology and Psychiatry*, vol 9, p 327.

Harriss, J. (2002) *Depoliticizing development: The World Bank and social capital*, London: Anthem Press.

Hartman, A. and Laird, J. (1983) *Family centred social work practice*, New York: Free Press.

Hatfield. A. (1982) 'Therapist and families: worlds apart', *Hospital and Community Psychiatry*, vol 33, no 7, p 513.

Hatfield, A., Spaniol, L. and Zpple, A. (1987) 'Expressed emotion: a family perspective', *Schizophrenia Bulletin*, vol 13, pp 221-6.

Hawkley, L., Thisted, R., Masi, C. and Cacioppo, J.T. (2010) 'Loneliness predicts increased blood pressure: five-year cross-lagged analysis in middle-aged and older adults', *Psychology and Aging*, vol 25, pp 132-41.

Healy, K. and Hampshire, A. (2002) 'Social capital: a useful concept for social work?', *Australian Social Work*, vol 55, no 3, pp 227-38.

Hedges, F. (2005) *Introduction to systemic therapy with individuals: A social constructivist approach*, Basingstoke: Palgrave Macmillan.

Heelas, P. and Lock, A. (1981) *Indigenous psychologies: An anthropology of the self*, London: Academic Press.

Herman, J. (1992) *Trauma and recovery*, London: Pandora.

Hill, A. and Shaw, I. (2011) *ICT and social work*, London: Sage Publications.

Hillier, J. and Rooksby, E. (eds) (2002) *Habitus: A sense of place*, Aldershot: Ashgate.

Hochschild, A. (1990) *The second shift: Working parents and the revolution of the home*, New York: Viking.

Hochschild, A. (2003) *The commercialization of intimate life: Notes from home and work*, Berkeley, CA: University of California Press.

Hodgkinson, T. (2008) 'With friends like these', *The Guardian*, 14 January (www.guardian.co.uk/technology/2008/jan/14/facebook).

Hoffman, L. (1985) 'Beyond power and control: towards a "second order" family systems therapy', *Family Systems Medicine*, vol 3, no 4, pp 381-96.

Hoggett, P. (2001) 'Hatred of dependency', in *Emotional life and the politics of welfare*, Houndmills: Macmillan, pp 159-80.

Howard, C. (2007) *Contested individualization: Debates about contemporary personhood*, New York: Palgrave Macmillan.

Huffaker, D. and Calvert, S. (2005) 'Gender, identity and language use in teenage blogs', *Journal of Computer-Mediated Communication*, vol 10, no 2, Article 1 (http://jcmc.indiana.edu/vol10/issue2/huffaker.html).

Jameson, F. (1991) *Postmodernism, or the cultural logic of late capitalism*, Durham, NC: Duke University Press.

Jamison, K. (2009) *Nothing was the same*, New York: Knopf.

Jarre, R. (2011) *Louis Althusser: Hailing, interpollation and the subject of mass media* (http://ezinearticles.com/?Louis-Althusser:-Hailing,-Interpellation,-and-the-Subject-of-Mass-Media&id=614657).

Jenkins, A. (2009) *Becoming ethical: A parallel, political journey with men who have abused*, Lyme Regis: Russell House.

Jones, C. (2001) 'Voices from the front line: state social workers and New Labor', *British Journal of Social Work*, vol 31, no 4, pp 547-62.

Jones, A. and May, J. (1995) *Working in human service organizations: A critical introduction*, Melbourne: Longman.

Jordan, J., Kaplan, A., Miller, J.B., Stiver, I. and Surrey, J. (1991) *Women's growth in connection: Writings from the Stone Center*, New York: Guilford Press.

Jung, C. (1946) 'The psychology of the transference', in *The practice of psychotherapy. The collected works*, vol 16, London: Routledge.

Kawachi, I. and Berkman, L. (2003) *Neighbourhoods and health*, New York: Oxford University Press.

Keene, J. (2001) *Clients with complex needs: Inter-professional practice*, Oxford: Blackwell Science.

Keene, J. and Li, X. (2005) 'A study of a total social service care population and its inter-agency shared care populations', *British Journal of Social Work*, vol 35, pp 1145-61.

Khan, M. (1975) 'Introduction' in D.W. Winnicott *Through paediatrics to psychoanalysis: The international psycho-analytical library*, 100:1-325, London: The Hogarth Press/Institute of Psycho-Analysis (http://pep.gvpi.net/document.php?id=ipl.100.0001a&type=hitlist&num=15&query=zone1%2Cparagraphs|zone2%2Cparagraphs|author%2C%22Winnicott%2C+D.W.%22).

Kipnis, L. (2003) *Against love: A polemic*, New York: Vintage Books.

Kohut, H. (1959) 'Introspection, empathy and psychoanalysis', *Journal of the American Psychoanalytic Association*, vol 7, pp 459-83.

Lasch, C. (1977) *Haven in a heartless world: The family besieged*, New York: Basic Books.

Lasch, C. (1979) *The culture of narcissism*, New York: W. W. Norton.

Layard, R. (2005) *Happiness: Lessons for a new science*, London: Penguin.

Leonard, P. (1984) *Personality and ideology: Towards a materialist understanding of the individual*, London: Macmillan.

Levinas, E. (1987) *Time and the other*, Pittsburgh, PA: Duquesne University Press.

Lewis, G. and Ronan, K. (2010) 'Improving the outcome of cognitive behavioral therapy in the treatment of schizophrenia', *Psychotherapy in Australia*, vol 16, no 4, pp 70-6.

Liebow, E. (1967) *Tally's corner*, Boston, MA: Little, Brown & Co.

Lindner, H., Menzies, D., Kelly, J., Taylor, S. and Shearer, M. (2003) 'Coaching for behavior change in chronic disease: a review of the literature and the implications for coaching as a self-management intervention', *Australian Journal of Primary Health*, vol 9, nos 2 and 3, pp 1-9.

Lipsky, M. (1980) *Street level bureaucracy*, New York: Russell Sage.

Longres, J. (2000) *Human behavior in the social environment*, Itasca, IL: Peacock Publishers.

LSE (London School of Economics) (2006) *The depression report: A new deal for depression and anxiety*, London: LSE Mental Health Policy Group.

Mackay, H. (2002) 'The best intimacy money can buy', *The Age*, 8 June, p 14.

McBeath, G. and Webb, S. (2005). Post-critical social work analytics, in J. Fook, S. Hick & R. Pozzuto (Edits.) Social Work: A Critical Turn, Thompson, Toronto, pp 167-187.

McColl, E. (1948) *Dirty old town*, Vanguard VS-9110 (www.wirz.de/music/washfrm.htm).

McGilchrist, I. (2011) *The master and his emissary: The divided brain and the re-shaping of western civilization*, New Haven, CT: Yale University Press.

McGoldrick, M. (2011) *The genogram journey*, New York: W.W. Norton.

McMahon, M. (1992) 'Dangerousness, confidentiality and the duty to protect', *Australian Psychologist*, vol 27, pp 12-16.

Maris, P. (1998) *The politics of uncertainty: Attachment in private and public life*, New York: Routledge.

Marmot, M. (2005) 'Social determinants of health inequalities', *The Lancet*, vol 365, pp 1099-104.

Marsh, P. and Doel, M. (2005) *The task book*, Abingdon: Routledge.

Marshall, T. and Soloman, P. (2000) 'Releasing information to families of persons with severe mental illness: a survey of NAMI members', *Psychiatric Services*, vol 51, pp 1006-11.

Maslow, A. (1943) 'A theory of human motivation', *Psychology Review*, vol 50, pp 370-96.

Maslow, A. (1970) *Motivation and personality*, New York: Harper & Row.

Mathews, F. (1995) *The ecological self*, London: Routledge.

Mayer, J. and Timms, N. (1970) *The client speaks: Working class impressions of casework*, London: Routledge & Kegan Paul.

Mehrabian, A. (2007) 'Communication without words', in C.D. Mortenson (ed) *Communication theory*, Piscataway, NJ: Transaction Publishers, pp 193-200.

Menzies, I. (1961) *The functioning of social systems as a defense against anxiety*, London: Tavistock.

Miller, A. (1983) *The drama of the gifted child and the search for the true self*, London: Faber & Faber.

Miller, J. (1978) *Living systems*, New York: McGraw-Hill.

Miller, J., Donner, S. and Frazer, E. (2004a) 'Talking when talking is tough: taking on conversations about race, sexual orientation, gender, class and other aspects of social identity', *Smith College Studies in Social Work*, vol 74, no 2, pp 377-92.

Miller, S., Duncan, L. and Hubble, M. (2004b) 'Beyond integration: the triumph of outcome over process in clinical practice', *Psychotherapy in Australia*, vol 10, no 2, pp 32-43.

Mills, C. Wright (1959) *The sociological imagination*, Oxford: Oxford University Press.

Minuchin, S. (1974) *Families and family therapy*, Cambridge, MA: Harvard University Press.

Mitchell, J. (2009) 'Inferences about other minds', *Philosophical Transactions of the Royal Society B*, vol 364, pp 1309-16.

Mitchell, S. (1988) *Relational concepts in psychoanalysis*, Cambridge, MA: Harvard University Press.

Mitchell, W. (2011) Quoted from his official publisher's website (www.super-selfhelp.com/inspiration-motivation.pdf).

Morgan, C., Burns, T., Fitzpatrick, R., Pinfold, V. and Priebe, S. (2007) 'Social exclusion and mental health', *British Journal of Psychiatry*, vol 191, pp 477-83.

Morris, K. and Barnes, M. (2008) 'Prevention and social exclusion: new understandings for policy and practice', *British Journal of Social Work*, vol 38, no 6, pp 1194-211.

Morss, J. (1996) *Growing critical: Alternatives to developmental psychology*, New York: Routledge.

Mottarella, K., Philpot, C. and Fritzsche, B. (2001) 'Don't take out this appendix! Generalizability of the Global Assessment of Relational Functioning Scale', *The American Journal of Family Therapy*, vol 29, no 4, pp 271-80.

Mowbray, M. (2004) 'The new communitarianism: building great communities or Brigadoonery', *Just Policy*, vol 32, pp 11-20.

Napier, A. and Whitaker, C (1978). The family crucible, New York: Harper & Row.

Nie, N. (2001) 'Sociability, interpersonal relations and the internet', *American Behavioral Scientist*, vol 45, no 3, pp 420-35.

O'Brien, M. (1981) *The politics of reproduction*, London: Routledge & Kegan Paul.

O'Connor, T. and Zeanah, C. (2003) 'Attachment disorders: assessment strategies and treatment approaches', *Attachment and Human Development*, vol 5, no 3, pp 223-44.

OECD (Organisation for Economic Co-operation and Development) (2003) *Ageing, housing and urban development*, Paris: OECD.

Offer, A. (2006) *The challenge of affluence: Self-control and well-being in the USA and Britain since 1950*, Oxford: Oxford University Press.

Orbach, S. (1999) *Towards emotional literacy*, London: Penguin.

Ornstein, E. and Ganzer, C. (2005) 'Relational social work: a model for the future', *Families in Society*, vol 86, no 4, pp 565-73.

Owusu-Bempah, K. (1999) 'Confidentiality and social work practice in African cultures', in B. Compton and B. Galaway (eds) *Social work processes*, Pacific Grove, CA: Brooks/Cole, pp 166-70.

Page, T. (2007) 'Parallel play: a personal history', *The New Yorker*, vol 83, no 24, pp 36-41.

Parton, N. (2008) 'Changes in the form of knowledge in social work: from the "social" to the "informational"', *British Journal of Social Work*, vol 38, pp 253-69.

Parton, N. and O'Byrne, P. (2000) *Constructive social work: Towards a new practice*, Basingstoke: Palgrave/Macmillan.

Paterson, T. (1996) 'Leaving well alone: a systemic perspective on the therapeutic relationship', in C. Flaskas and A. Perlesz (eds) *The therapeutic relationship in systemic therapy*, London: Karnac Books, pp 15-33.

Pawsey, R. and Firestone, A. (1983) 'BIAS: the Bouverie Information and Assessment schema', *The Journal of Strategic and Systemic Therapies*, vol 2, no 1, pp 31-43.

Pease, B. (2010) *Undoing privileged: Unearned privilege in a divided world*, London: Zed Books.

Pentony, P. (1981) *Models of influence in psychotherapy*, London: Collier Macmillan.

Perine, S., Titov, N. and Andrews, G. (2008) 'The climate sadness program of internet-based treatment for depression: a pilot study', *E-Journal of Applied Psychology*, vol 4, no 2, pp 18-24.

Perlerz, A., Furlong, M. and McLachlan, D. (1992) 'Family work and acquired brain injury', *Australian and New Zealand Journal of Family Therapy*, vol 13, no 3, pp 145-53.

Perlman, H. (1979) *Relationship: The heart of helping people*, Chicago, IL: University of Chicago Press.

Phillips. A. and Taylor, B. (2009) *On kindness*, London: Penguin.

Pierce, J. (1996) 'Rambo litigators: emotional labor in a male dominated occupation', in C. Cheng (ed) *Masculinities in organizations*, London: Sage Publications, p 1-28.

Pilgrim, D. and Rogers, A. (2008) 'Asylums: the social situation of mental patients and other inmates', *Journal of Health Services Research and Policy*, 13(11): 47-9.

Pilgrim, D., Rogers, A. and Bentall, R. (2009) 'The centrality of personal relationships in the creation and amelioration of mental health problems: the current interdisciplinary case', *Health: An Interdisciplinary Journal for the Social Study of Health, Illness and Medicine*, 13(2): 235-54.

Pilgrim, D. (2011) 'The hegemony of cognitive-behavior therapy in modern mental health care', *Health Sociology Review*, vol 20, no 2, pp 120-32.

Putnam, R. (2000) *Bowling alone: The collapse and revival of American community*, New York: Simon & Schuster.

Rapaport, N. and Overing, J. (2000) *Social and cultural anthropology: The key concepts*, London: Routledge.

Relationships Foundation, London (www.relationshipsfoundation.org/Web/).

Riesman, D. (1956) *The lonely crowd: A study of the changing face of American character*, New York: Doubleday.

Rogers, C. (1969) *On becoming a person: A therapist's view of psychotherapy*, London: Constable.

Rollnick, S. and Miller, W. (1995) 'What is motivational interviewing?', *Behavioral and Cognitive Psychotherapy*, vol 23, pp 325-34.

Rose, N. (1989) *Governing the soul*, London: Routledge.

Rose, N. (1999) 'Interrogating the psychotherapies: an interview with Nikolas Rose', *Psychotherapy in Australia*, vol 5, pp 40-6.

Rose, N. (2000) 'Government and control', *British Journal of Criminology*, vol 40, pp 321-39.

Rosenstein, B. (2011) 'Work-life lessons from the legendary Peter Drucker' (www.businessknowhow.com/growth/drucker.htm).

Rosier, P. (2001) *Workwise: A guide to managing workplace relationships*, Christchurch: Canterbury University Press.

Ruch, G., Turney, D. and Ward, A. (2010) *Relationship-based social work*, London: Jessica Kingsley Publishers.

Ryff, C. and Singer, B. (2001) *Emotion, social relationships, and health*, New York: Oxford University Press.

Said, E. (1978) *Orientalism*, New York: Pantheon.

Said, E. (2001) 'The public role of writers and intellectuals', The Alfred Deakin Lectures, Melbourne Town Hall, 19 May [transcript].

Saleebey, D. (2009) *The strengths perspective in social work practice*, Boston, MA: Pearson/ Allyn & Bacon.

Schmitz, C. and Schmitz, E. (2010) *Building a love that lasts: The seven surprising secrets of a successful marriage*, New York: Jossey-Bass.

Schizophrenia.com (2011) Schizophrenia Daily News Blog (www.schizophrenia.com/sznews/archives/003633.html).

Seedhouse, D. (2002) *Total health promotion: Mental health rational fields and the quest for autonomy*, Chichester: John Wiley & Sons.

Selvini-Palazzoli, M., Boscolo, L., Cecchin, G. and Prata, G. (1980) 'Hypothesizing-circularity-neutrality: three guidelines for the conductor of the session', *Family Process*, vol 19, no 1, pp 3-13.

Sharp, G. (2009) 'To market, to market: telecommunications and the road to growth', *Arena*, vol 100, pp 35-42.

Silver, A. (1990) 'Friendship in commercial society', *American Journal of Sociology*, vol 95, no 6, pp 1474-504.

Silver, E. (1991) 'Should I give advice? A systemic view', *Journal of Family Therapy*, vol 13, pp 295-309.

Simon, F., Steirlin, H. and Wynne, L. (1985) *The language of family therapy: A systemic vocabulary and sourcebook*, New York: Family Process Press.

Smith, M. (1975) When I say no, I feel guilty: How to cope using the skills of systematic assertiveness Therapy

Snyder, N.R. (1997) 'Person-in-environment: the PIE classification system for social functioning problems', *Social Work*, vol 42, no 5, p 536.

Sommer, D. (1998) 'The re-construction of childhood: implications for theory and practice', *European Journal of Social Work*, vol 1, no 3, pp 311-26.

Spinelli, E. (2010) 'Coaching and therapy: similarities and differences', *Psychotherapy in Australia*, vol 17, no 1, pp 52-8.

Steinbeck, J. (1965) *Cannery Row*, from *The short novels of John Steinbeck*, New York: The Viking Press, pp 355-469.

Steinberg, D.M. (2010) 'Mutual aid: a contribution to best-practice social work', *Social Work with Groups*, vol 33, pp 53-68.

Szalavitz, M. and Perry, B. (2010) *Born for love: Why empathy is essential – and endangered*, New York: William Morrow.

Szreter, S. and Woolcock, M. (2004) 'Health by association? Social capital, social theory and the political economy of public health', *International Journal of Epidemiology*, vol 33 no 4, pp 650-67.

Taket, A., Crisp, B., Nevill, A. and Lamaro, G. (2009) *Theorizing social exclusion*, London: Routledge.

Thompson, N. (2001) *Anti-discriminatory practice*, Basingstoke: Palgrave.

Todman, L. (2004) 'Reflections on social exclusion: what is it? How is it different from US conceptualizations of disadvantage and, why might Americans consider integrating it into US social policy discourse?', 'City Futures: An International Conference on Globalism and Urban Change', Chicago, IL, 8-10 July (www.uic.edu/cuppa/cityfutures/papers/webpapers/cityfutures papers/session2_3/2_3refectlions.pdf).

Tomm, K. (1988) 'Interventive questioning', *Family Process*, vol 27, pp 1-15.

Tönnies, F. (2001) *Community and civil society*, New York and Cambridge: Cambridge University Press.

Trevillion, S. (2000) 'Social work, social networks and network knowledge', *British Journal of Social Work*, vol 30, pp 505-17.

Trevithick, P. (2003) 'Effective relationship-based practice: a theoretical exploration', *Journal of Social Work Practice*, vol 17, no 2, pp 163-76.

Triandis, H.C. (1995) *Individualism and collectivism*, Boulder, CO: Westview Press.

Trompenaars, F. and Hampden-Turner, C. (2002) *Riding the waves of culture: Understanding cultural diversity in business*, London: Nicholas Brealey Publishing.

Turnell, A. and Edwards, S. (1999) *Signs of safety: A solution and safety-oriented approach to child protection*, New York: Norton.

Twenge, J. and Campbell, K. (2009) *The narcissism epidemic: Living in the age of entitlement*, New York: Free Press.

Uchino, B. (2004) *Social support and physical health: Understanding the health consequences of relationships*, New Haven, CT: Yale University Press.

Ungar, M. (2005) 'A thicker description of resilience', *The International Journal of Narrative Therapy and Community Work*, vol 3, pp 89-96.

van der Veer, G. (2000) 'Empowerment of traumatized refuges: a developmental approach to prevention and treatment', *Torture*, vol 10, no 1, pp 8-11.

VicHealth (2005) *A plan of action: Promoting mental health and wellbeing*, Melbourne: Victorian Health Promotion Foundation.

VicHealth (2010) *VicHealth history: Major events and milestones*, www.vichealth.vic. gov.au/About-VicHealth/VicHealth-History-Major-Events-and-Milestones. aspx

VicServ (2008) *Pathways to social inclusion*, Psychiatric Disabilities Services of Victoria (www.vicserv.org.au/uploads/documents/pathways/pathways_full.pdf).

von Foerster, H. (1984) 'On constructing a reality', in P. Watzlawick (ed) *The invented reality. How do we know what we believe we know? Contributions to constructivism*, New York: Norton, pp 41-61.

Ward, N. (2009) 'Social exclusion, social identity and social work: analyzing social exclusion form a material discursive perspective', *Social Work Education*, vol 28, pp 237-52.

Watson, R. (2010) *Future minds*, London: Nicholas Brealey Publishing.

Warner, R. (1985) *Recovery from schizophrenia: Psychiatry and political economy*, London: Routledge & Kegan Paul.

Watzlawick, P., Weakland, J.H. and Fisch, R. (1974) *Change: Principles of problem formation and problem resolution*, New York: W.W. Norton.

Weakland, J. (1983) 'Family therapy with individuals', *Journal of Strategic and Systemic Therapy*, vol 2, no 4, pp 1-9.

Weber, M. ([1906] 2002) *The Protestant ethic and the spirit of capitalism*, London: Penguin Books (translated by Peter Baehr and Gordon C. Wells).

Weingarten, K. (1991) 'The discourses of intimacy: adding a social constructionist and feminist view', *Family Process*, vol 30, no 3, pp 285-306.

Wender, P. (1968) 'Vicious and virtuous cycles: the role of deviation amplifying feedback in the origin and perpetuation of behavior', *Psychiatry*, vol 31, pp 309-24.

Wenger, E. (1999) Communities of practice: Learning, meaning and identity, Cambridge: Cambridge University Press.

Westacott, E. (2011) *The virtues of our vices: A modest defence of gossip, rudeness, and other bad habits*, Princeton, NJ: Princeton University Press.

Westen, D. (2008) *Psychology: Brain behaviour and culture*, New York: Wiley.

White, M. (1988) 'Saying hello again: the incorporation of the lost relationship in the resolution of grief', *Dulwich Centre Newsletter*, Spring, pp 7-11.

White, M. (1992) *Experience, narrative and imagination*, Adelaide: Dulwich Centre Publications.

White, M. (1994) 'Michael White and the narrative perspective in therapy: an interview', *The Family Journal: Counseling and Therapy for Couples and Families*, vol 2, pp 71-83.

White, M. (2000) *Reflections on narrative practice*, Adelaide: Dulwich Centre Publications.

White, M. (2002) 'Addressing personal failure: (Part 2) Refusal', *The International Journal of Narrative Therapy and Community Work*, vol 3, pp 46-52.

White, M. (2004) *Narrative practice and exotic lives*, Adelaide: Dulwich Centre Publications.

White, M. (2007) *Maps of narrative practice*, New York: W.W. Norton.

Wilkinson, R. and Marmot, M. (eds) (2003) *Social determinants of health: The solid facts* (2nd edn), Geneva: World Health Organization Regional Office for Europe.

Wilkinson, R. and Pickett, K. (2009) *The spirit level: Why more equal societies almost always do better*, London: Allen Lane.

Wirtz, H. and Schweitzer, R. (2003) 'Groupwork with men who engage in violent and abusive actions', in *Responding to violence: A collection of papers relating to child sexual abuse and violence in intimate relationships*, Adelaide: Dulwich Centre Publications, pp 187-202.

Wodak, R. (1997) *Gender and discourse*, London: Sage Publications.

Wolf, B. (1952) *Limbo*, New York: Random House.

Wolfe, T. (1975) *The new journalism*, London: Pan Books.

Woolfolk, R. and Saas, L. (1989) 'Philosophical foundations of rational-emotive therapy', in M. Bernard and R. DiGuiseppe (eds) *Inside rational-emotive therapy: A critical appraisal of the theory and therapy of Albert Ellis*, San Diego, CA: Academic Press, pp 9-26.

Yeatman, A. (2007) 'Varieties of individualism', in C. Howard (ed) *Contested individualization: Debates about contemporary personhood*, New York: Palgrave Macmillan, pp 45-60.

Subject index

L

labels, demoralizing 72–3
language, careful use of 72
lawyers, family court 141
leading questions 165–6, 216
learning to act well relationally 213–51
  coaching clients 225–8
  mediated forms of relating 240–5
  relating exercise 222–5
  specific engagements for 228–40
  working up an etiquette 214–22
legal issues
  achieving adulthood 260
  and confidentiality 103, 193
  and detention in secure settings 246
  impossibility of family or group files 103
legal privilege 191
letters 152, 239, 250
liberating research 79
life cycle 93, 121
living arrangements, sharing information
  about 195, 200
locally social 5, 22–5
  and interpersonal politics 42–3
  practitioners' awareness of 83
  regard being given to 19
  see also interpersonally local
location
  choices about 30
  and geographic exclusion 55
  and quality of relationships 49
logotherapy 239
loneliness
  asking about 173
  and autonomy 51–4
  and cooperation with others 61–2
  cycles of, interrupting 78–80
  increasing 1, 66
  professionals do not help 254
  as a risk factor 20
  in secure units 247
long term practice 150–4
longer term practice 8
longer-term goals and needs 126, 131
losers 34, 71–4, 265

M

male-stream thinking 3, 89, 238
managers, role of 6, 10, 206–12, 263
manners 39
Maori populations 202
Marx, Groucho 159
Marx, Karl 14, 43, 64, 66, 259
material aid agency 262–3
materialism 265
me-first attitude 76
me-first maneuver 232–5
me-first opportunism 79
mediated forms of relating 24, 240–5

medications, sharing information about 184,
  195
medium term contact 148–50
medium-term goals and needs 126
men, violent, group work with 204–5
mental health
  Lennie vignette 124–31
  loss of autonomy by consumers 70–1
  measures of recovery, lack of social
    connectedness in 56–7
  and relational support 2
  residential unit vignette 220–2
  and social factors 20
  use of Global Assessment of Relational
    Functioning Scale 161
mental illness
  clinical approaches to 20
  and social cognition 217–18
  and social exclusion 36
  see also anxiety; depression; psychiatric illness;
    schizophrenia
mental representations/internalized images 82
Milan group 148
Mind Australia 207
mission statements 206, 207
  and sharing information 197
Mitchell, Anne 206
modernity 76
  and constant questioning of relationships 68
  criticism of 256
  individualization as master idea of 27
  process of rationalization is characteristic
    of 94
  and total self-reliance 34
modernization 29–30, 64–5
moral development, men's and women's 41
moral duty 34
morality, relational 238
mothers and daughters 40–1
multipartial alliance 98
multiperson sessions, conducting 186–90
  see also conjoint work
mutual aid tradition 205

N

naming-and-then-moving-on option 150
narcissism 76, 230
narrative practitioners 172, 201
narrative therapy 23, 174, 214, 262
  acknowledge the power of language 172
  discussions around division of labor 239
  emphasizes personal accountability 93
  values interdependence 201
  witnessing circles 201–2
National Happiness Index 112
needs, Maslow's hierarchy of 90–2
negative emotions, pathologizing 93
neighbors, vignette with 223–5
Netherlands, dying alone in 59

psychiatric illness
  and problems with social cognition 230
  and secure detention 246
  see also mental illness
psychoanalytic ideas
  use of 49-51, 69, 77, 92, 197-198,
    inappropriate, can be 197-8
  relational approach 4
psychobiological theories 92
psychodynamic theory 92, 93, 262
psychologists 1, 5
psychology
  ideological role of 96
  traditions of 92
psychology of separation 92, 93, 210
psychopathic personality 230
psychopathology, Western textbooks on 112
psychopaths, economically successful 35
psychotherapists 126-8, 261-2
psychotherapy 88-96
  has negative impact on relationships 88
  in Jarvis vignette 158
  and Maslow's hierarchy 90-2
  reprioritization of the relational 261-2
  rescuing the patient 96-9
  traditions of 92
public health 5, 22
public safety
  and privacy 190
  and secure settings 247

Q

questions
  circular questioning 148
  direct, in coaching 226
  interventive 147
  leading 216
    to map social relations 165-6
  in longer-term practice 151
  as naming others 171-4
  in one-off sessions 145
  to prompt client embeddedness 145-6,
    147-8

R

racism, reduction in 38
rational-emotive theory 92-3
reasonableness, psychotherapy ignores 95
record keeping 208, 244, 263
recovery
  mental health 56-7
  promoting, in mission statements 207
  sexual abuse 57
recruiting an audience 201
reflective exercises
  clarifying your values 120-1
  improving client's social relations 124-31
  leading questions 216
  values of connection and separation 131-2

refugees 36
rehabilitation 245-6, 250-1
rejection, assumptions of 61
relational
  definition 4-5
  doubts about psychotherapists 262
  hard to discern 2
  and material aid agency 262-3
  thinking relationally 118-32
  women's mode of being 40-1
relational agenda
  and confidentiality 197
  in practice frameworks 209
  see also relationship-building agenda
relational approach, psychoanalytic 4
relational base, clients 1, 3, 210, 253, 254
  building, for ex-inpatients 251
  and practice frameworks 209
  working with significant others 98
relational beings, addressing clients as 171-6
relational capacity 66, 228-40
relational context 161-7
relational domain, women's locus in 41
relational exclusion 55
relational impact of personal choices 261
relational mode of being, feminist perspectives
    on 40-2
relational self 3, 155, 175
  balance with autonomous self 156-61, 261
relational work, advanced 200-6
relationally-oriented/focused practice
  and cultural differences 105-10
  decision points in 133-54
  organizational constraints 101-5
relationship building
  and personal accountability 239
  practitioners' opportunities for 133-9
  relating exercise 222-5
  in secure settings 245-51
  and traditional models of practice 261-3
relationship review table 226-8, 244
relationship-building agenda 81
  in a forensic setting 245
  group work advances 204
  lack of monopoly on 5
  with various therapies 262
  see also relational agenda
relationship-building capacity 209
relationship-building path 263
relationship-building practice
  advanced examples of 200-6
  attitudes and skills which support 117-18
  in secure settings 245-51
  and traditional models 261-3
  as unproblematic add-on 81
relationship-building skills 169-212
  addressing the client 171-6
  advanced work 200-6
  being creative with confidentiality 190-200

Author index